THE VIRTUE OF HOPE

THE VIRTUES: MULTIDISCIPLINARY PERSPECTIVES

Series Editor
Nancy E. Snow
Professor of Philosophy, The University of Kansas

Justice
Edited by Mark LeBar

Humility
Edited by Jennifer Cole Wright

Integrity, Honesty, and Truth-Seeking
Edited by Christian B. Miller and Ryan West

The Virtues of Sustainability
Edited by Jason Kawall

The Virtue of Harmony
Edited by Chenyang Li and Dascha Düring

The Virtue of Loyalty
Edited by Troy Jollimore

The Virtue of Solidarity
Edited by Andrea Sangiovanni and Juri Viehoff

The Virtue of Hope
Edited by Nancy E. Snow

THE VIRTUE OF HOPE

Edited by Nancy E. Snow

OXFORD
UNIVERSITY PRESS

OXFORD
UNIVERSITY PRESS

Oxford University Press is a department of the University of Oxford. It furthers
the University's objective of excellence in research, scholarship, and education
by publishing worldwide. Oxford is a registered trade mark of Oxford University
Press in the UK and certain other countries.

Published in the United States of America by Oxford University Press
198 Madison Avenue, New York, NY 10016, United States of America.

© Oxford University Press 2024

CIP data is on file at the Library of Congress

ISBN 978–0–19–006958–2 (pbk.)
ISBN 978–0–19–006957–5 (hbk.)

DOI: 10.1093/oso/9780190069575.001.0001

Paperback printed by Marquis Book Printing, Canada
Hardback printed by Bridgeport National Bindery, Inc., United States of America

Grateful acknowledgment is made to Oxford University Press for permission to reprint
"Focus Theory of Hope" by Andrew Chignell in *The Philosophical Quarterly*
Volume 73, Issue 1; to Routledge, Michael D. Matthews, and Richard M. Lerner for
permission to reprint portions of "Hope for the Future" in *The Routledge International
Handbook of Multidisciplinary Perspectives on Character Development*
(edited by Michael D. Matthews and Richard M. Lerner) by Nancy Snow; and to
Cambridge University Press for permission to reprint a modified version of the
Introduction to *Hope: A Literary History*, by Adam Potkay.

CONTENTS

CONTENTS

SERIES EDITOR'S FOREWORD

Typically, having a virtue means being disposed to having certain kinds of perceptions, thoughts, motives, emotions, and ways one is inclined to act. The end of the twentieth and the beginning of the twenty-first centuries have seen an upsurge of interest in the topic of virtue. This is true not only in philosophy but also in a variety of other disciplines, such as theology, law, economics, psychology, and anthropology, to name a few. The study of virtue within disciplines is vitally important, yet the premise of this series is that the study of virtue in general, as well as of specific virtues, can be enhanced if scholars take into account work being done in disciplines other than their own.

Cross-disciplinary work can be challenging. Scholars trained in one field with its unique vocabulary and methods do not always move seamlessly into another discipline and often feel unqualified to undertake the task of serious cross-disciplinary engagement. The upshot can be that practitioners of disciplines can become "siloed"— trapped within their own disciplines and hesitant to engage seriously with others, even on important topics of mutual interest.

This series seeks to break open the silos, with fifteen volumes on specific virtues or clusters of virtues. For each book, an introduction by the editor highlights the unity of writings by identifying common themes, threads, and ideas. In each volume, the editor seeks to include a chapter from a "wild card" discipline, a field one would not expect to see included in a collection of essays on a particular virtue. We do this both to highlight the diversity of fields in the study of specific virtues and to surprise and challenge readers to broaden their horizons in thinking about virtue.

The audience for this series is practitioners of different disciplines who seek to expand their thinking about virtue. Each volume contains chapters that are accessible and of interest to scholars from many disciplines. Though the volumes are not comprehensive overviews of the work on virtue that is occurring in any given field, they provide a useful introduction meant to pique the curiosity of readers and spur further engagement with other disciplines.

Nancy E. Snow
Professor of Philosophy, the University of Kansas

CONTRIBUTORS

Andrew Chignell is Laurance S. Rockefeller Professor at Princeton University, with appointments in the University Center for Human Values, Religion, and Philosophy. His research interests include early modern philosophy, philosophy of religion, moral psychology, the ethics of belief, and food ethics. He was the co-director of a four-year $5 million grant, "Hope and Optimism: Conceptual and Empirical Investigations."

Lisa M. Edwards is a professor of counselor education and counseling psychology at Marquette University. Edwards' research primarily focuses on understanding factors that promote well-being among ethnic minority youth and adults, particularly Latinas/os. Edwards also conducts research about hope, and she is currently a co-editor of the *Handbook of Positive Psychology* (3rd edition).

Lewis R. Gordon is Board of Trustees Distinguished Professor of Philosophy and Global Affairs and Head of the Department of Philosophy at the University of Connecticut. He is also Honorary President of the Global Center for Advanced Studies and Distinguished Scholar at The Most Honourable PJ Patterson Centre for Africa-Caribbean Advocacy at The University of the West Indies, Mona. He is the author of many books, including, more recently, *Freedom, Justice, and Decolonization* (Routledge, 2021); *Fear of Black Consciousness* (Farrar, Straus and Giroux in the USA, and Penguin-UK 2022); *Black Existentialism and Decolonizing Knowledge: Writings of Lewis R. Gordon*, edited by Rozena Maart and Sayan Dey (Bloomsbury, 2023); and *"Not Bad for an N—, No?"/ "Pas mal pour un N—, n'est-ce pas?"* (Daraja Press, 2023).

Liz Gulliford is an associate professor for the Jubilee Centre for Character and Virtues in the School of Education at the University of Birmingham. She is also an associate fellow of the Oxford Character Project. Her PhD (Queens' College, University of Cambridge) established a firm critical foundation for interdisciplinary theoretical and practical work in positive psychology, upon which she has progressively built an international reputation. Since completing her doctorate, she has carried out extensive conceptual and empirical work in positive psychology and moral education. She has a long-standing interest in research on character strengths and virtues, including gratitude, forgiveness, compassion, courage, and hope, and her work has been published in a range of journals in psychology, education, and philosophy.

Béatrice Han-Pile studied at the Ecole Normale Supérieure (Paris) and taught at various French universities (Paris-Sorbonne, Reims, and Amiens). She is now a professor of philosophy at the University of Essex. She writes mostly on twentieth-century European philosophy (in particular Foucault and phenomenology), Nietzsche, agency, and ethics. Between 2015 and 2018 she was principal investigator on a large AHRC-funded grant, The Ethics of Powerlessness: The Theological Virtues Today. Among other things, she published a paper, "Hope, Powerlessness and Agency" (2017). In 2018 she took part (with Judith Wolfe and Robert Stern) in an episode of *In Our Time* (BBC Radio 4) on hope.

Michael Lamb is the F. M. Kirby Foundation Chair of Leadership and Character, executive director of the Program for Leadership and Character, and an associate professor of interdisciplinary humanities at Wake Forest University. He is also a research fellow with the Oxford Character Project. He is the author of *A Commonwealth of Hope: Augustine's Political Thought* (2022), which offers a new interpretation of Augustine's virtue of hope and its relevance for politics. He has also published on the virtue of hope in the work of Thomas Aquinas. An award-winning teacher, his research and teaching focus more generally on leadership, character, and the role of virtues in public life. He is a co-editor of *Cultivating Virtue in the University* (2022) and *Everyday Ethics: Moral Theology and the Practices of Ordinary Life* (2019). His work has been published in edited volumes and academic journals across numerous disciplines, including the *American Political Science Review*, *Journal of Religious Ethics*, *Journal of Moral Education*, and *Journal of Character Education*. He holds a PhD in politics from Princeton University, a BA in political science from Rhodes College, and a second BA in philosophy and theology from the University of Oxford, where he studied as a Rhodes Scholar. He is currently a principal investigator on major grants to educate character at Wake Forest University and other U.S. colleges and universities.

Kat R. McConnell is a doctoral candidate in the Counseling Psychology Program at Marquette University. Her research interests include culturally informed health psychology practice, the study of grief and loss, and end-of-life care. McConnell also conducts research in the areas of peer mentoring for doctoral students.

Gabriele Oettingen is a professor of psychology at New York University. She is the author of more than two hundred articles and book chapters on thinking about the future and the control of cognition, emotion, and behavior. She received her PhD from the Ludwig Maximilian University and the Max Planck Institute for Behavioral Physiology. Her major contribution to the field is research on the perils of positive thinking and on mental contrasting, a self-regulation technique that is effective for mastering one's everyday life and long-term development. Oettingen's work is published in social and personality psychology, developmental and educational psychology, health and clinical psychology, organizational and consumer psychology, as well as neuropsychological and medical journals. Her findings contribute to the burgeoning literature on behavior and lifestyle change, and educational institutions have increasingly become interested in the application of her research. In her recent work, Oettingen analyzes a phenomenon she calls "misplaced certainty" or "paradoxical knowing," which is a shortcut to knowledge leading to antisocial and fanatical behavior. Her first trade book is *Rethinking Positive Thinking: Inside the New Science of Motivation* (2014). For more information, see www.woopmylife.org.

Adam Potkay is William R. Kenan, Jr. Professor of Humanities at the College of William and Mary in Virginia; he has also been Laurance S. Rockefeller Visiting Professor for Distinguished Teaching at Princeton University and Hurst Distinguished Visiting Professor at Washington University, St. Louis. His most recent book is *Hope: A Literary History* (2022); other books include *Wordsworth's Ethics* (2012) and *The Story of Joy from the Bible to Late Romanticism* (2007), awarded the Harry Levin Prize for best book in literary history and criticism by the American Comparative Literature Association and translated into several languages. He is currently editing a volume covering the seventeenth through nineteenth centuries for *The Cambridge History of Rhetoric*, a five-volume work scheduled for publication in 2025.

Nancy E. Snow is a professor of philosophy at the University of
Kansas. She was co-director of The Self, Motivation & Virtue Project,
a $2.6 million research initiative on the moral self, and the Principal
Investigator of The Self, Virtue, and Public Life Project, a $3.9 million
research initiative. She is the author of *Virtue as Social Intelligence: An
Empirically Grounded Theory* (2009) and over forty-five papers on
virtue and ethics more broadly. She has edited or co-edited eight
volumes, and is the series editor of "The Virtues," a fifteen-volume
interdisciplinary series on virtues published by Oxford University
Press. She is the co-author, with Jennifer Cole Wright and Michael
T. Warren, of *Understanding Virtue: Theory and Measurement* (2021)
and the author of *Contemporary Virtue Ethics* (2020). She is currently
writing a book on hope as a democratic civic virtue.

Robert Stern is a professor of philosophy at the University
of Sheffield. In the history of philosophy, he has published
widely on German Idealism and K. E. Løgstrup, and is currently
researching the Lutheran tradition in philosophy. He has also
worked on transcendental arguments, ethical realism versus ethical
constructivism, and accounts of moral obligation. In 2018 he took
part in an episode on hope for the BBC Radio 4 series *In Our Time*,
along with Judith Wolfe and Béatrice Han-Pile. He was elected a
Fellow of the British Academy in 2019.

Willa Swenson-Lengyel is the Holmes Rolston III Chair in
Religion and Science and an assistant professor of religious studies
at Davidson College, where she teaches in the Religious Studies and
Environmental Studies departments. She held a Catherine of Siena
Postdoctoral Fellowship in Ethics at Villanova University from 2018
to 2022 and received a PhD with distinction in theological ethics
from the University of Chicago Divinity School. She is the author
of several articles and chapters on hope, moral psychology, and the

climate crisis, and she was the guest editor of the January 2021 issue of the *Journal of Religion* on death and afterlives.

Allen Thompson is a professor of ethics and environmental philosophy at Oregon State University. His research concerns broadening our conception of environmental virtue and moral responsibility as a part of understanding human excellence in adapting to the Anthropocene. In addition to teaching and writing journal articles and book chapters, Thompson is the editor-in-chief of the journal *Environmental Ethics*, a past president of the International Society of Environmental Ethics, and a co-editor with Stephen M. Gardiner of and contributor to *The Oxford Handbook of Environmental Ethics* (2017) and co-editor with Jeremy Bendik-Keymer to *Ethical Adaptation to Climate Change* (2012).

Darren Webb is a senior lecturer in education at the University of Sheffield. His research straddles the fields of utopian studies, educational studies, and hope theory. He is especially interested in the pedagogical practices of the "utopian" educator. How does a committed utopist bring this commitment to bear on their role as an educator? Can there be such a thing as utopian pedagogy? Or a utopian pedagogue? Where and how can/should utopian pedagogy best operate? These are the questions he is currently working through.

Introduction

NANCY E. SNOW

The present volume is a collection of work on hope from a variety of disciplines. It adds to the vibrant literature on hope, providing background in fields as diverse as literature, philosophy, theology, psychology, utopian studies, and environmentalism. As background for many of these contributions, and to parallel the history of hope in literature offered by Adam Potkay in chapter 1, I begin with a selective history of hope in Western philosophy, then turn to the plan of the book.

I.1 A BRIEF HISTORY OF HOPE IN WESTERN PHILOSOPHY

I.1.1 Introductory Comments

What is hope? In the history of Western philosophy to the present day, there is tremendous disagreement about the answer to this seemingly simple question. Most philosophers in the Western tradition see hope in a positive light, though others think it is negative.[1] If we attempt to trace the history of thought about hope in Western philosophy, we should start with the story of Pandora. Hesiod wrote of Pandora in

Nancy E. Snow, *Introduction* In: *The Virtue of Hope*. Edited by: Nancy E. Snow, Oxford University Press.
© Oxford University Press 2024. DOI: 10.1093/oso/9780190069575.003.0001

both the *Theogony* and *Works and Days*. Pandora was the first woman, created as a "beautiful evil" by Zeus as a punishment for Prometheus' theft of fire. Pandora is told not to open a jar, but her curiosity gets the better of her and she opens it. All of the evils that beset humanity fly out, but as she closes it, one item remains: she closes the jar on 'hope' (*elpis*) (see https://en.wikipedia.org/wiki/Pandora). The difficulties of interpreting this story abound.[2] Is hope an evil or a good—the antidote to evil, prevented from being released into the world?

Whether hope is good or bad, and whether we should focus not on hope, but on hopes, hoping, or hopefulness, as some contemporary philosophers contend, are contested questions. However, there is agreement on one key point: hope is about that which is unsettled. Typically, we have hopes for the future—that the weather will be good for the parade tomorrow, that I'll have a good biopsy outcome, that the exam will be easy, and so on. But we can have hopes for the past. We might hope that a certain tyrant died a slow, painful death. There is, of course, a fact of the matter about whether the tyrant did indeed die in this manner. If we knew this fact, it would not make sense for us to hope. Our hope that the tyrant died a slow, painful death would either have been fulfilled or dashed.

This discussion indicates two things: first, that hope is about what is not settled and, second, that what we can know is important for hope. Since the future is not settled, and we cannot know how it will turn out, it makes sense for us to have hope for the future. The medieval philosopher, theologian, and saint of the Roman Catholic Church Thomas Aquinas expands on this idea by saying that hope is an intermediate state between two extremes that are either sins or vices—presumption and despair.[3] Presumption is thinking that something for which I hope is a certainty; despair is thinking I will never attain it. Hope occupies a middle ground—since I am uncertain of attaining the object of my hope, whether I attain it or not is a matter that is unsettled.

The contemporary philosophical literature on hope, like philosophical accounts of hope in the history of philosophy, is robust, complex, and full of interesting debates.[4] Trying to review all of this literature, even in barest outline, is well beyond the scope of any introduction. I focus on work in the history of philosophy that has, to my mind, had the greatest influence on the most important contemporary philosophical work on hope and has influenced the contributors to this volume. Moreover, I focus only on work on the concept of hope, not on that on hopefulness or whether hope is a virtue, and if so, what kind—moral, intellectual, or political. I believe the most fruitful conceptual work currently being done on hope is in contemporary analytic philosophy.

Proponents of phenomenology and pragmatism might contest this. Notice should be taken, if only briefly, of an important trend that emerges in both traditions, and that we see resonate with similar ideas from thinkers in other traditions.

The trend is that of thinking of hope as a deep-seated orientation that makes possible more specific hopes with particular objects, such as the hope that there will be good weather tomorrow for the parade. In this vein, the contemporary phenomenologist Matthew Ratcliffe (2008, 2010, 2013), explores what he calls "pre-intentional hope." Ratcliffe (2013, 604) understands this as a deep existential feeling of openness to future possibilities, and contends that without it, specific, intentional hopes would make little or no sense, presumably because a person without pre-intentional hope would not care enough to have intentional hopes. The analytic philosopher Cheshire Calhoun (2018) draws on Ratcliffe to articulate a similar notion that she calls 'basal hope.' Other approaches to hope as a *sine qua non* of meaningful human life and agency are found in the Thomist Josef Pieper's (1997) notion of 'fundamental hope,' and in the idea, developed by the East German Marxist Ernst Bloch, that hope is a kind of deep-seated hunger (1986). The commonality among these views is the identification of a kind of hope that operates at a very deep level of the human psyche and is a very general orientation toward life. However, these views about general hope at a deep level, which are contextualized within different traditions, differ in many respects. For example, Pieper presupposes a theistic worldview with unification with God at the eschaton as the ultimate end of hope, and Bloch, the achievement of a Marxist classless society.

Work on hope is also evident in the pragmatist tradition.[5] Shade (2001) also furnishes a pragmatist account of hope. In my view, Shade's (2001, 136) most important contribution is his view that "hopefulness is an attitude or general orientation toward the future which defines how we respond to life's trials." In the generality of its orientation, hopefulness according to Shade (2001) seems similar to the deep-seated orientations discussed by Ratcliffe, Calhoun, Pieper, and Bloch. In its reference to hopefulness as an orientation that defines our response to life's trials, it is similar to the view of the French Christian existentialist Gabriel Marcel (1978). Shade (2001), of course, adopts neither a theistic nor a Marxist perspective. We should take care to note that fully understanding the various views of hope that these philosophers present depends on understanding how they are embedded within larger philosophical frameworks. The brief mention made here of commonalities should not blind us to the fact of deep differences—differences that lay far beyond the scope of the present discussion.

I.2 A SELECTIVE PHILOSOPHICAL HISTORY OF HOPE

Unlike most contemporary analytic philosophers who write about hope, most historical thinkers offer accounts of hope that are embedded in larger theoretical frameworks; what is presented here should be read with that in mind. This selective overview of historical work is chosen with an eye to those accounts that have most influenced contemporary debates in analytic philosophy.[6] Much interesting work, is, of necessity, left aside.[7] I also leave aside challenges to hope found in historical philosophers, such as Nietzsche, the pessimist tradition, and some existentialist philosophers, who had negative views about hope's value (see Blöser and Stahl 2017a; Dienstag 2006).

I begin with Aquinas, who believes that hope is both a theological virtue and a passion. The theological virtue of hope "denotes a movement or stretching forth of the appetite towards an arduous good" (*Summa Theologica*, II-II, Q. 17, a. 3). The good is eternal happiness, both ours and that of others. Hope is the mean between the extremes of despair and presumption (II-II, Qq. 20 and 21). Despair is a grievous mortal sin, a turning away from God (II-II, Q. 20, aa. 1, 3). It is a failure of the will, and not unbelief (II-II, Q. 20, a. 2). The other extreme, also a sin, is presumption. This is not turning away from God, but the assumption that we can attain salvation through our own powers. It is immoderate hope (II-II, Q. 21, a. 1), and involves pride.[8]

Aquinas also regards hope as a passion. Joy, sadness, hope, and fear are the four main passions. Joy is felt when obtaining a perceived present good; sadness, when faced with a perceived present evil. Hope is felt at the prospect of obtaining a perceived future good, and fear is felt when faced with a perceived future evil (I-II, Q. 25, a. 4). The object of hope is some perceived future good which is difficult but possible to attain (I-II, Q. 40, a. 1; a. 2; a. 5).

Despair and fear are contraries of hope, though for different reasons (I-II, Q. 40, a. 4). Fear and hope are contraries because their objects, evil and good, are contraries (I-II, Q. 40, a. 4, reply obj. 1). We fear an evil we do not know will befall us, and hope for a good we do not know we can attain. As regards hope and despair, hope is attraction for a perceived future good that is difficult to attain; despair is repulsion or withdrawal when we realize just how difficult attaining that future good would be (I-II, Q. 40, a. 4).

Most contemporary philosophers adopt Aquinas' basic definition of hope as desiring (in some sense) an end and believing that it is possible to attain it. Many contemporary philosophers continue to view fear and despair as hope's opposites.[9]

Like Aquinas, modern philosophers think of hope as a passion.[10] Spinoza and Hume view hope as a passion, and think it is intertwined with fear. Both explain hope in terms of joy, and fear, in terms of sorrow or grief. Spinoza claims that "*Hope* is a joy not constant, arising from the idea of something future or past, about the issue of which we sometimes doubt" and makes parallel claims about fear as "a sorrow not constant, arising from the idea of something future or past, about the issue of which we sometimes doubt" (Wild 1958, 270; italics Spinoza's). Spinoza thus acknowledges the impact of knowledge on our hopes (and fears). We can, he thinks, intelligibly hope for something that is past when we do not know how it turned out. Essential to hope, then, is that we doubt an outcome, whether past or future.

Hume offers an analysis similar in some ways to Spinoza's. According to Hume (1978, 439-448), both hope and fear are primarily explained by reference to joy and grief on the one hand and the probability of an event occurring on the other. Probability can be either objective, when the event is uncertain as a matter of fact, or subjective, when it is certain as a matter of fact but uncertain according to the agent's judgment. Both kinds of probabilities cause fear and hope due to the "uncertainty and fluctuation they bestow on the imagination" (Hume 1978, 444).

Joy and grief can intermingle, as can hope and fear, which are mixtures of joy and grief. Hope can slide into fear, and vice versa, depending on the probability of an event occurring. Hume (1978, 444) contends: "'Tis a probable good or evil, that commonly produces hope or fear; because probability, being a wavering and unconstant method of surveying an object, causes naturally a like mixture and uncertainty of passion." In sum, probability influences how we see an object; variations in how we see the object caused by variations in probability cause mixed emotions.

Kant has also influenced contemporary hope theorists, in particular, the work of Adrienne Martin (2014). Blöser and Stahl (2017b) offer an excellent and concise discussion of hope in Kant's work, as well as some of the influences it has had on contemporary work.[11] According to them, in his early work (the *Anthropology*), Kant offers a definition of hope in keeping with the tradition of viewing hope as a passion, that is, as a non-cognitive attitude.

More complexity arises in Kant's later work. Blöser and Stahl (2017b) maintain that Kant focuses on hope as an attitude that allows us to take a rational stance on that which is not guaranteed by experience. In the *Critique of Pure Reason*, Kant asks the question, "For what may I hope?"

Blöser and Stahl (2017b) write that he gives three answers. First, in the *Critique of Pure Reason*, Kant claims that we may hope for our own, individual happiness that we deserve because of our moral conduct, though there is no guarantee that our moral conduct will result in our happiness. This uncertainty provides room for hope. Second, in a much later book, *Religion within the Limits of Reason Alone*, Kant thinks we may hope for our individual moral improvement, which requires changing our fundamental maxim from bad to good. If my fundamental maxim is bad it is hard to see how moral improvement could be possible. Instead, it is something for which I can only hope. The hope for moral improvement can have two objects. The first is to achieve moral improvement through our own efforts; the second is hope for God's help to change what we cannot change on our own. Finally, in his political and historical writings, Kant argues that we may hope for progress toward a morally better, more peaceful future.

Blöser (2020), who goes into even more detail than Blöser and Stahl (2017b), provides a framework for understanding what Kant means by the question, 'For what may I hope?' He is interested in rational hope. Blöser (2020, 67) identifies two key elements of rational hope: (a) the recognition that we cannot achieve our hoped-for ends by ourselves; and (b) the necessity that our grounds for hope be more than mere wish. Our grounds for hope are not theoretically rational, since we lack sure knowledge of whether these grounds exist. They are practically rational. They are operable in our lives and based on assumptions, such as trust and moral belief, that are practically necessary for the hoped-for ends mentioned above.

I.3 CONTEMPORARY ANALYTIC PHILOSOPHERS ON HOPE

Contemporary debates about hope began in earnest with Day (1969).[12] Day (1969, 89) holds the view that hope is a belief-desire complex, contending: "'A hopes that P' is true if and only if 'A wishes that P, and A thinks that P has some degree of probability, however small' is true."[13] This has been called the 'standard' or 'orthodox' view, as well as 'superficial' hope; in other work, I have referred to it as the 'bare-bones' conception of hope.[14] For the sake of consistency, I will call it the "standard" account.

We should notice two points about Day (1969). First, he argues that a belief/desire complex is both necessary and sufficient for hope. Second, and following from this, he contends that hope is not an emotion. The short version of his argument for this claim is this: "since a hope is identical with a desire plus a probability-estimate, and neither desires nor probability-estimates are emotions, hope is not an emotion either" (Day, 1969, 89). He situates this reductionist account of hope within a schema of what he claims are four contraries of hope: fear, resignation, despair, and desperation, which are also ana-lyzed as composites of desires and probability-estimates. Thus, like Aquinas, Spinoza, and Hume, Day (1969) takes pains to analyze hope vis-à-vis its opposites but departs from them in not viewing hope as an emotion.[15]

Many contemporary analytic philosophers approach hope in the following ways. (1) Some criticize the standard account as being nec-essary but not sufficient for hope, with arguments for various suffi-ciency conditions;[16] (2) some criticize the criticisms of the standard account; that is, they criticize views that take the standard account to task, with arguments for different sufficiency conditions designed to address problems allegedly faced by both the standard account and views critical of it; (3) Milona and Stockdale's (2018) percep-tual theory of hope; (4) Milona's (2019) revised standard theory, which does not add sufficiency conditions, but delves further into the nature of desire in the belief/desire complex that constitutes hope; (5) Andrew Chignell's (2022) focus theory of hope, reprinted as chapter 3 in this volume; (6) later work by Milona (2022), in which he questions whether fully blown belief is necessary for hope; and (7) work by Blöser (2019) arguing that hope is an irreducible concept.[17]

I.3.1 Critiques of the Standard Account: Bovens (1999), Agency Theorists, and Pettit (2004)

Luc Bovens (1999), Victoria McGeer (2004, 2008), Margaret Walker (2006), and Philip Pettit (2004) all critique the standard account on the ground that the desire for an end and the belief that it is possible are necessary, but not sufficient, for hope, but each adds different suf-ficiency conditions.

Bovens (1999, 674) adds mental imaging, which is "devotion of mental energy to what it would be like if some projected state of the world were to materialize." Mental imaging isn't just imagining a future state of affairs, but includes the expenditure of mental energy in the process of hoping. Bovens (1999, 674) gives a now-famous example of a host hoping that Sophie will come to his party. He argues that the host would not be hoping that Sophie would come if he did not expend mental energy to looking at the clock and wondering whether she would come, checking whether she was among newly arrived guests, and so on.

Two philosophers whom I have called "agency theorists," McGeer (2004, 2008) and Walker (2006), develop accounts in which hope is connected with agency. Walker (2006, 47, 48) criticizes Day for not explaining the motivational force of hope, as well as for neglecting 'hope phenomena': desires, perceptions, and forms of attention, expression, feeling, and activity, that are characteristic of hope or associated with hope. McGeer (2004, 101) argues that hope is "a unifying and grounding force of human agency," and claims that "[t]o live a life devoid of hope is simply not to live a human life; it is not to function—or tragically, it is to cease to function—as a human being." Hope grounds effective human agency and enables us to project our agential capacities into the future.[18] It is neither wishful thinking nor imaginative fancy, but realistic engagement with our capacities as they are that enables us to bring those capacities to where we want them to be.[19] Drawing on psychologist Jerome Bruner's theory of parental scaffolding, McGeer (2004, 105–108) provides a backstory to our abilities to hope. Parental scaffolding—the kinds of support and encouragement parents provide their children—enables children to learn how to be effective agents. Though we eventually become independent agents, or "self-scaffolders," in McGeer's (2008, 108) terms, we never completely lose the need for supportive others in maintaining our agency and our hope.

Pettit (2004, 154) starts with a "lowest common denominator" analysis of hope as "belief that some prospect may or may not obtain, where one desires that it does obtain." This is, of course, the standard view. Pettit (2004, 155–157) calls this 'superficial hope,' but goes beyond it to develop what he calls substantial hope.' He defends the pragmatic rationality of substantial hope by noting its parallels with the rationality of precaution.

If we negotiate with a contractor to have a project done for $100,000, it's rational to adopt a precautionary assumption—that is, we take our belief that the total cost will be $100,000 "offline," and act as if we believe that we will have a cost overrun of $10,000. The precautionary assumption is pragmatically rational because it buffers us against potential upset due to changing information, thereby enabling us to stick with a plan to achieve a clearly articulated goal.

Substantial hope parallels this, and comes into play when someone's confidence that the hoped-for outcome will obtain is at a low level. It is a form of mental self-regulation that is or gives the agent cognitive resolve, and does this by enabling her to make an assumption and stick with it, despite new information (Pettit 2004, 159). It is pragmatically rational to have substantial hope because humans are deeply emotional creatures: "We are ruled by lymph and gland and brain stem, not just by the computational processing of the cortex" and "When it comes to dealing with the brass tacks of earthly life, we are something of a mess. We see everything, not through a glass darkly but through a glass that hangs in the mists and vapors of a biological mind" (Pettit 2004, 160). Our emotions can cause us to despair. Substantial hope is an antidote that allows us to maintain steady focus as we pursue our goals.

I.3.2 Criticisms of the Critiques (Meirav 2009) and Martin (2014)

The foregoing accounts have been challenged by philosophers who think they are flawed responses to the standard view. Many of these critics offer their own theories of hope. A number of philosophers can be included in this group, for example, Meirav (2009), Martin (2011, 2014), Blöser and Stahl (2017a), McCormick (2017), and Han-Pile (2017).[20] To my mind, the most influential have been Meirav (2009) and Martin (2014).

Meirav (2009) takes on Day (1969), Bovens (1999), and Pettit (2004) on the ground that their accounts cannot distinguish between hope and despair. His claim is that someone can believe that something can come about and desire it (the two factors necessary for hope) while either hoping or despairing of its coming about. To illustrate this, Meirav (2009, 222) gives the example of two characters, Andy and Red, from Frank Darabont's 1994 film, *The Shawshank Redemption*. Both are serving time for a brutal murder, both understand the circumstances of the prison, both are equally cognizant of the low chances of escape, yet neither has lost the desire to escape. Andy hopes to escape, however, but Red despairs. To distinguish hope from despair we need an "external factor" account of hope. In addition to a desired end and a probability assignment given to its attainment, we need to posit that, "hope involves a characteristic attitude towards an external factor, on whose operation the hoper takes the prospect's realization to depend causally" (Meirav 2009, 216).[21] To make his case, he invokes the notion of resignative desire: "having resignative desire for the prospect implies acknowledging that something *distinct from oneself* (as well as from the prospect itself)" will determine whether or not the prospect obtains (Meirav (2009, 229; emphasis his). In hoping for an end or despairing of it, I recognize that it is not completely within my control to bring it about. If I view the external factor as good, I'll hope; if I view it as not good, I'll despair (Meirav 2009, 230).

Let's turn now to Martin's (2014) "incorporation analysis" of hope. Martin (2014) purports to explain how and why it can be rational to have "hope against hope," that is, to hope in cases in which the probability of actually attaining one's end is very low. Martin (2014) argues that when someone is fully aware that the probability of attaining a hoped-for end is very low, it can still be rational for her to hope for it if she can incorporate it into the constellation of her other rationally held ends. For example, a cancer patient with a 1% chance of surviving through treatment could rationally hope to survive, provided that the end of surviving fits in with the patient's other rational ends, such as completing important projects, seeing her children grow up, and so on.

The incorporation analysis has two parts. The "licensing stance" involves the hoper seeing the probability she assigns to an outcome as "licensing her to treat her desire for the outcome and the outcome's desirable features as reasons to engage in . . . forms of planning, thought, and feeling" (Martin 2014, 35). The second part is the person "actually treating her desire and the outcome's desirable features as reasons to engage in said forms of planning, thought, and feeling" (Martin 2014, 35). These two elements explain how and why a hoper *stands ready to offer a certain kind of justificatory rationale for her hopeful plans, thoughts, and feelings* (Martin 2014, 36; emphasis hers). Writing in a Kantian vein, Martin (2014, 52–54) notes that we can take a reflective, higher-order stance on our immediate attractions. This stance enables us to distance ourselves from the immediacy of our desires and judge whether these attractions do provide us with reasons to think and act in certain ways.

I.3.3 A Perceptual Theory of Hope: Milona and Stockdale (2018)

Milona and Stockdale (2018) introduce their theory by noting a methodological deficit in the hope literature—it fails to take account of the resources afforded by the rich literature on emotions.[22] Taking hope as an emotion, they draw on perceptualist theories of emotion, rather than judgmentalist theories, to argue that hope is a kind of normative perception of the practical reasons to pursue a hoped-for end (see Milona and Stockdale 2018, 208ff., 216). Their theory incorporates some features of the standard account, but goes beyond it. For them,

> hope is an attitude that involves:
> 1. The desire for an outcome.
> 2. The belief that the outcome's obtaining is possible but not certain.
> 3. Seeing the possible-but-uncertain desired outcome as encouraging to varying degrees.
> 4. Hopeful feelings. (Milona and Stockdale 2018, 211).

In addition to the perception of the outcome as encouraging, several other features of their view should be noted. It is like Martin (2014) in that the authors believe that hope involves a normative assessment—that there are practical reasons to pursue a hoped-for end. Whereas Martin (2014) believes that hope involves the judgment on the part of the hoper that she has sufficient practical reasons to pursue the hoped-for end, Milona and Stockdale (2018) argue that the normative assessment is provided via the hoper's perception of practical reasons to pursue the end. Further departing from Martin (2014), they write, "In *perceiving* that one has practical reasons to pursue an end, one does not necessarily judge that one is justified in doing so" (Milona and Stockdale 2018, 216; emphasis theirs). Another point should be mentioned. Unlike most hope theorists, Milona and Stockdale (2018, 215–216) contend that it is more plausible to think that hope represents practical reasons to the hoper, and not the hoped-for end as good for the hoper.

I.3.4 *Revising the Standard Account: Milona (2019)*

In "Finding Hope," Milona (2019) claims that the standard account need not be augmented with sufficiency conditions. Taking his cue from Meirav's (2009) contention that the standard account cannot distinguish hope from despair, Milona (2019) argues that if we correctly understand desire as it is integral to hope in the standard account we can see that no sufficiency conditions are needed to distinguish hope from despair, or fully to explain hope itself, for that matter. Milona (2019, 716; emphasis his) contends:

> According to the *revised standard theory*, a person, S, counts as hoping that P if and only if S satisfies the following conditions:
> (1) S believes that P has a probability between 0 and 1 of attaining.
> (2) S has a desire that P which takes the belief as part of its cognitive base.

The novel idea in the revised standard account is that desires have cognitive bases. Milona (2019, 715) writes: "The cognitive base of a desire is composed of the mental states—beliefs, perceptions, imaginings, etc.—that directly causally influence the desire." He illustrates how this works with Cynthia, a diner who desires to order a piece of pie for dessert. At first, her desire is informed by the belief that she will certainly have a piece of pie. However, she is told that the restaurant often runs out of pie later in the evening. This changes the cognitive base of her desire. The belief that she will certainly have pie changes to the belief that she will only possibly have pie. This change in belief, according to Milona (2019, 715), transforms the desire. The now-transformed desire is hope-constituting, because the beliefs in the cognitive base of the desire—those that directly causally influence the desire—have changed. Not only the beliefs, but also the desire, have changed. There is now more urgency to Cynthia's desire to get pie, which could lead to actions on her part, such as ordering a piece of pie before the restaurant runs out.

Let's suppose that Cynthia comes to believe that she will not get a piece of pie. Accordingly, she despairs of getting pie. Cynthia might still have the belief that getting pie is possible and still might desire a piece of pie, even though she despairs of getting the pie. In this case, according to Milona (2019, 715; emphasis his), the belief that getting pie is possible might be co-present or simultaneous with the desire for a piece of pie, but "does not count as hoping because the belief is not among the mental states directly influencing the desire; the two have become psychologically disconnected. That is, in despairing over P, the desire that P is a *mere* wish."

I.3.5 *The Focus Theory of Hope (Chignell (2022)*

The focus theory of hope, introduced by Andrew Chignell (2022) and reprinted as chapter 3 in this volume, is formally stated as follows:

> [*Focus Theory*]: S hopes that *p* only if
> (*Cognitive*): S presupposes that *p* is metaphysically possible,
> (*Conative*): S desires that *p*, and
> (*Focus*): S is disposed to focus on O under the aspect of unswamped possibility (Chignell 2022, 54; emphasis his).

The focus theory is a version of the standard theory with a unique sufficiency condition, namely, the focus condition. The cognitive condition is not fully blown belief, but the weaker notion of 'presupposition,' which Chignell (2022, 47) thinks is more appropriate for mundane hopes.[23] The focus condition is novel: one must focus on a desired outcome under the aspect of unswamped possibility. This means that the hoper's attentional focus on the possibility of the outcome is not swamped or overcome by focusing on countervailing factors that might cast doubt on, or undermine, the possibility of the outcome. This is a psychological condition. Suppose, for example, that I hope that it will not rain tomorrow and the chances of rain in the weather report for tomorrow are 50%. If I focus on the 50% chance that it will rain, this focus swamps the hoped-for outcome of its not raining.

An advantage of the focus theory, according to Chignell (2022, 49–50), is that it can explain many challenges to the standard theory. Recall Andy and Red, characters in *The Shawshank Redemption*. The focus theory explains why Andy hopes to escape prison but Red despairs of it by contending that Andy focuses on the hoped-for outcome under the aspect of unswamped possibility, whereas Red despairs because he focuses on the countervailing factors against escaping. Chignell (2022) contends that the focus theory can explain this and other counterexamples to the standard theory, as well as Milona's (2019) revised standard theory.

Two other features of the focus theory should be mentioned. The first is that it is dispositional. This it can accommodate "the fact that our occurrent focus comes and goes" (Chignell 2022, 54). Red might have some glimmers of hope, but overall, he is disposed to despair just in case his focus across ordinary circumstances is on the impossibility of escaping (see Chignell 2022, 54). In those circumstances, his focus on the possibility of escaping is swamped by countervailing factors.

The second feature is that the focus theory can explain how and why both moral and pragmatic norms regulate hope in ways that differ from their governance of the belief/desire composite. Consider moral norms. Hoping is sometimes under our direct control in ways that our desires are not. Chignell (2022, 60–61) discusses this in terms of the case of Sadie, a born sadist. Since Sadie is a born sadist, she cannot rid herself of her desire to hurt Vickie, though she can control her hope to hurt Vickie, which is immoral. She can directly control her occurrent focus, though she might not be able directly to control her dispositional focus on the possibility of hurting Vickie. By directly stopping her occurrent focus on the possibility of hurting Vickie, perhaps by focusing instead on the aspect of its impermissibility, she might be able to control her *hoping*. As Chignell (2022, 61) puts it, "we directly control the attentional and salience patterns that manifest our hopes—and thereby exercise a degree of indirect control over the hopes themselves. In a phrase: if you mindfully control your hoping, you can slowly change your hopes."

Pragmatic norms also govern hope (Chignell 2022, 61). For example, we might want to win the lottery, even though we know that our chances of winning are barely possible. The focus theory explains why it would be foolish to hope intensely or in an all-consuming way for this outcome. Focusing on winning the lottery under the aspect of unswamped possibility can cause you to ignore other factors, including other economic opportunities, better uses for your money, and so on. Your attention is occupied and your actions can be guided in pragmatically irrational ways.

I.3.6 *Belief Might Not Be Necessary for Hope (Milona 2022)*

In an article that extends themes from Milona and Stockdale (2018), Milona (2022) argues that fully blown belief might not be necessary for hope. As with his work on the perceptual theory, Milona (2022) takes hope to be an emotion, and notes a problem that judgmentalist accounts of emotion have with explaining recalcitrant emotions. Judgmentalist accounts maintain that emotions require beliefs. Fear, for example, requires the belief that the object of our fear is dangerous. As Milona (2022, 192) explains, "An emotion is recalcitrant when it persists in the face of a conflicting evaluative judgment." I might be afraid of flying on a plane yet believe that flying isn't dangerous. A judgmentalist explanation of this recalcitrant emotion seems to require that I believe that flying is both dangerous and not dangerous—an ascription of beliefs that is incoherent.

Similarly, we have recalcitrant hopes. An example from Bovens (1999, 679) is hoping to see an accident at a race track while believing that one shouldn't have that hope. Milona (2022, 192) discusses hopes that are "rooted in an insensitivity to considered beliefs about the probability of what we hope for." This can happen in two ways. We can hope too little, by our own lights, for an outcome that we believe has a good chance of coming about; or we can hope too much, again by our own lights, for an outcome that we believe has very little chance of obtaining. Milona (2022, 192–193) illustrates this recalcitrance with two cases, "Championship Quest" and "Lucky 8s." In "Championship Quest," Jasmine, a longtime fan of a losing team, believes the odds that are put on her team's winning the championship this year, which are 5 to 1. She feels, however, that the win will almost certainly not happen, but reports that she should feel better about her team's chances, and hope more intensely for the victory. In "Lucky 8s," Jasmine, who frequently purchases one dollar scratch-off lottery tickets, buys a more expensive ticket called a "Lucky 8." She has had good luck with the number 8, and knows that the chances of winning big with a more expensive ticket are better. She also knows that the chances of winning a large amount of money are very low, and even that the chances of recouping the amount spent on the ticket are quite low. As Milona (2022, 193) puts it, "She tells herself that she should feel worse about her chances and hope less fervently to win big." With these examples, Milona (2022) seeks to mark a parallelism for hope with problems created for judgmentalist accounts of emotions. This leads him to argue to the following conclusion:

We have strong reason to believe that some hopes are not constituted by a belief about the probability of the hoped-for outcome.
(Milona 2022, 193)

In light of this, he asks how we should conceive of a probability assignment that is not a belief, and sketches a possibility using
Tamar Gendler's (2008a) idea of an alief, which is comprised of three
elements:

(a) the representation of some object or concept or situation or circumstance, perhaps propositionally, perhaps
non-propositionally, perhaps conceptually, perhaps non-
conceptually; (b) the experience of some affective or emotional state; (c) the readying of some motor routine. (Gendler
2008a, 643; quoted at Milona (2022, 194–195)

According to Gendler (2008a), these components are "associatively
linked"; that is, "they are systematically co-activated when certain
conditions are met" (Milona 2022, 195). Thus, aliefs, Milona (2022,
195) contends, are better described as units than as co-occurring
elements, and according to Gendler (2008b, 553), may be rooted in
evolutionary history, habits, and cultural priming.

The idea of an alief, Milona (2022, 195) argues, can help us to
understand both "Championship Quest" and "Lucky 8s." In both
cases, the non-doxastic probability assignment is not an alief, but is
naturally treated as part of an alief. In both cases, Jasmine has a non-
doxastic representation of the chances of winning that is rooted in
a history of "how things have tended to be" (Milona 2022, 195). In
"Championship Quest," her team has a history of losing that leads
her to represent her team as not likely to win. In "Lucky 8s," she
has a history of good luck with the number eight, which "triggers a
non-doxastic representation that she has a good chance to win big"

(Milona 2022, 195). In both cases, the non-doxastic representations are linked with motivation and affect, but are more resistant than beliefs to change based on evidence. Milona (2022, 195) adds that no new restrictions are placed "on the content of the uncertainty dimension of the hope." It can be represented as merely possible or in terms of probability. That said, "The specifics of the content of these non-doxastic representations will plausibly depend on [sic] upon the relevant history of the hoper" (Milona 2022, 195).

To conclude his article, Milona (2022, 196) claims that although he has sketched a way in which hope can be conceptualized without belief, his aim has been modest: to call into question the widely accepted idea that hope requires belief.

I.3.7 Hope Is an Irreducible Concept (Blöser 2019)

Blöser (2019) challenges the standard account of hope in an even more extensive way. She argues against the notion that belief and desire are necessary for hope, maintaining instead that it is a conceptually irreducible concept, multiply ontologically realizable, and that it is best explained by Wittgensteinian family resemblances.

After criticizing the standard definition and attempts to supplement it with sufficiency conditions, all of which she calls "compound accounts," Blöser (2019, 208–209) turns to a critique of the only other view on offer that views hope as a singular construct: Segal and Textor's (2015) view that hope is a primitive mental state. Segal and Textor (2015, 207) argue that compound accounts cannot explain hope's motivational force, and opt instead to understand it as irreducible and describe its functional role (see Blöser 2019, 208). Blöser (2019, 209) points out, rightly in my view, that the success of their argument that compound accounts cannot explain the motivational force of hope would require them to argue the point against every new compound account that emerges. Her second claim against them is that "many but not all realizations of hope enhance motivation" (Blöser 2019, 209).

She goes on to develop her strong position that neither belief nor desire is necessary for hope. Regarding belief, she argues for a non-doxastic position according to which it is false to claim that someone hopes only if she believes the hoped-for outcome is possible. Hoping could, instead, involve a suspension of judgment about whether a hoped-for outcome is possible. She notes the attraction of the common doxastic constraint on hope: that belief in the impossibility of attaining a hoped-for outcome would destroy hope. She writes: "If that is true, then rather than entailing a belief in the possibility of the object, hope would seem to entail the absence of a belief in its impossibility" (Blöser 2019, 209). Consequently, belief is not necessary for hope.[24] Regarding desire, she offers two arguments. In the first, she takes the position of Davidson (1963) and Smith (2008) that desire is only one of a number of "pro-attitudes." As Davidson (1963, 689) puts it, pro-attitudes are answers to the question, "Why did you do it?" (quoted at Blöser 2019, 210). On a comprehensive view of pro-attitudes, she claims, "hoping can be seen as a pro-attitude in its own right, just like desiring, wishing, valuing, and the like" (Blöser 2019, 210). But if so, desire is not necessary for hope. Her second argument is that "hope and desire are different types of attitudes that do not necessarily occur together" (Blöser 2019, 211). In making this argument, she relies on Smith's (2008) view that "desires are simply dispositions to act" (Blöser 2019, 210). She points out that hopes lack an essential link to action, and illustrates this with the case of hopes about the past or future states of affairs over which we have no power. She recognizes, however, that other views about desire claim only that desire represents its object as in some way good. If hope also represents its object in this way, she notes that it is harder to argue that hope can exist without desire (see Blöser 2019, 210n15).

Finally, though she maintains that hope is conceptually irreducible to beliefs, desires, and other factors, it is multiply ontologically realizable. What this means is that "we hope in a great variety of ways" (Blöser 2019, 212). She believes this can be explained in terms of Wittgensteinian family resemblances, but does not offer an account of hope in these terms.

Work on hope in analytic philosophy and other areas of philosophy is ongoing. Hope has been studied in other academic disciplines, and there is a robust popular literature on hope and neighboring concepts, such as positive thinking. The present volume adds to the robust multidisciplinary academic literature on hope.

I.4 PLAN OF THE BOOK

This volume is comprised of eleven chapters by scholars from different disciplines, each providing a unique perspective on hope. Chapter 1, "Virtue or Vice? A Short Literary History of Hope," by Adam Potkay, offers a magisterial overview of the complexities of hope that are found in literature from the ancient Greeks and Romans through the work of Franz Kafka in the twentieth century. The ancients see hope as largely negative. Potkay summarizes the five main points against hope in classical literature: (1) hope is deceptive, based on the uncertainties of an imagined future that rarely arrives; (2) hope is morally corrosive because its objects, such as wealth, sensual pleasure, beauty, and glory, are often unworthy; (3) we are passive in relation to hope when it is considered as a passion—we have either no or insufficient control over it, and thereby lose or compromise our rational agency; (4) as a corollary to (3), in being susceptible to hope, we are also susceptible to fear, as well as to sorrow and disappointment; and (5) hope for the future alienates us from the present, over which we do have some control.

By contrast, the Judeo-Christian tradition believes hope to be a virtue. For Hebrew thinkers, hope is individual and collective. Indivduals, and the Israelites as a people, hope for justice, righteousness, a relationship with God, a promised land, a leader, and an enduring kingdom. For Christian thinkers, hope orients us toward unification with God at the eschaton. Faith, hope, and charity are the three theological virtues; in this life, the virtue of hope is the choice of confidence in God and the promise of eternal life. The elevation of hope as a theological virtue is contrasted with worldly hopes in the mid-seventeenth-century dialogue poem "On Hope" by Abraham Cowly and Richard Crashaw. Crashaw raises a cognitive challenge for Christian hope: how can we know what eternal life will be like? The object of Christian hope—eternal life—is determinate yet unspecific, whereas the objects of worldly hopes can be both determinate and specific. Yet in the later seventeenth and eighteenth centuries, heaven was imagined in increasingly worldly terms, including chronological time and individual personality. Alexander Pope challenged this view, writing in *An Essay on Man* that eschatological hope is a gift, with its proper object of eternal life being determinate but unspecific.

Interestingly, Potkay notes that Samuel Johnson creatively misreads Pope on the joys to be hoped for in heaven. Pope writes of hope for the afterlife, but Johnson focuses on hopes in this life and in human psychology. He thereby places himself alongside modern philosophers, including Hobbes, Locke, Mandeville, and Hume, that psychologizes hope. In this vein, hope's function is to keep us moving forward from one temporary satisfaction to another.

The psychologizing of hope gives way, Potkay argues, when read against the transformative hope for social justice that began with the French Revolution and continued in the work of the Romantics. Both Wordsworth and Emily Dickinson are noteworthy in this tradition. "Romantic-era hope does not supersede or displace the orthodox theological virtues," Potkay writes, but "it does supplement or vie with them" (Potkay, this volume). Yet it is also coupled with despair, and is in close contact with past traumas and tragedies. In that respect, Potkay observes, it is similar to the African American tradition of hope grounded in the work of W. E. B. Du Bois and expressed by Joseph R. Winters with the term "melancholic hope."

During the twentieth century, hope never quite sheds this negative pall. Kafka, Beckett, Woolf, and Wisława Szymborska, for example, explore the small hopes held by ordinary people in their everyday lives. Analyses of hope in the Holocaust complicate this story. Authors such as Borokowski are bitter and negative, whereas Viktor Frankl writes of the dignity afforded to those who held 'expressive hope.' This seems akin, Potkay notes, to 'radical hope,' which outstrips our imaginative capacities, and finds a place among the horrors of destruction. Potkay underscores the ambivalence of hope in the literary history he analyzes. As a final, haunting question, he refers to authors who write of experiences of hope and hopelessness in the Nazi death camps: was hope the only possible expression of value in a hopeless situation, or was it, instead, a cause of hopelessness?

Chapter 2, "Is Hope a Secular Virtue? Hope as the Virtue of the Possible," by Béatrice Han-Pile and Robert Stern, takes up the question of whether hope can be considered a virtue outside of religious contexts. The authors argue that it can. They identify three main criteria for a trait to be a virtue: it is good for its possessor, it stands between two vices, and it can be cultivated and actualized. They rebut objections to hope's being considered a virtue on each count. The authors adopt a broadly Aristotelian conception of virtue according to which a virtue is a disposition which, in virtuous action, is exercised appropriately and skillfully in specific circumstances and is reinforced through repeated actualizations. The virtue renders its possessor sensitive to certain reasons to act and can have characteristic feelings or emotions associated with its actualization, though it is not reducible to them. Han-Pile and Stern offer the following characterization of how hopes relate to desire:

> Hopes involve a desire which, in conditions of subjective uncertainty about whether the desired end will obtain or can be obtained, is responsive to reasons to think that the end will obtain (or not), and whose strength is not directly proportional to the weight of these reasons.

They then go on to note that this raises the question of whether hope is good for its possessor, and proceed to outline objections to each of the criteria for a trait's being a virtue. The rest of the chapter is devoted to extensively addressing these concerns. One of the most interesting aspects of their view is an extensive account of hope, intentionality, and agency. By way of final comment, they note that, on their view, epistemic and ethical skills are required for exercising hope. This can preclude young children who lack these skills from having the virtue of hope, though they can be in a state of belief and desire commonly attributed to hope, as described above. The hopes of young children are one of several mental states commonly thought of as hope that are not hope in a full, robust sense. The authors maintain that hope in the full, robust sense is always a virtue.

Chapter 3 reprints "The Focus Theory of Hope," by Andrew Chignell. A discussion of this theory is provided in the previous section.

In chapter 4, "A Black Existential Reflection on Hope," Lewis R. Gordon shifts our attention from conversations about hope as a virtue and the standard theory of hope and alternatives to a broader field of vision. Stating at the outset that he is not a fan of hope, he begins with a personal anecdote about his hope that his mother would be alive after being informed by a hospital administrator that her condition was critical. As it happened, his mother had died;

the administrator wanted him to be told in person. Reflecting on his hopes after the fact, he was struck by their naivete, and by the notion that hope highlights our lack of control over outcomes—in short, our vulnerability. It can be said that the entirety of the Black existentialist tradition is an extended meditation on hope as a reflection of the vulnerability of Black people to oppression. Gordon, however, begins his analysis with a meditation on a different tradition in which hope and vulnerability have dynamic interplay—that of stories found in Kierkegaard's *Fear and Trembling.* Gordon finds in Kierkegaard the start of an argument for taking a leap of faith—making a commitment—to a desired state of affairs without regard for the outcome. Thus, Gordon, like Kierkegaard, finds faith superior to hope.

That is by no means the end of his analysis. Referring to different traditions, such as the tradition of Black Christian thought embodied in thinkers like Dr. Martin Luther King Jr. and former president Barack Obama, as well as traditions of Judaism and Islam, in which hope is problematized, he turns to the work of the Zen Buddhist thinker Nishitani to urge us to overcome the self/Being dichotomy that is found in Kierkegaard and, indeed, in all Abrahamic religions. If we overcome that dichotomy, we need not leap. Nor should we hope, for, as with all Buddhists, we must give up our egocentric attachments and with them, our hopes for particular outcomes. The upshot is that we give up not only hope, but also despair. Where does this leave us? It leaves us with the freedom to make a radical existential commitment, such as were made by the people who endured the Middle Passage. This kind of commitment entails continuing to live when no life is possible—continuing to exist as people when personhood is denied. This commitment entails a movement beyond the self to some greater good which one cannot know will obtain but toward which one strives nonetheless. Herein lies the possibility of deep and enduring hope—hope, expressed in one's aspirations and actions—for the possibility of loving relations even with putative enemies. Hope against enmity, made possible by radical freedom and the choice of aspirational commitment, might then lay claim to being a virtue.

Chapter 5, "Created and Fallen Hope: Theological Anthropology and Human Hoping," by Willa Swenson-Lengyel, takes up the question of hope as a virtue as well as hope's orientation toward certain kinds of goods in light of features of the human condition. She is concerned specifically with protestant thinking about hope in a way that distinguishes it from faith, yet takes seriously protestant accounts of faith. She does this by rooting her analysis not in eschatological reflection, but in theological anthropology. This offers a framework for interpreting hope's role in human life without contending that hope, like faith, is certain.

She begins with an analysis of created hope. Creatures are finite and recognize their limitations. Yet we, as finite creatures, we also have desires that extend beyond our limitations. Hope is one created, good response that helps us to make sense of this tension and gives rise to many of our emotions and actions. According to Swenson-Lengyel, in hoping, we acknowledge and affirm a desire as good for us now, analyze and interpret the limitations to achieving the object of the desire, evaluate those limits, and determine to invest in the desire, that is, to dedicate time, attention, emotion, and activity to the desire and its object. Created hope, she thinks, is a way of responding to the tension between our limitations and desires that enables us to invest in goods that are beyond us.

The fall has implications for created hope. It affects all aspects of hoping: our desires, our understanding of our limitations, and our willingness to invest. Our fallenness warps our hope. Both individuals and their communities are stuck in this existential failing. The fall also affects how we should understand hope as a virtue. Hope can be a Christian virtue only by responding to the vicissitudes of earthly life: fallenness, temptation, and sin. Christian hope can orient one to one's earthly vocation—to be a Christian living a finite life in our best imitation of Christ. I have hope in the here and now for that which is uncertain—that earthly evils will be confronted and overcome and the gospel brought to the world. I hope that God's word will be actualized in the present moment, but I have faith in God's ultimate justice—that His will ultimately will be done. Thus, hope is always uncertain, whereas faith is certain. Moreover, the Christian virtue of hope is possessed by finite creatures in the here and now whose this-worldly understandings are necessarily limited, both by their creaturely nature and by the damages of the fall.

Is fallen hope a virtue? In the last part of her chapter, Swenson-Lengyel takes up this question. It is not in itself a virtue, she claims, though it can be used virtuously as part of our this-worldly efforts to combat the evils of fallenness, and to orient ourselves to Christ. This, I take it, is a call to activism. As Christian hopers, we have a vocation: We are called actively to shape ourselves and the world around us—fallen though we may be—to that to which Christ calls us. Though we see through a glass darkly, we can in fact see. Virtuous hoping, with its careful attention to our fallen nature, our limitations, and our desires, helps us to see and to act in the world as Christians.

Chapter 6, by psychologist Liz Gulliford, is titled "Hope: An Interdisciplinary Examination." Gulliford looks at hope and the neighboring concept of optimism using perspectives from philosophy, theology, and psychology. She begins with a brief review of hope and optimism in works in psychology and philosophy that highlight optimism's reliance on objective evidence to support probabilities in contrast with hope's broader scope of yearning toward that which is unlikely, though possible. Gulliford succinctly captures the essence of this distinction by saying that optimism is a concept of the "head," whereas hope engages the "heart" by being an emotional orientation to a desired future. Turning then to positive psychology, she reviews the idea of learned helplessness, then introduces the notion of explanatory style, which includes optimistic and pessimistic explanatory styles. Explanatory styles are patterns according to which people seek to explain the causes of events in their lives. Learned optimism relies on the notion that an optimistic explanatory style can be cultivated by "examining and changing cognitive attributions" (Gulliford, this volume). The premise of learned optimism is that individuals can exert a high degree of control over how events affect them. People with optimistic explanatory style typically attribute failure to external factors and regard failures as impermanent and specific. By contrast, those with pessimistic explanatory style typically attribute failures to internal factors and regard them as more permanent, global, and pervasive. Neighboring concepts of learned optimism include C. R. Snyder's agency-pathways theory of hope, according to which high hopers are able to set their sights on hoped-for goals and exert agency in finding the means to achieve them. Closely related is Carver and Scheier's theory of dispositional optimism, according to which optimists confidently believe their goals can be achieved and persist in pursuing them. All of these theories regard hope and optimism as intrapersonal constructs, identified as virtues of self-regulation or self-management. In the rest of the chapter, Gulliford explores themes of hope, time, and waiting, and, most important, draws on psychoanalytic and religious perspectives to make the point that hope and optimism are not only intrapersonal, but can be interpersonal. This can occur when we "hope in" another—when we trust in that other and rely on her to open us to imaginative possibilities that we could be unable, perhaps because of mental illness, to access by ourselves. In a world in which the future is uncertain and out of our control, hope, according to the Jesuit priest and psychoanalyst William Lynch, reaches to the outside world for help. Thus, hope can be collective and dependent on others.

Psychologists Lisa M. Edwards and Kat R. McConnell are the authors of chapter 7, "The Influence of Culture on Psychological Hope." In this essay, they describe in some detail psychologist C. R. Snyder's influential agency-pathways theory of hope and how it functions in various cultural contexts. The agency-pathways theory is a primarily cognitive account of how individuals can achieve goals, with feelings playing an important but subsidiary role. According to this psychological account, hope is not a virtue—the goals toward which agency and pathways are directed need not be moral, but can be neutral or even morally bad. Edwards and McConnell focus on psychological hope, specifically, on how cultural influences can shape it. Exploring these issues requires a word about measurement, in particular on construct equivalence. After taking up measurement issues, the authors discuss various cultural influences on hope, including those of nationality, collectivism and individualism, generational differences, race and ethnicity, religion and spirituality, disability status, and refugee status. Forty years of research has yielded insights into the agency-pathways theory and how it differs in various populations both as regards behaviors and how people experience hope in their lives. Yet as the authors conclude, more research needs to be done to plumb the depths of how hope operates both between and within cultural groups.

Chapter 8, "Positive Fantasies about the Future Breed Hope," by psychologist Gabriele Oettingen, offers a definition of hope as "positive thoughts and images (fantasies) about the future that can even occur when a person's subjective probabilities (expectations) of reaching the desired future are low." After a review of literature in psychology showing that positive fantasies alone will not enable us to reach a desired future, but instead, will actually make us less successful in doing so, Oettingen turns to Fantasy Realization Theory (FRT). According to FRT, what will help us to reach a desired future is the thought process called 'mental contrasting.' Mental contrasting occurs when we fantasize about a desired outcome, but also consider practical obstacles that stand in the way of our realizing it. If the obstacles are perceived as surmountable, we can plan ways to overcome them and achieve our desired outcome. If they are not perceived as surmountable, we can let go of our hopes and perhaps seek other outcomes that we think we can attain. Importantly, disengaging from a desire for an outcome and shifting our mental resources to another is a wise strategy when we have a choice of actions. Sometimes, however, we have no choice—we are in an "inescapable context"—we cannot do anything; our actions are stymied. Oettingen gives the COVID-19 pandemic as an example. We could not stop the pandemic. Our choices were severely restricted. In such cases, indulging in positive fantasies can help us to patiently await a better future and avoid frustration, aggression, and depression. Oettingen closes her chapter by noting respects in which her conception of hope is similar to hope as a virtue.

Darren Webb, an education theorist, is the author of chapter 9, "Hope and the Utopian Impulse." Webb urges us to take a closer look at the assumption that hope is always an unmitigated good or is necessarily aligned with utopianism. Hope, he maintains, can be broadly understood as a positive orientation toward an uncertain future good that is open to disappointment. He understands the utopian impulse as a shift that occurs within social life that leads us toward imaginary and better futures. He then examines five different modes of hoping—patient hope, critical hope, sound hope, resolute hope, and transformative hope—with an eye to explicating whether, and if so, how, they align with utopian impulses. He concludes with a case study to illustrate the application of the modes of hoping.

Patient hope, as found in the work of the French Christian existentialist philosopher Gabriel Marcel (1978) and attributed to the Crow chief Plenty Coups by the philosopher Jonathan Lear (2006), orients us toward an objective reality that we cannot imagine. It enjoins patient waiting—the expectation that we will be delivered from our trials by forces beyond the self. Since the utopian impulse requires imagination and desire, patient hope possesses, according to Webb, an anti-utopian functionality. Critical hope is evident in the writings of the Protestant theologian Jürgen Moltmann. It urges us to protest the suffering of the world, to be in conflict with the world as a way of moving toward a better future which we cannot imagine. Sound hope, championed by J. P. Day, is familiar from discussions in contemporary Anglo-American analytic philosophy. Hope is defined as a desire for an outcome plus a probability estimate of the likelihood of the outcome's being attained. Sound hope, which can be undermined by low probability estimates, is unlikely to be transformative. Resolute hope, as found in the work of the analytic philosopher Philip Pettit, focuses on cognitive resolve, which indemnifies us against the derailing effects of negative evidence and low probabilities of attaining our hoped-for outcome. The psychologist C. R. Snyder also offers a theory of resolute hope, as does the pragmatist philosopher Patrick Shade. All of these theories focus on the hope of the individual, and all, according to Webb, bolster social stability and, thus, serve a socially conservative function. Finally, transformative hope is seen in the writings of the philosopher Richard Rorty and the Catholic liberation theologian Gustavo Gutierrez. As with resolute hope, transformative hope is hope against evidence. Unlike resolute hope, which is individual hope, transformative hope is collective. It inspires collective social action to create a better world.

Can we hope for a better world in the face of environmental damage wrought by climate change? This is the broad topic of chapters 10 and 11, by Allen Thompson and Michael Lamb, respectively.

In chapter 10, "Adapting Environmental Hope," philosopher Allen Thompson provides an in-depth discussion of climate change and, given its consequences for our planet, of the kinds of environmental hopes we can have. He understands hopefulness as the disposition to hope well, and views it as a virtue that is compatible with both the Aristotelian and the Humean tradition of virtue ethics. Environmental hopes, Thompson argues, have been and continue to be shaped within three different kinds of narrative frameworks for environmentalism in North America since the late nineteenth century: the protection narrative, the system failure narrative, and the post-apocalyptic narrative. Environmentalists, such as John Muir and Theodore Roosevelt, who adopted the protectionist narrative, sought to protect nature, including wilderness, from disruption by human forces. They hoped that nature, wilderness, and natural resources, especially in the American West, would be preserved by limiting the effects of human encroachment. The system failure narrative is based on the view that disturbance is the norm. The more optimistic strand of system failure environmentalists hope to decrease pollution and waste, slow deforestation and water depletion, and stop species extinction. The point of hopefulness is to avoid collapse and the loss of natural systems, or more positively, to work toward a "green awakening." The system failure narrative, according to Thompson, is arguably the most prominent in our day and age, but the post-apocalyptic narrative is emerging. Proponents of this narrative believe that we cannot avoid environmental catastrophe. Thompson asks a pointed question: What happens to traditional environmental hopes when we give up on saving nature?

Thompson offers an extensive discussion of this question, analyzing tactics for dealing with the post-apocalyptic narrative as well as advancing moral arguments for keeping hope alive in the face of evidence that we are causing serious and irreversible environmental damage. Ultimately, he thinks that we can adapt hope for a post-apocalyptic narrative. We can opt for a bold, transformative vision of social change. We can, like the Crow chief Plenty Coups, hope for a future that outstrips our imaginative capacities of how to lead flourishing lives. We can hope that Stoicism, which valorizes rational

INTRODUCTION

self-control, empowers people to endure hardships. As he eloquently states:

> We can hope that other innate human capacities for flourishing are resilient and that ideals of justice, equality, and human rights are not left behind in the wreckage but instead serve to form the basis of new societies that promote the development of core human capabilities.

Finally, based on recent evidence in restorative ecology, we can hope that non-historic ecosystems reassemble themselves in new ways, giving credence to the hope that in the long run, nature is resilient in ways we have yet to imagine.

The volume concludes with chapter 11, "Difficult Hope: Wendell Berry and Climate Change," by Michael Lamb. Lamb explicates Berry's complex conception of hope and how it relates to concepts such as optimism, pessimism, and despair. Importantly, health is the standard at which virtues aim, according to Berry. By 'health,' Berry means a complex system in which people, communities, societies, and nature are holistically integrated. Optimally, we should realize that we are all 'members' of this complex system, and that the health of the system as a whole is that at which any virtue aims. This has implications for hope as an environmental virtue in light of climate change, both constraining what can legitimately be hoped for, as well as encouraging appropriate hopes both proximate and long term. Hope avoids optimism, an oversimplification that confuses fantasy with reality and presumes that all will be well, and pessimism, that is, prematurely giving up because a negative outcome is seen as inevitable, thereby inviting despair. Both optimism and pessimism license refusing to work for the desired outcome.

Berry's virtue of hope is practical in several respects. Without going into all of these, we should note that perhaps the most

35

important is hope's stabilizing influence. As with Pettit's notion of cognitive resolve, hope steadies us against fluctuations of emotion and fortune.

Though the enactment of hope can be difficult, expressing hope publicly can help us to discover grounds of hope in ourselves. We are right to act hopefully, that is, virtuously, even when the expectation of good consequences is low. Berry illustrates this point in his discussion of an anti–Vietnam War poem by Hayden Carruth. Carruth was under no illusions that his poem would end the war, but he published it anyway, thereby publicly displaying his own reasons for hope and enlisting the aid of fellow citizens in the shared venture of protest. We need, Berry thinks, to hope in our fellow humans and to foster their hope. One way of encouraging hope is by identifying exemplars of hope. Famous people can be exemplars, but so, too, and perhaps most of all, ordinary people striving against the perils of environmental degradation, the destruction of family farms, and so on, exemplify hope. They find hope in their work and in their relations to one another.

I.5 CONCLUSION

The study of hope is ongoing in many disciplines. This volume, we trust, will be useful to scholars in many fields who wish to learn more about hope, and to contribute to the many discussions currently taking place.

ACKNOWLEDGMENTS

Portions of this introduction draw on "Hope for the Future," by Nancy E. Snow, which will appear in the *Multidisciplinary Handbook of Character Virtue Development,* edited by Michael D. Matthews and Richard M. Lerner (Routledge, forthcoming). Published here by permission.

A modified version of chapter 1 was published as the Introduction to Adam Potkay, *Hope: A Literary History* (Cambridge University Press, 2022). It is reprinted with permission of Cambridge University Press.

Chapter 3, "The Focus Theory of Hope," (2022) is reprinted from *The Philosophical Quarterly* 73 (1): 44–63. It is subject to the Creative Commons license (http://creativecommons.org/licenses/by/4.0/) and reprinted here under its terms.

NOTES

1. Philosophers in the Western tradition who are negative about hope include Friedrich Nietzsche and Arthur Schopenhauer, and a long tradition of pessimism that includes the latter. According to the pessimists, we are better off without hope, for it foments illusions about what we can achieve in life. We are better off with a clear-eyed realism about the limits of humanity and our capacities for achievement (see also Dienstag 2006). Though some work has been done on hope in Eastern philosophical traditions, e.g., Buddhism (see, for example, Dunlap 2020), my focus here is on Western philosophy.
2. See Cairns (2020, 28n37). Cairns (2020, 28) maintains that the standard interpretation is that Pandora's jar contained evils and one good—hope.
3. Presumption and despair are considered sins when Aquinas is writing of hope as a theological virtue. They are considered vices when he is writing of hope as a passion.
4. Contemporary philosophical work on hope here left aside includes Bobier (2017); Blöser and Stahl (2017a); Chae (2019); Cobb (2015); Cremaldi and Kwong (2022); DeYoung (2014); Dodd (2004); Döring (2014); Han-Pile (2017); Jackson (2021); Jeffrey (2017); Kadlac (2015, 2017); Kwong (2019, 2020, 2022a, 2022b, forthcoming); Lear (2006); Martin (2011); Mason (2021); McCormick (2017); Milona (2020); Milona and Stockdale (2021); Mueller (2019); Palmqvist (2021); Rioux (2021a, 2021b); Segal and Textor (2015); N. H. Smith (2008); Snow (2019, 2019, 2019b, 2019c, 2020); Stockdale (2019, 2021); and van Hooft (2011). For hope and climate

changes, see Thompson (2009) and Williston (2012). Recent work on historical conceptions of hope includes Bobier (2017); Chignell (2013); Forte (2016); Gravlee (2000); Lamb (2016a, 2016b, 2018, 2022); and Vogt (2017). For hope in political philosophy, see Blöser, Huber, and Moellendorf (2020); Huber (2019); Dauenhauer (1986); Moellendorf (2006); Sleat (2013); and Snow (2019). For hope in epistemology, see Benton (20, 2020) and Dodd (2017). For African American perspectives on hope, see Warren (2015) and Winters (2016). For multiple perspectives on hope, see the essays in Blöser and Stahl (2020); Dalferth and Block (2016); and van den Heuvel (2020). For more bibliographical references, see Blöser and Stahl (2017b).

5. Stitzlein (2020) offers a helpful overview which focuses on the classical pragmatism of Charles S. Pierce, William James, and John Dewey from the late nineteenth and early twentieth centuries, and includes commentaries on twentieth- and twenty-first-century pragmatists Richard Rorty, Patrick Shade, Judith Green, Cornel West, and Colin Koopman. In various ways, these thinkers view 'habits of hoping' as forms of life or orientations toward the world that are deeply social.

6. Blöser and Stahl (2017b) provide an overview of work on hope, including its history in Western philosophy. See also selected essays in Blöser and Stahl (2020) and van den Heuvel (2020).

7. Given difficulties of interpretation, I leave aside discussions of hope in ancient philosophy. Cairns (2020) provides an excellent discussion of the difficulties in interpreting the Greek term *elpis* as 'hope.' For example, Cairns (2020, 16) writes: "*Elpis* differs most obviously from hope in that it does not always focus on a positive outcome" and (Cairns 2020, 28), "From philosophical sources, one might get the impression that ancient Greeks had little interest in the moral psychology of hope." But see Gravlee (2020) on hope in ancient philosophy; Forte (2016) on hope in Plato's *Philebus*; Vogt (2017) on hope in the same dialogue; and Gravlee (2000) on hope in Aristotle. See also the discussion in Mittleman (2009). I also leave aside a discussion of hope in the Christian thinkers Augustine and Kierkegaard. For Augustine, see *The Enchiridion on Faith, Hope, and Love*. Lamb (2022) is an excellent new book on hope in Augustine's political thought; see also Lamb (2018). See Blöser and Stahl (2017) for references for work on Kant, Kierkegaard, and existentialism.

8. See also Lamb (2016a, 2016b).

9. See, e.g., Day (1969) and Govier (2011), though Day (1969) does not regard hope's opposites as either sins or passions, but as belief/desire complexes; Govier (2011) does not regard them as sins, but as attitudes.

10. Exactly how to understand a passion in the views of Aquinas as well as modern philosophers is here left aside. See, e.g., James (2003) and Martin (2014, 11–12, 77–82). For hope in modern philosophy, see Mittleman (2009, 27ff., 94–96) and Smith (2008).

11. See also Blöser (2020) on Kant.
12. Two previous publications on hope in the analytic tradition should be noted: Wheatley (1958), who attempts to distinguish wishing from hoping, and Downie (1963), who engages with Wheatley. Neither has been as influential as Day (1969).
13. See also Day (1991, 1998).
14. Meirav (2009) calls it the "standard" account; Martin (2014), the "orthodox" definition; and Pettit (2004), "superficial" hope. I call it the 'bare-bones' account. See Snow (2019, 2020).
15. On situating hope among contraries, see, for example, Govier (2011, 246–251). Govier (2011, 246) mentions Marcel (1978) and Godfrey (1987) on despair, and Schumacher (2003) on presumption, despair, and fear.
16. Just about all hope theorists take this tack. For exceptions in contemporary analytic philosophy, see Segal and Textor (2015), Milona (2019), and Blöser (2019).
17. I here leave aside a separate discussion of Segal and Textor (2015), who argue that belief and desire are not sufficient for hope; instead, they claim, hope is a primitive mental state, not reducible to other mental states, and is characterized by its functional role with respect to other mental states. I mention Segal and Textor (2015) in the context of my treatment of Blöser (2019), who convincingly critiques their account. I also leave aside Döring (2014), who argues that hope is an emotion.
18. McGeer (2004, 103) approvingly cites the psychologist C. R. Snyder's agency-pathways theory.
19. Martin (2011) calls the McGeer-Walker view the 'agential investment' account, and offers a conception of hope in which fantasy has roles to play.
20. McCormick (2017) argues for the rationality of hope in terms of both theoretical and practical norms. Han-Pile (2017) takes up the low-probability assignment problem (see Pettit 2004 and Martin 2014). She argues that the voluntarist, cognitivist conception of agency that their solutions presuppose is incompatible with the standard definition of hope. She calls her alternative "medio-passive" agency. *Contra* Martin (2014), Blöser and Stahl (2017a) argue that reasons for hoping are not exclusively instrumental. "Fundamental" hopes are partially constitutive of our practical identity, and are intrinsically valuable.
21. By 'prospect,' Meirav means the hoped-for end. Spiritual traditions of thought about hope, including Aquinas, acknowledge the role of attitudes toward external factors—for Aquinas, God—in the psychology of hope. See also Pieper (1997), Marcel (1978), and Moltmann (1967) in the Christian tradition; Fackenheim (1970) in Judaism; Bahmani, Amini, Tabei, and Abbasi (2018) in Islam; and the radical hope attributed by Lear (2006) to the Crow chief Plenty Coups. Meirav (2009, 217nn1, 2, 220n8, 228nn13, 14) is aware of

some of this work, but does not refer to the external factor as a deity or higher spiritual power in the body of his text.

22. See Milona (2020, 106–108) for his own summation of this view, as well as criticisms.

23. In maintaining that fully blown belief is not necessary for all hopes, Chignell (2022) is in company with Milona and Stockdale (2018), Blöser (2019), and Milona (2022).

24. Chignell (2022, 47n6) writes: "Blöser argues that since full-blown belief isn't required for hope, there is no cognitive necessary condition on hope at all. But that's a *non sequitur* given the availability of these other states." By this he means the position that he argues for, namely, that fully blown belief is not required for hope, only the presupposition that the hoped-for outcome is possible. However, his point could equally apply to Milona's (2022) view that alief, not belief, is all that is required to hope.

REFERENCES

Aquinas, T. 2021a. *Summa Theologiae: Prima Secundae Partis.* https://www.newadvent.org/summa/2.htm/.

Aquinas, T. 2021b. *Summa Theologiae: Secunda Secundae Partis.* https://www.newadvent.org/summa/3.htm.

Augustine. 2021. *The Enchiridion on Faith, Hope, and Love.* https://www.newadvent.org/fathers/1302.htm.

Bahmani, F., M. Amini, S. Z. Tabei, and M. B. Abbasi. 2018. "The Concepts of Hope and Fear in the Islamic Thought: Implications for Spiritual Health." *Journal of Religion and Health* 57 (1): 57–71.

Benton, M. A. 2020. "Epistemological Aspects of Hope." In *The Moral Psychology of Hope*, edited by C. Blöser and T. Stahl, 135–151. London: Rowman & Littlefield.

Benton, M. A. 2021. "Knowledge, Hope, and Fallibilism." *Synthese* 198: 1673–1689.

Bloch, E. 1986. *The Principle of Hope.* 3 vols. Translated by N. Plaice, S. Plaice, and P. Knight. Cambridge, MA: MIT Press.

Blöser, C. 2019. "Hope as an Irreducible Concept." *Ratio* 32: 205–214.

Blöser, C. 2020. "Hope in Kant." In *The Moral Psychology of Hope*, edited by C. Blöser and T. Stahl, 57–74. London: Rowman & Littlefield.

Blöser, C., J. Huber, and D. Moellendorf. 2020. "Hope in Political Philosophy." *Philosophy Compass* 15 (5): e12665.

Blöser, C., and T. Stahl. 2017a. "Fundamental Hope and Practical Identity." *Philosophical Papers* 46 (3): 345–371.

Blöser, C., and T. Stahl. 2017b. "Hope." In *The Stanford Encyclopedia of Philosophy*, edited by E. N. Zalta. https://plato.stanford.edu/entries/hope/.

Blöser, C., and T. Stahl, eds. 2020. *The Moral Psychology of Hope*. London: Rowman & Littlefield.

Bobier, C. 2017. "Hope and Practical Deliberation." *Analysis* 77 (3): 495–497.

Bobier, C. 2018. "Why Hope Is Not a Moral Virtue: Aquinas's Insight." *Ratio* 31 (2): 214–232.

Bovens, L. 1999. "The Value of Hope." *Philosophy and Phenomenological Research* 59 (3): 667–682.

Cairns. D. 2020. "Hope in Archaic and Classical Greek." In *The Moral Psychology of Hope*, edited by C. Blöser and T. Stahl, 15–35. London: Rowman & Littlefield.

Calhoun, C. 2018. *Doing Valuable Time: The Present, the Future, and Meaningful Living*. New York: Oxford University Press.

Callina, K. S., N. E. Snow, and E. D. Murray. 2018. "The History of Philosophical and Psychological Perspectives on Hope: Toward Defining Hope for the Science of Positive Human Development." In *The Oxford Handbook of Hope*, edited by S. Lopez and M. Gallagher, 9–26. New York: Oxford University Press.

Chae, L.-A. 2019. "Hoping for Peace." *Australasian Journal of Philosophy* 98 (2): 211–221.

Chignell, A. 2013. "Rational Hope, Moral Order, and the Revolution of the Will." In *Divine Order, Human Order, and the Order of Nature: Historical Perspectives*, edited by E. Watkins, 197–218. Oxford: Oxford University Press.

Chignell, A. 2022. "The Focus Theory of Hope." *Philosophical Quarterly* 73 (1): 44–63.

Cobb, A. D. 2015. "Hope as an Intellectual Virtue?" *Southern Journal of Philosophy* 53 (3): 269–285.

Cremaldi, A., and J. M. C. Kwong. 2022. "Bitterness without Hope." *Journal of Social Philosophy*, https://doi.org/10.1111/josp.12455.

Dalferth, I. U., and M. A. Block, eds. 2016. *Hope: Claremont Studies in the Philosophy of Religion Conference 2014*. Tübingen: Mohr Siebeck.

Dauenhauer, B. 1986. *The Politics of Hope*. New York: Routledge & Kegan Paul.

Davidson, D. 1963. "Actions, Reasons, and Causes." *Journal of Philosophy* 60 (23): 685–700.

Day, J. P. 1969. "Hope." *American Philosophical Quarterly* 6 (2): 89–102.

Day, J. P. 1991. *Hope: A Philosophical Inquiry*. Helsinki: Philosophical Society of Finland.

Day, J. P. 1998. "More about Hope and Fear." *Ethical Theory and Moral Practice* 1: 121–123.

DeYoung, R. K. 2014. "Practicing Hope." *Res Philosophica* 91 (3): 387–410.

Dienstag, J. F. 2006. *Pessimism: Philosophy, Ethic, Spirit*. Princeton, NJ: Princeton University Press.

Döring, Sabine. 2014. "What May I Hope? Why It Can be Rational to Rely on One's Hope." *European Journal for Philosophy and Religion*, Autumn, 117–129.

Dodd, James. 2004. "The Philosophical Significance of Hope." *Review of Metaphysics* 58 (1): 117–146.

Dodd, Jordan. 2017. "Hope, Knowledge, and Blindspots." *Synthese* 194 (2): 531–543.

Downie, R. S. 1963. "Hope." *Philosophy and Phenomenological Research* 24 (2): 248–251.

Dunlap, R. 2020. "A Zen Buddhist Conception of Hope in Enlightenment." In *The Moral Psychology of Hope*, edited by C. Blöser and T. Stahl, 209–226. London: Rowman & Littlefield.

Elliot, D. 2017. *Hope and Christian Ethics*. New York: Cambridge University Press.

Fackenheim, E. L. 1970. "The Commandment to Hope: A Response to Contemporary Jewish Experience." In *The Future of Hope*, edited by W. H. Capps, 68–91. Philadelphia: Fortress Press.

Forte, J. 2016. "Explaining Hope in Plato's *Philebus*." *International Philosophical Quarterly* 56 (3): 283–295.

Gendler, Tamar Szabó. 2008a. "Alief and Belief." *The Journal of Philosophy* 105 (10): 634–663.

Gendler, Tamar Szabó. 2008b. "Alief in Action (and Reaction)." *Mind & Language* 23 (5): 552–585.

Godfrey, J. J. 1987. *A Philosophy of Human Hope*. Dordrecht: Martinus Nijhoff.

Govier, T. 2011. "Hope and Its Opposites." *Journal of Social Philosophy* 42 (3): 239–253.

Gravlee, G. S. 2000. "Aristotle on Hope." *Journal of the History of Philosophy* 38 (4): 461–477.

Green, J. M. 2008. *Pragmatism and Social Hope: Deepening Democracy in Global Contexts*. New York: Columbia University Press.

Han-Pile, B. 2017. "Hope, Powerlessness, and Agency." *Midwest Studies in Philosophy* 41: 175–201. https://en.wikipedia.org/wiki/Pandora.

Huber, J. 2019. "Defying Democratic Despair: A Kantian Account of Hope in Politics." *European Journal of Political Theory* 20 (4): 719–738.

Hume, D. 1978. *A Treatise of Human Nature*. Edited by P. H. Nidditch. Oxford: Clarendon Press.

Jackson, E. 2021. "Belief, Faith, and Hope: On the Rationality of Long-Term Commitment." *Mind* 130 (517): 35–57.

James, S. 2003. *Passion and Action: The Emotions in Seventeenth-Century Philosophy*. Oxford: Clarendon Press.

Jeffrey, A. 2017. "Does Hope Morally Vindicate Faith?" *International Journal for Philosophy of Religion* 81(1–2): 193–211.

Kadlac, A. 2015. "The Virtue of Hope." *Ethical Theory and Moral Practice* 18: 337–354.

Kadlac, A. 2017. "Hope(s) and Hopefulness." *American Philosophical Quarterly* 54 (3): 209–221.

Koopman, C. 2009. *Pragmatism as Transition: Historicity and Hope in James, Dewey, and Rorty*. New York: Columbia University Press.

Kwong, J. M. C. 2019. "What Is Hope?" *European Journal of Philosophy* 27 (1): 243–254.

Kwong, J. M. C. 2020. "Hope and Hopefulness." *Canadian Journal of Philosophy* 50 (7): 832–843.

Kwong, J. M. C. 2022a. "How to Theorize about Hope." *European Journal of Philosophy* 30 (4): 1426–1439.

Kwong, J. M. C. 2022b. "The Phenomenology of Hope." *American Philosophical Quarterly* 50 (3): 313–325.

Kwong, J. M. C. Forthcoming. "Despair and Hopelessness." *Journal of the American Philosophical Association.*

Lamb, M. 2016a. "Aquinas and the Virtues of Hope: Theological and Democratic: Aquinas and the Virtues of Hope." *Journal of Religious Ethics* 44 (2): 300–332.

Lamb, M. 2016b. "A Passion and Its Virtue: Aquinas on Hope and Magnanimity." In *Hope: Claremont Studies in the Philosophy of Religion Conference 2014*, edited by I. U. Dalferth and M. A. Block, 67–88. Tübingen: Mohr Siebeck.

Lamb, M. 2018. "Between Presumption and Despair: Augustine's Hope for the Commonwealth." *American Political Science Review* 112 (4): 1036–1049.

Lamb, M. 2022. *A Commonwealth of Hope: Augustine's Political Thought.* Princeton, NJ: Princeton University Press.

Lear, J. 2006. *Radical Hope: Ethics in the Face of Cultural Devastation.* Cambridge, MA: Harvard University Press.

Marcel, G. 1978. *Homo Viator: Introduction to a Metaphysic of Hope.* Chicago: Gateway.

Martin, A. 2011. "Hopes and Dreams." *Philosophy and Phenomenological Research* 83 (1): 148–173.

Martin, A. 2014. *How We Hope: A Moral Psychology.* Princeton, NJ: Princeton University Press.

Mason, C. 2021. "Hoping and Intending." *Journal of the American Philosophical Association* 7 (4): 514–529.

McCormick, M. S. 2017. "Rational Hope." *Philosophical Explorations* 20 (1): 127–141.

McGeer, V. 2004. "The Art of Good Hope." *Annals of the American Academy of Political and Social Science* 592: 100–127.

McGeer, V. 2008. "Trust, Hope, and Empowerment." *Australasian Journal of Philosophy* 86 (2): 237–254.

Meirav, A. 2009. "The Nature of Hope." *Ratio*, n.s., 22 (2): 216–233.

Milona, M. 2019. "Finding Hope." *Canadian Journal of Philosophy* 49 (5): 710–729.

Milona, M. 2020. "Discovering the Virtue of Hope." *European Journal of Philosophy* 28 (3): 740–754.

Milona, M. 2022. "Does Hope Require Belief?" *American Philosophical Quarterly* 59 (2): 191–199.

Milona, M., and K. Stockdale. 2018. "A Perceptual Theory of Hope." *Ergo: An Open Access Journal of Philosophy* 5 (8): 203–222.

Mittleman, A. 2009. *Hope in a Democratic Age: Philosophy, Religion, and Political Theory.* New York: Oxford University Press.

Moellendorf, D. 2006. "Hope as a Political Virtue." *Philosophical Papers* 35 (3): 413–433.

Moltmann, J. 1967. *Theology of Hope.* New York: Harper and Row.

Mueller, A. 2019. "Hopeless Practical Deliberation—Reply to Bobier." *Analysis* 79 (4): 629–631.

Palmqvist, C.-J. 2021 "Analysing Hope: The Live Possibility Account." *European Journal of Philosophy* 9: 685–698.

Pettit, P. 2004. "Hope and Its Place in Mind." *Annals of the American Academy of Political and Social Science* 592: 152–165.

Pieper, J. 1997. *Faith, Hope, Love.* San Francisco: Ignatius Press.

Ratcliffe, M. 2013. "What Is It to Lose Hope?" *Phenomenology and the Cognitive Sciences* 12 (4): 597–614.

Rioux, C. 2021a. "Hope as a Source of Grit." *Ergo: An Open Access Journal of Philosophy* 8 (33): 264–287.

Rioux, C. 2021b. "Hope: Conceptual and Normative Issues." *Philosophy Compass* 16 (3): e12724.

Schumacher, B. 2003. *A Philosophy of Hope: Josef Pieper and the Contemporary Debate on Hope.* Translated by D. C. Schindler. New York: Fordham University Press.

Segal, G., and M. Textor. 2015, "Hope as a Primitive Mental State." *Ratio* 28 (2): 207–222.

Shade, P. 2001. *Habits of Hope: A Pragmatic Theory.* Nashville, TN: Vanderbilt University Press.

Sleat, M, 2013. "Hope and Disappointment in Politics." *Contemporary Politics* 19 (2): 131–145.

Smith, N. H. 2008. "Analysing Hope." *Critical Horizons: A Journal of Philosophy and Social Theory* 9 (1): 5–23.

Snow, N. E. 2019. "Faces of Hope." In *Theories of Hope: Exploring Alternative Dimensions of Affective Experience,* edited by R. M. Green, 5–23. Lanham, MD: Lexington Books.

Snow, N. E. 2020. "Is Hope a Moral Virtue?" In *The Moral Psychology of Hope,* edited by C. Blöser and T. Stahl, 171–187. London: Rowman & Littlefield.

Snyder, C. R., ed. 2000. *Handbook of Hope: Theory, Measures, and Applications.* San Diego, CA: Academic Press.

Stitzlein, S. M. 2018. "Hoping and Democracy." *Contemporary Pragmatism* 15: 228–250.

Stitzlein, S. M. 2020. "Pragmatist Hope." In *The Moral Psychology of Hope,* edited by C. Blöser and T. Stahl, 93–112. London: Rowman & Littlefield.

Stockdale, K. 2019. "Social and Political Dimensions of Hope." *Journal of Social Philosophy* 50 (1): 28–44.

Stockdale, K. 2021. *Hope under Oppression*. New York: Oxford University Press.

Thompson, A. 2009. "Radical Hope for Living Well in a Warmer World." *Journal of Agricultural and Environmental Ethics* 23 (1–2): 43–55.

van den Heuvel, S. C., ed. 2020. *Historical and Multidisciplinary Perspectives on Hope*. Cham, Switzerland: Springer.

van Hooft, S. 2011. *Hope*. Durham, UK: Acumen.

Vogt, K. M. 2017. "Imagining Good Future States: Hope and Truth in Plato's Philebus." In *Selfhood and the Soul: Essays on Ancient Thought and Literature in Honour of Christopher Gill*, edited by R. Seaford, J. Wilkins, and M. Wright, 33–48. Oxford: Oxford University Press.

Walker, M. U. 2006. *Moral Repair: Reconstructing Moral Relations after Wrongdoing*. New York: Cambridge University Press.

Warren, C. L. 2015. "Black Nihilism and the Politics of Hope." *CR: The New Centennial Review* 15 (1): 215–248.

Westbrook, R. B. 2008. *Democratic Hope: Pragmatism and the Politics of Truth*. Ithaca, NY: Cornell University Press.

Wheatley, J. M. O. 1958. "Wishing and Hoping." *Analysis* 18 (6): 121–131.

Wild, J., ed. 1958. *Spinoza Selections*. New York: Charles Scribner's Sons.

Williston, B. 2012. "Climate Change and Radical Hope." *Ethics and the Environment* 17(2): 165–186.

Winters, J. R. 2016. *Hope Draped in Black: Race, Melancholy, and the Agony of Progress*. Durham, NC: Duke University Press.

Chapter 1

Virtue or Vice?

A Short Literary History of Hope

ADAM POTKAY

Is hope a virtue? Not necessarily. We hope for many things, some of them good, some bad. What we do or don't do about our hopes may also reflect on us, for better or for worse. One might hope for world peace or an end to poverty, and these appear to be worthy if improbable objects. Yet hoping for such things is not a good, or much of a good, in and of itself. Merely passive hope scarcely seems a virtue; it may appear an idle daydream. Hope for the good becomes meritorious when coupled with exertion: "I am hopefully helping, in my small way, to make good things happen." In earlier English, "I aspire to do good." Conversely, passive hope for bad or morally dubious things—"I hope he breaks a leg"—seems less blameworthy than actively trying to trip up a rival or envied other. To ancient moralists, as well as many people today, the hope for revenge might seem perfectly acceptable behavior; indeed, the failure to avenge a slight is in many contexts dishonorable or shameful. Yet there are hopes that far fewer would condone, for instance, in President Truman's account, the Nazis' "hope to enslave the world."[1] Politically, people can and

Adam Potkay, *Virtue or Vice?* In: *The Virtue of Hope.* Edited by: Nancy E. Snow, Oxford University Press.
© Oxford University Press 2024. DOI: 10.1093/oso/9780190069575.003.0002

do hope for the success of persecuting regimes, for the elimination of foes and foreigners. Envy, hatred, revenge, self-aggrandizement, and injustice of every kind are no less salient as motives and objects of hoping than their opposing virtues.

Is hope pleasurable or comforting? Again, not necessarily. It sometimes is, as reflected in Samuel Johnson's definition of the word in *A Dictionary of the English Language* (1755): "Expectation of some good; an expectation indulged with pleasure" (definition 1). Hope typically involves an expectation that falls short of certainty: we also desire the things for which we hope,[2] and this desire is itself, arguably, pleasurable. Ancient Greek metaphors often present hope (*elpis*) as a sweet and warm feeling (even though it was, as a cognitive state, something of which they largely disapproved) (Cairns 2016, 44). Emily Dickinson, in one of the best known poems on hope ("Hope is the thing with feathers"), reifies it as "the little bird/That kept so many warm." Johnson may be drawing for his definition of hope on Aristotle's *The Art of Rhetoric*, where desire involves pleasure: "whether we are remembering desires that were satisfied in the past or looking forward to their satisfaction in the future, we do feel a kind of pleasure" (book 1, chapter 11, 137b14). The point, however, is arguable. Jayne M. Waterworth maintains that hope is not clearly an emotion, as it lacks the "characteristic feelings" associated with other emotions, for example, "cowering in fear" (Waterworth 2004, 41). Contra Aristotle, Waterworth argues that it is not "necessarily the case that one who hopes should experience any hedonic tone at all" (Waterworth 2004, 57). But we can go further: hope may not only not involve pleasure, but rather involve anxiety and pain. As a Google search amply reveals, poets often invoke "anxious hope" and "fearful hope." And one of Nobel Laureate Olga Tokarczuk's protagonists reflects: "I still had hope but it was a stupid hope, so painful" (Tokarczuk 2019, 219).

Hope, then, depends for its moral status and hedonic tone (if any) on a variety of contexts, including the particularities of what is hoped for, the likelihood of attaining what is desired, and how an agent acts or does not act on her hopes. Why, then, is *hope* apt to sound like an immediate *good* to many people? If hope appears an unqualified good to you, independent of any specific context, it is likely for one of two reasons:

1. You belong to or have been influenced by one of the Abrahamic faiths (Judaism, Christianity, Islam), in which faith-based hope counts as a virtue.
2. You are a political liberal who hopes for social justice, however you may conceive of it—and the fuzzier your conception, the better hope may sound. As I will explain later in this chapter, starting with supporters of the French Revolution— and extending through Barack Obama's 2008 "Hope" poster—"hope" has served as shorthand for hope in progressive politics.

Because hope's positive connotations are now prevalent in the West, I start this compressed history with the classical counterpoint, in which hope is at best problematic, something in need of regulation and restraint if not extirpation. I then turn to Judeo-Christianity, and next to European and American Romanticism, offering a preliminary sketch of the reasons why hope features as a good thing in these overlapping but distinct contexts, religious and political. Since the rise of Christianity, hope has been a double-edged concept: on one hand, it is a worldly passion or emotion, and its contrary is either fear or despair. As an emotion (or an emotion-like motive), hope was widely criticized in classical antiquity through the Renaissance and Enlightenment as an illusion, a distraction from the present moment, the occasion for irrational and self-destructive thinking, and a presumption vis-à-vis God or the gods: in short, a vice. On the other hand, within Christianity hope of a specific kind is one of three theological virtues, and its opposite, despair, is the unforgiveable sin. As a theological virtue—the anticipation of sharing eternally in the glory of God—hope is always a good thing in Christian cultures, and more generally in the Abrahamic faiths.

After paying some attention to the Enlightenment transformation of hope, along with the other passions, into a morally neutral motivational psychology, I focus on the grander claims made on behalf of hope during and after the French Revolution. Hope becomes in the Romantic era a new, semi-secularized virtue: the hope for more life, a better or perfected condition of the individual, of the nation, or of the species, in time or eternity. This new and indeterminate hope often directs us toward a receding horizon, be it imaginative, ethical, or, most typically, political. Romantic-era authors direct us beyond clear conceptualization, for example, William Wordsworth's "something evermore about to be" (*The Prelude* [1805 text], 6:542); Percy Shelley's hope for "arts, though unimagined, yet to be" (*Prometheus Unbound,* act 3, scene 3, line 56). Turning at last to the twentieth century, I address the attenuation of hope in literary modernism before and after Auschwitz, including Kafka's tragi-comic parables of "vanishingly small, almost non-existent hope" (Kafka 2009, 100).[3]

Surprising as it now may seem, for thousands of years many if not most writers viewed hope with suspicion or outright disapproval. Personal hopes, claimed sages from Mesopotamia to China, Socrates to the Stoics, typically involve unworthy or impious objects and thus, whether fulfilled or unfulfilled, end in disappointment if not disaster. Vain human hopes or wishes—hope and wish are closely linked concepts[4]—include those for riches, reputation, remembrance, or significant worldly improvement. It may be acceptable in difficult situations rationally to endorse good outcomes, but it is better not to hope, taking hope to have emotional force.

The case against hope sometimes derives from one of two conservative assumptions: first, that we should not desire what the gods have not given or do not allow us; or second, what history shows to be impossible. The first of these is prominent in one of Pindar's odes from the fifth century BCE, which revisits the myth of the healer Asklepios—who fatally desires the enrichment that would come from bringing a man back from the dead—to condemn "hunting impossibilities on the wings of ineffectual hopes" (Pindar, *Pythia* 3, line 23). Asklepios' vain hope is impious, impossible, and punished as such. But even without the gods, history teaches humility through its repetitive and all-effacing force. All things pass, and all things recur. Nothing satisfies for long and nothing will be remembered. The historical case against hopes or wishes appears strongly in Ecclesiastes, an outlying book of the Hebrew Bible, probably from the fifth–fourth centuries BCE but legendarily attributed to King Solomon: "I the Preacher was king over Israel in Jerusalem. . . . I have seen all the works that are done under the sun; and, behold, all is vanity and vexation of spirit. That which is crooked cannot be made straight: and that which is wanting cannot be numbered" (1:12–15). Rather than harboring trust in God's promises or hope in Israel's future, Ecclesiastes depicts natural and historical cycles at odds with the human orientation toward aims or goals, including those of achievement and remembrance. The wishes we do have, from generation to generation, are for objects that are distributed not according to merit and justice but rather "time and chance" (9:11), and, even if attained, bring no enduring satisfaction. Such hopes are for wisdom itself (1:18), power, wealth, palaces, aesthetic delights, and long life. The characteristic advice of Ecclesiastes or the Preacher is to work or apply oneself (4:9, 9:10), not with an eye to ultimate accomplishment, but rather to be able to enjoy the simple pleasures of the present, "to eat, and to drink and to be merry" within a family setting (8:15).[5]

With relation to the gods or to the historical laws that serve as their proxies, hope appears symptomatic of human ignorance and impotence. Even Homer's Odysseus, the avatar of effort and expectation, foresight and craft, who succeeds in returning home from war after twenty years away, errs under the sway of hope: he stays his men in the Cyclops' den for the exciting guest-gift he imagines might come his way. The Cyclops, lacking all sense of hospitality, promptly eats two of Odysseus' men, and we know the story from there (*Odyssey*, book 9). The story of Pandora's jar is an interpretive crux in Hesiod's *Works and Days* (80–105): what does it mean that amid the evils associated with the jar (prominently, labor and sickness), hope alone is preserved for us? Is hope another evil, perhaps the greatest of evils—or the last remaining good, an antidote to evils—or, somehow, both?

The vanity of most or all hopes is commonplace in the Stoic and Epicurean philosophical traditions and the Latin poetry they inspired. The Stoic Seneca, in his more temperate moods, recommends, "let us restrict the range of hope" in order to avoid disappointment and anger.[6] Less moderately, he advises against hope entirely: "cease to hope . . . and you will cease to fear."[7] Boethius concurs in *The Consolation of Philosophy* (book 1, poem 7, lines 27–31): "Fly from hope and sorrow. The mind is clouded, bridled and bound, where these things reign."[8] For Horace, in Ode 1.11, the uncertainty and brevity of life preclude "long hopes" (*spem longam*), and so he famously counsels, "seize the day, trusting the future as little as possible" (*carpe diem, quam minimum credula postero*).[9] These quotations remain commonplaces through the eighteenth century; *carpe diem* is one of the few Latin tags widely known today.

Two generic exceptions to the classical case against hope would seem to be (1) the golden-age scenarios of Greek and Roman literature, recursions to a just natural state where property and labor will either vanish or become less divisive and less strenuous; and (2) the

Greek-language novels of the Roman era, which reward, after many arduous trials, the reunion hopes of two virtuous lovers, who then live happily ever after. Both cases, however, are purely fanciful, self-consciously literary creations. Of the five complete Greek novels (including, most famously, the *Aethiopika* and *Daphnis and Chloe*), Laurel Fulkerson notes that it is in any case only the central lovers whose hopes are fulfilled, with ancillary characters (other suitors, parents) left frustrated (Fulkerson 2016, 82). In golden-age returns, including parts of Hesiod's *Works and Days* (lines 109–120, 213–237) and Virgil's fourth *Eclogue* (often referred to, in the Christian era, as the "Messianic Eclogue"), we find exhortations to greater justice clothed in the implied promise (Hesiod) or the explicit, fantastical representation (Virgil) of cyclical return. Virgil's cycling back is a dialectical preservation of the most refined luxury of his day—for example, to save people the rigors of dying cloth, sheep will spontaneously change their fleeces to purple and saffron (lines 42–45)—in a way that is the more appealing for being more flamboyantly impossible. Since hope is desire for the possible, then neither the early novel nor the golden-age recursion reflects hope.

In summary, the classical case against hope may be divided into five main points:

1. Hope is fundamentally deceptive, based on an uncertain future that rarely arrives as we imagine it.

2. Hope is morally corrosive because most things that most people hope for are or tend to be unworthy, unsatisfying, impious and harmful, including riches, unstinting sensual pleasure, fame, beauty, glory, and long (or endless) life. The loci classici for this theme in the West are Ecclesiastes and Juvenal's Tenth Satire (the latter has spirited English translations by John Dryden and Samuel Johnson), though it underwrites as well the satiric aspect of utopian fiction from

More to Huxley. The ephemerality or illusive nature of most or all human hopes and wishes also features prominently in classical Indian (Brahman, Hindu, Buddhist) and Chinese (Confucian, neo-Confucian) philosophies.

3. Considered as a passion, hope is, like all the passions (love, fear, anger, etc.), something in relation to which we are passive. We have either no control or insufficient control over it. Therefore, in hoping we compromise or lose our rational agency.

4. As a corollary to point 3, susceptibility to hope—which may seem a better emotion than others—makes us susceptible to the negative future-oriented emotion of fear, as well as the negative present-oriented emotion of sorrow or disappointment.

5. Hope in the future alienates us from something over which we have some control: the enjoyment and/or proper use of the present day. Horace enshrines this point in one of his best-known odes, here in John Dryden's eighteenth-century couplet translation:

Happy the man, and happy he alone,

He who can call today his own;

He who, secure within, can say,

Tomorrow, do thy worst, for I have lived today.

Be fair or foul, or rain or shine,

The joys I have possess'd, in spite of fate are mine.

Not Heaven itself upon the past has power;

But what has been, has been, and I have had my hour.

(Horace, *Ode*, 3:29, in Dryden 1969, 83)

Judeo-Christianity is, by contrast, strongly prospective. In Christian theology, hope of a particular sort is indeed a *virtue*. No classical moralist considered it such; only in post–World War II literature (for example, Viktor Frankl) and some contemporary philosophy (Bovens 1999; McGeer 2004; Snow 2018) is hope tentatively explored as a possible *secular* value or virtue. In the Bible, however, hope is central to the moral life of a God-infused community. The Hebrew Scriptures feature both waiting (words derived from *yhl*) for the Lord, a stance of expectation that may be positive, and active and tense hoping (*kvh*), its object more often than not being God's justice (Mittleman 2009, 115–125). "Faith inaugurates a duty to hope," writes Alan Mittleman; "where there is faith, then, there are always good grounds for hope" (Mittleman 2009, 119). Hope is both individual and collective: individuals, and the Israelite people, hope alike for justice, righteousness, an unbroken or restored relationship with God, divine help against persecution and suffering, and, not least, a promised land, an inspired leader, an enduring kingdom.

In the Hebrew Bible, collective hope sometimes focuses on an anointed future king, hope in the Messiah (Hebrew) or Christ (Greek), who will reign over a restored or perfected nation or Mediterranean world (see, for example, Isaiah 9:1–7). According to the Christian Bible's New Testament, the Messiah has already arrived in the person of Jesus Christ, and he will come again in power and glory to usher in the final judgment and institute, for his elect, a new and perfected world. In the time preparatory to this second coming, the three crucial virtues for Christians—the three so-called theological virtues—are faith, hope (Greek *elpis*, Latin *spes*), and spiritual love (translated in the King James Bible as "charity," from the Latin *caritas*). St. Paul's best-known words are these from 1 Corinthians 13:12–13: "For now we see through a glass, darkly [dimly, imperfectly]; but then [at the end time, in an afterlife] face to face: now I know in part; but then shall I know even as also I am known. And now abideth faith, hope, charity, these three; but the greatest of these is charity." One reason for love's superiority is that, by most counts, it alone will abide in God's eternal presence, once faith in things unseen and hope for their unfolding in time are no longer needed. Now, in this life, hope is a virtue because it involves a deliberate choice, the choice of confidence in God and his promise.

Although any relationship to the future involves us in uncertainty, people of faith may consider eternal life a certain outcome, which involves an apparent paradox and the subordination of hope to faith. Dante, toward the end of his *Divine Comedy*, recounts his comprehension, in Paradise, of the true meaning of hope (derived from the theologian Peter Lombard):

"Hope," I said, "is the certain expectation
of future glory, springing
from heavenly grace and merit we have won." (Dante, *Paradiso*,
    25: 67–69)

Hope's religious opposite is despair, often interpreted as the unspecified, unforgivable sin of the gospels (Matthew 12:31–32). To despair is to abandon all merit and all possibility of grace (unmerited favor), and divine hope, once lost, is forever denied to one. In Dante, the words inscribed on the gate to Hell conclude: "ABANDON ALL HOPE, YOU WHO ENTER HERE" (Dante, *Inferno*, 3: 9).

Historically, hope as a theological virtue—philosophically formulated by St. Thomas Aquinas, poetically elevated by Dante, and crucial to Western literature through the eighteenth century—sits uneasily beside hope as a worldly emotion. As an emotion or motive, hoping—or wishing (the two are rarely, in practice, distinguished)—is dogged by classical disapprobation into the nineteenth century. In the Christian era there are two hopes just as there are two loves, carnal and spiritual, particular and universal, a division (or continuum) rooted in Diotima's ladder of love in Plato's *Symposium* and endlessly elaborated up to the present day.[10] Yet while the philosophical and literary-historical literature on love is extensive, the two hopes are as yet largely innocent to analysis.

The two hopes are brought into clear contrast in the dialogue poem "On Hope," written jointly by Abraham Cowley and Richard Crashaw in the mid-seventeenth century.[11] Cowley's stanzas (four out of the poem's ten) arraign hope according to classical and especially Stoic topoi: hope is a cheat, an illusion; a companion to fear; a prelude to disappointment and anger. Hope is "Fortune's cheating Lotterie" (Crashaw 1970, line 51) and "Brother of Feare!" (line 71). In response to Cowley's witty revisiting of classical authority, however, Crashaw provides interlaced stanzas (a preponderant six of the poem's ten) in praise of hope as a theological virtue. Hope sails above Fortune and the stars (lines 61–64); it is "*Faith's* sister!" and "Feares Antidote!" (81–82). Unsurprisingly, Christian hope—revealed as "true hope"—gets to close the poem: "True *Hope's* a glorious Huntress, and her chase/The God of Nature in the field of Grace" (89–90).

What true hope anticipates, of course, is eternal and spiritually perfected life. It also provides a foretaste of this anticipated state— hope is "our earlier Heaven!" (Crashaw 1970, 41)—and may even seem to collapse the present into that future, chronological time (*chronos*) into spiritual time (*kairos*):

> Sweet *Hope*! Kind cheat! Faire fallacy! by thee
> Wee are not where, or what wee bee,
> But what, and where wee would bee: thus art thou
> Our absent presence, and our future now. (67–70)

The question Crashaw raises in these rhymes is a cognitive one: how can we know, now, what eternal life will be like, and without this knowledge, how can hope be our future now? The object of Christian hope is *determinate*—eternal life—but it is also *unspecific*, as we can never know what that life will be like. (Hoping for a worldly good, by contrast, can be both determinate and specific.)

Not that lack of knowledge can keep us from *imagining* future life. Jacob Sider Jost has argued that, in the later seventeenth and eighteenth centuries, hell and divine judgment recede in importance, and heaven is increasingly imagined in terms of chronological time and individual personality. In contrast to a "theocentric heaven . . . in which human pleasures and relationships were subsumed in the overwhelming presence of God," John Bunyan and the *Spectator* papers popularized "a more humanized heaven in which licit human pleasures and relationships, particularly ties of kinship, marriage, and friendship, continue in a new form" (Jost 2015, 25).

However, this prosaic view of heaven—and, more generally, making assumptions about an afterlife—were not without detractors. In Alexander Pope's well-known lines from *An Essay on Man* (1733–1734), eschatological hope is a gift given to all, its proper object being determinate (eternal life) but unspecific. Since we don't know what eternal life will be like, Pope advises:

> Hope humbly then; with trembling pinions soar;
> Wait the great teacher Death, and God adore!
> What future bliss, he gives not thee to know,
> But gives that Hope to be thy blessing now.
> Hope springs eternal in the human breast:
> Man never Is, but always To be blest:
> The soul, uneasy and confin'd from home,
> Rests and expatiates in a life to come. (1950, epistle 1: 91–98)

Forty-five years after Pope wrote his lines on hope, Samuel Johnson creatively misread them, contributing to hope's earthward turn in the later eighteenth century. Pope had addressed the afterlife; Johnson applies a couplet of Pope's (taken out of context) to mortal life, and human psychology. I quote from Boswell's *Life of Johnson* (1791) and his entry for April 10, 1775:

> He this day enlarged upon Pope's melancholy remark, "Man never is, but always to be blest." He asserted that the present was never a happy state to any human being; but that, as every part of life, of which we are conscious, was at some point of time a period yet to come, in which felicity was expected, there was some happiness produced by hope. Being pressed upon this subject, and asked if he really was of opinion, that though, in general, happiness was very rare in human life, a man was not sometimes happy in the moment that was present, he answered, "Never, but when he is drunk." (Boswell 1980, 617–618)

Consciousness of the present moment is painful, Johnson claims, unless either the present is supplemented by futurity, or consciousness is abated by liquor. Drunkenness is stasis, while hope propels us and provides some tenuous, future-oriented "happiness" or pleasurable consciousness. Johnson is not moralizing here, satirizing human wishes—something he partly does elsewhere, notably in his poem *The Vanity of Human Wishes*, an imitation of Juvenal's third Satire, and in the sermon he ghost-wrote on Ecclesiastes 1:14, "all is vanity and vexation of spirit."[12] Yet even in these apparent satires, Johnson has been called a "satirist manqué," one for whom the distance necessary for satire collapses in sympathy with all-too-human nature (Bate 1970). For Johnson worldly hopes might be illusionary, but they are at the same time the only palliative for the ache or emptiness of the existential present.

In Boswell's *Life of Johnson*, Johnson speaks of hope as part of a social psychology in which desires prompt endeavors that are fundamentally self-interested. In doing so, he situates himself in the line of a mechanistic project that extends from Thomas Hobbes, for whom happiness is a psychological matter rather than, as for the ancients and Thomists, an ethical assessment of the life that is good or proper for human beings (*eudaimonia*). Hobbes maintains at the outset of *Leviathan* (1:11) that "felicity is a continual progress of the desire from one object to another, the attaining of the former being still the way to the latter"; there is, in his psychological model, no ultimate aim of life, no contentment or repose (Hobbes 2002, 75). Hobbes' mechanistic psychology, as developed by Locke and Mandeville, informs Johnson's secular view of human nature just as it does David Hume's (Potkay 2000, 61–75). According to this psychology, hope is a more or less neutral mechanism for moving the self-concerned individual forward in time from one temporary satisfaction to the next. As Addison will put it in one of his broadly popular *Spectator* essays (1712): "we have no sooner gained one Point but we extend our Hopes to another."[13] Hopes keep us going, individually, with no end or final aim in sight. It is a functional good, though not necessarily a moral one.

Yet the psychologizing of hope, as a light of literary history, pales next to its political and ontological incandescence in Romanticism. What we now think of as political hope—hope in the socially transformative power of representative government (as distinct from prophetic hope in a future ruler)—is, arguably, a product of the French Revolution. Social justice as we now understand it, as the state's distribution of goods to individuals irrespective of their merits or desert, arises during the French Revolution, along with our notion of hope as a distinctly political category. In 1841, Ralph Waldo Emerson divided politics between "the party of Conservatism and that of Innovation," representing "the opposition of Past and Future, of Memory and Hope."[14]

Political hope has had a special appeal, over the past 230 years, to young persons—starting, famously, with the great English Romantic poet William Wordsworth, who wrote of his early enthusiasm for the French Revolution:

> O pleasant exercise of hope and joy,
> For great were the auxiliars which then stood
> Upon our side, we who were strong in love.
> Bliss was it in that dawn to be alive,
> But to be young was very heaven! (*The Prelude*, 10:689–693
> [1805 version])

Part of why political hope appeals so much is, I think, its aspect of *indeterminacy*—although it may have certain determinate objects (legal equality, etc.), it also tends to exceed them, to become an attitude of general hopefulness toward general, unspecific changes and improvements. The hopes of youth are often indeterminate—a hopefulness without clear or consistent objects—and so are those of progressive politics. Nor, according to the Romantic account, should hope have a clear or determinate object or aim. For Wordsworth, the inability of experience to live up to our hopes proves not that our hopes are unreasonable (the classical conclusion), but rather that

> Our destiny, our nature, and our home,
> Is with infinitude—and only there;
> With hope it is, hope that can never die,
> Effort, and expectation, and desire,
> And something evermore about to be (*The Prelude*, 6:538–542).

Hope thus becomes a new, semi-secularized virtue: the hope for more life, a better or perfected condition of the individual, political society, or the species, in time or—depending on how far "evermore about to be" extends—eternity. This new and indeterminate hope directs us toward a receding horizon. It aims beyond any immediate hope, and beyond conceptualization. Emily Dickinson, Wordsworth's great heir as a poet of interminable hope, suggests its affective call, seemingly independent of clear or present semantic content, in the metaphor, "the tune without the words":

> "Hope" is the thing with feathers—
> That perches in the soul—
> And sings the tune without the words—
> And never stops—at all—

Part of the reason it never stops is that satisfaction is not achievable in the "actual" world, a point Dickinson makes in a subsequent poem ("Who never wanted—maddest Joy"):

> Within its reach, though yet ungrasped
> Desire's perfect Goal—
> No nearer—lest the Actual—
> Should disenthrall thy soul—

Our presumed attraction to the ever-out-of-reach, the thing enjoyed in imagination only, is proof for Schiller (*Hoffnung*, "Hope") that "we were born for something better" (*zu was besserm sind wir gebohren*) (Schiller 1995). Goethe's Faust strives upward perpetually, even in heaven (such is the claim, at least, of the problematic historian of hope, Ernst Bloch).[15] Percy Shelley imagines a resurrected hope that realizes its object beyond its own "wreck," or creates that object imaginatively in its very failure, urging us "to hope, till Hope creates/From its own wreck the thing it contemplates."[16] Do any of these authors believe in an assured or even possible afterlife, another world beyond our actual one? They tend in varying degrees to entertain the possibility, at least intermittently, and have certainly appealed to readers without as well as with religious faith. While Romantic-era hope does not supersede or displace the orthodox theological virtues, it does supplement or vie with them, and thus figures in the modern "differentiation" between religious and secular or poetic modes of authority.[17]

Artistically, the Romantics also rely on the drama of Christian autobiographical models. As in the best-known Christian autobiographies, from Augustine's *Confessions* to John Bunyan's *Grace Abounding to the Chief of Sinners*, the hope of Romantic-era authors features in relation to episodes of doubt, delay and despair. "Hope and dejection," M. H. Abrams claimed, are central to Romantic writing and its post-Enlightenment "reversion to . . . the violent conflicts and abrupt reversals of the Christian inner life . . . the extremes of destruction and creation, hell and heaven, exile and reunion, death and rebirth, dejection and joy, paradise lost and paradise regained" (Abrams 1971, 66, 442–448). Thus, Dickinson's indefinite hope counterposes her erotic-religious suffering and recourse to "the White Sustenance—/ Despair—." Wordsworth's hope in "something evermore about to be" arises in narrative context from the "dejection" he experienced in crossing the Alps without being aware of it, an immense anti-climax to imaginative expectation. At the time of his poem's composition his greater "sorrow, disappointment" was with the violent course of the French Revolution under Robespierre, leading to an "utter loss of hope itself/And things to hope for." Along the way, studying the rationalist-anarchist philosopher William Godwin did not help: "Sick, wearied out with contrarieties,/[I] Yielded up moral questions in despair."[18] Within Romanticism, hope and futurity are in close interchange with the traumas and tragedy of the past: Romantic hope is more akin to what, speaking of an African American literary tradition grounded in W. E. B. Du Bois, Joseph R. Winters calls "melancholic hope," as distinct from facile optimism (Winters 2016, 6).

Literary modernism is attuned to this historical dialectic between progress and loss, improvement and corruption, hope and more or less endless disappointment. The ancients' understanding of cyclical

repetition and the impotence of long hope is reborn in high modernism from Nietzsche's eternal recurrence to the daily, balked efforts of
Kafka's protagonist K. to make contact with the Castle, and Beckett's
perfectly free tramps daily awaiting the never-coming of Godot. In
the twentieth century authors from Kafka to Beckett, Virginia Woolf
to Wisława Szymborska, have focused on the small hopes of small
souls, hope straggling forward in diminished manner toward objects
of dubious worth or reality.

Far from religious hopes, and the secular-political hopes that
extend from the French to the Russian Revolution, Kafka's still
haunting fictive world features characters seeking acknowledgment or redress from structures of political or divine authority with
"almost non-existent hope." In *The Castle* (1925), Kafka's protagonist, known only as K., makes daily efforts to see the castle official
Klamm, who he hopes will offer final confirmation of his position
as the village's land-surveyor—or at least acknowledge his existence. Here is a typical conversation that K. has with a fellow vil-
lager, the landlady Gardena, who has earlier offered to take a letter
of K's to Klamm's secretary: "But you turned my offer down [says
Gardena], and yet there won't be any other way for you, only that
way. To be sure, after your performance today, after your attempt to
accost Klamm, you'll have even less chance of success. But this last
small, vanishingly small, almost non-existent hope is the only hope
you have." K. replies with surprise that Gardena now "urge[s] me
forward on the path to Klamm," but Gardena replies—apparently
contradicting her earlier offer of the smallest hope—"Urge you
forward? . . . Is it urging you forward if I say that your attempts are
hopeless?" (Kafka 2009, 100). Kafka himself, in response to his
friend Max Brod's query about whether there was hope outside of
the world that we know, famously replied, "Plenty of hope—for
God unlimited hope. Only not for us."[19] Modernism is to a great
extent a literature of no or of limited hopes, tragi-comic repetition

over advancement, minimal differentiation over moral or political transformation.

Kafka died a decade before the consolidation of Nazi power in Germany, and two decades before the peak working of the Nazi death camps across central Europe. In a way that has yet to be appreciated, literature is polarized by two conflicting responses to the role of hope in the *shoah* or Holocaust. Was hope a balm, indeed the only possible expression of value and of faith, or was it a part of the calamity? Tadeusz Borowski, in "Auschwitz: Our Home" (1946, Poland), takes the latter view, the one that Nietzsche might have taken. Borowski's bitter address to his contemporaries is tinged with self-reproach as a survivor of the camp:

> Despite the madness of war, we lived for a world that would be different. For a better world to come when all this is over. . . . Do you really think that, without the hope that such a world is possible, that the rights of man will be restored again, we could stand the concentration camp even for one day? It is that very hope that makes people go without a murmur to the gas chambers, keeps them from risking a revolt, paralyses them into numb inactivity. . . . Never before in the history of mankind has hope been stronger than man, but never also has it done so much harm as it has in the war, in this concentration camp. We were never taught how to give up hope, and this is why today we perish in gas chambers. (Borowski 1976, 121–122)

Borowski's argument is that in the camps despair or, better, *desperation* would have been more useful or effective than hope. Although hope may be connected to agency, Borowski asks us to imagine hopelessness, in a hopeless situation (if one can assuredly be perceived as such), as a superior motivation, because what may have been required was risking everything recklessly, rising up against armed oppressors with sheer numbers, without hope in a better future, without the future-oriented drive of self-preservation. Borowski sees hope, by contrast, as paralysis.

Borowski's denigration of hope finds its counterpoint in Viktor Frankl, *Man's Search for Meaning: An Introduction to Logotherapy*. Frankl asserts the value of hope in a "practically hopeless situation": "They must not lose hope but should keep their courage in the certainty that the hopelessness of our struggle did not detract from its dignity and meaning" (Frankl 2006, 83). Frankl prompts the philosopher Jayne Waterworth to see "hope as a symbolic act embodying meaning. That is, even if camp inmates believed that death was inevitable, and they also believed that any struggle was vain in terms of saving themselves, they could nevertheless hope that their deaths would not be in vain, individually, collectively or historically." Such a hope is *for others*: others who might survive and say "Never again." Frankl's "expressive hope," Waterworth concludes, "persists to express value in the face of . . . catastrophe" (Waterworth 2004, 105, 107). Such "expressive hope" is akin to the "radical hope" Jonathan Lear attributes to the truly hopeless—in his case, a Native American tribe facing extinction.[20] For proponents of radical hope—which may stretch back as far as Percy Shelley—there are possibilities beyond what can be imagined, and a certain amount of wrack and ruin must be endured before the imageless good can be realized.

In sum, the literary history of hope is not preponderantly hopeful or comforting. Literature amply reveals both the pros and cons of hope in one or more of its forms: worldly or other-worldly, definite or indefinite, psychological or political, individual or collective. Hope, especially within Christian and Romantic-political contexts, can be a key virtue, but it can also, in other situations and from other points of view, be an error, a shortcoming if not a vice. In Kafka it becomes a risibly mechanical habit and recurrent vanishing act in a fictive universe designed to obfuscate and frustrate. In the more brutal reality semi-fictively represented by authors who survived the Nazi death camps, hope appears in starkly opposing ways that call for further consideration: was it the only possible expression of value in a hopeless situation, or was it the cause of that hopelessness?[21]

NOTES

1. Truman's exact phrasing in his August 15, 1945, speech (on the bombing of Hiroshima) is "the Germans were working feverishly to find a way to add atomic energy to the other engines of war with which they hoped to enslave the world. But they failed." https://www.trumanlibrary.org/publicpapers/index.php?pid= 100, accessed November 5, 2019.

2. The Oxford English Dictionary's first definition of hope stresses the basis of desire, though in an oddly tautological and chiasmic way: "Expectation of something desired; desire combined with expectation." The philosopher Luc Bovens lists three necessary conditions for hope: non-confident belief that something may or will come about; desire for it to come about; and a "devotion of mental energy" toward or "mental imaging" of its coming about (Bovens 1999, 674).

3. Chapter 9.

4. Johnson's *Dictionary* defines "to hope" as "to live in expectation of some good" and "to expect with desire"; it then defines "to wish" as "to have a strong desire," noting secondarily that "wish" "has a slight significance of hope." Hope presupposes desire, and thus "to wish" in that word's primary sense ("a strong desire"); in its secondary sense wish blurs into the hope it "slightly" signifies. Yet wish is often interchangeable with hope, as in the variable locution "I wish/hope/pray to God." A wish can also be a superstitious hope invested in an external power or force: in a wishing well, for example, or the activity of "wishing upon a star." In these cases, at least, wishing for something involves a non-confident belief that it could, with some assistance, come to pass.

5. The Preacher ends his discourse at 12:8, "Vanity of vanities, saith the preacher; all is vanity"; the book ends with an editorial addition that speaks of the Preacher in the third person and that imposes a pious moral, "Fear God, and keep his commandments: for this is the whole duty of man" (12:13).

6. *In vicinum spes exeat*: from Seneca, *Moral Essays, De Ira/On Anger*, book 3, chapter 7, 1:272–273.

7. Quoting the Stoic Hecato, Seneca writes, *Desines, inquit, timere, si sperare desieris*: from Seneca, *Epistles: 1–65*, Epistle 5, 22–23.

8. My translation from Boethius 1973, 172: *Spemque fugato/Nec dolor adsit./ Nubila mens est/Vinctaque frenis,/Haec ubi regnant.*

9. My translation from Horace (1968, 32).

10. For an accessible intellectual history of love from the Bible to Proust, see May (2011).

11. Quoted from Crashaw (1970, 71–74). George Williams, in his editorial head-note to the poem, remarks that "On Hope" was probably written in the late 1630s or early 1640s, when Crashaw and Cowley were both at Cambridge.

12. Sermon number 12 in Johnson (1978, 127–136).

13. *Spectator* number 535, in Addison (1965, 4:409).

14. "The Conservative," in Emerson (1983, 173).

15. "Goethe's Faust gropes further for his goal even in heaven . . . expecting sheer future in the form of eternity," writes Ernst Bloch (1995, 2:824) in his gargantuan, Marxist-inflected defense of hope in an indefinite future, *Das Prinzip Hoffnung* (Frankfurt: Suhrkamp, 1959), translated into English in 1995. For a strong negative assessment of Bloch, see Eagleton (2015, 90–111). Bloch's project is fundamentally polemical rather than historical, and does not treat the classical and English-language works that are at the center of my ongoing study.

16. *Prometheus Unbound*, 4.573–574, in Shelley (2002).

17. On the modern era's "differentiation" between forms of cultural authority, and the relation of this to nineteenth-century literature, see Jager (2007, 28–29 and passim).

18. Wordsworth (1979), quotations from 1805 text, 6:491, 11:4–7, 10:899–900.

19. Kafka's February 23, 1920, conversation with Brod is quoted from Hayman (1982, 247–248).

20. Lear examines the response of the last great chief of the Crow tribe to the imminent ruin of his tribe's way of life, and his hope in an inconceivable future for his people. "Radical hope," for Lear, is the anticipation of "a good for which those who have the hope as yet lack the appropriate concepts with which to understand it" (Lear 2006, 103).

21. A modified version of this essay was published as the introduction to Adam Potkay, *Hope: A Literary History* (Cambridge University Press, 2022). It is reprinted with permission of Cambridge University Press.

REFERENCES

Abrams, Meyer H. 1971. *Natural Supernaturalism: Tradition and Revolution in Romantic Literature*. New York: Norton.

Addison, Joseph. 1965. *The Spectator*. Edited by Donald F. Bond. Oxford: Clarendon Press.

Aristotle. 2018. *The Art of Rhetoric*. Translated by Robin Waterfield. Oxford: Oxford University Press.

Bate, Walter Jackson. 1970. "Johnson and Satire Manqué." In *Eighteenth-Century Studies in Honor of Donald F. Hyde*, edited by W. H. Bond, 145–160. New York: Grolier Club.

Bloch, Ernst. 1995. *The Principle of Hope*. Edited by Neville Plaice. Cambridge, MA: MIT Press.

Boethius. 1973. *The Theological Tractates* and *The Consolation of Philosophy*. Edited by Hugh F. Stewart, Edward K. Rand, and S. Jim Tester. Loeb Classical Library. Cambridge, MA: Harvard University Press.

Borowski, Tadeusz. 1976. *This Way for the Gas, Ladies and Gentlemen*. Translated by Barbara Vedder. New York: Penguin.

Boswell, James. 1980. *Life of Johnson*. Edited by Robert W. Chapman. Oxford: Oxford University Press.

Bovens, Luc. 1999. "The Value of Hope." *Philosophy and Phenomenological Research* 59 (3): 667–681.

Cairns, Douglas. 2016. "Metaphors for Hope in Archaic and Classical Greek Poetry." In *Hope, Joy, and Affection in the Classical World*, edited by Ruth Caston and Robert Kaster, 13–44. New York: Oxford University Press.

Crashaw, Richard. 1970. *The Complete Poetry of Richard Crashaw*. Edited by George Walton Williams. New York: Norton.

Dante. 2000. *Inferno*. Translated by Robert Hollander and Jean Hollander. New York: Anchor.

Dante. 2007. *Paradiso*. Translated by Robert Hollander and Jean Hollander. New York: Anchor.

Dickinson, Emily. 1960. *The Complete Poems of Emily Dickinson*. Edited by Thomas H. Johnson. Boston: Little, Brown.

Dryden, John. 1969. *The Works of John Dryden*. Vol. 3: *Poems 1685–1692*. Edited by Earl Miner and Vinton A. Dearing. Berkeley: University of California Press.

Eagleton, Terry. 2015. *Hope without Optimism*. Charlottesville: University of Virginia Press.

Emerson, Ralph Waldo. 1983. *Essays and Lectures*. Edited by Joel Porte. New York: Library of America.

Frankl, Viktor E. 2006. *Man's Search for Meaning*. Translated by Ilse Lasch. Boston: Beacon Press.

Fulkerson, Laurel. 2016. "'Torn between Hope and Despair': Narrative Foreshadowing and Suspense in the Greek Novel." In *Hope, Joy, and Affection in the Classical World*, edited by Ruth Caston and Robert Kaster, 75–91. New York: Oxford University Press.

Hammond, Gerald, and Austin Busch, eds. 2012. *The English Bible, King James Version: The New Testament and The Apocrypha*. New York: Norton.

Hayman, Ronald. 1982. *Kafka: A Biography*. Oxford: Oxford University Press.

Hobbes, Thomas. 2002. *Leviathan.* Edited by Aloysius P. Martinich. Peterborough, NH: Broadview.

Horace. 1968. *Odes and Epodes.* Translated by C. E. Bennett. Loeb Classical Library. Cambridge, MA: Harvard University Press.

Jager, Colin. 2007. *The Book of God: Secularization and Design in the Romantic Era.* Philadelphia: University of Pennsylvania Press.

Johnson, Samuel. 1755. *A Dictionary of the English Language.* 2 vols. London: J & P Knapton.

Johnson, Samuel. 1978. *Sermons.* Edited by Jean Hagstrum and James Gray. New Haven, CT: Yale University Press.

Jost, Jacob Sider. 2015. *Prose Immortality, 1711–1819.* Charlottesville: University of Virginia Press.

Kafka, Franz. 2009. *The Castle.* Translated by Anthea Bell. Oxford: Oxford University Press.

Lear, Jonathan. 2006. *Radical Hope: Ethics in the Face of Cultural Devastation.* Cambridge, MA: Harvard University Press.

Marks, Herbert, ed. 2012. *The English Bible, The King James Version: The Old Testament.* New York: Norton.

May, Simon. 2011. *Love: A History.* New Haven, CT: Yale University Press.

McGeer, Victoria. 2004. "The Art of Good Hope." *Annals of the American Academy of Political and Social Science* 592 (1): 100–127.

Mittleman, Alan. 2009. *Hope in a Democratic Age: Philosophy, Religion, and Political Theory.* New York: Oxford University Press.

Pindar. 1976. *The Odes.* Translated by Richmond Lattimore. Chicago: University of Chicago Press.

Pope, Alexander. 1950. *An Essay on Man.* Edited by Maynard Mack. London: Methuen.

Potkay, Adam. 2000. *The Passion for Happiness: Samuel Johnson and David Hume.* Ithaca, NY: Cornell University Press.

Seneca. 1917. *Epistles: 1–65.* Edited by Richard M. Gummere. Loeb Classical Library. Cambridge, MA: Harvard University Press.

Seneca. 1928. *Moral Essays.* 3 vols. Translated by John W. Basore. Loeb Classical Library. Cambridge, MA: Harvard University Press.

Schiller, Friedrich. 1995. *Hoffnung/Hope.* In *Great German Poems of the Romantic Era: A Dual-Language Book,* edited and translated by Stanley Applebaum, 42–43. New York: Dover.

Shelley, Percy Bysshe. 2002. *Shelley's Poetry and Prose.* Edited by Donald H. Reiman and Neil Fraistat. New York: Norton.

Snow, Nancy E. 2018. "Hope as a Democratic Civic Virtue." *Metaphilosophy* 49 (3): 407–427.

Tokarczuk, Olga. 2019. *Drive Your Plow over the Bones of the Dead.* Translated by Antonia Lloyd-Jones. London: Fitzcarraldo.

Waterworth, Jayne M. 2004. *A Philosophical Analysis of Hope.* Houndmills: Palgrave Macmillan.

Winters, Joseph R. 2016. *Hope Draped in Black: Race, Melancholy, and the Agony of Progress.* Durham, NC: Duke University Press.

Wordsworth, William. 1979. *The Prelude: 1799, 1805, 1850.* Edited by Jonathan Wordsworth, M. H. Abrams, and Stephen Gill. New York: Norton.

Chapter 2

Is Hope a Secular Virtue?

Hope as the Virtue of the Possible

BÉATRICE HAN-PILE AND ROBERT STERN

While hope is one of the three theological virtues within the Christian tradition, alongside faith and love, its position as a virtue outside that tradition is more contested.[1] Indeed, doubts about the value of hope have been raised from Hesiod onward, through to Byron's claim that it is "nothing but the paint on the face of existence,"[2] and Nietzsche's denunciation of hope as "the worst of all evils, because it prolongs the torments of man,"[3] while a character from a Terence Rattigan play declares: "if you can live without hope, you can live without despair."[4] Although not completely critical, both Plato and Aristotle seem to have shared these reservations, Plato worrying that hope can make us gullible, while Aristotle refrained from listing it among the virtues, though he did explore its relation to courage and *megalopsychia* [greatness of soul].[5]

In this chapter, we examine in more detail the case against hope as a secular virtue, focusing on three main criteria of what makes something a virtue: namely, it is good for its possessor; stands between two vices; and can be cultivated and exercised. The status of hope as a

Béatrice Han-Pile and Robert Stern, *Is Hope a Secular Virtue?* In: *The Virtue of Hope*.
Edited by: Nancy E. Snow, Oxford University Press. © Oxford University Press 2024.
DOI: 10.1093/oso/9780190069575.003.0003

virtue can be questioned on each of these counts, but we aim to rebut these doubts, arguing that hope can and should be accorded this status after all. We will begin by briefly explaining what we take a virtue to be and so what it might mean to conceive of hope as a virtue, and then we will attempt to show how hope can meet each of the criteria of virtue outlined above, thereby defending this way of conceiving of hope as a virtue. Just as patience helps us to navigate the temporal, hope helps us to navigate the possible, and to flourish in situations of uncertainty.

2.1 WHAT IS A VIRTUE?

On our account, a virtue is a disposition or *hexis* (ἕξις)[6] which, in cases of virtuous acting, is actualized appropriately and skillfully in specific circumstances, and which is reinforced by repeated actualizations. The virtue makes the agent sensitive to certain reasons to act and may have characteristic feelings or emotions associated with its actualization, though given its dispositional nature, a virtue cannot be reduced to these feelings or emotions.[7]

In what follows, we argue that hope is a virtue understood in this manner. While we consider hope to be a unified phenomenon, for the sake of analysis we distinguish between: (a) hopefulness as background trust that at least some goods can obtain (where typically hopefulness is pre-reflective and therefore not propositional, although it can be put in propositional form); (b) hope as the (virtuous) disposition to hope skillfully; and (c) instances of hoping (hopes) as successful actualizations of this disposition relative to specific circumstances. We will say more in §§2.5 and 2.7 about what successful actualizations of this disposition consist in, including the claim that hope can be properly actualized in attitudes other than hopes.

It should be noted here that we are not including within the skills required for hoping as such the skill of assessing the objective value of the end in question, and thus whether some ends should be desired at all: we take such skills to be appropriate for being a virtuous practical reasoner in a general sense, rather than to the virtue of hope itself. Thus, we hold that a person could have the virtue of hope, but still have hope for what are in fact the wrong things, as their practical reasoning more generally is at fault (just as a person could be courageous, but in the wrong cause).[8] This person therefore fails to be fully virtuous or virtuous overall, but we allow that a person can possess one virtue without being virtuous overall, and so can be a good hoper while being a bad person.[9] However, because we believe that agents only ever act under the guise of the good, then insofar as a hoper is also an agent, a hoper can only have hope for what *appears to them to be good*, though of course it may not appear to them as a *moral* good, as they may not take such goods to be good at all.

Having characterized a virtue as a disposition, we will now consider whether hope can be considered a virtue in relation to three widely accepted fundamental features of the virtues. (1) To have a virtue is good for the person who possesses it, by getting the possessor to do the right thing in the situation by responding to the right reasons.[10] (2) A virtue will stand between two corresponding vices, a view that is most famously expressed in Aristotle's conception of 'the golden mean'.[11] (3) Secular virtues are capable of being cultivated and exercised by the agent, though this may also require a favorable social context if the agent is to do so properly.[12] Our focus now in what follows will be first to consider reasons to question whether hope meets these criteria, and then to rebut those concerns, which we take to raise the most fundamental objections to claiming that hope is a virtue.[13]

2.2 OBJECTION (A): HOPE IS NOT ALWAYS GOOD FOR THOSE WHO HOPE

While few would deny that hope can be good for an agent on some occasions, many have denied that it is always good, and thus have claimed that this disqualifies it as a genuine virtue—as we have mentioned, Hesiod condemns hope for encouraging us to be lazy, Plato thinks it can make us gullible, while Nietzsche thinks it can deceive us about the truth of our situation. It is worth considering in more detail what it is about hope that might make this worry plausible, which we think fundamentally relates to the way desire operates in relation to hope.

It is widely accepted that a necessary (although possibly not sufficient) condition for hoping is that we should see a prospect as good and have reason to think that it is possible, but not certain, that this prospect will obtain.[14] However, while someone who hopes will not be entirely unresponsive to reasons that the desired end will or will not obtain, it is plausible to hold that they will not be wholly determined by those reasons either. This is because hopes can only arise in conditions of perceived uncertainty about whether the desired outcome will obtain. In such conditions, if there is some reason to think that what is desired may obtain, this reason does not determine or fix the likelihood of its obtaining. As a result, the desire cannot simply be settled by the reason in this respect, and so instead involves some uncertainty for the agent, either because the probabilities are uncertain, or because we are in a probabilistic situation in the first place.

This suggests the following, preliminary way of understanding how hopes relate to desire:

Hopes involve a desire which, in conditions of subjective
uncertainty about whether the desired end will obtain or
can be obtained, is responsive to reasons to think that the

end will obtain (or not), and whose strength is not directly proportional to the weight of these reasons.[15]

But when hopes are understood in this way, the question about whether hope is good for the possessor may naturally seem to arise, given that the strength of the desires involved in our hopes is not directly proportional to the strength of the reasons they track: doesn't this make the hoping agent gullible and irrational, just as Plato and others have feared?

2.3 OBJECTION (B): HOPE DOES NOT STAND BETWEEN TWO VICES

The second objection centers on whether hope fits the model of the 'golden mean' which is central to many conceptions of the virtues, including of course Aristotle's. The issue concerns which vices can be contrasted with hope as a virtue in the appropriate way.

The two most obvious options would appear to be unwarranted optimism on the one hand,[16] and despair on the other.[17] Unwarranted optimism can plausibly be said to be a vice, as it is clearly bad in leading to rash exercises of agency and so only turns out well through moral luck. However, the position is arguably less clear when it comes to despair. For, it can be said, if circumstances are sufficiently dire, despair could be more fitting than hope, which would then itself look like unwarranted optimism. And if despair is the appropriate response under these conditions, it would follow that despair is not a vice, and so hope cannot stand between it and unwarranted optimism as a mean.

One example that would seem to raise this objection in a vivid way comes from Cormac McCarthy's novel *The Road*, in which under post-apocalyptic and extremely bleak conditions, the mother who commits suicide could be said to be right to despair and to see end-ing her life as the best way to act.[18] On this reading, she is the virtu-ous agent and the hope that leads the father to attempt to carry on and undertake a perilous journey with their son to the sea cannot be contrasted with the mother's despair as a vice, and indeed might itself be said to be no more than unwarranted optimism.

2.4 OBJECTION (C): HOPE CANNOT BE CULTIVATED OR EXERCISED

This third and final objection concerns another fundamental feature of a secular virtue, namely that it can be cultivated by the agent, in particular through practice and habituation,[19] and can also be exer-cised by them, thereby making both the hopes and the virtue of hope their own. The worry here is that hope does not fit this criterion of virtue, as hopes are not a matter of volitional control: an agent cannot instill hopes in themselves or will to hope, any more than an agent can will themselves to love. Nor are hopes a matter of evaluative con-trol, on the model of epistemic arguments. I may *conclude* that there are more reasons for the desired outcome to obtain in my situation than there are reasons for it not to obtain, but it won't *follow* that I will start hoping. Trying to make ourselves hope through an effort of will, or through argumentative reasoning, is self-defeating for a number of reasons. In particular, I can't bring myself to hope if I am aware that my motivation for hoping is instrumental (a variant of the so-called 'dynamic paradox'). Further, the very listing of reasons to hope may have the opposite effect, reminding me of how precarious my situ-ation is and making me more hopeless (just as trying to cheer up a depressed person often makes them more depressed). Given these difficulties of agency in relation to cultivating and exercising hope, it may then be hard to see how any agent can claim to own their hopes at all, and thus claim the associated virtue as their own. Indeed, it could be argued, this issue is one reason why the Christian tradition has treated hope as a *theological* virtue, which we cannot instill in ourselves, and so instead has made it a matter of divine grace.

2.5 RESPONSE (A): HOPE IS GOOD FOR THE POSSESSOR

Having laid out three reasons why hope might not be considered a virtue, we now turn to rebutting those reasons, and so to defending hope's status as a virtue instead, beginning with the worry that hope may not be good for the person who possesses it. For, as we have seen, it could be argued that hope is not always good for the possessor, as the desire involved in hoping is not determined by reasons to think the desired end will obtain, which can lead to unwarranted optimism and hence gullibility in some circumstances.

In response, we can begin by returning to our earlier, preliminary characterization of the relation between hope and desire:

> Hopes involve a desire which, in conditions of subjective
> uncertainty about whether the desired end will obtain or
> can be obtained, is responsive to reasons to think that the
> end will obtain (or not), and whose strength is not directly
> proportional to the weight of these reasons.

Notice, however, that as stated, this characterization does not allow for a differentiation between hope and unwarranted optimism (in the same way as the orthodox definition of hope does not allow for a differentiation between hope and despair).[20] The unwarranted optimist is precisely a person whose desire is so strong that it leads them to distort favorably the reasons they have to think that what they desire will obtain, and who is thus led by this desire to act rashly. In order to distinguish unwarranted optimism from hope, our preliminary characterization needs modification as follows:

> Hopes involve, in conditions of subjective uncertainty about whether the desired good will obtain or can be obtained, a desire which is *appropriately* responsive to, without being able to be determined by, the hoper's *subjectively warranted* epistemic reasons to think that the outcome will obtain (or not), and whose strength is therefore not directly proportional to the weight of those epistemic reasons, but is *appropriately* responsive to subjectively warranted practical reasons.

Our suggestion will now be that with these additional provisions, hope can avoid the concerns raised above. We will first comment on 'subjectively warranted epistemic reasons' and 'appropriately responsive', and then outline three possible ways for the disposition of hope to be successfully actualized.

By *subjective* epistemic reasons, we mean reasons that are first personal, that is, reasons from the perspective of the hoper and so reasons *for* them—hence their subjective aspect. For example, a voter can have reasons to hope that a politician will deliver on an electoral promise, even though a third person who knows the politician is aware that they have no real intention to do so. Nonetheless, to be reasons the voter must still be warranted in acting on them: they must be arrived at by an epistemically acceptable process. For example, the politician has been truthful up to now, and the voter believes the politician has reasons to tell the truth, such as a concern with integrity.

Hoping thus requires a range of epistemic skills, depending on the situation. These skills can be outward- or inward-facing. *Outward-facing* epistemic skills include induction, deduction, careful weighing of the available evidence, searching for new evidence, checking that all possible evidence has been obtained, careful balancing of reasons together, willingness to revise such weighing in the light of new information, and so on (this list is not intended to be exhaustive).[21] Note that it is not necessary to exercise all these skills at the same time, as some may be more appropriate to the situation than others, and that their exercise need not be reflective—indeed, as we shall see in §2.7, the more skilled the hoper, the less reflective the use of her epistemic skills. *Inward-facing* epistemic skills include in particular self-examination to guard against unconscious bias in weighing evidence due to the intensity of desire in hoping. Such bias can be positive (for example, making me overestimate the reasons for the outcome obtaining, overlook negative evidence, and so on); or it can be negative (for example, making me underestimate the reasons for the outcome not obtaining, overlook positive evidence, and so on). Both are failures to exercise the disposition to hope properly, because both involve a misrepresentation of epistemic reasons as being more conclusive than they are in one way or the other: excessively strong positive bias leads to unwarranted optimism; excessively strong negative bias, to despair.

Thus, in the situation of a hoper, the epistemic reasons do not conclusively settle one way or the other how things will be (whereas the unwarranted optimist will think they do, because they will see the situation as more settled than it is). Therefore, hope as a virtue also depends on the exercise of other, non-epistemic skills of practical understanding, in particular courage (either to sustain hope, or to abandon it), patience, and resilience, which takes us to the second set of skills needed in hoping: namely, the ethical skills which determine whether the hoper is *appropriately responsive* to their subjective warranted practical reasons.[22] While the epistemic skills at play in hoping will help us make as good an assessment of the likelihood of the outcome obtaining as possible, the situation is never sufficiently clear for there to be reasons that would settle what will happen, so that our desire can't simply be proportional to those reasons. This means that the hoper has to go beyond the epistemic evidence/reasons available—but given the circumstances, this does not in itself make them irrational or gullible as, unlike the optimist, they do not distort those reasons; rather, this just follows from the situation in which they find themselves as agents in conditions of uncertainty.

This means that there are three aspects of what is required of the skilled hoper in using their practical understanding in their response to this situation.

First, they must have the courage to face and balance two opposed risks: on the one hand, the risk of disappointment if they seek to sustain a hope for the outcome even though there is a lack of favorable evidence regarding that outcome; on the other hand, the risk of giving up this hope prematurely. On the background of their best assessment of outer circumstances and inner states, hopers must balance these opposed risks and have the courage either to commit to sustaining their hope and keeping open a sense of the possible even in the face of unfavorable odds, or giving up their hope without bitterness or resentment (more on these options below).[23]

A second aspect concerns maintaining this commitment to balancing risks over time, so long as the exercise of the hoper's epistemic skills does not track any significant changes in their reasons (not) to hope. This requires patience and resilience as our hopes tend to fluctuate with our emotions and with our understanding of our situation. Part of the skill in hoping consists in seeing the situation from a wider perspective and not letting oneself be discouraged (or excessively boosted) by these fluctuations.

Third, the skilled hoper needs to resist reactive emotions, as hopes are threatened by emotions of this kind, including not only anger, fear, cynicism, bitterness, or resentment, but also gratitude and forgiveness.[24] Resisting these emotions can help create an emotional space where hopes can develop or flourish, or can prevent us hoping for the wrong reasons. This itself requires a capacity to be aware of one's own emotional states (and so also the capacity to guard against unconscious bias in exercising the relevant inward-facing epistemic skills, as previously noted).

One may worry that our account makes the virtue of hope overly reflective and/or excessively rational, at the possible cost of distorting the phenomenology of hope. Regarding the first worry, note that for a skillful hoper the uses of practical understanding outlined above are typically pre-reflective. Unlike, for example, the sub-personal adjustments our brain makes to adapt our vision to changing light conditions, pre-reflective intentional attitudes are personal. While not propositionally articulated, they structure and give meaning to the agent's comportment: as explored by phenomenologists like Husserl and Sartre,[25] pre-reflective intentional attitudes are 'lived through' without needing to be conceptualized explicitly. For example, we can aim to bring about a certain outcome, and act accordingly, without being propositionally aware that we are doing so: having met an attractive person during my daily walk in the park at a certain time the day before, I may find myself taking the same route at the same time the next day so as to generate a 'chance' encounter, without being consciously aware that I am doing so. Yet contrary to sub-personal contents, pre-reflective attitudes are in principle available to our reflective awareness, should we focus our attention on what it is we are doing: thus I may shake my head and smile at myself when realizing why I have changed my routine today.

Phenomenological analyses of skillful comportment show that the more skilled a person is, the less reflective they become about the exercise of this skill.[26] While the novice will typically need to reflectively assess what the relevant aspects of a situation are and make conscious decisions about what to do, unless the situation is particularly tricky and reflection is required, the skilled person will immediately grasp the salient features of the situation and respond by doing the appropriate thing intuitively. Imagine two patients just diagnosed with cancer, one who was previously healthy and another whose years of coping with a chronic condition have turned her into an expert hoper. The challenges of hoping well in the new cancer situation may require the previously healthy patient to reflectively balance the opposite risks of disappointed hope or premature resignation; to commit explicitly to doing this over time, against the fluctuations of responses to treatments and test results; and to consciously seek to resist the reactive emotions which threaten hope. By contrast, the patient with a chronic illness or injury has become practiced at dealing with the ups and downs of an unstable condition. She is experienced enough to know pre-reflectively both how to keep her hopes up against changes in her physical and emotional states, and when to give up a particular hope—for example, that of complete recovery, or of a longer life span. She need not be aware that she is being courageous in balancing the risks involved in hoping; nor does she need to do this consciously. Such balancing structures her comportment without this being an explicit decision. It expresses itself in the way she takes in bad news about her latest round of chemo without breaking into tears and then asks about further options, or in how on the background of her hope she is able to focus on a happy moment without letting her fears for the future intrude. The patience and resilience involved in sustaining her hope over time (or giving it up at the right time) may show itself in kindness for her new failings, such as the starkly reduced scope of what she can now do, and in forgiveness for the awkwardness of others who do not know what to say to her and may sometimes show too much or too little hope for her, thus affecting her own. This skilled hoper need not tell herself to seek to resist reactive emotions: like the person who pre-reflectively modifies her daily walk routine, she avoids situations which would foster such feelings, for example engaging in former activities which would require abilities and strength she no longer has. Sustaining our hopes in this pre-reflective, context-sensitive way requires a great deal of practice and skill, but it is precisely this degree of practice and skill which removes the need for reflective assessment.

The second worry was that our account may be overly rationalist, turning hoping into a risk/benefit calculus whereby we would hope exactly in proportion to the reasons which are available to us. Recall, however, that by definition in the case of hope epistemic reasons will not settle how things will turn out (as otherwise there would be certainty, and so either expectation or resignation). The hoper needs additional, practical reasons to hope. Yet as we just saw, these reasons need not feature as such in a deliberative process: they help the hoper to *see* the situation in a such a light that a certain course of action appeals as the best one possible. So, a hope is not the outcome of a decision that the hoper would make based on the consideration of the reasons they have to hope. Conversely, while the virtuous hoper can, retrospectively, answer the question "Why do you hope?" by providing reasons, these reasons will not fully account for why they have this hope: hope requires a commitment which is not entirely transparent to the hoper.

Perhaps an analogy with love will help convey this point: we can, if asked, list reasons why we love someone. But even if we make this list as exhaustive as possible, we will still feel that there is something about our love which is not captured by the list: further reasons which we cannot articulate, if only because they exceed our current skills as articulators. And this is part and parcel of the phenomenon of love. In fact, the person hearing the list would likely feel that there is something lacking about our love if we could fully account for it by listing our reasons, as if it was a matter of ticking a number of boxes. And even if they agreed with our reasons, this would not make our listener love the person we love in the way we do. So, love is a commitment which may be made for reasons, but without all these reasons being reflectively available at the time to the lover: we commit to those we love without knowing entirely why.

In the same way, the commitment to hope (or not) is made, in situations of uncertainty, for reasons, but without all these reasons being reflectively available to the hoper, and without reflective consideration of the reasons available being able to account for the phenomenon, or make one hope. This means that hope is not entirely rational, if by that one means that each hope should be fully accounted for by reasons reflectively available to the hoper—a demand which, in relation to many important aspects of human life (such as love, but also, for example, aesthetic appreciation), may itself seem excessive. But this does not make hopes irrational in the way Plato feared in the *Timaeus*, because virtuous hopers can still give a warranted account of the reasons which are reflectively available to them, something which neither the despairing person nor the unwarranted optimist can do.

Moreover, it is important to recognize that sustaining their hopes is not the only option for the skilled hoper. We suggest that there are three ways in which the disposition involved in hope can be successfully actualized.

1. Hope in a mature way

Mature hope faces up to subjectively warranted reasons not to hope by courageously embracing the risk of disappointment. This stabilizes our hopes while preserving their strength. An example of this might be a cancer patient who retains their hope while facing the highs and lows of their treatment, and is helped by their hope to flourish.[27]

2. Redirect a hope

Redirected hope faces up to subjectively warranted reasons not to hope for a particular outcome by attaching itself to another outcome.

For example, a person might give up on their piano lessons because they recognize that they are very unlikely to ever to succeed in learning the piano, and so instead hope to do something else in the time this makes available, like write a book. In this case, the disposition to hope actualizes itself through redirection, just like the disposition to be courageous actualizes itself through redirection in the case of fleeing (rather than fighting) if this is for the right reasons.[28]

3. Give up a particular hope (without redirecting or succumbing to despair)

The hoper gives up a particular hope appropriately when they face up to subjectively warranted reasons not to hope for an outcome by giving up their desire for it, but without redirection or despair. Such cases may involve shifting one's desire to an outcome which one expects (not hopes) to happen, just being content with the present situation, or going from hope to stoical resignation.[29]

Finally, note that because the hoper always must go beyond reasons/evidence to hope, and because the warrant for these reasons/evidence is subjective, there is no one-size-fits-all answer to the question of whether it is right or not to form a hope in specific circumstances. For, as long as the reasons are subjectively warranted and the hoper exercises the relevant ethical skills appropriately, it is possible, and legitimate, for different individuals to respond to the same situation in different ways. This can be illustrated again with the example of *The Road*. In this case, both the father and the mother have considered all possible evidence and reasons, and each recognizes this of the other.[30] Yet they adopt very different attitudes, which from their respective points of view can be warranted as appropriate responses to the situation—as the reader is aware.[31]

Thus, we have argued, when hope is virtuous, each set of skills in hoping—epistemic and ethical—focuses on one of hope's combined intentional attitudes. The exercise of our epistemic skills provides subjective justification for (or grounds for rejection of) our belief that the outcome may obtain. This, in turn, affects our desire because of its sensitivity to reasons. The exercise of our ethical skills helps us relate to our desire in a way which either stabilizes it (if we courageously balance the risks toward sustaining our hopes), redirects it, or abandons it. In the virtuous hoper, it is precisely this range of skills that means that even though it is the case that hope cannot simply be determined by assessing the probability of an outcome, the skilled hoper is nonetheless protected from the damaging gullibility that Plato and others have feared. To this extent, we have therefore addressed the worry that hope is in this way detrimental to the person who possesses it.

However, even if we have shown that the skills involved in hope mean it should be distinguished from unwarranted optimism, the example of the mother from *The Road* nonetheless seems to cause another problem for the claim that hope is a virtue, namely that it can be better for the individual to despair rather than hope—and if that is so, that despair should not be put alongside unwarranted optimism as one of the two vices between which hope stands as a mean, but rather should be treated as a virtue in its own right.

2.6 RESPONSE (B): HOPE AS STANDING BETWEEN TWO VICES

As we have noted, the reader of *The Road* may well feel that in the extremely bleak situation in which the couple find themselves, the mother is perfectly right to feel despair, and to express that despair in her rejection of the hope shown by the father, which to her appears entirely deluded and damaging.[32] But what conception of despair (and of unwarranted optimism) does the objection rest on? And is the mother's comportment best described as an instance of despair? We will argue that it is not, and that on closer inspection, the following claims can be supported: (a) Despair and unwarranted optimism are always bad for the agent, and thus are vices. (b) But it doesn't follow that hoping for a particular outcome is always the best option for an agent, as in some cases resignation or expectation may be preferable. (c) But this doesn't undermine hope's status as a virtue; on the contrary, it is part of exercising the virtue of hope to recognize the particular cases in which other attitudes are more appropriate than hopes.

First, it can be argued that despair and unwarranted optimism are always bad for the agent as follows:[33] When in despair, the agent believes that their desire cannot be satisfied but retains the desire (otherwise they would be resigned, not despairing);[34] but they are unable to act on it, or even to believe in the possibility of the desired good obtaining on its own, which generates frustration and inner conflict.[35] On the other hand, when unwarrantedly optimistic, the agent believes her desire will be satisfied but lacks the subjective warrant for this belief, which generates expectations and actions that have little chance of fulfillment (where in both cases, the relevant belief need not be conscious, and is in fact often pre-reflective).[36]

But, it could be said, in some instances, even if despair is not good for the agent, isn't it better for them not to hope? So, doesn't that show that hope is not always good for the agent, and so a vice? This brings us to our second response, which is to suggest that while hope is a virtue, it does not follow that it is always right to sustain particular hopes. Indeed, knowing when to stop hoping and to adopt another attitude is precisely part of the virtue of hope. One way for this to happen is when we rightly move from a hope to an expectation: for example, immediately after trying to repair my kettle, and knowing my relatively limited electrical skills, I turn it on hoping it will work; but after seeing it work successfully for several days, I now expect it to work when I turn it on, rather than merely hoping it will. At the other end of the spectrum, as it were, we can also rightly move from hopes to resignation, as when we become convinced that the outcome will likely not obtain, and as a result it seems better to drop the desire and thus the hope: for example, I keep trying but failing to repair my kettle, and give up on the project and buy a new one instead.

By considering the alternatives to sustaining hopes we can come to think of the mother in *The Road* in a different light, and show that it is wrong to think of her as a counterexample to our claim that hope is a virtue, on the grounds that she is said to exemplify the virtue of despair instead. For, on closer inspection, it seems wrong to say that she despairs: on the contrary, she gives up her desire to survive and so resigns herself to its unfulfillability as an outcome or goal, and re-directs her hope toward death as a realizable aim.[37] Rather than showing that it is better to despair than hope, and thus that despair might be a virtue, she shows it can be better to be resigned than fall for unwarranted optimism, and that the virtuous hoper will know when and how to re-direct their hopes accordingly. Her argument with the father is therefore not whether despair is better than hope, but whether their hopes should take on a different form—the hope of dying, versus the hope of getting to the sea. Of course, it may seem odd to say that death is an object of hope; but her point is that as their circumstances are sufficiently dire, this is all they can legitimately hope for, and (as we noted above), she is justified in making her case, even if the father can be justified in resisting it, as we have seen above.

Third, however, it could be objected that this still shows that hope is not a virtue, because if it were, it would be appropriate to hope at all times, rather than replace hope with some other attitude such as expectation or resignation—just as it would seem wrong to think of the virtuous agent as replacing courage with anything else. In response, we would argue that the virtue of hope allows for the agent not to hope on a particular occasion, where having the virtue of hope is precisely knowing when this is appropriate—but such examples do not show that the virtue of hope itself is to be given up. For example, while a good hoper will be hopeful in general that bad news will be met with a sympathetic response, it is also part of hoping virtuously to know not to hope for such sympathy if one has reasons to believe that the other person is not well disposed. However, this response might provoke a more radical objection: such examples show that what should be given up is hopefulness as the background trust which we see as an enabling condition for hope as a virtue. In response to this, we would argue that such trust is a necessary condition for agency,[38] and thus cannot be given up by any agent themselves, even though it could be destroyed in them by extreme circumstances. Thus, our view can allow that while the background trust cannot be given up by the agent, sometimes it could be more appropriate for them to be resigned to some event not happening rather than for them to hope it will, and being a virtuous or skilled hoper of the sort we discussed in §2.5 is to know when this is so.[39]

We thus propose understanding unwarranted optimism and despair as vices, insofar as they are two opposite ways of failing to hope. Unwarranted optimism involves a desire which leads the agent to overlook or favorably distort the epistemic reasons *against* thinking that the desired end will or will not obtain, leading the agent to act rashly. Despair involves a desire which leads the agent to overlook or unfavorably distort the epistemic reasons *for* thinking the desired end will or will not obtain, leading the agent to miss opportunities to act. Both of these extremes are deleterious for the agent. The unwarranted optimist is so driven by their desire that they overlook the practical consequences of their rashness, while the despairing person keeps desiring the good but without being able to act to bring it about because they think it is unobtainable, or that it cannot obtain on its own. Their desire is therefore experienced as a painful longing for the (subjectively) impossible, brought on by this inner conflict.

Thus, in dealing with these first two objections to the claim that hope is a virtue, we have argued as follows: hope is always good for the possessor, and it stands between the vices of despair and unwarranted optimism; and we argued for this on the basis that its exercise requires both epistemic and ethical skills, and that its exercise can result in mature hope, redirected hope, or the giving up of hope, while at the same time despair and unwarranted optimism are always vices. If this is correct, we have shown how hope meets the first two criteria for being a virtue in the classical sense. We now need to examine whether it meets the last one.

2.7 RESPONSE (C): THE CULTIVATION AND EXERCISE OF HOPE

As specified at the beginning, on our account a virtue is a disposition which, in cases of virtuous acting, is exercised appropriately and skillfully in specific circumstances, and which is developed like a habit, through intentional practice. Yet in §2.4 we noted that hoping is a matter of neither volitional nor evaluative control. But if we can neither will ourselves to form hopes, on the model of basic actions, nor come to such hopes as the conclusion of an argument about why we should hope, how can we exercise hope and cultivate it through hoping? And if we cannot do this, how can hope then be a virtue?[40]

In reply to both problems, we grant that hopes are not a matter of direct or even indirect control and introduce a new notion, 'aspirational control', as more appropriate to the two main ways in which our relation to hopes may be understood: (a) actualizing the disposition by seeking to generate specific hopes, and (b) finding oneself hoping already and seeking appropriately to maintain this existing hope. We thereby develop the phenomenology of the agency at work in generating particular hopes, and in already hoping.

It is clear that hopes are not a matter of direct control, where direct control may be defined by the agent's efforts to φ sufficing to ensure that they φ.[41] Making efforts to hope does not suffice to ensure that one hopes. However, it seems intuitively plausible that hopes may be generated in more indirect ways, such as representing the situation in the best possible light, seeking information that supports the likelihood of the desired outcome obtaining, surrounding oneself with positive people, and so on. So, is this a case of what is usually called 'indirect control'? Zimmerman defines the latter as follows: "one has indirect control over something just in case one has control over it by way of having control over something else" (2006, 593). Zimmerman gives the following example:[42] Smith and Stith are equally skilled assassins. They both fire their guns but only Smith kills his target because a bird unexpectedly flies in the path of Stith's bullet. Zimmerman concludes: "as I have depicted their cases, the assassins have merely indirect control over the ensuing events. This is because whether the ensuing events occur is not in their control at all, except insofar as the first one [pressing the trigger] is. Indirect control . . . requires the cooperation of factors . . . outside of one's control, factors whose cooperation is not required by direct control" (2006, 598).

Prima facie, generating hopes looks like a case of indirect control: the agent devises and implements steps designed to generate a hope, but this requires the cooperation of factors outside of their control. However, there is a key difference: an agent in indirect control has the default *expectation* that, all things being equal, a certain sequence of events will be triggered by the action they are in control of. If this does not happen it is seen, as in the case of Stith, as a freak accident. Thus, in indirect control the agent's implicit probability assessment of the likelihood of the desired outcome obtaining is very high. By contrast, agents seeking to generate a hope do not have such a high probability assessment: they are aware that even if they implement the relevant steps there is a significant chance of failure. Consequently, they only have the (second order) *hope*, not expectation, that implementing the relevant steps will yield the desired result. This difference can be brought out in the following way: if an agent exercising indirect control fails to achieve their goal, they will be disappointed and surprised (like Stith). But if an agent who seeks to generate a hope fails, they will be disappointed, but not surprised. They knew from the start that there was no guarantee of success.

Thus, the generation of hopes is a case of neither direct nor indirect control. Yet it has a clear intentional structure: the agent devises and takes steps toward a certain goal in the hope, but not the expectation, that they will achieve this goal. We propose to call this intentional structure 'aspirational control'. In cases of direct control, the agent achieves Y by doing it; with indirect control, the agent does X with the expectation of achieving Y; with aspirational control, the agent does X with the hope of achieving Y. Aspirational control is a form of *control* because it involves instrumental reasoning: agents do not act at random. They have reasons to undertake the steps chosen, and these reasons warrant their hope that these steps will succeed. However, this control is *aspirational* because none of these reasons is compelling: this is why agents can only hope, but not expect, to succeed. This hope is, however, enough to rationally motivate the attempt. Thus, an artist may seek to create a good artwork, and devise and take steps toward this goal. Yet there is no default expectation on their part that they will succeed: they know that they could put a lot of effort into the work and still fail. Similarly, we may seek to generate a hope by taking steps such as the ones outlined above, but with only the hope, not the expectation, that we will succeed: we are all too aware of the fragility of our hopes, at least when it comes to significant matters. Importantly, note that as it is only rationally and psychologically possible to exercise aspirational control in a situation where the agent no longer seeks direct and indirect control, it then follows that in order to successfully cultivate hope, the agent has to have given up on volitional or evaluative control (more on this below).

But, one may object, why is indirect control not suitable in the case of the generation of hopes? And if aspirational control constitutively involves hoping, rather than expecting, that a hope can be generated in this way, does this not create a regress in the sense that the generation of hopes relies on a further hope?

Regarding the first objection, exercising indirect control would require the agent to expect that they will be successful in generating hope about the success of the desired outcome. Yet the agent would not seek to generate hope in the first place if they were not uncertain about the possibility of the desired outcome obtaining: a cancer patient would not seek to generate hope in the success of their treatment if they were confident that the treatment will work. And the uncertainty about the desired outcome extends to the likelihood of generating hope for it. So, the very fact that the agent seeks to generate hope by aspirational control is by itself an indication that indirect control is not suitable, because there can be no expectation of success, neither about the desired outcome, nor about hoping for it.

Regarding the second objection, it is important to clarify the sense in which there might be a regress. In a way there is no regress, as the generation of my hope for a certain outcome does not presuppose hope for that outcome, but for the success of the process of hope-generation itself. However, one may worry that this hope for successful generation may itself be taken as an object of further hoping, and this, ad infinitum. Our reply is that while it is possible in theory, such regress is very unlikely in practice. Taking one's hope for successful generation as a further object of hoping would presuppose that the agent is doubtful about the steps devised for the first-degree generation. Yet if this was the case, the steps would not appear to them *as steps*, and so could not feature as appropriate means in the instrumental reasoning required for the generation of a particular hope. It is possible that an agent should revise the steps intended to such hope, for example in the light of new information which retrospectively reveals their hope in the original steps being successful as unwarranted optimism.[43] But this is not tantamount to engaging in a regressive process: it is a further adaptation of the proposed means to the end.

We now turn to the second way of relating to hopes: cases where we find ourselves hoping, without our hoping being the result of any conscious intentional act, and seek to maintain our existing hope appropriately. Finding oneself hoping is very common: you discover that a good prospect is possible for you and find yourself hoping for its realization. Or, you say something wise to me and I find myself hoping upon listening to you. Either way, the experience seems one of becoming aware of hope dawning spontaneously, without the agent having done anything, and hence being able to own this hope.[44] It is therefore important to develop an account of the phenomenology of the agency at work in the hopes we become reflectively aware of, as the issue of how we can own our hopes arises here too.

We submit that the hopes we find ourselves having do in fact result from an exercise of agency, albeit not a standard one. This is not the carrying out of a prior intention, but rather a response to the solicitations of a particular situation, which are disclosed to us *as* solicitations by our understanding of the situation and of ourselves. Such understanding is pre-reflective and dependent on a set of abilities and dispositions which are specific to the agent and make certain features of the situation salient and relevant to them.[45] To see this, let us return to our examples. You could say the same things to someone else in a similar situation and not elicit hope from them because they take your words as empty reassurances. My hoping upon listening to you speak to me is not the passive obtaining of a state caused by hearing your words. Rather, it is a pre-reflective actualization of my disposition to hope, made possible by my understanding your words as wise. In responding to your words by hoping I have already exercised the relevant epistemic and ethical skills: I have pre-reflectively assessed your words as appropriate to my situation and exercised the courage to face the risks involved in hoping accordingly. Your words have allowed me to hope, and I have let myself hope. Similarly, your hoping upon discovering a good new prospect is not mindless, like a knee jerk resulting from the knock of a medical hammer on the patellar tendon: it rests on your having pre-reflectively assessed this prospect as good and exercised the relevant ethical skills in balancing the risk of hoping for it with that of not doing so, or of being disappointed.

Thus, a person's disposition to hope is different from a glass' disposition to break: the latter is entirely triggered by relevant circumstances, and all (non-shatter-resistant) glasses would break in such circumstances. By contrast, not all agents would hope hearing the same words, or discovering the same information. This is, as we saw, because particular hopes arise, not merely causally from certain circumstances obtaining, but from the circumstances being understood in a certain way by certain agents, who in turn can influence and develop such understanding. So, we can specify in which sense the hopes we find ourselves having are, in fact, a matter of agency: in hoping for a particular outcome I am doing something already, not in the sense that I am carrying out an intention to hope, but in the sense that I am responding to the situation as I understand it through the actualization of my disposition to hope, thereby making the hope my own. The actualization of the disposition is passive in the sense that it is dependent on external circumstances (a good, new prospect; my hearing your voice). But it is active in the sense that these circumstances can only afford the agent a solicitation to hope if they are pre-reflectively interpreted by means of a set of skills and abilities developed through years of engagement with self and world, and through previous instances of hoping. Without the right circumstances, nothing would happen; but without the circumstances registering on an agent made responsive by their previously developed abilities and skills, nothing would happen either. Hoping is neither active, nor passive: it is what might be called medio-passive (Han-Pile 2009, 2013, 2017).

Thus, properly understood, the phenomenology of existing hopes is no obstacle to viewing hope as a virtue, albeit a medio-passive one. On this basis, maintaining an existing hope appropriately is best characterized as another exercise of aspirational control: I seek to sustain, redirect, or abandon an existing hope by devising steps which I can only hope, but not expect, to work. A structural reason for this is that there is a constitutive link between hope and anxiety (Han-Pile 2017): hoping is a response to anxiety about a situation of perceived uncertainty. It also makes us anxious in itself (by raising the stakes in case of disappointment). In seeking to cultivate hope, we are constantly vulnerable to the possibility of these anxieties overwhelming us.

This, in turn, brings out an important aspect of the psychology of aspirational control in general, and of hoping as a virtue in particular: agents must develop, and act in the light of, a keen awareness of their dependence on, and vulnerability to, circumstances beyond their control. It is this awareness which motivates their giving up direct or indirect control in relation to hope. Those who hope, or seek to cultivate hope, do not understand themselves as self-assured, autonomous agents but as relatively fragile selves, who exercise their agency medio-passively, in the full awareness that their success (if any) will depend at least as much on the cooperation of the world as on themselves.[46]

In closing this chapter, we should acknowledge that on our account, exercising hope requires epistemic and ethical skills. This leaves open the possibility of hopes as states (as opposed to resulting from an exercise of agency). Such states obtain when a person believes uncritically in the possibility of an outcome they desire. Young children, who do not yet have the skills required to exercise hope, may thus be said to be in this state of belief and desire, but to lack the virtue of hope itself, which thus prevents the state being *theirs* in the manner of hopes. We should also note that this account does not commit us to a counter-intuitive 'infallibility view', whereby whenever we find ourselves hoping we would be hoping virtuously. It does not follow from the fact that all hopes are (virtuous) actualizations of the disposition to hope that all the intentional states we *think* of as hope are virtuous. Since it is a trademark of unwarranted optimism that it must present itself as hope (for otherwise it would be self-defeating), many instances of our finding ourselves hoping may well turn out to be exercises of unwarranted optimism. This is compatible with saying that hope, properly understood, is always a virtue.[47]

NOTES

1. For a rich historical discussion of different ways in which hope has been treated, both negative and positive, see the chapter by Potkay (2024: this volume).
2. Byron, letter to Thomas Moore, October 28, 1815, in Byron (2015, 195).
3. Nietzsche, *Human All Too Human,* section 71.
4. This is said by Mr. Miller in Terence Rattigan, *The Deep Blue Sea* (1952)—who then advises the main character to "get beyond hope, it is your only chance."
5. Plato, *Timaeus* 69d; Aristotle, *Nicomachean Ethics,* 3.6 1115a35 and 3.8.1117a10, and *Rhetoric,* 2.12.1389a16–34. On Aristotle, see Gravlee (2000).
6. See Aristotle, *Metaphysics,* 5.1022b.
7. Thus, courage is a disposition which, in the case of courageous acting, is actualized appropriately or skillfully by (for example) fighting a battle which the disposition discloses to the agent as worth fighting, where this may be accompanied by certain characteristic affects (such as a feeling of comradery with fellow fighters, fear, or excitement).
8. Cf. Kant's view that 'qualities of temperament' on their own, unless conjoined with the good will, can be for the bad, such as the courageous thief (*Groundwork for the Metaphysics of Morals* 4:393). For debate on this issue in relation to hope, see Kadlac (2015) and Snow (2019).

THE VIRTUE OF HOPE

9. This therefore means that we are denying the unity of the virtues in one sense, namely that having one virtue does not entail having all—though what we say is compatible with the unity of the virtues in a weaker sense, namely that for a fully rational agent, they will possess all of the virtues and not merely some.

10. Here we are focusing on practical virtues; we are happy to allow that there are also epistemic virtues, which relate to what it is right to believe, rather than to do.

11. Aristotle, *Nicomachean Ethics*, 1106a26–b28.

12. See McGeer (2004).

13. Another objection that can be found in the literature, but which we do not take to be so fundamental, is that hope cannot be a virtue because it is an emotion (see, for example, Bobier 2017). While we do not have space to develop the response here, we believe this objection fails, because while hope certainly can have affects, it seems too narrow to reduce hope to just these, while on the other hand virtues can have affective aspects, as noted above.

14. For various versions of the so-called orthodox definition, see, for example, Day (1969, 89), "A hopes that p is true if and only if A wishes that p, and A thinks that p has some degree of probability, however small." See also Downie (1963, 249): "there are two criteria which are independently necessary and jointly sufficient for 'hope that'. The first is that the object of hope must be desired by the hoper.... The second . . . is that the object of hope falls within a range of physical possibility which includes the improbable but excludes the certain and the merely logically possible." Pettit (2009, 153) and Martin (2014, 4) summarize the 'lowest common denominator of analysis' or the 'orthodox definition' in the following terms (respectively): "I can be said to hope that something is the case . . . so far as I want the scenario to materialize and believe that it is possible but not inevitable that it does materialize: I assign a nonzero, non-unit probability to that desired prospect"; "[on this account hope is] the combination of the desire for an outcome and the belief that the outcome is possible but not certain."

15. So, I can hope strongly even though my reasons to hope are objectively weak, or hope weakly even though my reasons are objectively strong.

16. For some further discussion of the relation between hope and optimism, see the discussion by Liz Gulliford in her chapter in this volume (Guilliford 2024).

17. Just to briefly mention two challenges to this view here: First, within the theological tradition, the situation may seem rather more complicated, as *presumption (praesumere)* is also taken to be a vice which stands opposed to hope in a different way, as taking ourselves to have control over our salvation in a way that makes hope redundant—so that it is similar to but different from unwarranted optimism in this respect. While this introduces potential complications which we cannot consider fully here, and which anyway are tangential to our more secular focus in this paper, it could also be said that presumption

operates at a higher and more general level, as a kind of 'Ur-vice' that is the source of all vices (for Augustine it is at the root of the Fall), and so is not a vice that stands in relation just to hope as such. (In his chapter in this volume, Michael Lamb (Lamb 2024) discusses presumption in a more secular sense, but as he allows this is very close to what we would call unwarranted optimism, for example when one presumes that climate change will be solved more easily than is the case.) Second, within the secular tradition, it might be said that as well as despair, hope can also be undermined by other attitudes such as fear and cynicism, which therefore also potentially stand in opposition to hope as vices, in addition to despair (see Govier 2011). However, in our view, while fear and cynicism may make hope more difficult, they are not genuine contradictories to hope: for, while one cannot say "I both hope and despair that p," one can say that one hopes that p while also saying that one fears p or has a cynical attitude toward it (for example, "I hope he will turn out to be a decent politician, though frankly I have my doubts given the way politicians behave these days"). It is only if this fear or cynicism has generated despair that hope becomes impossible, which is why it is despair that is the best candidate for a vice that stands as a contrary to hope.

18. *The Road* describes the journey south taken by a young boy and his father in world that has been destroyed by an unspecified cataclysm, leaving people to fend for themselves after the breakdown of all civilization and in desperate and dangerous conditions. Early on in the book, the woman who is the wife and mother of the family urges the father to let them all kill themselves as the only escape; when he refuses, she commits suicide alone. The father and son undertake their journey to the sea, which they manage to reach despite many threats and difficulties, though the father dies exhausted by his efforts and illness, and the boy is taken up by another family.

19. Of course, the right upbringing, social circumstances, and material conditions may also be required for this cultivation to be fully successful.

20. Imagine that a group of patients is told that statistically the chance of recovery for people with similar diagnoses is 10%. A 10% recovery chance fits the two criteria of the orthodox definition of hope: the patients believe that recovery is possible, and it has a probability assignment between (and excluding) 0 and 1. Yet some patients will hope, and others will despair, depending on whether they think of themselves as potentially included in the 10% or not. A much discussed case raising the same issue is the one taken from *The Shawshank Redemption*, concerning the contrast between Andy (who hopes) and Red (who despairs) despite both sharing the same desires (to escape prison) and the same estimation of the difficulty of doing so (see Meirav 2009).

21. Recall that we have previously argued (in §2.1) that the ability to hope for the good is not a skill that falls within the virtue of hope as such, but is part of

the wider virtue of practical wisdom, and so is excluded from our analysis of hope here.

22. While taken on their own, these capacities might be considered virtues, we call them skills here because they are being used in the service of hope, rather than deployed in their own right.

23. Note that there are also risks that attach, not just to the situation, but to hoping itself. For, on the one hand, in some cases the mere fact of hoping may increase the likelihood of the desired outcome being realized; on the other hand, their very hoping can also increase the magnitude of the possible disappointment. The courage lies in facing the risks attached to the situation, and to hoping itself, lucidly, and without ever having the grounds to be certain that one is doing the right thing in seeking to sustain or give up hope.

24. Regarding the latter two: gratitude may lead one to be content with what one has, rather than hope for more; likewise in premature forgiveness one may no longer hope for better from a person, while in feeling entitled to be forgiven one will fail to hope for forgiveness, but instead just expect it.

25. See, for example, Husserl (2008, 130): "every act is consciousness of something, but there is also consciousness of every act. Every act is 'sensed,' is immanently 'perceived' (internal consciousness), although naturally not posited." The following is a *locus classicus* for Sartre: "if I count the cigarettes which are in that case, I have the impression of disclosing an objective property of this collection of cigarettes: *they are a dozen*. This property appears to my consciousness as a property existing in the world. It is very possible that I have no positional consciousness of counting them. Then I do not know myself as counting. Yet at the moment when these cigarettes are revealed to me as a dozen, I have a non-thetic consciousness of my adding activity. If anyone questioned me, indeed, if anyone should ask, 'What are you doing there?' I should reply at once, 'I am counting'" (1943, 19–20; 1956, liii). For a collection of recent discussions of pre-reflective consciousness, see Miguens, Preyer, and Morando (2019).

26. A seminal model was given by Dreyfus and Dreyfus (1986). This model has been widely discussed in the phenomenological tradition and also exported to other contexts; see, for example, Benner (1984) for applications to nursing practice.

27. Cf. Groopman (2018, xiv): "Without hope, I would have been locked forever in that prison of pain. But I also sensed that hope had done more than push me to take a chance and not give up. It seemed to exert potent impalpable effects not only on my psychology but on my physiology. As a scientist, I distrusted my own experience, and set out on a personal journey to discover whether the energising feeling of hope can in fact contribute to recovery. I found that there is an authentic biology of hope."

28. Similarly, a person injured in a car accident may initially hope for a full recovery, then realize this will not happen and hope that their new, chronic condition can be managed well enough for them to live a normal life.

29. Examples of each of these cases (in the same order) are as follows: (a) I am hoping to have seabass at my favorite restaurant but it turns out they didn't get any at the market today, so I give up the hope and order squid instead with the full expectation of enjoying it because I've had it many times there. (b) I was hoping to go for a walk but the weather is bad and I'm happily reading a book instead. (c) I was hoping that chemo would work but it hasn't, so I give up the hope for a cure and set my affairs in order instead.

30. In the scene in which the mother and father confront one another, the mother states: "You have no argument because there is none," showing how she has used her skills in evaluating reasons—there is no argument *left*, she has reviewed them all. And the father accepts this point in the next passage: "She was gone and the coldness of it was her final gift. She would do it with a flake of obsidian. . . . And she was right. There was no argument. The hundred nights they'd sat up arguing the pros and cons of self destruction with the earnestness of philosophers chained to a madhouse wall" (McCarthy 2006, 59–60).

31. The mother (a) hopes for survival; (b) realizes through exercise of her evaluative skills that survival is possible but *very unlikely*, so courageously gives up her hope for survival; so (c) redirects her hope toward eternal nothingness; and (d) this hope helps her exercise her agency in seeking death. Cf. McCarthy (2006, 59): "As for me my only hope is for eternal nothingness and I hope for it with all my heart." By contrast the father (a) hopes for survival; (b) realizes through exercise of his evaluative skills that survival is very unlikely but *possible*, so courageously sustains the hope; (c) this hope helps him exercise his agency in going to the sea.

32. McCarthy (2006, 57–58): "What in God's name are you talking about? We're not survivors. We're the walking dead in a horror film. . . . Sooner or later they will catch us and they will kill us. They will rape me. Theyll rape him. They are going to rape us and kill us and eat us and you wont face it. You'd rather wait for it to happen. . . . You say you cant? Then don't do it. That's all. Because I am done with my own whorish heart and I have been for a long time. . . . [D]ont ask for sorrow now. There is none."

33. In her chapter for this volume (note 42), Swenson-Lengyel raises the question whether despair might not be fitting or appropriate, even though she agrees it is not a virtue as it does not enable the agent to flourish in this world, for the reasons she gives. As we are asking whether despair might be a secular virtue, we do not consider this as a challenge to our view. Further, it is not clear that "in protest [they] continue to desire that which they have every right to desire" is best described as a case of despair. For, while the person does retain the original desire, this very retaining is made possible by the fact that the

holding of the desire is now understood as a protest. But a protest is an attempt at communication, which would not make sense if the protester did not pre-reflectively hold out the hope of the protest being noticed, and understood for what it is; in which case the person who retains the impossible desire in protest has, in fact, redirected their hope. Finally, Swenson-Lengyel seems to assume that despair may be more fitting than resignation, as the former can be combined with appropriate anger or rage; but it can be argued that resignation is also compatible with these responses. If resignation is understood as the giving up of a desire for what one takes to be impossible, it seems that this could be combined with anger or rage directed at whatever has made this impossible and so compelled one to give up the desire.

34. Throughout this chapter we are looking at despair as a matter of agency, as otherwise it could not be a candidate for virtue (since virtues are dispositions of agents, as we have argued in §2.1). This means we are leaving aside other instances of what is sometimes called despair, such as the apathy of deep depression, where no desire can register significantly on the individual, so that they are deprived of agency in this respect.

35. Kwong (2023, 13) rejects "accounts of despair that construe it as a loss of belief in the possibility that the outcome can be realised," citing our paper as an example of such an account. On his view, *hoping* is "a matter of register-ing that one has . . . a desire one believes to have some possibility or chance of obtaining" (Kwong 2021, 6). By contrast, *hopefulness* consists in a person's positive orientation toward the possibility that the desired outcome will obtain. On Kwong's view, then, a despairing person still views the desired outcome as possible, but does not view its chances of obtaining in a positive light. So, while for Kwong despair *requires* hope and is the opposite of *hopeful-ness*, for us despair and hope are mutually exclusive, while hopefulness is just a disposition to hope (a view which Kwong also rejects). We would like to offer two thoughts in reply. Firstly, Kwong's view is explicitly grounded in the claim that "the sentence 'I hope that x but I'm not hopeful about x' is neither redundant nor senseless" (Kwong 2021, 3). However, our view is that a more intuitive and coherent phrasing of the thought would be "I hope that x but I'm not *optimistic* about x," which itself strongly suggests that Kwong is wrong in thinking there is a distinction between hope as a neutral state and hopefulness as an exercise of agency, as this is why instead another kind of term has to be used. Second, Kwong's main argument against our thought that a despairing person views the desired outcome as impossible (while still desiring it) is that "this construal goes against the way despair is commonly treated in the litera-ture, which postulates that despair presupposes that a person believes that it is possible for the desired outcome to obtain" (Kwong 2023, 13). This, however, is a misconstrual of the examples Kwong refers to, because it does not distin-guish between general and first-personal senses of possibility, namely whether

something is possible for a group or is possible for me, from my own perspective. It is true that Red in *The Shawshank Redemption* or Alan the cancer patient in *Martin* (2014) despair even though they believe that the desired outcome is *generally* possible, if unlikely. But the reason why they despair is that they view the desired outcome as impossible for *them*, that is, as first-personally impossible. By contrast, Bess, the other cancer patient, is able to hope because she thinks "I'm going to be one of the 1%!" and so sees the desired outcome as first-personally possible for her. This aligns with our own thought that the reason why the despairing person despairs is that they view the desired outcome as first-personally impossible, a thought which, it turns out, is entirely consistent with the existing literature after all.

36. Of course, this does not rule out both states leading to the good of the agent by chance—for example, through my despair I could fail to act in a way that then means I avoid some harm, or through following my faulty subjective reasons I could still get what I desire after all. But we are assessing the value of these states as possible virtues, which are dispositions—so they need to be assessed in the long run, not on the basis of individual cases where things work out by chance.

37. See again McCarthy (2006, 59): "As for me my only hope is for eternal nothingness and I hope for it with all my heart."

38. We would again argue that this is evidenced by the example of the mother, who despite abandoning many specific hopes, cannot act at all without trusting that she will be able to take her own life.

39. We are particularly grateful to David Batho for comments that helped us clarify these issues throughout the chapter.

40. It should be noted that in asking this question, we are very much focusing on whether hope can be cultivated *as a virtue*, not just whether on a particular occasion, an agent might be able to instill a feeling of hope in themselves, for example by focusing only on some features of the situation. We do not deny that a temporary feeling of hope could be generated this way, but this approach could not apply to hope as a virtue, first because it will involve ignoring some of the relevant information and so is more like optimism than hope, and second, because of the kind of irrationality involved, it could not offer a long-term strategy for a virtuous agent.

41. Cf. Lockhart and Lockhart (2018, 313): "It seems (at least pre-reflectively) absurd to maintain both that an agent was in control of having φ-ed and to maintain that her efforts to φ were not enough to ensure that she φed. If an agent's efforts to bring about a goal cannot bring about that goal, if she has to rely, once her efforts are exhausted, on some contribution of the world which goes beyond that which her efforts can ensure, then she lacks control over the realization of her goals to the extent that the realization of those goals depends on that which is beyond her efforts."

42. Zimmerman here reinterprets Thomas Nagel's example of Smith and Stith, originally introduced in the context of a study of moral luck, as a case of indirect control: see Nagel (1993).

43. For example, I may have thought that surrounding myself with positive people would help me find hope that there is a way out of a bad situation, but I now realize that this just depresses me, and that what I took for hope in the success of this strategy was unwarranted optimism.

44. See Bobier (2017).

45. See Rousse (2018).

46. Note that we do not consider hope a necessary condition of possibility on all exercises of agency. Many of the things we do (for example, bodily movements and basic actions) are carried out with an *expectation* (not hope) of success. To pick up on a previous example, in normal circumstances I do not hope that my kettle will boil if I turn it on: I expect that it will. We also act on faith, or trust, without hope (because of the higher degree of certainty which attaches to faith and trust). So, if someone I trust tells me that they will meet me at a certain time at a certain place, in normal circumstances I do not hope that they will be there: I trust that they will, and this is enough to warrant my ensuring that I am at the right place at the right time. Hope is required for agency only when the agent is uncertain about their circumstances or the exercise of their agency (or both).

47. We are very grateful to those who kindly commented on previous drafts, including the audience of the Max Charlesworth lecture at Deakin University, where Robert Stern presented a distant ancestor of this chapter; the other members of the workshop for contributors to this volume; colleagues David Batho, Paul Faulkner, Wayne Martin, and Dan Watts; and to Nancy Snow as editor.

REFERENCES

Benner, Patricia. 1984. *From Novice to Expert: Excellence and Power in Clinical Nursing Practice*. Menlo Park, CA: Addison-Wesley.

Bobier, Christopher A. 2017. "Why Hope Is Not a Moral Virtue: Aquinas's Insight." *Ratio* 31 (21): 214–232.

Byron, George Gordon. 2015. *Byron's Letters and Journals: A New Selection*. Edited by Richard Lansdown. Oxford: Oxford University Press.

Day, J. P. 1969. "Hope." *American Philosophy Quarterly* 6 (2): 89–102.

Downie, R. S. 1963. "Hope." *Philosophy and Phenomenological Research* 24 (2): 248–251.

Dreyfus, Hubert L., and Stuart E. Dreyfus. 1986. *Mind over Machine: The Power of Human Intuition and Expertise in the Age of the Computer*. Oxford: Basil Blackwell.

Govier, Trudy. 2011. "Hope and Its Opposites." *Journal of Social Philosophy* 42 (3): 239–253.

Gravlee, George S. 2000. "Aristotle on Hope." *Journal of the History of Philosophy* 38 (4): 461–477.

Groopman, Jerome. 2018. *The Anatomy of Hope: How People Prevail in the Face of Illness*. New York: Random House.

Han-Pile, Béatrice. 2009. "Nietzsche and Amor Fati." *European Journal of Philosophy* 19 (2): 1–38.

Han-Pile, Béatrice. 2013. "Freedom and the 'Choice to Choose Oneself' in Heidegger's *Being and Time*." In *The Cambridge Companion to Being and Time*, edited by Mark A. Wrathall, 291–319. New York: Cambridge University Press.

Han-Pile, Béatrice. 2017. "Hope, Powerlessness and Agency." *Midwest Studies in Philosophy* 41 (1): 175–201.

Husserl, Edmund. 2008. *On the Phenomenology of the Consciousness of Internal Time*. Translated by John B. Brough. London: Springer.

Kadlac, Adam. 2015. "The Virtue of Hope." *Ethical Theory and Moral Practice* 18 (2): 337–354.

Kwong, Jack. 2022. "How to Theorize about Hope." *European Journal of Philosophy* 30 (4): 1426–1439.

Kwong, Jack. 2023. "Despair and Hopelessness." *Journal of the American Philosophical Association* 1–18.

Lamb, Michael. 2024. "Difficult Hope: Wendell Berry and Climate Change." In *Hope: A Virtue*, edited by Nancy Snow. Oxford: Oxford University Press.

Lockhart, Jennifer R., and Thomas Lockhart. 2018. "Moral Luck and the Possibility of Agential Disjunctivism." *European Journal of Philosophy* 26 (1): 308–332.

Martin, Adrienne. 2014. *How We Hope: A Moral Psychology*. Princeton, NJ: Princeton University Press.

McCarthy, Cormac. 2006. *The Road*. London: Picador.

McGeer, Victoria. 2004. "The Art of Good Hope." *Annals of the American Academy of Political and Social Science* 592 (1): 100–127.

Meirav, Ariel. 2009. "The Nature of Hope." *Ratio* 22 (2): 216–233.

Miguens, Sofia, Gerhard Preyer, and Clara B. Morando, eds. 2019. *Pre-Reflective Consciousness: Sartre and Contemporary Philosophy of Mind*. London: Routledge.

Nagel, Thomas. 1993. "Moral Luck." In *Moral Luck*, edited by Daniel Statman, 57–72. Albany: State University of New York Press.

Pettit, Philip. 2009. "Hope and Its Place in the Mind." *Annals of the American Academy of Political and Social Science* 592 (1): 152–165.

Potkay, Adam. 2024. "Virtue or Vice? A Short Literary History of Hope." In *Hope: A Virtue*, edited by Nancy Snow. Oxford: Oxford University Press.

Rattigan, Terence. 1985. *The Deep Blue Sea*. London: Methuen Publishing.

Rousse, B. Scot. 2018. "Self-Awareness and Self-Understanding." *European Journal of Philosophy* 27 (1): 162–186.

Sartre, Jean P. 1956. *Being and Nothingness*. Translated by Hazel E. Barnes. New York: Philosophical Library.

Snow, Nancy. 2019. "Is Hope a Moral Virtue?" In *The Moral Psychology of Hope,* edited by Claudia Blöser and Titus Stahl, 171–189. New York: Rowan & Littlefield.

Swenson-Lengyel, Willa. 2024. "Created and Fallen Hope: Theological Anthropology and Fallen Hoping." In *Hope: A Virtue*, edited by Nancy Snow. Oxford: Oxford University Press.

Zimmerman, Michael J. 2006. "Moral Luck: A Partial Map." *Canadian Journal of Philosophy* 36 (4): 585–608.

Chapter 3

The Focus Theory of Hope

ANDREW CHIGNELL

3.1 INTRODUCTION

We speak of hope in many ways. One of the main ways depicts hope as a propositional attitude toward a desired state or outcome. We say that we

hope that it will not rain tomorrow,
hope that our friend will recover from their illness,
hope that the Earth will not warm more than 2 degrees.

Hopes like these are *specific*: they are directed toward discrete and often measurable outcomes (did it rain or did it not?). Such hopes are also *episodic*. Sometimes they consist in a single episode:

There's a runaway horse—I hope it doesn't collide with that bicyclist!

The collision occurs or it doesn't, and then our hope is replaced with either horror or relief. But most episodic hopes are grounded in dispositions that manifest repeatedly under various conditions:

I hoped all last year that the students would find jobs.

Andrew Chignell, *The Focus Theory of Hope* In: *The Virtue of Hope*. Edited by: Nancy E. Snow, Oxford University Press. © Oxford University Press 2024. DOI: 10.1093/oso/9780190069575.003.0004

This hope led to certain actions when they needed practice interviews, and to certain feelings when they were having real ones.

Recent work in the now-active field of elpistology[1] has led to near-consensus about one thing: *specific, episodic hopes* like these are not adequately characterized by the standard belief/desire theory of hope that we find in classical authors like Hobbes. That account (call it 'the Standard Theory') says that hope involves a desire for an outcome accompanied by the belief that the outcome is possible.[2] Beyond the rejection of the Standard Theory, however, there is little consensus about how to revise or replace it. Here I will argue that we need a third element: in addition to the cognitive and conative elements, hope involves the disposition to *focus on* a desired outcome as one whose possibility is psychologically 'unswamped' by the salience of countervailing considerations. The result of adding this *focus* element to the Standard Theory is the 'Focus Theory' of hope. There is a counterpart Focus Theory of despair—I will gesture at it here but save a detailed discussion for another time.

I begin by distinguishing the varieties of hope in more detail (section 3.2) and then go on to describe the Standard Theory (section 3.3) and a couple of the best-known objections to it (section 3.4). In section 3.5, I look at an important recent effort to salvage the Standard Theory, before introducing the Focus Theory and the notion of 'swamping' (section 3.6). I wrap up by briefly considering (in section 3.7) some questions about the nature and aspect of the focus involved, and how the theory accounts for some of the unique norms on hope.

3.2 SPECIFIC HOPE AND BASAL HOPE

Specific episodic hope comes in degrees, and along at least two dimensions: *significance* and *intensity*. Often these two dimensions are correlated: if I invest a great deal of *significance* in some outcome—the survival of my child who has been stricken with a terrible disease, say—then my hope for it will probably be very *intense*. But they can also diverge: I might fervently hope to play a game of snooker with Mark Johnston-Allen someday, and yet openly admit that the whole thing is quite trivial. The fervency or intensity of episodic hope is largely a function of how powerful the desire is—I *really* want to play with Johnston-Allen, and this manifests in a degree of what we might call 'speratic[3] feeling': a phenomenology that is familiar if hard to describe.

At the lowest end of the scale of significance are the banal hopes of daily life (e.g., that it will not rain tomorrow). Toward the top end are the extremely significant specific hopes (e.g., that the Earth won't warm by more than 2 degrees). At the apex are the most significant kinds of life-structuring hopes—the hope to have fulfilling relationships, the hope to make a positive difference, the hope to have a meaningful life, and so on. For many people, hopes regarding the afterlife also fit here at the apex: post-mortem bliss or beatitude is one of the central objects of hope in many religious traditions. Specific hope for a very significant and yet extremely *unlikely* outcome is sometimes referred to (following St. Paul) as "hope against hope."[4] Such hope always has a high degree of intensity.

Note, further, that the same outcome can be the object of banal, insignificant hope for some people, moderately significant hope for others, and apex-level, life-structuring hope for still others. For example, the sentence

I hope that it will not rain tomorrow

uttered by you while planning a picnic expresses a banal hope. Uttered by me when the best man at an outdoor wedding, it expresses a quite significant hope. Uttered by residents of the community on the banks of a raging, overflowing river, the sentence expresses a still more significant hope. The significance, again, is at least partly a function of how invested the hoper is in the outcome.[5] This explains why significant hopes are often, though not always, accompanied by intensity of speratic feeling.

Another and very different way in which we speak of hope refers not to an episodic state but to a broad existential stance: an anticipatory openness to or embrace of an indeterminate range of possible futures. Cheshire Calhoun describes this *basal hope* as "the phenomenological idea of the future" (2018, 74). Basal hope has no specific object, does not involve a disposition to have specific mental episodes, and is not typically under our control. Authors ranging from Calhoun to the Christian existentialist Gabriel Marcel to the Jewish Marxist Ernst Bloch have depicted basal hope as an essential element of finite agency.

It seems possible for some of our most significant life-structuring hopes to start off specific but become so abstract that they 'go basal'— the hope to have a meaningful life or the hope to be happy, for example. So there is some vagueness here about the boundary between significant specific hope and basal hope. Some theorists propose to analyze hope in such a way that their account applies to both specific and basal hope (Milona and Stockdale 2018). In what follows, however, I set aside basal hope and focus on specific episodic hope (hereafter just 'hope'). I leave it open whether a version of the Focus Theory might extend to basal hope as well.

3.3 THE STANDARD THEORY

As mentioned earlier, the Standard Theory says that hope has two key elements—a *Cognitive* element and a *Conative* element (Hobbes [1651] 1994; Downie 1963; Day 1970).

The *Cognitive* element is a presupposition that the hoped-for outcome is *possible*—i.e., that it *could* obtain. Advocates of the Standard Theory typically speak of full-blown belief here (Hobbes calls it an 'opinion'). But this is too strong: some hopes (especially banal quotidian ones) require merely that the outcome be *epistemically possible* for us, or that we *take for granted* that the outcome is possible, or, weaker still, that we simply *lack certainty that it is impossible.*[6] So it is better to say that the requirement here is a mere 'presupposition of possibility'.

Hope contrasts with *wish* on this score: we can wish for outcomes that we take to be clearly *impossible*—that I had been born to different parents, that the losing candidate had won, that the virus were made of ice cream, and so on. But we cannot hope for such things.[7] Many people do hope for miracles, however, even though they take them to be violations of the laws of nature. So the kind of possibility that hope presupposes must be metaphysical rather than physical/causal.[8]

Some Standard Theorists add the condition that we cannot hope for what we take to be certain. I find this dubious: if you ask me whether I hope that the sun warms the earth today, my answer will be "Obviously, yes!" But I am also certain that this will happen and so it would be strange to go around expressing that hope unbidden—it would give people the impression that I take solar malfunction to be a genuine concern. The lesson here, in my view, is that we can and do hope for what we take to be certain, but there is a norm against *asserting* that hope in most contexts. I've discussed this in more detail elsewhere (Chignell 2013); here I will just leave the uncertainty clause out of the analysis.

The *Conative* element of hope is simply the desire for or 'attraction' to the outcome in question.[9] This is different from mere *intention*: suppose that my boss has scheduled a long meeting today, so

I get on my bike and head to the office. I clearly intend to go to the office, but only grudgingly: this isn't genuine hope.[10]

The *Conative* element of hope is also not merely a *preference*. I may have the standing preference that party P wins elections, and so prefer that P wins in Podunk tonight. But I live far from Podunk and haven't given their election much thought; to be honest, I probably won't even feel disappointed to learn that P did not win in Podunk. I may still have a contrastive preference for P-victory in Podunk, but that too isn't genuine hope.

These reflections indicate that hope differs from both intention and preference by necessarily involving a non-contrastive desire for its object. And again, this desire is typically manifested in a degree of phenomenological 'pull' or speratic feeling. That said, there may be latent or sub-conscious episodic hopes that lack all occurrent phenomenology, just as there may be latent or sub-conscious desires. Often such hopes manifest later—in pleasure when they are fulfilled, or in disappointment when they are dashed. Thus Timothy Williamson infers that hope is not a self-transparent (or 'luminous') state:

> I believe that I do not hope for a particular result to a match, I am conscious of nothing but indifference; then my disappointment at one outcome reveals my hope for another. When I had that hope, I was in no position to know that I had it. (1995, 535)[11]

This seems psychologically realistic.

The Standard Theory can be stated as a pair of core necessary conditions, where *p* is a proposition describing a specific outcome:

[**Standard Theory**]: S hopes that *p* only if
(**Cognitive**): S presupposes that *p* is metaphysically possible
and
(**Conative**): S desires that *p*.

Articulated in this way, the Standard Theory has at least two main theoretical virtues (in addition to a storied past).

First, it is *elegant*: it has just two conditions, and they are intuitive. At the same time, the Standard Theory can allow that particular hopes (or kinds of hope) typically have additional features or are accompanied by additional states and behaviors. If you hope to get out of jail, or hope to fetch some water in a pail, then you *probably* also (a) have certain emotions and feelings regarding the outcome, (b) endorse those feelings and emotions as justifying certain actions, (c) keep your eye out for pathways to the outcome, (d) are *prima facie* inclined to take those pathways when they present themselves, (e) will be resilient or "gritty" in the face of setbacks with respect to the outcome, and so on. In order to avoid ready counterexamples, the Standard Theory says that these are frequent concomitants or effects of hope, but not essential to it.

Second, the Standard Theory is *ontologically neutral*. In other words, the theory can remain noncommittal regarding whether the presupposition of possibility and the desire are *constituents* of hope, even though many Standard-bearers assume that they are (e.g., Hobbes [1651] 1994; Downie 1963). Earlier I said that hope 'involves' these elements, just as it 'involves' an outcome. But hope also involves having a mind, and it's not clear that we should construe the latter as a constituent of hope. The Standard Theory can avoid all this by claiming merely that Cognitive and Conative are *core* necessary conditions on hope—they are always involved with hope, whether or not they partly or entirely constitute it. This is compatible with hope being a 'primitive' or 'irreducible' state distinct from the subject's beliefs, emotions, and desires (Segal and Textor 2015; Blöser 2019), or a passion or emotion (Aquinas [1265–1274] 1920; Walker 2006; Bobier 2018), or even a kind of perception (Milona and Stockdale 2018).

As we will see, these theoretical virtues (though not the storied past) also characterize the Focus Theory of hope that I present below.

3.4 CHALLENGES TO THE STANDARD THEORY

Two main kinds of challenge to the Standard Theory can be found in the recent literature:

> a. There appear to be *Counterexamples* that indicate that the Standard Theory is unable to distinguish hope from despair.
> b. There appear to be *Different Norms* governing hope, on the one hand, and the presupposition-desire pair described by *Cognitive* and *Conative*, on the other. This indicates that there is more to hope than the Standard Theory allows.[12]

Regarding challenge (a), consider the now-standard counterexample that was first introduced into world literature by Leo Tolstoy (via Stephen King) and into the hope literature by Luc Bovens:

> *Prisoners*: Andy and Red are in the same jail cell. Both believe that escape is unlikely but possible; both desire to escape to the same very high degree. Still, Andy hopes while Red despairs.[13]

We can set aside the details of the film (and in particular the background context involving race and the history of incarceration in America) and stipulate that in *Prisoners*, the *Cognitive* and *Conative* conditions are met *in precisely the same way* by both people. If it still seems plausible that Andy hopes and Red despairs, then the Standard Theory is in trouble.

Regarding the *Different Norms* challenge in (b), consider a different case:

> **Born Sadist:** Sadie is an otherwise fairly normal member of the moral community, but she was born with an ineradicable desire occasionally to inflict pain on certain people. She finds that she has this desire with respect to victimizing Vickie, and also sees that it is possible.[14]

Friends of 'ought-implies-can' will deny that Sadie has a *direct* duty—right now, in the moment—to banish her desire to hurt Vickie, since that's not something she can do. They will also deny that Sadie has an *indirect* duty to dismantle her sadistic desire, since by hypothesis this is also something that she cannot do—it's ineradicable after all. But does she have a duty not to *hope* to hurt Vickie? I think there is an intuitive difference in the norms here. Sadie is not a complete sociopath; although she was born with these ineradicable desires, she's still sensitive to moral rules. As a result, this sounds like a sensible admonition for us to give her:

> **Admonition:** Look, it's clear that you *can* hurt Vickie, and we know that you can't help but *want* to do so. All the same, you shouldn't *hope* to hurt her.

If *Admonition* is coherent, it suggests that some of the norms on hope differ from the norms on the presupposition-desire pairs described by *Cognitive* and *Conative*. It also suggests that hope is (or is at least taken to be) in some way voluntary, even when the presupposition-desire pair is not. And those features suggest that the Standard Theory is in trouble once again.

Some elpistologists take cases like *Born Sadist* to indicate not just that the norms on hope come apart from those on desire, but also that the norms on hope coincide with the norms on desire-*endorsement*. Although Sadie has no duty not to want to hurt Vickie, she ought not *endorse* that desire, and that is why she has a duty not to hope to hurt Vickie. Such theorists thus take endorsement or rational 'incorporation' to be one of the key constituents of hope.[15] But a variation on *Born Sadist* shows that this is too strong: suppose Sadie is aware that she hopes to hurt Vickie and yet does *not* endorse the desire involved. Her hope is thus *recalcitrant*, but it is hope nonetheless. We need an account that makes sense of the different norms, but does not rule out the possibility of recalcitrant hope.[16] The Focus Theory satisfies this constraint, as we will see in section 3.6.

3.5 REVISING THE STANDARD THEORY?

Suppose that these objections to the Standard Theory are sound. There are two main kinds of remedy. The first involves *revising* the two Standard conditions such that they do, together, succeed in handling the objections. The other involves *augmenting* the Standard Theory by adding another element to the list of core necessary conditions.[17] In this section I'll consider a recent revisionary effort by Michael Milona; in the sequel I'll present my own augmentation effort.

Milona's view—which he explicitly characterizes as a version of the 'Hobbesian' Standard Theory—includes an account of the *Conative* element that is supposed to help with the challenges above. He articulates the two core necessary conditions this way:

[**Revised Standard Theory**]: S hopes that p only if

(1) S's belief that *p* is possible is *in the cognitive base of*
(2) a hope-constituting desire that *p*.

Here is his gloss:

> In other words, a hope-constituting desire that *p* is **directly caus-
> ally influenced** by a belief that *p* might come (or be) true in such
> a way that the **desire defeasibly leads the agent to behave and
> attend as if *p* might come (or be) true.** (2018, 6; my emphasis)

It's a complicated idea, even when glossed. To illustrate it, Milona
provides the example of pie-loving Cynthia, who is presently din-
ing at a restaurant and wants a slice of pie. Initially it's just a desire,
but then Cynthia is told by an authoritative source that the kitchen
is liable to run out of pie this late in the evening. Suddenly "what was
once an ordinary desire transforms into a hope" (6). This transformation involves not just a new belief about the improbability of pie-
acquisition, but an 'affective shift':

> The desire for a slice is now such that it motivates her to perform
> new actions, e.g. to flag the waiter as soon as possible to beat
> other patrons to what may be the final slice. (6)

In other words, the belief that having pie is possible becomes part
of the 'cognitive base' of the desire. And that desire counts as 'hope-
constituting' because it (defeasibly) leads Cynthia to 'behave and
attend' in ways that are responsive to the pie possibility.

The inclusion of a defeasible connection to action and attention gives Milona's Revised Standard Theory (RST) a response to
Born Sadist. Sadie's desire to harm Vickie, when influenced by her
belief that it is possible, just *is* the hope to harm Vickie, according
to RST. Since these desires and beliefs are by hypothesis ineradicable, she has no duty not to hope. But RST can account for the
Different Norms intuition by saying that Sadie has a duty to prevent

the 'hope-constituting desire' from leading to certain patterns of action and attention. In other words, Sadie ought to make sure that the defeasible connection is in fact defeated: *that* is what is under her control—indirectly or directly. In effect, then, RST resolves the *Different Norms* challenge by denying that it exists: there are *not* different norms, and the intuitive sense that there are can be explained by the requirement to 'defeat' the connection to action and attention. Sadie inevitably hopes to hurt Vickie, but she ought not act or attend as if she might do so.

Although this is a coherent model, it would clearly be preferable to preserve our intuitive idea that there are different norms expressed in *Admonition*—that is, there are different norms on presupposition-desire pairs than there are on hope. The Focus theory can do that, as we'll see.

A second concern about RST is that it requires a full-blown modal belief to play the causal role specified. But as noted earlier, it's controversial in elpistological circles that a full-blown modal *belief* is required for hope. My own view is that what the presupposition in *Cognitive* minimally requires is simply the *absence of certainty that* p *is metaphysically impossible* (see Chignell 2013). But it's hard to see how a mere absence of certainty can play the causal role that Milona wants the belief to play in condition (1)—that of 'directly causally influencing' a desire. The Focus theory doesn't suffer from this problem, as we'll see.

Third, there are contexts in which RST renders the wrong verdict. Consider:

> **Smoker:** I notice that you have a pack of cigarettes in your
> pocket at the evening reception, and I know that you're
> a fairly generous person and that we've smoked together
> at receptions for years. So I see that it's possible for me

to smoke, and this produces a strong urge to smoke with you. I keep my eye on you at the reception, watching to see whether you are heading outside for a smoke. But I also reflect on my promise to my spouse that I will not come back to the hotel room smelling like cigarettes, and so in the end I resist the desire and try not to follow you when you head for the doors. This time, you smoke outside alone.[18]

In *Smoker*, my awareness that it's possible for me to smoke with you 'directly causally influences' my desire. That desire is then liable to 'lead me to act and attend as if' the proposition *I am going to go out and have a smoke* 'might come (or be) true.' In the end the defeasible connection is defeated: I made a promise *not* to smoke, and my desire to keep my promise wins out in the end. It seems clear, in such a case, that I hope *not* to smoke. But do I *also* hope to smoke? RST says yes, but this is implausible: of course I still *want* to join you for a cigarette, but my hope is directed elsewhere.

In order to avoid this problem, RST could stipulate that only our *top* desire is a hope-constituting one.[19] But in the absence of some sort of endorsement condition, this seems ad hoc—why wouldn't our other modally informed desires also constitute hopes? The Focus Theory does a better job with *Smoker*, as we'll see.

Finally: even if RST can overcome the objections raised so far, it is still too weak. For merely *behaving and attending as if p might come (or be) true* is not sufficient in many cases to distinguish hope from despair. Here we can simply go back to *Prisoners*: suppose Red's top desire is to escape, and this leads him to watch Andy digging behind the toilet month after month—he attends as if the escape might occur. RST says that Red therefore hopes. But that's the wrong verdict: due to his estimation of how unlikely escaping would be, and how risky the effort is, Red despairs of ever doing so.

3.6 INTRODUCING FOCUS

There is more to say about the Standard Theory and the various efforts to revise or augment it.[20] Here, however, I will simply move on to develop my own augmentation.

The key element of hope that is missing from the Standard Theory, in my view, is this: in addition to the presupposition that a desired outcome is metaphysically possible, hope involves a disposition to *focus on* or *attend to* that outcome in a specific way. To use a scholastic-sounding phrase: a subject hopes for a desired outcome when she is disposed to focus on it *under a certain aspect.* The aspect here is modal: a subject who hopes is disposed to focus on a desired outcome under *the aspect of unswamped possibility.* 'Unswamped' in this context is a psychological notion rather than an epistemic or logical one: the possibility of an outcome is unswamped for a subject as long as no countervailing considerations—for example that it *ought not happen,* or is *very unlikely* to happen, or involves *extreme risk*—tend to be more psychologically salient for her than its possibility. I'll say more about swamping and salience below.

The addition of this third element immediately resolves *Prisoners:* Andy desires to be free and believes it's just barely possible. But he is also disposed to attend to the imagined escape *as* possible. Red desires freedom to the same degree, and takes it to be possible in just the same way. But he is disposed to focus on the outcome in a different way—under the aspect of its *improbability.* We hear this difference in the way they intone the same proposition:

Andy: "It's just a one-in-a-million chance, but *IT'S POSSIBLE!*"
Red: "It's possible, but it's *JUST A ONE-IN-A-MILLION CHANCE!*"[21]

For Andy, the possibility of escape is unswamped; for Red, the possibility of escape is swamped by its improbability.

Note that the modal aspect of a subject's focus on a desired outcome need not be static or fixed in order for him to count as having hope or despair with respect to it. Inevitably, both Andy and Red fluctuate in their focus (everyone has good days and bad days). But the kind of attention that they are *disposed* to pay under ordinary circumstances reveals that Andy hopes to escape, whereas Red despairs.

Taking 'O' to be the outcome described in *p*, then, we can now add the third core condition on hope:

[*Focus Theory*]: S hopes that *p* only if
(*Cognitive*): S presupposes that *p* is metaphysically possible,
(*Conative*): S desires that *p*, and
(*Focus*): S is disposed to focus on O under the aspect of unswamped possibility.

Some further clarifications:

1. **'Disposed to'**: first, as just noted, the dispositional formulation accommodates the fact that our occurrent focus comes and goes. Jill still hopes that she will succeed in fetching a pail of water during her walk with Jack this afternoon, even if she is not *presently* focused on that outcome at all.

The disposition in question is also not exceptionless: there might be times when a subject is focused on the relevant outcome, but under a different aspect. Suppose Jill momentarily focuses on water-fetching under the aspect of its *improbability* (perhaps she is thinking about the big hill they will have to climb, and how heavy the pail will be, and how uncooperative Jack is in such situations). As long as she is *disposed* across ordinary circumstances to focus on the outcome under the aspect of unswamped possibility, then *Focus* is satisfied and Jill has hope.

A limit case of this would be a subject who is disposed to focus under the aspect of possibility even if in fact he *almost always* focuses on it under a different aspect. Pops hopes that his kids will live to be at least eighty years old, and his psychological dispositions are such that he is likely to focus on that outcome under the aspect of unswamped possibility. In fact, however, Pops almost never brings it to mind, and when he does it is usually because of some threat to his kids' future (posed by climate change, for example). So *in fact* Pops almost always focuses on the desired outcome under the aspect of improbability or precarity. Still, he is *disposed* to focus on it as an unswamped possibility; thus Pops hopes.[22]

Conversely, we can at times engage in the mental activity that is characteristic of hope—namely, focusing on an outcome under the aspect of possibility—but still not hope for it, given the state of our dispositions. The English language doesn't have another good term for the characteristic speratic mental activity, so I propose to simply call it 'hoping.' *Hoping* is what Red does when he gets talking to Andy some days: for a fleeing moment, he does what Andy and other hopers do—he focuses on the outcome in such a way that countervailing considerations are no longer the most salient for him. So Red is indeed *hoping* at those moments, but his dispositions reveal that he doesn't *hope*. That's because Red is more inclined, across ordinary circumstances, to focus on the outcome under the aspect of improbability or risk.[23]

2. **'Unswamped possibility'**: Recall that 'swamping' in this context is not a logical or epistemic relation but rather a psychological one: the possibility of an outcome is swamped for a subject when she is disposed to regard a countervailing consideration as more salient than its possibility. So when a possibility is swamped, that is not because the subject comes to view the outcome as metaphysically *im*possible. More generally:

> **Swamping:** The possibility of an outcome O is *swamped*
> for S iff it is less salient in the aspect of S's focus than a
> countervailing consideration regarding O.
>
> A *countervailing (or 'swamping') consideration* is a
> consideration, typically based in an apparent feature of O,
> that distracts or detracts from the thought that (a) O will
> obtain or (b) it would be a good thing (for S or some other
> subject) for O to obtain.

Leading candidates for swamping considerations include O's perceived improbability, riskiness, harmfulness, precarity, or impermissibility. I can *believe* that O is improbable or impermissible and still hope for it, obviously—that happens all the time. But if, in the very aspect of my dispositional focus on O, the improbability or impermissibility of the outcome is more salient than its possibility, then I do not satisfy *Focus* and I do not hope for O.

These two components of the Focus Theory—the dispositional quality of the focus together with the 'unswamped' salience of the outcome's possibility—allow it to resolve tricky cases like *Smoker*. Addicts often need to recognize that and when satisfying their craving is possible—this is what they learn in the various 'Anonymous' groups. So we can allow that our smoker is indeed disposed to focus on smoking at the reception as possible. However, he is also disposed to see its prohibited character as its most salient feature. So when the disposition is manifested, he focuses on smoking under the aspect: possible-but-*PROHIBITED*. In other words, the salience of the outcome's possibility is swamped: yes, I *want* to smoke and it seems *possible* to do so with my colleague, but it also much more saliently seems prohibited and bad. So I do not hope to smoke.[24]

The Focus theory can also account for *recalcitrant* hopes. Luc Bovens (in conversation) describes the case of someone at a Formula 1 race who is horrified to find himself moving up to sit near the sharp bend in the track—clearly in the hopes of witnessing a fiery crash. One thing we might say here is that the subject does not really hope but is just momentarily *hoping*, and is then aghast to find himself hoping in that way. But suppose we allow that he genuinely hopes, and just wishes that he didn't. Then the hope is recalcitrant.

In such cases, the Focus Theory can say that the subject's dispositions are such that the bad-making features of the outcome do *not* swamp its possibility. He also knows that the outcome is likely to be very bad for the driver, and may even focus on it as bad-but-POSSIBLE. Still, the possibility of the fiery crash is the most salient feature for him and so it remains unswamped for the subject; thus the subject hopes to witness a fiery crash at the racetrack.

All this is still compatible with *wishing* at a higher-order level that the bad-making features *were* more salient to him, and even with trying to adjust the aspect of his focus so that they do become more salient. In other words, the subject wants the possibility of a deadly crash to be psychologically swamped for him by its badness: he wants it to seem possible-but-*BAD* rather than bad-but-*POSSIBLE*. And so his hope is recalcitrant. Because the Focus Theory does not require the agent to endorse the desire or the aspect of the focus, it can account for recalcitrant hope in this satisfying way.

A final point about swamping: it occurs only when *countervailing* considerations are more salient in the subject's dispositional focus than the outcome's possibility. If a consideration that works *in favor* of the thought that *O will obtain* or *would be a good thing if it obtains* is the most salient aspect of the subject's focus, the possibility remains unswamped. For example, when I focus on the outcome <*Me Not Smoking*> as *possible-and-COMMENDABLE*, its commendableness is more salient to me than its possibility. But the possibility remains unswamped, and so I hope not to smoke.

We saw earlier that the Focus Theory shares with the Standard Theory the virtue of elegance: it does not incorporate much into the analysis of hope *simpliciter*. But it can likewise allow that the manifestation of hope (i.e., *hoping*) often involves or leads to further states: images, fantasies, associations, and so on. Hope also further disposes us in a wide range of circumstances to *act* in various ways (assert, act as if, look for pathways, take pathways when they open up, be resilient or gritty,[25] take various risks), to *feel* in various ways (anticipate joy, fear disappointment), and even to evaluate in various ways (to endorse the presupposition-desire pair as reason to act and feel in certain ways).[26] Because these neighboring states and dispositions are so common, elpistologists have been tempted to include one or more of them in the analysis of hope *simpliciter*. This has led to endless conceptual trouble, typically in the form of counterexamples. It is a crucial part of the Focus Theory that these further dispositions are *not* necessary for hope, but rather common concomitants of it.

That said, the Focus Theory is not *as* simple as the Standard Theory: it has three rather than two core necessary conditions. A friend of the Standard Theory might try to exploit this by arguing that the *Conative* condition can simply absorb the *Focus* condition. If desire can have a modal focus built into it, then the Standard theorist can say that hopers simply *desire an outcome under the aspect of unswamped possibility.*

This would yield a better version of the Standard Theory, one that is close to RST,[27] but at the cost of building a lot into the concept of desire. The account would also raise questions about whether it is the *same* desire that persists when we shift between focusing on an outcome as possible, or as improbable, or as impossible. Can the *same* desire constitute different patterns of salience over time, and thus constitute hope, despair, expectation, and wish? I'm not sure that's coherent. An alternative would be to proliferate desires: one desire is the perception of an outcome as possible, another desire is a perception of it as impossible, another desire is a perception of it as probable, and so on. That too seems to work against the elegance of the Standard Theory.

In the end, then, I think the Focus Theory has the advantage here: it can say that there is typically just one persistent desire accompanied by a *distinct* disposition to focus on the outcome. It's the focus, not the desire, that comes and goes, or fluctuates in aspect. What the *Focus* condition adds in terms of surface-level complexity, then, is made up for by this kind of explanatory elegance. (I'll note some further advantages of keeping the focus element distinct in the next section.)

A related point: although the Focus Theory says that the *Cognitive, Conative,* and *Focus* elements are distinct, it also acknowledges that they interact in various ways. If Jill's desire for an outcome is very strong, that will typically lead her to focus on it. If she is disposed to focus under the aspect of unswamped possibility, then she hopes for it—in this case intensely, fervently hopes. If she is disposed to focus on it under the aspect of improbability, then she despairs of it—in this case, fervently despairs (extremely intense despair could plausibly be called *desperation*). Other things equal, the more improbable we take an outcome to be, the less likely we are to hope for it—the improbability easily swamps the possibility. But other things are not always equal: sometimes we hope against hope for things that we take to be extremely unlikely—just barely possible—by fixing our focus in a way that sidelines the long odds. Often this happens when and because the desire is very strong.

Conversely, when we focus on a good outcome under the aspect of possibility, that can generate or intensify our desire for it, thereby 'awakening hope' (or making our existing hope more intense). Because fervent hopes are more likely to lead to action, this is one of the ways in which intentionally guiding our focus can sustain our practical resolve.[28]

As stated, *Focus* is a synchronic condition: it is part of an account of what it is for S to hope that *p* at a specific time *t*. But there is a diachronic corollary. S counts as having hope that *p* over t_1-t_n only if S's dispositions over that interval remain such that S is predominantly disposed to focus on O under the aspect of unswamped possibility. When ascribing such diachronic hope to people, we often speak of them *being hopeful that* p.[29] *Hopefulness*, in turn, is the trait of being hopeful with respect to various desired outcomes across many different contexts. In some but not all traditions, hopefulness regarding permissible outcomes is commended as a virtue.[30]

3.7 FOCUS, MODALITY, AND THE WILL

In this section I briefly address a few questions that naturally arise regarding the Focus Theory. There is more to be said about each question, but this is at least a start.

a. What is the mental focus in question? Here it is hard to do more than simply rattle off close synonyms: 'selective attention', 'concentration', 'responding to salience', and so on. But in this we are in good company: William James, too, took the notion of 'attention' as basic and obvious:

Everyone knows what attention is. It is the taking possession by the mind, in clear and vivid form, of one out of what seem several simultaneously possible objects or trains of thought. Focalization, concentration of consciousness are of its essence.[31]

James says here that focalized attention is *sometimes* under the direct control of the will—the mind 'takes possession' of an object or thought. We shouldn't conclude from this, however, that focus is always voluntary: again, sometimes we want an outcome so badly that it *commands* or *occupies* our attention. But even when our focus is compelled by desire in this way, its *aspect* may still be up to us.

b. What is the aspect in question? It is common to distinguish between a perceptual state *simpliciter* (such as *seeing*), and a perceptual state that takes its object under a sortal aspect (*seeing as a pail*, say) or an evaluative aspect (*seeing as valuable*). Focus Theorists needn't claim that hope is a perceptual state—that's just one of the ontological options that is compatible with the analysis. But the focus involved in hope is like sortal perception in taking its object 'under an aspect'. In this case, as we have seen, the aspect is modal: a hoping subject is disposed to focus on the desired outcome as *possible*—or, more precisely, *as probable to a non-zero degree*.[32] The aspect is not merely a function of the *Cognitive* modal presupposition, however, since the subject can presuppose that an outcome is metaphysically possible and yet still despair of it. Instead, speratic focus itself has an adverbial aspect under which it presents an outcome: *as* one whose possibility is more salient than any countervailing considerations.

c. What accounts for the aspect? We have seen that the focus involved in hope is often guided by our desire for the object. We have also noted that the desire is sometimes so strong that it *commands* our attention, or even *compels* us to regard the outcome under a certain modal aspect. For example: I *really* want the students to get the jobs for which they are interviewing today, and so cannot help but focus on the fact that they just might.

In other cases, however, I may have a weak desire for an outcome, or no desire at all, and yet still manage to focus on the outcome as possible. Perhaps I callously don't care who gets the job, and would prefer to be focused on other things, but am grudgingly keeping my promise to a colleague to send the students 'good karma' during the interview today. Maintaining such modal focus in the absence of desire for the outcome is quite difficult. But the fact that we sometimes have such control indicates once again that the focus required for hope need not be or even be based in a first-order desire.

A third kind of case is mixed: sometimes our focalized attention is commanded by a strong desire, but its *aspect* remains under our control. In such circumstances, we lack control over *whether* to focus on a desired outcome, but still have control over *how* we do so. Sadie may not be able to avoid focusing on the prospect of victimizing Vickie, but she may still be able to control *how* she focuses on that outcome. That leads to the next point.

d. Are there moral norms on hope? The fact that speratic focus (or at least its aspect) is sometimes under our control is key to resolving the *Different Norms* challenge. In *Born Sadist* it is stipulated that Sadie's desires are ineradicable: she was born a sadist and will always be one—that's unfortunate, but not her fault. Still, as *Admonition* illustrates, it is intuitively plausible that Sadie nonetheless has a duty *not* to hope to hurt Vickie. We saw that RST employs the distinction between hope (conceived as *Cognitive* plus *Conative*) and the attention and action patterns characteristic of hope to explain away the intuition. On RST, Sadie has no duty not to hope to hurt Vickie, but rather a duty not to attend or act as if she might do so. In other words, the 'defeasible' connection between her hope-constituting desire and these further states of attention and action should be defeated.

The Focus Theory can say all of that. But unlike RST, the Focus Theory can also preserve our intuitive sense that Sadie has a duty not to *hope* to hurt Vickie. It does so by emphasizing the connection between a direct duty to control our *hoping* (our occurrent patterns of attention) and the indirect duty, over time, to modify our impermissible *hopes*. What Sadie is *disposed* to focus on, and how, may not be under her direct control. But she may still be able to control whether she *presently, occurrently* focuses on the opportunity to hurt Vickie.

Or, if she can't help but presently focus on it, then she may be able to control the aspect of her occurrent focus.

More generally, because hope involves a distinct disposition to focus in a certain way (*Focus*), we may be able to change that disposition over time, even if we can't change the modal presupposition (*Cognitive*) and desire (*Conative*). A commonplace way to change or dismantle a disposition is to exert mindful, sustained control over its manifestations—to try to block it from manifesting. So in *Born Sadist*, Sadie (indirectly) ought to seek to change her hope by (directly) exercising control over her *hoping*—the occurrent, actual patterns of attention. She ought to stop occurrently focusing on the possibility of victimizing Vickie, or at the very least focus on it primarily under the aspect of its impermissibility.

More generally, unlike the Standard Theory, the Focus Theory of hope explains how we can have indirect duties to dismantle hopes for morally impermissible outcomes, even if the relevant modal presuppositions and desires are completely entrenched. It does so by emphasizing that in many cases we directly control our *hoping*—that is, we directly control the attentional and salience patterns that manifest our hopes—and thereby exercise a degree of indirect control over the hopes themselves. In a phrase: if you can mindfully control your hoping, you can slowly change your hopes.

5. Are there pragmatic norms on hope? The discussion so far has been about moral norms, but an analogous point can be made about pragmatic norms. We might presuppose that some permissible *p* is just barely possible and desire *p* to be true. But typically it would be foolish to hope in an intense or all-consuming way for the outcome described in *p*. The Focus Theory explains why: it is foolish to let a massively unlikely outcome (winning the lottery, say, or making it safely down the double black diamond slope) occupy a great deal of your attention under the aspect of its possibility. That's not because *p* is impossible; it's because focusing on such an outcome as possible makes you liable to ignore more likely outcomes, or take unreasonable risks, or fail to take precautions. An all-consuming hope to win the lottery will occupy your attention and influence your actions in ways that are liable to lead to poverty.

Note that I am not suggesting that it is *always* foolish to focus on massively unlikely outcomes in a hopeful way; sometimes there is good reason to do so. Very ill patients might get great pragmatic benefit from cultivating ongoing, fervent hope to survive. But when there isn't such reason—when the hope is pragmatically irrational—it is often precisely because of the way the outcome *occupies* our attention under the aspect of unswamped possibility.

3.8 CONCLUSION

Cases like *Prisoners* and *Smoker* depict situations in which a subject satisfies both the *Cognitive* and the *Conative* conditions on hope, but still does not hope—precisely because they do not satisfy *Focus*. So the Focus Theory can deal with the *Counterexamples* challenge to the Standard Theory.

The Focus Theory deals with the *Different Norms* challenge raised by cases like *Born Sadist* by highlighting the additional rational constraints on our patterns of mental focus, over and above the norms on presupposition and desire. Again, even if Sadie can't help but desire to hurt Vickie when she spies the opportunity, she may still have an indirect duty *not* to hope to do so, and that's because she shouldn't attend to that outcome under the aspect of unswamped possibility.

Finally, the Focus Theory can remain neutral on ontological questions about what hope is *constituted* by, and say simply that hope always satisfies the *Cognitive*, *Conative*, and *Focus* conditions. The disposition described in *Focus* is often manifested when the desired outcome becomes occurrently salient by being perceived, imagined, mentioned, associated with, and so on. Such hope may further dispose us to act in various ways (assert, pretend, look for pathways, take pathways when they open up, be resilient, take various risks), to reason in various ways (i.e., take the presupposition, desire, or occurrent focus to *justify* various other states and actions), and to feel in various ways (anticipate joy, fear disappointment, feel nervous or 'on edge,' etc.).[33] But according to the Focus Theory, none of these additional dispositions, actions, thoughts, or feelings is *necessary* for hope *simpliciter*.[34]

NOTES

1. From Greek *elpis*. The Greek concept seems to conflate two contemporary concepts—that of hope and that of expectation. See Cairns (2020) and Chignell (forthcoming).
2. Hobbes: "Appetite with an opinion of attaining is called HOPE" ([1651] 1994, I.vi.14). Aquinas: "Hope is a movement of appetite aroused by the perception of what is agreeable, future, arduous, and possible of attainment" ([1265–1274] 1920, I-II, Q. 40, A. 1).
3. From Latin: *spes*—hope.
4. An outcome whose probability is just utterly inscrutable to the subject might also be the object of such hope against hope.
5. There may of course be rational constraints on how significant a particular hope *ought* to be.
6. See Chignell (2014) as well as Blöser (2019) and Benton (2021) for further discussion of this issue.
7. On hope vs. wish, see Wheatley (1958) and, in a Kantian context, Englert (2017).
8. See Chignell (2013) for an argument that the precise formulation of the minimal *Cognitive* condition is "not being certain that *p* is metaphysically impossible."
9. 'Attraction' is Martin's preferred term for the conative element; she thinks that the notion of desire is both too familiar and too contested in the moral psychology literature (2014, 52).
10. This sort of case causes trouble for views (such as that in Bobier 2017) according to which hope is *required* for practical deliberation. It seems like we can deliberate regarding an action without hoping to perform it. Compare Mueller (2019).

11. I don't take a position on the question of whether one can have a hope without *ever* manifesting it—that goes to a deep debate in the dispositions literature that I can't address here.

12. Moellendorf (2006) makes this point, and Martin (2014) elaborates on it.

13. The canonical statement of the case (which is taken from the movie *Shawshank Redemption* and the Stephen King story of the same name, which is itself inspired by a Tolstoy story) is in Bovens (1999). Meirav uses the case to sharpen the point in his (2009).

14. I first encountered Sadie in a talk delivered by Sharon Street. Here we are considering a version of Sadie who is not just a sadist but a born one.

15. This sort of Endorsement Theory of hope is suggested by Moellendorf (2006) and, in a much more elaborate way, by Martin (2014), who calls it the Incorporation Theory.

16. Bovens (1999) makes this point and Milona (2019) develops it as an explicit critique of the Incorporation Theory of hope found in Martin (2014).

17. A third remedy would be to abandon the idea that *Conative* and *Cognitive* are the core necessary conditions on hope, and look for an entirely different approach that declines to analyze hope at all. See Segal and Textor (2015) and Blöser (2019). I won't explore these alternatives here.

18. My thanks to Professor Richard Cross for numerous experiences at American Philosophical Association meetings over the years that inspired this example (though I think he never actually ended up outside alone).

19. Thanks to two anonymous referees for suggesting this amendment to RST.

20. There by now are many 'third condition' proposals in the literature, including Bovens (1999), Pettit (2004), Moellendorf (2006), Meirav (2009), Martin (2014), Kwong (2019), Palmqvist (2020), and Rioux (2022). For the sake of space I have had to set aside critical engagement with most of them here, just in an effort to get the Focus Theory on the table.

21. This way of putting the point is inspired by Martin's discussion of *Prisoners* (see 2014, 15ff.), as well as Meirav's lottery case (2009, 222–224). Palmqvist, by contrast, suggests that such a state could not count as hope because the chances are too low and thus the outcome is not a "live possibility." He thus adjusts the chances to one-in-twenty (2020, 11n). But I can't see what motivates this; surely we can and do hope for outcomes that we take to be less probable than one-in-twenty.

22. As noted above, I stay neutral here on the question whether he can still count as having hope if he *never* manifests the disposition. Thanks to Ryan Darr and an anonymous referee for discussion of this case.

23. I don't offer an account here of how to analyze the notion of the dispositions involved, but it's natural to think of exceptionable dispositions in terms of conditionals combined with probabilities. Something like this: *If* S focuses on O, then S is *likely* to focus on it under the aspect of unswamped possibility. The

tricky part is how to determine which worlds to consider when evaluating the antecedent.

24. Thanks to Gabriel Citron and an anonymous referee for discussion of this aspect of the case.

25. See Rioux (2022) for an account that emphasizes the grittiness of certain kinds of hope.

26. This last disjunct refers to Martin's Incorporation Theory of hope (2014).

27. See Milona and Stockdale (2018) for an elaboration of how desire can be 'perceptual' in this sort of way.

28. See Rioux (2022) for an account of the connections between what she calls 'substantial practical hope' and 'gritty' action ('substantial practical hope' is a concept that Rioux takes from Calhoun).

29. In English, there's no clear counterpart for despair here: 'despairful' is not a word. But the state of despairing that p over time surely obtains. The same thing can be said, *mutatis mutandi*, for 'despairfulness.'

30. On the moral value of certain kinds of attention and attention-patterns, see Weil (1986). On whether hope is a virtue, see Walker (2006), Lamb (2016), Bobier (2018), and Pinsent (2020).

31. James (1891, 403–404). Compare Bradley (1886). For a comprehensive discussion, see Watzl (2017).

32. Note: the focus is not *on the probability estimate*; rather, it is on the outcome *as probable to some non-zero degree*, rather than *as improbable*.

33. Note that these feelings would be over and above any desiderative 'speratic feeling' involved in the *Conative* element itself.

34. This paper first appeared in *The Philosophical Quarterly* (2022). It is subject to the Creative Commons licence (http://creativecommons.org/licenses/by/4.0/) and reprinted here under its terms. For feedback on earlier drafts, I am grateful to members of audiences at Goethe University-Frankfurt, University of Cologne Center for Contemporary Epistemology in the Kantian Tradition (CONCEPT), Humboldt University-Berlin, Calvin University, University of Manchester, Princeton's University Center for Human Values, and the Princeton Project in Philosophy and Religion. For helpful written comments I am grateful to Silvia De Toffoli, Alex Englert, Brendan Kolb, Nancy Snow, and two anonymous referees.

REFERENCES

Aquinas, T. (1265–1274) 1920. *The Summa Theologiæ of St. Thomas Aquinas.* Translated and edited by Daniel Sullivan. Chicago: English Dominicans.

Benton, M. 2021. "Knowledge, Hope, and Fallibilism." *Synthese* 198: 1673–1689. https://doi.org/10.1007/s11229-018-1794-8.

Bobier, C. 2017. "Hope and Practical Deliberation." *Analysis* 77 (3): 495–497. https://doi.org/10.1093/analys/anx102.

Blöser, C. 2019. "Hope as an Irreducible Concept." *Ratio* 32 (3): 205–214. https://doi.org/10.1111/rati.12236.

Bobier, C. 2018. "Why Hope Is Not a Moral Virtue: Aquinas's Insight." *Ratio* 31 (2): 214–232. https://doi.org/10.1111/rati.12161.

Bovens, L. 1999. "The Value of Hope." *Philosophy and Phenomenological Research* 59 (3): 667–681.

Bradley, F. H. 1886. "Is There Any Special Activity of Attention?" *Mind* 11 (43): 305–323. https://doi.org/10.1093/mind/os-XI.43.305.

Cairns, D. 2020. "Hope in Archaic and Classical Greek." In *The Moral Psychology of Hope*, edited by C. Blöser and T. Stahl, 15–36. London: Rowman & Littlefield.

Calhoun, C. 2018. *Doing Valuable Time: The Present, the Future, and Meaningful Living*. New York: Oxford University Press.

Chignell, A. 2013. "Rational Hope, Moral Order, and the Revolution of the Will." In *The Divine Order, Human Order, and the Order of Nature*, edited by E. Watkins, 197–218. Oxford: Oxford University Press.

Chignell, A. 2014. "Rational Hope, Possibility, and Divine Action." In *Religion within the Bounds of Mere Reason: A Critical Guide*, edited by G. E. Michalson, 98–117. New York: Cambridge University Press.

Chignell, A. Forthcoming. "Hope but Not Optimism: The Kantian Mind at the End of All Things." In *Hope: The Kantian Legacy*, edited by A. Z. Ezekiel and K. Mihaylova. New York: Bloomsbury.

Day, J. P. 1970. "The Anatomy of Hope and Fear." *Mind* 79 (315): 369–384.

Downie, R. S. 1963. "Hope." *Philosophy and Phenomenological Research* 24 (2): 248–251. https://doi.org/10.2307/2104466.

Englert, A. 2017. "Dutifully Wishing: Kant's Re-evaluation of a Strange Species of Desire." *Kantian Review* 22 (3): 373–394. https://doi.org/10.1017/s13694 15417000139.

Hobbes, T. (1651) 1994. *Leviathan: With Selected Variants from the Latin Edition of 1668*. Edited by E. Curley. Indianapolis, IN: Hackett.

James, W. 1891. *The Principles of Psychology*. New York: Henry Holt.

Kwong, J. 2019 "What Is Hope?" *European Journal of Philosophy* 27 (1): 243–254. https://doi.org/10.1111/ejop.12391.

Lamb, M. 2016. "A Passion and Its Virtue: Aquinas on Hope and Magnanimity." In *Hope*, edited by I. Dalferth and M. Block, 67–88. Tübingen: Mohr Siebeck.

Lear, J. 2006. *Radical Hope: Ethics in the Face of Cultural Devastation*. Cambridge, MA: Harvard University Press.

Martin, A. 2014. *How We Hope*. Princeton, NJ: Princeton University Press.

Meirav, A. 2009. "The Nature of Hope." *Ratio* 22 (2): 216–233.

Milona, M. 2019. "Finding Hope." *Canadian Journal of Philosophy* 49 (5): 710–729. https://doi.org/10.1080/00455091.2018.1435612.

Milona, M., and K. Stockdale. 2018. "A Perceptual Theory of Hope." *Ergo: An Open Access Journal of Philosophy* 5 (8): 203–222. http://dx.doi.org/10.3998/ergo.12405314.0005.008.

Moellendorf, D. 2006. "Hope as a Political Virtue." *Philosophical Papers* 35 (3): 413–433.

Mueller, A. 2019. "Hopeless Practical Deliberation—Reply to Bobier." *Analysis* 79 (4): 629–631. https://doi.org/10.1093/analys/anz009.

Palmqvist, C.-J. 2020. "Analyzing Hope: The Live Possibility Account." *European Journal of Philosophy* 29: 685–698. https://doi.org/10.1111/ejop.12584.

Pettit, P. 2004. "Hope and Its Place in Mind." *Annals of the American Academy of Political and Social Science* 592 (1): 152–165.

Pinsent, A. 2020. "Hope as a Virtue in the Middle Ages." In *Historical and Multidisciplinary Perspectives on Hope*, edited by S. C. van den Heuvel, 47–60. Cham, Switzerland: Springer Nature.

Rioux, C. 2022. "Hope as a Source of Grit." *Ergo: An Open Access Journal of Philosophy* 8 (33): 264–287.

Segal, G., and M. Textor. 2015. "Hope as a Primitive Mental State." *Ratio* 28 (2): 207–222. https://doi.org/10.1111/rati.12088.

Stockdale, K. 2021. *Hope under Oppression*. New York: Oxford University Press.

Walker, M. U. 2006. *Moral Repair: Reconstructing Moral Relations after Wrongdoing*. New York: Cambridge University Press.

Walker, M. U. 2018. "Hope(s) after Genocide." In *Emotions and Mass Atrocity: Philosophical and Theoretical Explorations*, edited by T. Brudholm and J. Lang, 211–233. Cambridge: Cambridge University Press.

Watzl, S. 2017. *Structuring Mind: The Nature of Attention and How It Shapes Consciousness*. Oxford: Oxford University Press.

Weil, S. 1986. "Attention and the Will." In *Simone Weil: An Anthology*, edited by S. Miles, 211–216. New York: Grove Press.

Wheatley, J. M. O. 1958. "Wishing and Hoping." *Analysis* 18 (6): 121–131. https://doi.org/10.1093/analys/18.6.121.

Williamson, T. 1995. "Is Knowing a State of Mind?" *Mind* 104 (415): 533–565. https://doi.org/10.1093/mind/104.415.533.

Chapter 4

A Black Existential
Reflection on Hope

LEWIS R. GORDON

I offer here some reflections on hope. Specifically, I will explore some existential paradoxes of hope as a virtue, and I will contextualize them through some challenges raised from Black existentialism, a philosophy of existence and freedom attuned to the challenges to thought and action posed by Euromodern colonialism and its concomitant commitment to antiblack racism. Black existentialism asks us to reflect on what it means to be human, to be free, and to justify thought in historical contexts of dehumanization, colonization and enslavement, and crises of hypocritical thought.

I should like to state at the outset that I am not a fan of hope. That sentiment left me, frankly, on the day my mother died. I received a call that she had been in a car accident and that her condition was "critical." Racing to the hospital—a bit of a contradiction under the circumstances—I reflected on what to do to help her through what I expected to be a difficult period, but along the way it occurred to me that "critical" may mean teetering on the verge of death. I *hoped* I was wrong, and in the process began to think about all I would give

Lewis R. Gordon, *A Black Existential Reflection on Hope* In: *The Virtue of Hope*. Edited by: Nancy E. Snow, Oxford University Press. © Oxford University Press 2024. DOI: 10.1093/oso/9780190069575.003.0005 up simply for her to be alive. The hospital official had, as it turned out, used the term "critical" to enable me to be told in person of her passing from an accident in which her death was instant.

Declarations of hope have since then smacked me with an air of naivete. After all, one hopes often when one lacks control over what could be and at other times promises to be an awful outcome. Hope, in other words, arises in moments of crisis and vulnerability. Often confused with optimism, hope sometimes seems to be a feature of people with access to something others may not have. Believing that one is somehow without access to that information, one may decide to give some credence to the agent of hope's chosen path. This poses a problem, however, since if there were some secret knowledge upon which one were acting, hope loses its gravitas. Oddly enough, hope may then be possible where pessimism reigns. That logic, however, falls apart when one realizes that optimism and pessimism are bedfellows. Both, after all, depend on the logic of expected outcomes and prediction. Optimism concludes favorable probabilities of positive outcomes; pessimism, negative ones. Acting on either constitutes investment, whether positive or negative. Hope stands back from both with a form of admission of *what one wants the outcome to be.* Wanting and having do not, however, always meet. An existential struggle then ensues between hope and faith. The latter, I will argue, in agreement with Kierkegaard, requires a movement of infinite resignation. By that, he means the realization of there being no chance of receiving what one wants. Hope does not entertain radical or infinite resignation. If I were told in advance that my mother had passed, my drive to the hospital would have been without hope. It would have been one marked by sorrow and the struggle to live with that reality.

Hope arises where there is mediation, where there is, in a word, actual possibility on the basis of what one knows or is aware. Is hope, then, more connected to the paradoxically life-affirming dimensions of the tragic, where there is ethical mediation? Beyond material outcomes, one could have hope in, for example, doing the right thing under the given, challenging circumstance. It is this link of mediation, I will argue, on the verge of spiraling into the abyss, that connects hope to virtue. Faith, although extolled by the likes of Kierkegaard and a good portion of people, may fail as virtue except for the isolated satisfaction of leaping across the impossible, but there are so many paradoxes there since, lacking mediations—even to the self— it won't work as virtue because the ethical conditions of virtuous life require mediation, disclosure, and appearance.

There are, however, other considerations than hope, since human beings, as in countries with chattel slavery and others with radical struggles with powerlessness and nihilism, may argue against even the relevance of many avowed ethical and moral norms. They may argue that, with such mediations pushed to the wayside in such societies, all is suspended and what the afflicted are left with is not hope but other actions and dispositions through what is best characterized as political commitment.

4.1

There seems to be an obsession with hope in the USA. This is at least the case among those who—as we saw in Jesse Jackson's speech at the Democratic Convention in Atlanta, Georgia, in 1988 and President Obama's in Boston in 2004—would like to believe that good outcomes are inevitable. As President Obama stated in 2012 in a speech that began in the midst of a downfall of rain: "If you still have hope, if you're still willing to go, I'm asking you for your vote." The weather offered him good timing. As it stopped raining, he concluded: "We'll win Wisconsin. We'll finish what we started and we'll remind the world that the United States of America is the greatest nation on earth. The sun's going to come out." The mythopoetics of the sun coming through receding clouds functions as an allegory for the complex dynamics of hope. The sun, after all, was there behind the clouds. Jackson's earlier speech stood in relation to Obama as a hope for racial progress, and for a time, Obama's achievement of the highest executive officer in the land was mistakenly taken as a fulfillment of that hope shining through receding clouds of racial hatred. Yet, as we know, prophetic declarations can also be fleeting through misreading one sign or another as their fulfillment. "Hope," after all, is sufficiently vague and far-reaching for it to exemplify whatever the hearer wishes. Jackson may have thought of racial progress, but President Obama was first elected in a hemorrhaging economy in which for many the life and world ended. The successes of his second term were overshadowed by those clouds of racial hatred and agents of misinformation and other forms of chicanery through which his successor exemplified a reassertion of disgust and, for many, despair. Former Vice President and (at the writing of this essay) President Joseph Biden faces what appears to be a futile, Sisyphean situation struggling to break into the realm of dialectical possibility.

The COVID-19 pandemic exacerbates this situation beyond the confines of the U.S. context from which some of these reflections are born. Across the globe, so many lamented a short time ago about the absence of vaccines; now, worldwide, there is lamentation about the continuation of the disease because of either refusals from those who have access or economic conditions and policies that limit access to those in need. Pessimism accompanies optimism as disasters loom. Add the many catastrophic effects of climate change, humanity lives the folly of a species with access to knowledge and technologies to reach for the stars but, instead, remains wedded to value systems and understandings of the self that are at home in the past. In the midst of such challenges, responses to what is to be done take forms of a desperate search for return to imagined perfect pasts, on one hand, and to seeking, through realizing that perfection was never a feature of humankind, possibilities to make things better, on the other. Both represent actions in which there is a belief that something can be done, but in both cases, hope succeeds instead of motivates action. In other words, it is once the dice has been cast that either, in a word, awaits the meaning of what their consequences offer.

In *Fear and Trembling*, Kierkegaard, that great sage of melancholia, offered the following observation: "[H]e who always hopes for the best becomes old, and he who is always prepared for the worst grows old early, but he who believes preserves an eternal youth" (1941, 7). Kierkegaard cleverly reveals the shortcomings of hope and pessimism, although it is clear that he regards pessimism as the worse of the two. He also makes this observation from a perspective in which hope is less than faith. Here hope is a wishful desire the investment in which requires much life energy. Kierkegaard is, of course, examining how in each instance one is located so much beyond the present that one fails to live, and investments in the worst require additional investments of life. Oddly enough in this regard, one may wish to think about those who are proverbially born old. Such maturation often carries insight through which, as they age, some people grow young. As this is a mark of sages, it no doubt offers a sense of virtue. But, by contrast, Kierkegaard's understanding of the hopeful reeks more of vice. Thus, at least from his existentialist perspective, hope *as a virtue* smacks of contradiction.

Kierkegaard's position is challenging. Writing through Johannes de Silentio, one of his pseudonyms that hardly function as such, its namesake alerts the reader to the silence at the heart of faith. We should bear in mind the long etymology of Johannes to the ancient Hebrew *y'hohanan* ("YHWH has favored" or "YHWH is gracious"); we have the silence from whom G-d has favored or to whom G-d is gracious. Beginning with a series of retellings of the *Akedah* or the Binding of Isaac, Kierkegaard draws forth a series of paradoxical reflections. From various vantage points, he explores why Abraham did not disclose his intentions while Isaac and he trekked up Mount Moriah. He raises the epistemological problem of what Abraham was doing when he obeyed the order to take Isaac up to the sacrificial altar as an offering. He asks what was going through Abraham's mind when he bound Isaac, drew his knife, and proceeded before being stopped by the Angel (Messenger)/G-d and, upon seeing the ram in the thickets, sacrificed it instead. I often ask my students about what that descent from the mountain must have been for Isaac.

Through Johannes Silentio, Kierkegaard says he does not—indeed *cannot*—understand Abraham. His action offers an existential paradox, which involves doing the impossible. How could he, while proceeding with the initial act that required *his agency*, also believe that the deity who promised him he would be a father of a nation through Isaac was not also a deceiver? He had no way of forecasting the outcome. If he were to explain what he was doing along the way, most observers then and now would see him as attempting the murder of his son. Although there were ancient societies that permitted filicide, most, such as Rome, required insolence on the part of the offspring. This was not the case with Isaac. To disclose his actions would make Abraham accountable to the universal dictates, or at least expectations, of moral law. Yet, as we know, Abraham was a good person, and he loved his son. What makes the case even more complicated is that G-d is also good. So, what is the status of such a command? The answer, Kierkegaard was trying to show, does not rest in an affirmation of the universal. To do so would be to subordinate G-d to moral law—at least as conceived of by human beings. But even more pointed, that Abraham could place himself into a relationship with a commandment that would be challenged if disclosed meant he was in a peculiar relationship with that commandment that stood above universal commandments. In Kierkegaard's words, it was to face an absolute relationship with the Absolute *absolutely*. This, of course, limits the question of "how" this is possible, since such an explanation would collapse back into the mediations of universal, communicative action. Abraham faced this problem, in absolute terms, alone.

Kierkegaard described this moment as one of a teleological suspension of the ethical. The absoluteness of the relationship to the Absolute absolutely meant there was no room for other forms of legitimation to enter. To make matters worse, without such mediations there was no bridge or ferry to carry Abraham over to the Absolute. With nothing in between and yet facing a divide, that chasm was infinite. This meant there was no epistemological bridge as well. Isaac's situation, at that moment, was grim. Since Abraham was carrying out the action, each step signified Isaac's inevitable loss. This is not a case of mere resignation, where there could be the proverbial ray of hope. In such instance there would be possibility. If Abraham invests in the idea that G-d might intervene, his action would be one of hope. For the tale to work, there must be no chance of hope. The resignation must be, in a word, infinite. Kierkegaard famously argued that infinite resignation is a bridgeless abyss with seemingly nothing beyond, which requires a leap of faith. Why so? Because there is no guarantee that the faithful will be secured and drawn into the embrace of salvation. Kierkegaard contrasts this with the tragic hero. Such an individual acts for the sake of right, moral law, or the universal. As a consequence, that person is disclosed. That person could resign herself or himself to the loss, but it is so for the greater good. What is different about Abraham, whom Kierkegaard refers to as a Knight of Faith, is that the loss would not only be of Isaac but also of himself if his leap comes to naught. For the tragic hero, there can be consolation from the community who recognizes the disclosed act not only as tragic—because, as we should remember, tragic heroes must be innocent or at least good— but also as what must be done affirms the goodness or virtue of the agent. The tragic hero suffers, but he, as in the case of Agamemnon, who sacrificed his daughter Iphigenia (in some versions she sacrificed herself) to appease the goddess Artemis to facilitate winds for the ships to sail to Troy, is not lost.

At this point, Kierkegaard makes some striking observations. First, clearly the Absolute is "higher" in every sense than the universal. One could look at this logically. A universal is simply what covers or can be mapped onto a particular domain. The Absolute is beyond all domains. Second, because of the ability to leap toward the Absolute, the individual in this case transcends the universal and is thus also, as Kierkegaard through Johannes de Silentio argues, higher than the universal. Third, the teleological suspension taken in such a leap— teleological because it has an aim, end, or purpose—transcends the universal, but strikingly its goal is not the eradication of ethical life. There is thus paradoxically an ethical suspension of ethics. In other words, the leap toward G-d is not an effort to fall into the arms of iniquity. Fourth, the stakes are high for what is to be lost—namely, *everything*—but what is "saved" as well is everything, which includes the faithful.

Although Abraham's trial has a happy ending, Kierkegaard also examines the curious tale of Agnes and the Merman before he returns to examples of salvific, redemptive, and eschatological outcomes. The Merman is a demon who devours maidens he seduces at the edge of the sea. He falls in love with Agnes, however, which raises the question of protecting her from his "nature," since to receive her requires him consuming her. When she decides to throw herself into his arms at the risk of losing all, he refuses and, instead, dies from failing to enact his nature. He was not lost, but this is so paradoxically in his demise. His destruction is his salvation without assurance of Agnes's survival. She could, after all, have still thrown herself into the sea from despair. Kierkegaard's final example of Sarah and Tobias has a different outcome; the lovers, who faced a wedding-night demon who would consume the groom, risked it all and, miraculously,

through some hitherto unknown but wise counsel from an angel, survived. They lacked the epistemic forecast of the resources the angel
gave Tobias to ward off the demon, which meant their action—their
faith—was their commitment to be with each other. In both tales,
Kierkegaard reminds us that we could take a leap of faith into the
arms of the demonic. Had he structured the argument in which the
guarantee of faith was to land in the arms of the divine, the reader's
relationship to the text would not be one of fear and trembling. What
can we surmise when "the highest passion in man," as Johannes de
Silentio claims, could also make us higher than the universal in the
form of the demonic?

Despite Kierkegaard's concerns for faith, ethics, and aesthetic
dimensions of life, his reflections offer implications beyond those
confines. In my book *Disciplinary Decadence*, for example, I argue
that disciplines—committed to epistemic practices of generating
laws or viable generalizations—often turn away from transcendent
reality and onto themselves into methodological fetishization. This
leads to an ontologizing of disciplines and their practices. Breaking
out of such silos, I argue, requires teleological suspensions of disciplinarity. These leaps beyond disciplines could take the form of
communicating with other disciplines, which brings humility to
one's own discipline, or they could, depending on the circumstance,
demand going beyond commitments to disciplines entirely. Similar
to the realization that a teleological suspension of the ethical does not
entail a rejection of ethical life, so, too, the willingness to leap beyond
disciplinarity need not require the elimination of an outcome that
may take the form of a discipline. Indeed, among the many striking
conclusions of Kierkegaard's analysis is the challenge it offers to theodicy. The Absolute in a theodicean sense requires the elimination of
its accountability to infelicity, injustice, or evil. There is a cleansing of
what functions as the divine. Yet, as we saw, Kierkegaard did not make
the theodicean case since it really was the case that Isaac was being

taken up Mount Moriah to be sacrificed; it really was the case that Agnes was going to throw herself into the clutches of the Merman; it really was the case that Sarah faced Tobias' being consumed by the conjugal demon. These aren't the only examples he discusses, but I offer them for the sake of brevity.

Theodicy, we should bear in mind, depends on demonstrating the compatibility of a given deity with a world of injustice or evil. A good, omniscient, and omnipotent deity should, it seems, do something about an infelicitous reality. Classic responses from antiquity to the present involve two main defenses. The first is that finite beings are unaware of the greater goals of an Infinite or Absolute one. The problem, in other words, is an expression of our own limitations, not the Divine's. The second is that a truly good, loving divinity would afford us freedom. That leaves us with the options of committing good and evil, right and wrong. The Divine's abstaining is a function of respect and love for our dignity and freedom. We needn't explore the limitations of those arguments here. The main thing is that the Divine is left intact. Transferring such arguments to what we treat as divine has the same effect. Idols ranging from deified knowledge systems to officials and social orders receive similar rationalizations. Think about how President Donald Trump's genuine followers rationalize his malfeasance. He is either the Divine's will or the Divine endowed with special knowledge or simply never wrong but is instead facing the wrongdoings of the rest of us. Similar rationalizations are rife among authoritarian adherents in countries ranging from Brazil to Belarus to Hungary to India. We needn't limit our case, of course, to malignant executives of state. This could occur with anything we treat as intrinsically perfect or sacred. Kierkegaard reminds us, in at least his treatment of our relationship with the Absolute, that *we do not have to take that leap.* His point is that its possibility raises questions for those of us who don't. We could rationalize that we cannot do otherwise, but this would mean to subordinate ourselves to what we have the capacity to transcend. His argument, in other words, is a defense also of human freedom.

4.1.1 What, then, does this analysis have to do with hope?

First, we already see that Kierkegaard regards faith as higher or better than hope. He does not by this mean that we must place our faith into everything or anything willy-nilly. He does, however, argue, second, that hope in some way compromises our humanity even though it is, ironically, an expression of it. Other animals may expect, through repetition, certain outcomes, but it is human beings who, to our knowledge, add hope to the expectations through an awareness of their possible failure. We cease to flourish—a key feature of virtue— in some way through hopeful investments than those of faith. Why is this so? He already hints at it in the burdens lost through faith versus those incurred in hope. We could look at it this way. If one acts from the commitment without regard for the outcome, then the journey itself would be worth doing. If one leaps and is not saved, the appropriate response would not be "I was wrong!" while plummeting into the abyss but, instead, simply without regret for trying. This observation requires further analysis.

4.2

I devoted attention to Kierkegaard's analysis because of his Lutheran—that is, Protestant—conceptual framework, which, as we know, connects him to dominating models of the self upon which much of Euromodern philosophical anthropology and psychology are built. His reflections enable us to examine hope through the subject who hopes and the alternatives, given that subject's desires and wishes, at her or his disposal. Hope, after all, is a guiding feature of eschatological religions, of which Christianity is one. Having faith in Christ is one thing. Hoping for his return is another. For many official denominations of Christianity, the two are inseparable.

It is as a Christian, for example, that Martin Luther King Jr. wedded hope to social transformation, as we see in the essay that serves also as the overarching title of his posthumous collection of writings, *A Testament of Hope*. Whether King's courage was premised on hope, faith, or both is worthy of reflection. What is clear is that Christianity's idea of the Divine made flesh, persecuted, executed, and then resurrected with the promise of a return leaves its faithful also waiting in riveted hope. With faith, so many from Kierkegaard to Martin Buber in Judaism to Ali Shariati in Islam have argued, faith could offer meaning through which to go on with our lives without the worry of hope.

4.2.1 What, however, if we were to particularize that framework and, in doing so, transcend it?

To begin, Judaism has a complicated relationship with hope. On one hand there is the concept of the Promised Land and the Messiah. Promises, as we know, lead to awaited fulfillment. The Messiah is also a promise, which raises questions of hope. Yet Judaism is antipathetic to the idea of an image of G-d. The idea of G-d being made flesh is anathema. One cannot even touch Torah with one's flesh but instead must use a Kosher implement (the yad). Judaic antipathy to idolatry, to imagery, is such that there are restrictions on even divine interpellation. This leads to a complicated aspect of Judaism that baffles many Christians—namely, the idea of Jews who reject G-d as an ontological being but not as an ethical obligation. The radicality of Judaism, under this view, is that a Jew is one who has taken up the responsibility for the presence of G-d as an ethical reality. This is, in other words, *the responsibility for ethical responsibility.* G-d therefore does not have to "appear" ontologically for the responsibility to hold. The ethical calling suffices. For such Jews, there is no act of hoping, no expectation of a Messiah, no search for a Promised Land (which is why there are Jews who, for example, reject Zionism). G-d in this sense "is" responsibility. I place the scare quotes to challenge the ontological meaning of the copula offered here by virtue of the English language. A good friend once stated this point of view to me this way: "I don't go to synagogues because I believe in G-d."

I take this segue through Judaism to raise the question of thinking about concerns of hope and faith beyond ontological investments. The Kierkegaardian discussion did, after all, have G-d as *out there;* his analyses did return to the realm of being, as it were. The Jewish reflection, however, offers a teleological suspension of the ontological *and* a critique of the universal. There are Jews who debate this last point, as we know, since there are those who look at *Halakah* (Jewish law) in an absolute sense. There are others, however, who focus on important dimensions of *Halakah* premised on *Mitzvoth* (roughly translated as commandments) in which kindness, dignity, and compassion offer exemptions. There is a profound sense of reasonability here instead of rigid, blackletter following of law. This leads to a paradox in Jewish ethics. Although there are Jews who believe in resurrection and eternal life—think of the Prophet Elijah, who did not die but simply ascended to Heaven—radically taking on the responsibility for responsibility makes such aspirations and hopes irrelevant. In fact, the responsibility is all the more so where there is no expectation of reward, which would make belief in no afterlife an even stronger support for acts of *Mitzvoth.*

This is not to say that Jews never have hope. It's just that the basis of such does not bear out in Judaism. Think, for instance, of the main difference between Jewish and Christian prayer. Jewish prayer is more about acknowledging and thanking G-d than to make requests or express desired wishes, although there are ample examples of appealing to G-d for grace and mercy. Even at times of mourning, there is an acknowledgment rather than an expression of hope for the deceased. In fact, there is no mention, at least in the Mourner's Kaddish, of the dead. Even in the Jewish interpretation of the case the Akedah is affected by the status of Abraham, Sarah, and Isaac as prophets, as later on others, such as Moses, through which their subjectivity is not a function of hope but "election" (in Hebrew, *bachar*), which is, as I have been arguing, a call to take responsibility for responsibility.

This brings us to two considerations. What would happen to hope if we were to, contra Kierkegaard, reject the self and Being through which the self is understood as a being and toward which the Absolute is treated also as a being or, in some cases, Being?

This question is posed not only against Christianity. Islam is, after all, eschatological and offers models of the self with two-dimensional material and spiritual sides in which, as Ali Shariati argued in *Man and Islam*, a third modeled on freedom could grow out of the second: Bashar (being) and Ensan (becoming) and Ithar (ability to choose other than oneself). Islam also admonishes idols, as well as images of the Prophet and the Divine.

There are also African exemplars such as among the Akan in which the self faces the inevitable birth of ancestry or the Yoruba among whom also ancestry and becoming an ancestor offer different normative challenges. Then there are the transformed Africans into African diasporic elements to consider, especially since this essay not only offers three African American models (Jackson, Obama, and Du Bois) but also because the author is also of the African diaspora. I will return to this consideration at the conclusion.

Nowhere is the critique of the self and Being more evident than in Buddhism, especially Zen Buddhism. As there are many exemplars, for the sake of brevity I will here focus on one. In *Religion and Nothingness*, Keiji Nishitani offers a powerful critique of thought invested in Being and by extension beings such as the self and its possessions.

Hope is to some extent a form of clinging to that in which the self is invested. The loss of the hoped-for object could result in the loss of the self, but where the self maintains the investment, there can then become a form of forlonging in which a self is maintained through hope as a defense against despair. This requires, unfortunately, extraordinary acts of self-deception where nihilism may be at the door if the self lets go. In the face of such a possibility, a search for meaning may follow, but if that search is premised on a form of grounding of being, then what is kept at bay may require paradoxically a form of normalized pathology. One could hope to the point of failing to live, which would hardly be virtuous. Sometimes to live there are attachments of which we must let go. In doing so, we learn to live with an awareness of what we have been trying to avoid. And what ultimately may that be? For Nishitani the answer is reality.

It is because of their investments in self and Being, even where they raise questions of lost meaning, that Nishitani argues Euromodern (so-called Western) philosophers aren't radical enough in their reflections on reality. They don't, as he illustrates through the Zen Buddhist example of "light under foot," step back. What, in other words, lies beneath our feet? The answer transcends the ground. Religion, he argues, addresses the "real self-awareness of reality"—that is, the reality beneath reality, which is radical emptiness. He proffers the Sanskrit word Śūnyatā instead of the Japanese Rōmaji word Kū. Part of his decision was to throw his reflection into the realm of that with which one is not quite at home. To some extent this displacement is similar to Kierkegaard's indirection and use of pseudonyms. Unlike forms of thought that ask from which being or Being did reality, including us, come, Nishitani asks us to address a basic insight of our once not having existed and that we will go out of existence. We can extend this to all living things and then all material things all the way through to energy itself and even the initial transformation in physics known as the Big Bang. The scientific view is a distinction that works with its own premises, but the lived view is haunted by the before-living and after-living. We often look *at* reality instead of getting involved in it, although we can experience living reality, which is often overwhelming; Cartesianism, for example, materializes the world, which leads to radical egological investment. Nishitani regards contemporary, hegemonic humanity as suffering from an ego problem. We need what he calls "existential thinking" (1982, 15). We already see here that hope, even for others, brings forth our own subjectivity. It is an attachment instead of a divestment.

This understanding—that reaching to reality requires forms of detachment—leads to one of Nishitani's startling observations. Being "covers over" reality (1982, 16). *Nihility* (no-place, no-thing), he argues, opens us to the radicality of reality beneath reality, or *Śūnyatā*. As this reality beneath reality is not Being, this means that forms of thinking that address *Śūnyatā* are more radical than those attached to Being. Religion, as Nishitani interprets it, offers such. It requires facing not Cartesian doubt but instead more radical forms beyond theoretical reflection, which, for him, are wedded to beings and Being.

If hope is an attachment to realization in the form of being or Being, then it serves as a source of investment in what falls short of reality. It inflates our sense of possibility with the hubris of containing instead of relating to what always transcends our grasp. What, then, would letting go of that idol entail?

Where there is not optimism, pessimism, or hope, it doesn't follow that all is lost. Not taking oneself too seriously lets go of the ego, which some people eventually learn, has a nasty habit of getting in the way of reality. Where hope dies, it doesn't follow that action cannot succeed. Commitment, especially to doing what is right, could offer meaning without expectations of a takeaway, since the action's value is already achieved on its own terms. This deontological under-standing of hopelessness transcends optimism and pessimism. With meaning in commitment, another malediction of overinvestment lacks a home—namely, despair.

4.3

At this point, the reader may wonder why I have opted to work through religious existential analyses in this reflection on hope. An ongoing concern of mine is the tendency of philosophy to denude religious and theological concepts of their meaning while pressing on either with their terms or their grammatical structure. Much of Euromodern political philosophy, for example, offers arguments that are theodicean in form. This leads to placing a concept such as jus-tice as John Rawls did, for instance, as axiomatic in political inquiry without paying attention to many miserable though avowed just soci-eties; the lack of concern for the misery wrought from settler colo-nialism and racialized enslavement as even part of the deep structure of American societies (from North to South), especially the United States, is mind-boggling. Liberal political theory in that regard pretty much ignores that a healthy society requires a degree of justice, but a society governed by justice may do so to the point of ignoring health. When pressed, it may be the case that most human beings may prefer living in a healthy society, or at least one in which both health and jus-tice prevail. But a justice-centered analysis leads, inevitably, to ratio-nalizations of the basic structure of the designated society, which, as with classic theodicean arguments, externalizes its contradictions.

It is no accident that a society such as the U.S. celebrates mes-sages of keeping hope "alive" while strengthening its resolve to break the spirit of those it degrades. What is hope in that regard but a call for an alignment of the dispositions that maintain the social fabric of an oppressing society? The call to keep hope alive is premised on the false dilemma that abandoning hope means closing off the possibility of actions for change. Yet there is a double-sided effort in such pleas, for at the moral level it is a call for systemic redemption through the unfolding of history. Isn't that eschatological? Yet redemptive narratives are primarily for those in need of redemption. For those who don't seek such, what point would such serve? Beneath calls of hope, then, is also the ironic hope for a loss of hope for those whose only presumed option is despair, apathy, and, thus, inaction.

What, however, about those for whom a lack of hope facilitates commitment? Without the seduction of keeping hope alive, they live through infinite resignation with the existential paradox of commitment. Since I began in the United States, I will close there, although what I'm about to say applies to any society premised upon the maintained exclusion, exploitation, or degradation of the humanity of certain groups of people with a dangling promise of their eventual inclusion. Such a promise often hides a pernicious condition of its aim: the oppressed population's disappearance.

Given the criticisms I have waged against hope, how, the reader might ask, could this illuminate or be of help to anyone? How could a lack of hope be a good—even a virtue? I have already argued for existential commitment as a consideration. Can one be both hopeful and existentially committed? The movement of infinite resignation entails not. This is because a commitment is realized, ultimately, when hope wanes. Why cannot commitment be an expression of hope? One can commit oneself to that for which one hopes, but it is when hope is lost and commitment continues that the difference becomes evident. We return to existential paradox.

The enslaved racialized peoples of the eighteenth through early nineteenth century saw global forces against their liberation. The brutality of the institutions of enslavement across the Americas was such that historians perusing the archives often required the salvation of therapy. The scale of depravity from the kidnapping of peoples on the African continent to their suffering on the Middle Passage across the Atlantic to the lash and other instruments of torture deployed by the "owners" offered no hope for most of the enslaved. Yet, many acted. Their actions ranged from the mundane to the spectacular. Despite the seeming futility and certain brutality of life, they managed to produce, through creativity and courage, their humanity in terms often not intelligible to those who persecuted them. They had marriages that were not legally recognized as such because of their legal status as enslaved peoples; they offered love to one another under systems that determined them worthless beyond being commodities; they produced pleasure in a world that argued they could only feel pain; and they committed a multitude of actions no longer known except beyond their having served as a condition of possibility for the present. As many became Christians, there were certainly many with hope—especially for an afterlife. Given the small number of people who hasten to the afterlife upon learning of it, I take it that a focus on their life on earth should be the focus of hope, even among most Christians. Given that, it was unlikely that those enslaved racialized peoples of the past acted on the basis of themselves being liberated—although those who found themselves prosperous were no doubt thrown into reflection on the miraculous.

The movements into hopelessness and action despite that condition were reflected upon by African diasporic intellectuals under conditions of profound suspicion. After all, as Frantz Fanon showed in *Peau noir, masques blancs* (*Black Skin, White Masks*), there is, for every black person, danger through contact with whites in antiblack societies. This continues to be so, as I show in *Fear of Black Consciousness*. Encountering white people who turn out not to be antiblack is, for most black people, a pleasant surprise. This charged situation of mundane dangerous encounters raises the question of why black people bother to take such risks. For some, there could be a lack of awareness; for others, it could be naivete; others, the force of having no options; and, beyond all those, there is, at times, a simple commitment to making human relationships possible. From the writings of Frederick Douglass through to Anna Julia Cooper, W. E. B. Du Bois, and all the way through to Fanon, el-Hajj Malik el-Shabazz/Malcolm X, Angela Y. Davis, and so many others, these considerations take a path from what Du Bois called "double consciousness" to what Jane Anna Gordon calls "potentiated double consciousness."

Double consciousness involves a form of infinite resignation of antiblack racist society as it is. In that regard, black people are what antiblack societies say black people are. This is often negative or abject. The consciousness of such blacks is marked by an awareness of antiblack people's views of blacks and black people's views of their lived reality. That consciousness is marked by a form of melancholia that's a consequence of hopelessness. It is an awareness of the creation of societies that transformed African and varieties of other peoples into blacks, which makes them indigenous to those antiblack societies *as blacks*. The melancholia—and hopelessness—emerges from the realization that such societies mark the elimination of blacks as an aspiration of their legitimacy. Blacks, in that sense, face the neurotic situation of not belonging to societies in which their identity is indigenous. If they fail to act beyond such systems, what remains is the condition of nonbelonging.

Among the many problems of double consciousness is a failure to question the legitimacy of the societies that force blacks into abjection. That failure entails a naïve acceptance of black people as what Du Bois called "problems." Where, however, the humanity of black people comes to the fore, the question that follows is whether it is legitimate for any society to make people into problems. Understanding people as facing problems instead of *being problems*, the focus of critique becomes the society. If the argument leads to being critical of an unhealthy society, then the project becomes social transformation and the actions necessary for such change. In the course of such actions is the realization that the initial guise of completeness and universality offered by the antiblack society is a fraud. That realization particularizes the society through spelling out its contradictions. This leads to a dialectical unfolding of contradictions through which possibility follows through potentiated action. This potentiality is marked by commitment, since its actors may never experience the proverbial Promised Land. What happens in this case is that, released of expectations of self-fulfillment, a commitment of acting for what is greater than the self follows. Instead of an individual's actions or hopes being assessed by themselves, there is retrospection on action over the course of commitments. Failure, for example, becomes a feature not of an individual's actions but, instead, of something to determine across the course of actions. The existential paradox here is that the assessment may come from those who, at the time of the initial set of actions, were anonymous. All of us today were anonymous to those on whom our lives, literally, depended. Failure and success are, with regard to challenges of world-transforming significance, always to be determined; their historical meanings aren't fixed but, as the saying goes, a work in progress.

The grammatical structure of theodicy, which underlies Euromodern rationalizations of justice in avowed liberal democracies, is evident in double consciousness. Potentiated double consciousness offers a critique of theodicean rationalization. The former insists on hope while producing hopeless situations; the latter rejects hope through a commitment to changing the world under circumstances where even failure won't devalue the importance of action. In this regard, the critical consciousness wrought from potentiated double consciousness rejects black melancholia through posing political commitment to actions by which the openness of dialectical possibility transforms blacks into Blacks, into, in other words, agents of history and producers of meaning and value.

There is, however, despite its many pitfalls, a possible hope for hope. These reflections focus on getting the self out of the way so that certain actions could come to the fore. Self-centeredness often devolves into narcissism, where the value of others is reduced to a projection of the self. Narcissistic love, for example, involves loving only those who are analogues of oneself. Human beings have the capacity, however, for non-narcissistic or radical love, in which others need not be reduced or become analogous to the self to be valuable. The radical difference of those who are not like the self can be such that acts of loving premised on their freedom and life follow. This form of loving could take the form of a commitment to actions of sociality through which love is made manifest through forms of goodwill that embody wishes for others' flourishing. Hope, in this sense, is an act of blessing, even where there is no power to affect outcomes. The hope I had on that tragic drive on the day of my mother's passing is a case in point. This kind of hope, marked by what Nancy Snow calls "social intelligence," involves bringing to one's commitments aspirations that are basically good, even when one's efforts appear futile. Beyond personal loved ones, receivers of such hope often see, in a socially situated way, that those who offer it are not their proverbial enemy. Commitments against enmity are indeed virtuous, and it may be in that sense, because marked by action, that hope may receive its place among virtues.

REFERENCES

Du Bois, W. E. B. 1903. *The Souls of Black Folk: Essays and Sketches.* Chicago: A. C. McClurg.

Fanon, Frantz. 1952. *Peau noire, masques blancs.* Paris: Éditions du Seuil.

Gordon, Jane Anna. 2014. *Creolizing Political Theory: Reading Rousseau through Fanon.* New York: Fordham University Press.

Gordon, Lewis R. 2006. *Disciplinary Decadence: Living Thought in Trying Times.* New York: Routledge.

Gordon, Lewis R. 2022. *Fear of Black Consciousness.* New York: Farrar, Straus and Giroux.

Kierkegaard, Søren. 1941. *Fear and Trembling.* Translated by Walter Lowrie. Princeton, NJ: Princeton University Press.

King, Martin Luther, Jr. 1986. *A Testament of Hope: The Essential Writings of Martin Luther King, Jr.* Edited by James Washington. San Francisco: Harper and Row.

Nishitani, Kejii. 1982. *Religion and Nothingness.* Translated by Jan Van Bragt. Foreword by Winston L. King. Berkeley: University of California Press.

Shariati, Ali. 2005. *Man and Islam.* Translated by Fatollah Marjani. North Haledon, NJ: Islamic Publications International.

Snow, Nancy E. 2010. *Virtue as Social Intelligence: An Empirically Grounded Theory.* New York: Routledge.

Chapter 5

Created and Fallen Hope

Theological Anthropology and Human Hoping

WILLA SWENSON-LENGYEL

5.1 INTRODUCTION

This volume asks if hope is a virtue. As the Christian theological ethicist among our cohort, it may seem my task is the easiest. It was, after all, the Christian tradition that first included hope among the virtues.[1] Perhaps my contribution to this collection could simply be "Yes!" followed by citations from Paul and Augustine through to Thomas Aquinas and beyond.[2] There is undoubtedly a live tradition of Christian thought that does so argue that hope is a virtue. This strain of thought comes primarily out of the Catholic tradition, using Thomas Aquinas as a central guide to provide an account of hope in human life and its nature as a theological virtue within Christian life.[3]

The Thomist tradition's account of hope depends upon a particular understanding of the distinction between hope and faith. For Thomas, faith is intellectual assent to a truth not demonstrated by the individual, given limits to knowledge;[4] the virtue of (Christian) faith is assent to the truth of God, grounded in divine authority, and

Willa Swenson-Lengyel, *Created and Fallen Hope* In: *The Virtue of Hope*. Edited by: Nancy E. Snow, Oxford University Press 2024. DOI: 10.1093/oso/9780190069575.003.0006 infused in the human by God's grace.[5] Hope, contrastingly, assesses a good as arduous, possible, and future and produces in us a tendency toward that good;[6] the virtue of (Christian) hope is a habit of the will to strive for the good of eternal happiness,[7] understood as possible and infused in us as a habit by the means of grace.[8] Eternal happiness is taken to be *possible* due to divine assistance; it is, however, not secured, as it depends upon one's own merits (to believe it secured would be presumption).[9] For Aquinas, then, the distinction between faith and hope is one of (a) intellectual assent to truth versus striving for a good[10] and (b) certitude versus uncertainty.[11] One has faith that God is true; one hopes that in the end one will participate in the beatific vision.[12]

This, however, is but one tradition of thought within a diverse Christian communion. If we turn to another strand of theological reflection, namely, magisterial protestant thought coming out of the sixteenth-century Reformation, it becomes somewhat more difficult to answer the question of this volume. Is hope a virtue in such protestant thought?[13]

Consider Martin Luther. His definition of faith differs from the Thomistic account significantly. Faith in God is not first and foremost intellectual assent to God's truth, but is certainty that God is 'for me.'[14] Understood this way, one can see that Luther cannot accept the Thomistic account of distinct theological virtues of faith and hope, as delineated above. On Luther's account, faith *is* certainty of one's salvation, made actual through Christ's alien righteousness rather than one's own merits.[15] There is no place, then, for a theological virtue of hope as Thomas defines it.[16] It cannot be a *virtue* to hope in uncertainty regarding one's participation in eternal life; to do so would be to misunderstand faith, to treat one's salvation as *not* secured.[17] This suspicion regarding hope does seem to come out, for instance, in the fact that hope is rarely examined in its own right in Luther's writings.[18]

With this, though, we face a bit of a conundrum. What can hope be, if it is not as Thomas defines it, and is it a good? If hope is tied to uncertainty, and if uncertainty regarding my salvation is not an appropriate attitude, then is hope simply *not* good? But, if that is the case, what do we make of the biblical witness and the tradition that elevates hope?[19]

A common approach taken in response to this conundrum is to transform what hope is for the Christian, making it 'assured,'[20] a future-oriented faith that patiently awaits[21] or revolutionarily orients one to[22] the kingdom of God.[23] One can see this throughline up to today, in Jürgen Moltmann's claim that "Christianity is wholly and entirely confident hope, a stretching out to what is ahead, and a readiness for a fresh start. . . . It is in the creative *expectation* of Christ's coming that our everyday experiences of life take place" (Moltmann 2004, 88). This understanding of hope in the eschaton is certain, unshaken by what seems to be the case, but holding fast to that which is not yet, but coming. This is not to say that this account of Christian hope has no sense of the troubles or uncertainties that attend life—certainly current life is full of strife, pain, and confusion, but, insofar as individuals are *successful* in their hope *as* Christians, they feel assured and confident in the hope that is truly expectation.[24] God's promises are sure, and so one lives in 'certain hope' for the good to come.

I am dissatisfied with this way of responding to the conundrum. It is unclear to me why we should call the activity described above hope, as opposed to faith.[25] If we are certain that God's eschaton is inaugurated and coming, why call this certainty 'hope'? Yes, such a conviction may face 'evidence to the contrary' in our world that one needs to stand certain against, but that is the case for all faith commitments: one will need to stand confident in the certainty, despite the world, that there is a creator, that that creator is good, and that that creator is in some intimate way related to Jesus. These are all matters of faith, and if my relation to the eschaton is like my response to all of these other articles, why call it a hopeful relation rather than a faithful one?[26] I see no truly functional difference between the terms on these accounts. Furthermore, such an elision between faith and hope requires that there be a sharp distinction *in meaning* between general human hope and Christian hope, which strains the term definitionally.[27] If hope, in common parlance, deals with the possible rather than the certain, then why does it deal with the opposite for Christians? Last, and most important for this investigation, we are simply not certain creatures. We are not the kind of creature that knows the future with any certainty, but with at best tentative evaluation of limitations and possibilities. To claim that 'Christian hope' (often understood as 'proper human hope')[28] is a matter of certainty seemingly denigrates our human capacities and our human limitations. In essence, it seems that identifying *proper* hope as fundamentally eschatological and assured (and graced!) requires deeming our finitude itself problematic.

Given this dissatisfaction and this conundrum, the task of this essay is to provide an alternative reading of hope's role in human and Christian life, that takes the protestant account of faith seriously and yet does not ultimately elide hope and faith. To do so, I turn away from eschatological reflection to theological anthropology, in order to offer a different interpretation of the place and importance of hope in human life. I argue that hope should be understood as a crucial created capacity of the human as a limited and desirous creature, that helps one make sense of one's own life amid a world beyond us. Simultaneously, this capacity is, in reality, fallen and warped in significant ways along many axes, making hope a fundamentally ambivalent reality in human life.[29] Understood in this way, I end the essay by considering again the question of the volume. Is hope virtuous—both for humans generally and for Christians specifically? I will suggest that, given my analysis of hope, hope *can* be virtuous in the human, but is always incompletely so and requires explicit defense against the tendencies of fallen hope. And I will suggest that Christian hope, as a species of hope, should be understood as a distinctly this-worldly and non-assured activity, geared toward projects and commitments to goods in this world.[30] With this, I turn to unpack the idea of hope as a created, good capacity.

5.2 CREATED HOPE

Above all, by 'created,' I mean to point to the divine affirmation of the goodness of all finite being (Genesis 1). With regard to human createdness, the symbol of creation includes several additional facets: first, that humans had, in some meaningful sense, the potential to live well as finite creatures—without asserting themselves for the sake of security against others, without violent strife, without desperate pride, and so on;[31] second, that it is not nonsense to try to distinguish between finitude and moral evil, despite their historic entanglement; and third, that how we should be (as opposed to how we are) is in some way more real, more human, than how we are today. While envisioning our created state will always be imaginative, it can be subject to criteria. Namely, I take accounts to be better if they (a) minimize differences in capacities and characteristics between pre- and postlapsarian humanity, avoiding 'superman' accounts of createdness;[32] (b) do not depend upon a historic account of the fall;[33] and (c) maintain clear distinctions between finitude and the problems of finitude, on the one hand, and sin and the problems of sin, on the other.[34]

With regard to creation and hope, I will argue that humans were made with a basic (good!) tension within themselves, between their recognizable, finite limitedness and their capacious, expandable desirousness.[35] A large part of what it means to live a human life is working out, interpreting, and responding to this tension in ways that are peculiar to oneself and productive for one's life. Hope, in creation, should be understood as one essential responsive strategy for interpreting and navigating that tension between our limitations and desires, that helps one to orient one's existence in relationship to those limits and desires and, in so doing, grounds much of one's life, actions, and activities. In particular, in hope, (a) one acknowledges and affirms one's desire as good for me now; (b) analyzes and interprets the limitations one faces in realizing the object of one's desire as potentially defeasible, only possibly obtaining, or partial; (c) evaluates the potentially defeasible, partial, or possible limits as genuinely possible to overcome, avoid, or live with *for oneself*; and (d) consequently determines to invest in various activities, emotions, and actions.[36]

I will first examine our limitations and desires, as they are in tension, to provide the grounding for my account of hope.

5.2.1 Limits

It seems self-evident to say that humans are limited in their power and knowledge. Our power over others is constrained: that I desire the United States to invest more in clean energy does not mean it is in my power to accomplish this. Our power over the world is dramatically restricted: that I want it to be sunny says nothing about my ability to moderate a downpour. And our power over ourselves meets resistance: that I want to become an operatic singer does not necessitate that I can be. Similarly, our knowledge of others, the world, and ourselves has significant boundaries—past, present, and future. We cannot know the hearts of others, we cannot predict with particular accuracy the long-term future, and we cannot know how we will feel, for instance, at the time of our own deaths.

These human limits seem diverse in character, both in themselves and as we interpret them.[37] There are those limits that are or that seem absolute to me: death, finiteness itself. But there are also limits that are or that seem potentially defeasible to me: limits to communication seem potentially overcome by speech; limits to our capacity to predict the future seem potentially overcome by weather forecasting systems. There are also limits that may only possibly obtain—I might realize that, in the end, I may well lose a game if my opponent's skill ultimately limits my success. Last, there are those limits that seem basically partial in nature: e.g., there might be a limit on the kind of knowledge I can have regarding the past, even as I can come to have genuinely partial knowledge. The latter three forms of limits—those that are potentially overcome, those that may possibly apply, and those that are partial—are different sides of the same reality, although they point to different subjective experiences.[38]

It is the reality of limits that are or that seem potentially non-absolute that provides the context for possibilities for persons. If I had no limitations, I would have no possibilities—only actuality would attend my life. Non-absolute limitations create the conditions for possibility and uncertainty rather than simply realized outcomes or merely impossible wishes.

5.2.2 Desires

That brings us to a second created reality about humans, in tension with the first: that we are expansively desirous creatures. As a species we desire goods that include and extend far beyond those required for meeting immediate needs. I desire sleep and nutrition, just as I desire musical excellence, increased clean energy investment, knowledge of my spouse's heart, and sunshine. We are created to want that which is beyond our power as much as what is immediately needful; we are even created to want the divine, to desire that which we can do nothing to fully fulfill, here and now. And not only that, we are made to desire that which we can only (potentially) accomplish together: reciprocal love, social justice, communion. Our desires, then, are expansive and expandable—we desire more and more, as we overcome various limitations.[39] This does not seem to be a fault, but the nature of human creatures as such. A given desire filled does not sate us, but often leads us on to another desire beyond it. One's desire to learn how to play the flute may lead one to desire to excel at a whole range of skills (sight reading, embouchure, tuning, etc.), which in turn may lead one to desire to master the Lowell Liebermann sonata, and so on.

5.2.3 The Problem This Presents

This is the crux: we know we are limited and yet we desire goods beyond our limits. This dynamic in itself is not due to the fall, but is simply part of our finite creatureliness. However, this means that our desires and limits, in combination, present as a problem to us and how we navigate this problem is a main task of living: How will we understand the limits we face? How will we relate ourselves to our desires in light of those limits? How will those limits in turn affect our desires? In response to the dynamic between the two, what desires and limits will we let shape our lives significantly? The answers to these questions can only be finally determined by the individual in her own life, and the answers are to a significant extent what make up that individual's life.

Envision a person with a talent for cycling, and a desire to excel at cycling. She recognizes some hurdles, some possible limits to her cycling career-possibilities: for example, a weak knee. Perhaps she recognizes limits that, while potentially surmountable, may, in the end, prove absolute for her: for instance, the potential limit of others' excellence. These limits as she recognizes and interprets them, along with her desires, are in tension with one another: she wants that which goes beyond what she can obtain easily without fear of failure, frustration, or harm. However, the mere fact of this tension does not determine her life; rather, her attitude, her life decisions, or her actions must be navigated in light of this dynamic. Her responses will be decisive for how she spends much of her life, for how she thinks of herself and the world around her.[40] I should note here that I am not suggesting that she chooses it 'on her own' or in some radically free or isolated way; she may respond in light of all sorts of pressures, factors, and relations outside of her control. However, she is not simply determined to respond in any given way, due to her social conditioning and genetic makeup, for instance. There is a non-necessity to her response that remains tied to her own life decisions.[41]

In other words, responses to tensions between desires and limits are called for, and these responses shape how one spends one's life. My argument is that we have been created with a repertoire of ways-of-being in response to these tensions in relation to the nexuses between limits and desires. These various methods of responding help us to orient and guide our lives amid these tensions. In this, they are part of our God-given, created nature, used by the individual in the process of living out her own life. There are several of these responses that include, at the very least, despair and desired expectation in addition to hope.[42] However, here I will focus on hope's role alone.

5.2.4 The Response of Hope

Hope, then, can be understood as one created good response, given to help us make sense of the tension between our desires and the limits we face, which gives rise to concrete emotions and actions that make up much of our living.[43] To recall from earlier in the essay, in hope, (a) one acknowledges and affirms the desire as good for me now;[44] (b) analyzes and interprets the limitations one faces to achieving the object of one's desire as potentially defeasible, merely possible, or genuinely partial; (c) evaluates those limits as genuinely possible to overcome, avoid, or to live with for oneself; and (d) consequently determines to invest in that desire in various activities, emotions, and actions.[45]

Let us take these criteria briefly in turn. Hope requires acknowledgment and affirmation of a desire one has as good for oneself now. A person does not hope for all things she desires, but only from desires she deems good.[46] Moreover, there are desires one deems good, but may not deem good either 'for now' or 'for me'. For instance, a person could be confronted with a situation in which she has conflicting desires, between sleep and continued conversation with a friend. These conflicting desires cannot be both affirmed and pursued in the same way at the same time; she will have to arbitrate between the desires she has for these two possible futures. Whichever desire she ultimately deems good for her now would be that which she takes into hope, even if the other desire continues to 'nag.' While sleep, for instance, is good for her, she may deem it not good for now, and as she arbitrates between her desires, she hopes she will be able to stay awake to continue her conversation, thus affirming her desire for continued conversation and taking that desire up into her hope for that desired state of affairs.[47] This reality of conflicting desires, and consequent competition and arbitration, are not due to the fall, but due to finitude. This is a crucial point, because it makes clear that arbitrating between desires is a good human capacity, and that conflict between desires is not simply due to the fall.

This 'deeming good for me now' is informed by the second criterion, the analysis of the limitations facing one. Discussed earlier, in hope one interprets the limitations one faces as overcomeable, merely possible, or partial, *rather* than as absolute or non-existent. This requires assessing the evidence around one and interpreting it; it is usually not self-evident how best to understand limitations, even as there are better and worse interpretations. For instance, to return to the cyclist, as she assesses evidence around her, she may determine that her weak knee is a final blow to her racing desires or she may, in consultation with a doctor, determine it a non-final setback. This determination is rooted in evidence and yet does not simply follow as a consequence of a given set of evidence. For instance, the doctor may say she has a 10% chance of strengthening the knee fully through physical therapy, and she could either say: 'well, that's like no chance at all' or, alternatively, '1/10 shot it is, then!' Her interpretation of the hurdles she faces as absolute or non-absolute is not in itself determined by the evidence, even as it should be informed by the evidence.

Moreover, her position toward the limitations she faces is not fully determined by her evaluation of that evidence. Even if she identifies the limitation of her weak knee as something that could be *potentially* overcome, given the doctor's assessment, she could still treat that possibility as *not* good enough for her to hope for, but instead respond with a variety of other strategies. She might, for instance, instead despair of cycling excellence, or choose to curtail her desire—treating it as no longer good for her now.[48] If she hopes for cycling excellence, it is because she evaluates the limitations she faces to obtaining her desired outcome as not final or absolute, and sees those non-absolute limits as non-fatal hindrances to treating her desire's object as potentially obtainable, realizable, or possibly true.[49]

Last, to hope, this in turn must result in a determination to invest in the desire in light of and despite the limitations facing one, and as such engage in some activity, emotion, or action.[50] By 'invest' in the desire, I mean simply that, in hope, one devotes time, attention, emotion, and activity to the affirmed desire and its object, in large and small, fleeting and sustained ways. Much of our daily life is made coherent by the hopes we have, small and large, because responding to the limits and desires we have in hope warrants a range of behaviors and emotions.

Here is a brief and very non-exhaustive list of the sorts of invested activities and emotions that can arise out of hope. The hoper may engage in hopeful fantasies or imaginings.[51] Alternatively, hoping may ground tentative planning or patient waiting.[52] Some hoping may also lead to "embodied imagination," where a person rehearses behavior that mimics that which is hoped for.[53] Additionally, one may long for that which is hoped for, or feel anxiety over whether it will happen or not, or feel excitement.

I argue in particular that one form of investment in response to created hoping is a form of human agency essential to living in this world. Namely, created hope is that response to our limits and desires which grounds much intentional action for uncertain goods. When I intentionally act for that which I desire, I act to bring that desire to fruition. However, we live in a world that is not particularly hospitable to human desire (hence, the limits we face). In such a world, acting for that which I desire without expectation for success is an essential human activity; we must act while recognizing the limits we face, and yet with simultaneous investment in that good we desire.[54] This form of agency is 'hopeful'. It is agency that is supported by our hopes. When I act to try to learn the Liebermann sonata, I act out of my hope that I can overcome the limits I have as a flutist while recognizing and responding to those limits. When the cyclist continues to practice her sport, despite the weak knee (and in light of it!), she acts hopefully. Much of created human action and human projects— and certainly all of our collective and collaborative ones—rely upon actions undertaken amid limitations and consequent deep uncertainties, where the intention in acting is buoyed by the hopes we have.[55]

The diverse array of activities and emotions, coupled with this form of agential action, arise from the response of hope. Hope thereby allows for or gives rise to these activities in life.[56] Of course, it is important to note that no given hope requires any particular activity, action, or emotion to arise in response to it; however it is our hopes that give rise to these emotions, activities, and agencies.[57]

5.2.5 *Hope's Necessity*

Created hope is then that way of responding to the tension between our limitations and desires that enables us to invest our lives variously in goods we desire that are beyond us. It allows for a way of relating to the world and our desires that helps us to avoid many inhumane forms of living. Without hope, as humans, we would be far worse off. For instance, because the objects of my desires are so often 'beyond me,' I might deem it better to simply ignore or repress them and focus solely on that which is easily treated as certain to obtain or expectable, constraining my life significantly. Hope prevents this total constraint of our desires to that which seems easily satisfiable. Contrarily, I could, despite limits, choose to live as if all my desires will be fulfilled, and live in optimistic expectation at all times. Consequently, I would be met with constant frustration as those expectations go unmet. Hope helps me to nuance my relation to my desires and avoid this constant frustration at our world and ourselves. Last, I could live in total despair given the hurdles we so often face, treating all my desires as unobtainable even as I continue to desire them. Instead, hope allows for investment in desired goods when one faces genuine limitations to obtaining them; it allows for living in light of our limitations without simply acquiescing to them. As such, it supports genuinely human life in a world beyond us and helps us to shape our own lives as we navigate those limits and those desires we have.[58]

5.3 FALLEN HOPE

My argument is that while we are created, we are also fallen creatures, whose created capacities are askew, warped in a variety of ways. As I understand it, the fall is at minimum a tripartite symbol that represents the ideas (a) of moral and existential shortfall of human persons; (b) that humans were intended otherwise, i.e., that the shortfall keeps us from how we were made to be; and (c) humans are in some way stuck in the position of moral and existential shortfall. This is, therefore, a rather minimal account of the fall, but one that does allow for the possibility that our moral, cognitive, and volitional capacities can be and are affected in mutually exacerbating ways, from social and internal sources.

I argue that the fall affects every aspect of our hoping: our desires, our understanding of the limits we face, and our willingness to invest.[59] By so affecting it, hope simultaneously continues to operate in our lives as an essential capacity, helping us to respond to the limits and the desires we have in ways productive for our lives *and*, in practice, provides evidence of and exacerbates problematic ways of being in the world. This basic bivalence of hope helps us to understand hope's power and its peril, its crucial nature and its constant vulnerability.[60] I turn now to give examples of the variety of ways in which hope can be corrupted.

5.3.1 *Desires*

First, our desires are variously askew in reality, in small and large ways that misdirect our hoping and, consequently, our lives.

For instance, many of our desires, while not bad nor bad for us *in themselves*, can be inordinately held, which may in turn result in hopes held as excessively important to individuals, guiding much of their daily lives and activities in ways that misshape and skew their existences.[61] Here we can think of a desire for excellence in one's work turning into a hope for true dominance in one's field, discarding or ignoring all other projects, goals, and values that might lead to a well-rounded life, for the sake of one's central over-investment in this hoped-for good. Or the desire for comfort, which may not be bad in itself, can be inordinately held, the central desire of one's life, such that one in turn may hope for such comfort, as well as for all sorts of more specific hopes—for more and more luxury goods, for instance—that in turn further misform one's identity and the content of one's life, as one fantasizes, pursues, or plans for these desires' fruition.[62]

Of course, we do also have hopes rooted in desires that we *ought* to deem bad in themselves or that we do in fact *in some way* deem bad ourselves.[63] For instance, a white nationalist's hope for a white state is rooted in a vicious desire for the oppression of others that should never be affirmed. Or, more mundanely, I might find myself hoping with anticipated schadenfreude for someone I dislike to fail at a project, even though, on the whole, I myself may deem such a desire morally problematic.[64]

Last, in the fall, our desires are deeply skewed and limited by the social structures and histories of which we are a part. We can imagine a housewife in the 1950s unable to hope for what would be her genuine good, precisely because she doesn't have the social support to *know* what she desires in the world, outside of marriage and children. Or, we can imagine people's desires formed by consumerism, grounding hopes that are not ultimately good for them—limited by what our culture tells them they should desire, rather than what would be truly liberatory.[65]

In the reality we know, the desires we have are far more complicated than they ought to be. Moreover, our ability to properly affirm or deny, to take up or ignore any given desire seems compromised, to say the least, and that compromise affects our hopes and much of our living. The desires we end up taking into hope, as well the resulting activities and emotions of our daily living, do not guide us in ways that lead straightforwardly to our flourishing in the lives we have formed for ourselves.

5.3.2 Interpreted and Evaluated Limitations

So too, our relation to the limits we face is corrupted, both in terms of our interpretation of those limits and our evaluation of them.

We can interpret limits falsely.[66] This is in distinction from the fact that it can always turn out that we were mistaken regarding the limits we face (i.e., they may turn out to be absolute, when we thought them merely partial or provisional). Instead, in fallenness our assessment of limitations can be driven by concerns other than veracity itself. For two examples: one might be driven by untoward self-interest or others' interests. One might, in self-interest, ignore or deny limitations, given the way in which those limits affect the goodness or possibility of that which one desires. For instance, people may ignore the evidence regarding climate change and the potential limitations it raises for human endeavors, because of the way in which such evidence pressures the 'good for now'-ness of certain desires they have (e.g., for a life made meaningful through buying products).[67] Or, one may ignore the evidence because of the way in which such evidence puts new limitations on the realization of one's desire.[68] In other words, a concern for one's self and one's interests infiltrates one's acknowledgment and assessment of the evidence.

For a socially formed example, very different in nature, a person may falsely interpret the limits facing her due to others' concerns or interests. For instance, an abused individual may learn to interpret the limitations she faces in her life as very often absolute, given the lack of support she receives from her closest relatives. She may interpret as absolute what, on most reasonable interpretations, ought to be treated as merely possible limitations and, consequently, she falsely relates herself to that which is beyond her. This example in particular is important insofar as it emphasizes that our hoping is corruptible and harmed, not due solely to our identity or decisions, but because we are formed and deformed by our communities and societies, and our innermost beings are vulnerable to the vices of others, individually and collectively.

Not only are the interpretations of our limits affected by the fall; so too are our evaluation of those limits as genuine, partial, or surmountable for *ourselves*. So, to keep with the two examples above, the climate-denier, as I emphasized above, may misdiagnose the limitations she faces (i.e., she may ignore the evidence around her). Or, she could treat the limitations, which she recognizes, as·not genuine hurdles to her hopes or expectations. So, she may recognize climate science's predictions as reliable, and yet not relate those predictions to her more proximate desired expectations. Often called implicatory denial, she deems the limitations overcomeable, merely possible to obtain, without a genuine reckoning of the implications of the evidence she encounters.[69]

So too, with regard to the individual who experiences abuse, she may genuinely misidentify the limitations she faces, seeing them as greater than she should, as emphasized above. Or, she may recognize the limitations relatively accurately, but not evaluate them as then genuinely possible for her to overcome. So, for instance, she may interpret the hurdles adequately as non-absolute (e.g., she knows of the programs and friends that could help her), but evaluates the hurdles as not genuinely conquerable *for her*.

Our interpretation and evaluations of the limitations we face in our lives is an essential element to our ability to live well in hoping. Our capacity to honestly undertake these tasks, in the world we live in, is compromised by our own self-interest and others' influence, individual and collective. This too means that while our hopes still help us to navigate and respond to the limits we face, often we live with hopes that are constituted by denial, fantasy, or delusion regarding the world around us. Rather than helping us to realistically invest in a world that is beyond us, we or others very often manipulate the world to suit our own or others' ends, resulting in hopes that misguide and harm us.[70]

5.3.3 Investment

Our ability in hope to appropriately invest in activities, emotions, and actions is also corrupted by our fallenness. For instance, while I may hope to become an operatic singer (and recognize at some level that this hope depends on my activity), this hope may result, in my life, in a lot of imagining and fantasizing, some anxiety and excitement, and little practice.[71] In the fall, the kinds of activities, emotions, or actions that one undertakes in hope may not be those most suited to the nature of the hope itself.[72] Insofar as this is the case, hope-grounded life, the substance of much of my daily existence, may be misshapen, inappropriate, whether or not the hopes I have are themselves worthwhile.

It is important to note that throughout all of these various examples, our hopes are variously informed and deformed by the social formation we receive. One's hopes for field domination or for travel in retirement are not simply one's own, sui generis, but are, in many ways, products of the hopes and actions of others, individually and collectively. The kinds of hopes we have are often those supported and validated by the communities of which we are a part or, alternatively, are those that are permitted by our community.[73] These communities, themselves inheriting and extending fallen forms of social existence, insinuate themselves into the individual and her hoping.

5.4 HOPE: A VIRTUE?

5.4.1 Hope's Basic Bivalence

I have given a breakdown of some of the ways in which hope goes wrong in our world, in order to give a picture of hope as variously and intricately warped, both internally and externally. That said, a rough-and-ready overall vision of fallen hope could be described in the following ways. In our created-and-fallen world, hope still operates in our lives as a way we try to make sense of the desires and limitations we have, and respond with continued investment despite those limits. However, hope responds in ways that are warped variously by social influence and internal flaws, into forms that in fact often support unsuitable ends and unhelpful practices, or it gets lost in denial, frustration, constraint, and despair. Through our hopes, we do make our lives, but the forms of life that come out of these hopes fall short and warp us from who we could be.

For instance, very often people use their hopes to secure their identities, making such securing an end-all goal, to be won however is necessary. Created hope does seem to have an element of such securing in it, insofar as it anchors the self to certain paths, pursuits, and desires, creating through that anchoring an identity. In created hope, this determining of the self is good precisely as it allows you to live *as* yourself, a finite human agent capable and yet constrained. The determination is therefore always provisional, just as the human creature can expect, given the world's independence and human finitude.[74]

However, in fallenness, rather than understanding hopes as precisely what they are, one may well use one's hoping as a strategy to completely insulate oneself to change. It becomes a way of making oneself determined, set against flux, imposition, or change, by validating and preserving the sense of oneself and one's projects over time. One identifies oneself with hopes that are set, ossified, no longer responsive to the world's changing landscape. To so secure oneself, one manipulates one's own sense of the world around one, in order to protect that self from threats. As discussed above, we see this in the climate deniers of various sorts, for instance.[75] Their sense of themselves as tied to their hopes drives (at least in part) their unwillingness to reckon anew with the limitations that climate change may bring and how that might alter the desirability or plausibility of some of their hopes.[76] They would rather secure their own sense of self through the preservation of their hopes than risk living in a world where their lives (or the lives of their children) could crumble, ignoring rather than reckoning with the limitations thrown up by the possibility of drastic climate change. This sort of securing easily leads into living apart from the actuality of the world in fantasy.[77] This, in turn, can easily lead to frustration or despair as the world around one and one's hopes for it clash.

Contrarily, hoping in some lives may, in fallen reality, be a thwarted or unsupported activity, seen as dangerous itself. Rather than hope becoming a means for absolute self-securing, it is an activity insufficiently invested in, unsupported by the world, leaving one constrained or despairing when one shouldn't have to be. The hopes one has are too little, too weak, too constrained by oppression. Rather than having the freedom to orient one's life by one's hope, one is denied hopes by social formation and the structures of one's society.

One reason hope is able to be so manipulated in these ways is because it is a matter of judgment—it requires recognizing and interpreting the limits we face and being able to weigh one's desires well, and, in so doing, it requires responding with the proper kind of investment. So, to be able to hope well requires both being willing to hope when one *should* and being able to use that hope to ground the appropriate actions, emotions, and activities.[78] As such, it is vulnerable to misjudgment coming from a variety of sources.

And yet, hope remains essential to our lives, even in its ambiguity. This bivalence, I believe, can help us to understand the complexity of hope as it operates in human lives. It is, at once, a concerted attempt to respond to the world around us and it is a warped one, which often harms us and the world, rather than helping.

5.4.2 A Partial and This-Worldly Good

Hope therefore is not *in itself* a virtue. It is an ambivalent capacity we have to shape and orient our lives. Given the fall, the mere presence of hope does not constitute a good, flourishing life that helps one to respond well to the surrounding world. Moreover, even if we can imagine the possibility of hope *being used* virtuously, it will be, in reality, significantly limited—whether Christian or not[79]—by this reality of fallenness.

Regarding human hope, if it is to be used virtuously in any way, it will need to be in response to these realities of sinfulness. Virtuous hoping actively resists that temptation to security and ease, where one's hopes are used to reinforce one's identity and one's power, rather than responding to a changing and uncertain world. Virtuous hoping will need to push back on false estimations of what is possible and impossible, whether that is an abuser's estimation of one's possibilities or a society's claims about what is 'realistic' politically. Virtuous hoping will need to interrogate desires and investments to consider their value and worth as paths to orient one's life by.

All of these will be imperfect, but insofar as this hope is about the good formation and direction of one's own life—self-creation—it will be hope oriented by vocation. One finds oneself to have certain talents, tendencies, desires, predilections, and one needs to respond to those in ways that fulfill rather than deny or warp or thwart one. In this, one is responding to a natural call—a call of the self to the self—to be who one ought to be and could become.[80] Vocational hope, then, could be virtuous hoping, guiding a person toward what and who they ought to be.[81]

I suggest there is a Christian hope, too, that *can be* virtuous (although not fully sanctified). However, on the analysis I have given here, this hope would be distinctly this-worldly, as an aspect of this vocational self-creation, in situations of uncertainty, limits, and possibility.[82] For Christians, the virtue of hope will still need to combat fallen tendencies and can still help one orient the self to the creation and fulfillment of one's vocation. As Christian, however, one's vocation is to be oneself, fully alive, and, at the same time, *in imitatio Christi.*[83] One's hopes can orient one in this process.

Writing this piece while in COVID-19 quarantine, the world reminds me of what it believes to be the limits we face as a society and as individuals. It reminds me that the scope of the possible and desirable for many is a 'healthy economy,' that to these actors there seem to be inevitable limitations to who can be saved and who cannot (usually, historically oppressed or already-vulnerable populations) to accomplish their hoped-for ends. And it reminds me how easy it is to acquiesce to these senses of limits and possibility.[84] In response to these realities, I have *faith* that, in some way, the final word will contradict this; it will be a last word of love, justice, and peace, and in some way *I* will participate in that triumph. However, as a *hoper*, I am here and now desiring and trying to form the world around me and myself to be that which Christ calls us to: my hopes are or should be for good news to the poor, for liberation to the captives, for the end of oppressions in this world.

Here and now this means something specific—my hopes are not for the eschaton, but for the release of prisoners in America who are currently being exposed in dangerous, unjust ways to infection. This is a hope; I have no faith that this will be realized, and the death count continues to rise among prisoners. Again, my hopes are not for the *ultimate* dignity for those in poverty (I have faith that their dignity can be violated but never alienated), but precisely for that dignity to be recognized today in the form of sufficient economic and medical aid, in a society not driven by capital (alone, at the very least), but by the welfare of people. I hope for the good news, not that they will someday be saved, but for some liberation here. This hope is not just "thy kingdom come" but "thy will be done on earth."[85] The hope is not for God's *final* word of justice and love—I have faith that God will have the last word—but for the word to be somehow realized in some partial way now.

And these are hopes. They are desires that I hold to, despite and in light of the limitations I see, in light of and despite the powers

CREATED AND FALLEN HOPE

and principalities arrayed against their realization.[86] I hope in them precisely because they are possible as I interpret the world around me—I interpret them as possible both in car caravans circling county and city jails and in the foolish self-immolation of those in power. But I also know they are *merely* possible, that the limitations arrayed against their realization are powerful and may, *for now*, be final. They are hopes that should orient my life and call me into who I ought to be, both idiosyncratically myself and in the likeness of Christ (as best as I can, sinner that I am).

Is hope a virtue? Is hope a *Christian* virtue? It can be, but is not of necessity. Moreover, that possible virtue is one that is (a) always partial and defensive[87] and (b) always of *this* world, of finite and uncertain creatures who can orient their lives by their desires and according to their understandings of the world around them.[88] For protestant traditions, it may be time to put the eschaton into the halls of faith and put hope back here on earth, giving us a way of living well amid the limits of this world.[89]

NOTES

1. See, for some discussion of ambivalence about hope outside the Christian tradition, Adam Potkay (this volume) and Beatrice Han-Pile and Robert Stern (this volume).
2. See, e.g., 1 Cor. 13:13 (*NRSV*); Augustine 1999; Aquinas, *ST* I-II.62.
3. See, for a sampling of twentieth- and twenty-first-century Thomistic accounts of hope, Elliot (2017); Griffiths (1990); Pieper (1977); Lamb (2016a).
4. Aquinas (1960, 287–289).
5. *ST* II-II.4.8.
6. For example, I may desire to be a virtuosic pianist in the future, understand that it is difficult to become one, yet believe it to be possible through my arduous striving. For Thomas' analysis of natural human hope, see *ST* I-II.20. See the following for my critique of aspects of this definition: Swenson-Lengyel (2017a, 421n27). While the natural passion of hope is not a virtue for Thomas, it is not necessarily vicious either and is open to habituation. As such, given the strength

of the Thomist tradition on hope, I am not sure I can agree fully with Potkay's characterization of Christianity's assessment of worldly hope, as "the occasion for irrational and self-destructive thinking, and a presumption vis-à-vis God or the gods: in short, a vice" (this volume). That said, his historical research may well have uncovered voices that do so treat this-worldly hopes as necessarily vicious. Those sources would not be strictly Thomistic, on my reading.

7. It is a habit of the will, rather than a passion, because, as Elliot points out, "since God is not a body, such hope seeks an *intelligible* good and properly resides in the will rather than the passions" (2017, 62, italics added), where the will is understood as a rational appetite.

8. *ST* II-II.17.1–2, 5.

9. See *ST* I-II.62.4 and II-II.17.1, 4. See Elliot (2017) as well for discussion regarding the distinction between hope and presumption as it relates to uncertainty, especially 120–121.

10. *ST* II-II.1.3.

11. *ST* II-II.4.7–8.

12. Thomas does have several crucial distinctions between the natural capacities and theological virtues of hope and faith. First of all, as Michael Lamb has emphasized, it is crucial to understand that theological faith and hope are not the perfections of the natural capabilities (which are not in themselves virtues of even the natural variety). Moreover, Thomas emphasizes that while faith and hope are acts performed by humans by their own powers, the theological virtues are habits infused by God's grace. See Lamb (2016b); *ST* I-II.62.

13. For the purposes of this paper, I set to one side the Reformation's unease with virtue language generally. See, for discussion, Jennifer Herdt's discussion of Luther (Herdt 2008, 173–196). She writes, "To think wrongly of faith as a virtue, as a created habit, even if infused by grace, supports in Luther's eyes a false sense of independence from God" (187). I will simply be asking, more generally, what hope is for this tradition and whether it is a good, for the human and for the Christian.

14. As Luther writes in his *Preface to the Epistle of St. Paul to the Romans*, "Faith is a living, bold trust in God's grace, so certain of God's favor that it would risk death a thousand times trusting in it" (Luther 1962, 23–24).

15. For example, see Martin Luther (1963, 4–9).

16. As Luther writes in his *Lectures on Galatians*, "Let us thank God, therefore, that we have been delivered from this monster of uncertainty. . . . Here I cannot have any doubts unless I want to deny God altogether" (Luther 1963, 387).

17. For Luther, to hope for salvation, while remaining uncertain of attainment, would easily lead to a posture of 'works righteousness' in the individual, where they seek to do 'good' in order to get something they want—namely to gain heaven and avoid hell—and in so doing, they would evacuate their actions of moral or spiritual significance.

18. As Jeffrey Silcock succinctly puts it, "Luther does not develop a theology of hope because hope is not the central driver of his mature theology. Central for him is rather faith in the promise of God" (Silcock 2017).

19. Griffiths argues that this conundrum essentially means that protestants (he particularly discusses Calvinists) simply do not have *Christian* hope. His argument, in my estimation, is not sufficiently defended and is unwarrantedly dismissive of a branch of Christian thought. He writes, "There is no place for what I have picked out as Christian hope in Calvinism," and "It may be that Calvinists have a use for the term hope, which picks out something quite different . . . but it is not Christian hope" (Griffiths 1990, 458, 461).

20. For instance, Luther writes, "Such experience engenders a sure hope, which does not doubt that they are God's children and belong to him" (Luther 1961, 151).

21. As Luther writes, "This is the hope; here the holy cross begins. Our life should be arranged in such a way that it is nothing else than a *constant longing and waiting for the future life*" (Luther 1967, 214, italics added).

22. See Webb (this volume) for a helpful related discussion of the ways in which different attitudes and emotions arise in relation to hope, especially his account of 'patient hope' and 'critical hope'.

23. Potkay in fact argues that Dante and other earlier thinkers similarly argue that hope can be assured, suggesting that this shows "the subordination of hope to faith" (this volume).

24. As such, it is usually considered a sin to despair—for instance, Moltmann writes, "[Despair] is the sin which most profoundly threatens the believer" (Moltmann 1967, 24).

25. Gabriele Oettingen gives a helpful overview of the ways in which contemporary psychology also tends to elide expectation and hope, as well as helpful evidence about 'laymen's' distinction between the two in their own lives. This, I believe, supports my discomfort with this strategy of responding to the protestant conundrum. See Oettingen (this volume).

26. Andrew Chignell asks a similar question in his essay, "Kantian Philosophies of Hope, History, and the Anthropocene" (2023).

27. This is, I take it, one of the strengths of Thomas' account. He provides continuity between what hope means generally and what hope means specifically in a Christian context, while also being attentive to and analyzing what he takes to be the discontinuities.

28. If redemption recovers humanity from sin, then Christian hope is seen as human hope as it was meant to be, apart from the fall, and is consequently understood to be 'proper human hope.'

29. Several of the contributors to this volume share with me the understanding of hope as potentially good or bad, virtuous or vicious, although not all. See Potkay and Webb (both this volume). I, however, am suggesting something a

bit more fundamental—that all experiences of hope *here* are ambiguous, that even the best of postlapsarian hopes are not unambiguously good and fully virtuous.

30. There can be protestant accounts of hope in line with my analysis, that include hope in the eschaton. This could be accomplished via emphasizing the uncertainty of the timing of the eschaton, where one hopes that it will come, for instance, in one's lifetime. I have suggested this as another possibility in an article in the *Journal of Religion*, "The Coming Kingdom: The Future and Human Responsibility" (2021). One could have faith that the eschaton *will* come, while having hope for projects here and now, as well as hope that the eschaton will come *sooner rather than later*. Alternatively, one may have faith that one is saved (what this would mean would need to be explained, of course) and yet be intellectually uncertain regarding the end of the cosmos being one of fulfillment. If this were the case, then one might have hope in the eschaton as I will describe hope in this chapter.

31. A note regarding meaningful potential. 'Meaningful potential' does not mean that anyone in history has actually lived amid finitude well (with the exception of Jesus, who is symbolized as the new Adam precisely because he lived a proper, finite human life). In other words, by meaningful potential, I mean that nothing in our created nature *demanded* sin. In this, I am very sympathetic to Paul Tillich's account of creation and fall. For him, we—as created—have a basic anxiety, due to existing between 'poles of existence' that we ourselves must balance. While, in theory, we could have balanced these well, in history, we have not, so our actual historical existence is always estranged from our createdness. See, e.g., Tillich (1959, 29–59).

32. In other words, while our faculties are variously warped in the fall, they remain the same faculties. Moreover, it is not as if we have become *different* creatures in terms of our physical capabilities, with, e.g., less strong eyesight or capacity to run long distances. While the fall insinuates itself in all aspects of our lives, it does so by our own choices and via social communication.

33. The historic fall is subject to the same sort of problems as a 'God of the gaps,' where the significance and truth of God-statements is made dependent upon (a lack of) scientific evidence. If we take the fall to be significant only insofar as it 'happened' in some historic moment, the meaningfulness of the concept is made dependent upon historic evidence. Moreover, it is not needed to get at the anthropological, moral, and spiritual significance of our estrangement from that which we should be.

34. There is, of course, a strong tradition throughout Christian thought that does elide these two, through divine punishment for the fall, as discussed in the above notes, where our experience of finitude has been *made* more acute by God. There are, however, other strategies for dealing with finitude if one sees it as a problem, without eliding finitude with sin, through, for instance, theosis or

divinization, i.e., a process of spiritual growth by which the human is brought into unity or communion with God. I do not here unpack these possibilities.

35. I grant that this sounds somewhat similar to Reinhold Niebuhr's conception of humans as finite and free or Tillich's 'poles' of existence, as mentioned in note 32. It does have this heritage. A couple of notes, however. (1) Contra Niebuhr's dichotomy, I am not suggesting that there is a tension between finitude and freedom (see Niebuhr 1996, 13–18). Rather, I am saying that our 'freedom' (whatever that may be), or rather more particularly simply one's life, is worked out in response to two kinds of partial givens: our desires and our world-situations; both of these are not solely givens, but in significant ways are not up to us. (2) Tillich's poles that we must balance in our own lives, of individualization-participation, dynamism-form, freedom-destiny, are somewhat closer to what I have in mind. I am simply pointing out another way in which we are pulled as creatures—between recognizing limits on our lives and affirming and pursuing desires we have that go beyond those limits.

36. See Swenson-Lengyel (2017a) for my engagement with this philosophical literature on the definition of hope.

37. I presume that there are, in the end, facts of the matter with respect to the absoluteness or defeasibility of limitations. Moreover, I presume that our interpretations of these can be better and worse, insofar as they map on to the evidence we have available to us. However, the interpretive element of them—given that they are interpretations precisely of things *we don't know*—will almost always be fallible.

38. In other words, all three are limitations that are non-absolute, uncertain, and revisable as I engage and respond to them over my life.

39. Here one may hear an echo of the Romantics' claim that, as a creature, we are always hoping for more, beyond what is. For instance, see Potkay (this volume). However, there is a turn to indeterminacy and an inability to conceptualize that which one desires in these nineteenth-century accounts that this analysis of hope does not necessarily share.

40. I am not simply suggesting that the 'choice' here is experienced as straightforwardly voluntary. It is not as if one can, in an abstracted and uninvested way, reflect between potential options in response to tensions between the limits facing one and the desires one has, and then decide between them. A person is always responding with hope (or despair or expectation) *in media res*, with habits, history, and character traits already up and running that inform their responses. As Han-Pile and Stern (this volume) helpfully emphasize, a person often cannot simply will themselves to hope for something, even if they *want* to hope for it. I grant this reality, but, as they themselves also emphasize with their discussion of 'aspirational control', I think that it is not the whole story. There is the capacity for the human to respond in hope with some kind of choice. We do not simply find ourselves hoping or despairing or expecting all

the time, and we can both recognize hopes we *want* or *ought* to have and can attempt to educate our ways of responding to the tensions between limitations we face and the desires we have, in order to so hope.

41. Liz Gulliford (this volume) helpfully emphasizes the interpersonal nature of stimulating hope and sustaining it. As social beings, our hopes are always formed in part by others and sustained by our social and relational contexts. Our senses of the possible and the desires we have are formed, at least in part, in the forge of social development, and so our hopes are never simply 'our own' in some radically isolated way. That said, social circumstances, relationships, and larger social systems do not *determine* the person's response to the limits and desires she has; she is not merely socially produced, but remains an individual in some way directing her own life.

42. Some may disagree with me on the necessity and fittingness of despair at times in the human life, for instance, Han-Pile and Stern (this volume). There is not sufficient space to fully defend my assertion here. What I will say is this: we live in a world in which there is tragedy due to finitude and exacerbated by sin and the fall. There are good desires that people may well have that they will (a) recognize as impossible to obtain and (b) continue to affirm as good desires. This response to the limits and desires one has may well result in forms of action, despite its not being end-oriented action, including actions of symbolic protest. It may be that I see the moral and meaningful life as less conducive to this-world flourishing than the virtue ethicists among us. I do not believe that resignation, which Han-Pile and Stern suggest is the appropriate relation to desires deemed impossible to attain, is always the fitting response to the world we find ourselves in. In death camps, should people simply be resigned in the face of their own unjust deaths, or in protest continue to desire that which they have every right to desire, even as they may well understand it as impossible to secure their own existence? And, apart from the fall and sin, it may well be appropriate to despair, rather than resign oneself to, the reality of certain tragedies of finitude—of, for instance, a life cut short due to injury or accident. As Dylan Thomas ardently exhorts, regarding the experience of death, "Do not go gentle into that good night./Rage, rage against the dying of the light" (Thomas 1952, 239).

43. One might hear resonances with this account of hope and the seventeenth- and eighteenth-century accounts of hope that Potkay describes in his work in this volume. He suggests that, for these thinkers, "hope is a more or less neutral mechanism for moving the self-concerned individual forward in time from one temporary satisfaction to the next." The resonance, presumably, would be in the way in which hope is functioning to orient the person in time in their own lives. I, however, am not suggesting that it is merely a neutral mechanism, nor a simply self-interested one, but a created capacity that helps us to live our lives well in response to the limitations we face in the world. Moreover, while

I am suggesting that desires are expandable, I am not suggesting that hope only deals with 'temporary satisfactions.' Last, hope, according to my account, is not solely about goal-orientation and attainment, but rather organizes our lives, emotions, and activities in a variety of ways (see later in this chapter for further discussion of this point).

44. It should be noted that, in hoping, one in fact does affirm the desire as 'good for one now' and not the object of the desire. For instance, the hope to be a mother includes a desire that one deems good for oneself now. One spends, perhaps, time imagining being a mother, for instance. One 'indulges' or 'affirms' the desire. This is completely compatible with not thinking that the object of the desire is good for oneself now. One may both hope to be a mother and not think that having a child now would be good for one.

45. I grant that the language used in this definition tends toward the cognitive and reflective. However, I do not mean to suggest that a person need always have conscious and intentional deliberation about their hopes. Probably most if not all of this work can be done pre-reflectively, rooted in a variety of habits about how one (a) pays attention, (b) tends to interpret situations, and (c) responds to one's desires. For a related position, see Han-Pile and Stern (this volume). They suggest there that retrospectively, a hoper can answer the question "Why do you hope?" with reasons, but that there may not have been a prior deliberative process. Rather, they may have simply "see[n] the situation in such a light that a certain course of action appears as the best one possible."

46. I am arguing that, as created, humans would hope only for objects of desire they deem good. However, this evaluative aspect becomes more fraught in fallen hope, to be discussed later in the chapter. Once we have desires for objects that are not simply 'not good for me now,' but are in some way deemed 'bad,' then a person may have hopes that respond to desires that they deem in some way bad. For instance, a parent whose child has been wronged may hope for vengeance against the perpetrator, even if that parent would not usually affirm such a desire for vengeance as good. They have a hope for vengeance that is in some way 'good for them now', and yet they may see that desire and the desired state of affairs as *not good* at their more reflective moments, for example. In other words, in a fallen world, hopes are often more complex evaluatively.

47. Of course, our desires are not fully within our intentional control. Her experience of the nagging desire for sleep is also a reminder that that non-intentional control is simply due to our finitude, not due to our fallenness. Because desires are not fully within our intentional control, we sometimes seem to hope for that which we don't want to hope for. So, again, the individual may well feel as if she has competing hopes, as the desires themselves compete for attention. Additionally, it is possible that she hopes for both. For instance, she could

hope to get 'enough sleep' even as she hopes to have a heart-to-heart with her friend. Or, she could vacillate between hopes.

48. See, for a related position, Martin (2014, 35–61).

49. This last particularly obtains for partial limitations. I might hope for my now-dead grandfather to have been madly in love with my now-dead grandmother. This is not a hope that can be overcome into certainty; the partial limit will remain. Yet, I look at the evidence and determine that the limitations preventing my knowledge need not determine that the desired end is impossible. I have evidence from stories about my grandparents that can provide a basis for my hope for their love. These do not determine my hope, yet can provide the basis for my interpretation of the limitations as not final in some way—I can live with the hope that my grandparents loved each other, given that it seems genuinely possible that they did.

50. See, e.g., Martin (2014, 22).

51. Oettingen (this volume), in line with Bovens (1999), argues that hope can be defined by fantasy or imagings, or that fantasizing can demonstrate the presence of hope. I am interested very much by the data regarding fantasizing and agency that Oettingen describes in her work in this volume, as it very relevant to thinking through the value of hope as well as the ways in which activities and emotions that come out of hope relate one to another. Yet, I do not think that we can define hope as necessarily tied to fantasy or imagining. While it is certainly an activity hopers engage in, one may well have a hope without such fantasy. For instance, a person may hope that a friend was successful at a job interview, without spending time fantasizing about what that success would be like or the results of that success.

52. Martin (2014, 22).

53. Walker (2006, 58).

54. For another argument regarding the relation between hope and agency, see McGeer (2004). McGeer and I agree that hope is deeply tied to agency. However, McGeer gives a developmental account of hope and agency that ties hope to *successful* agency much more intimately than I am prepared to do. This developmental account grounds her claim that "hoping [in adult agents] always has an aura of agency around it because hoping is essentially a way of positively and expansively inhabiting our agency" (2004, 104). I would argue that while some hoping may be agency-expanding, in the sense that hope can support agential activity, very often, hoping is connected to recognizing limitations to one's agency. While created hoping can support a form of agency that is hopeful, it also supports many non-agentially focused activities that help us to deal with those things we cannot control. For example, when one hopes for it to be sunny, one hopes precisely as a creature with limited agency, and when one hopes for democratic processes to continue in your country, it is precisely because of your limitations as an individual agent that you so hope.

55. This form of action in relation to one's hopes will be complicated by the fall. I am arguing that, in creation, action for uncertain goods is (nearly always) supported by hope. However, in fallen reality, there are certainly actions for uncertain ends that do not arise from hope. For instance, people often act for non-certain ends that they do not deem good for themselves now. When a person acts to obtain a cigarette to smoke, while (a) deeming it not certain that they can get a cigarette and (b) not wanting to want the cigarette, they act in a more complex fashion than simply 'hopefully'. They may well hope in some way to *not* locate a cigarette, even if they are currently acting under uncertain conditions to obtain a cigarette. As such, while it is action for an uncertain end one desires, it is not action that straightforwardly arises in response to hope.

56. This is not to suggest that other responses to the tension between limitations and desires, such as desired expectation and despair, do not give rise to related or, at times, even externally indistinguishable activities. For instance, a person may have a 'despairing fantasy' for a good they desire but which they deem unattainable. It is simply to point out that often many of our daily activities and emotions are supported by the hopes we have.

57. This way of understanding created hope and its resulting activities and emotions differs from many accounts of 'virtuous hope' that demand that 'virtuous hope' be active in some way, and that 'passive hope' is in some way less than or not virtuous. See, e.g., Potkay, Gulliford, and Lamb (all this volume). All of these texts suggest that hopes that do not result in effort are in some way empty or idle.

58. Han Pile and Stern (this volume) have a vision of hope that shares some similarities with mine. For instance, they describe hope in the introduction thus: "Just as patience helps us to navigate the temporal, hope helps us to navigate the possible, and to flourish in situations of uncertainty."

59. David Kelsey (2009), in *Eccentric Existence*, provides a related account of sin's effect on 'hopeful existential hows,' i.e., the ways of living that come out of hoping. His analysis is that sinful 'existential hows' arise from various improper responses to God's relating to us. For instance, he emphasizes that people can relate in distorted ways to the objects of their hope, by treating them as ultimate when they are not, and can ground their hopes inappropriately in historic processes and evidence, rather than in "a future (*adventus*) grounded in God's *already* inaugurating radical transformation" (572). There are resonances between Kelsey's account and my own here, but we differ most deeply, I believe, on the ground for sinfulness. Kelsey takes it that we sin in our hoping when we do not respond to God's 'already and not-yet fully actualized eschatological fulfillment' coming into our proximate contexts. I am less certain that eschatological relation is built into human existence as it is meant to be, such that, to be a virtuous hoper, one must respond (appropriately) to

that eschaton. More generally, here I give a primarily morally focused account of hope's fallenness, whereas Kelsey's account is theocentric.

60. It is interesting that throughout much of history, we see an ongoing argument about the value and goodness of hope, with some saying it is harmful and others that it can be a virtue. See Potkay (this volume) for a historical accounting of this diversity of assessment. Understanding hope's bivalence as I've described it here, I believe, can perhaps go some way to making sense of these dueling assessments.

61. Given the length of this essay, I cannot here defend the possibility of inordinately held desires. That said, I think the idea holds intuitive plausibility. There are many goods in the world that *are* genuine goods, but are held in too high a regard by many. Money seems an obvious example, although any example will be controversial, insofar as evaluation itself is a contentious activity.

62. In this section, I am describing the way in which our desires can be skewed. Hope is a matter of affirmed desires we deem good for ourselves now, where the limits to obtaining the object of desire are deemed provisional, partial, or conquerable. Therefore, insofar as we bring skewed desires into our hopes, our hopes are warped *via* our skewed desires.

63. While hope is always for desires I in some way deem "good for me now," in the fall, I have far less control over my desires and am a far more divided creature, such that I might find myself hoping in ways I deem morally problematic.

64. This realization, given hope's evaluative aspect, may lead me to try to reform my hoping here.

65. For instance, in the fall, one may not be formed socially to desire genuine revolution to social justice, but rather to desire comfort via consumer products and to desire economic success at others' expense.

66. In this volume, Gulliford's psychological review of hope in its interpersonal aspects seems particularly useful in understanding the way in which our understandings of our limits can be malformed. She suggests, using William Lynch's studies, that very often one may, on one's own, feel 'out of possibilities' and 'out of hopes,' but that community and relationships can re-enliven one's hopes by helping the individual imagine new possibilities. This section here is about this possibility *and its inverse*—the possibility of the individual whose community has helped to inculcate in them a false understanding of limitations and possibilities. Our hopes can be and are malformed both internally and externally, in mutually exacerbating ways. We are, as hopers, dependent on and vulnerable to our social supports and relationships in ways that can both help and hurt.

67. In other words, a person may practically ignore the evidence regarding just limitations to individual consumption due to global scarcity of, for instance, available CO_2 emissions (prior to predicted drastic climatic change), in order to continue to affirm their hope for consumer luxury.

68. For instance, people may desire that climate change not turn out so badly, and without significant sacrifice or harm to themselves or their family. That desire may itself put blinkers on their reception of predictions and evidence regarding drastic climate change, such that their interpretation of the limitations facing them is guided more by their desire than by the evidence they have available to them.

69. See Cohen (2001, ch. 1).

70. See Webb (this volume) in particular for discussion of the ways in which the sense of the possible can be manipulated, particularly by the power structures of a society. This is both in specific cases of what is determined to be possible, as well as in the sense of what sources and evidence people draw on to determine possibility. He provides helpful discussion of the way in which understandings of what is possible (usually tied to accounts of what is 'realistic') can be used to produce conservative hopes that tie individuals to inhumane systems.

71. Oettingen's research, presented in this volume, regarding the relationship between fantasizing and agency seems very relevant here. She shows that people who engage in fantasizing about their desires are less likely to act on and achieve their desires. It may be the case that, in the world as we know it, people actually have quite a tendency to overinvest in fantasy and consequently underinvest in action, in relation to the hopes we have. So, rather than simply being a single example presented here, it may be a strong tendency in many people's lives.

72. Due to Kelsey's focus on the sinful 'existential hows' of hoping or, in other words, on the lived practices that arise from hoping, this is where our analyses meet most closely. In his account of hope, he emphasizes problematic practices that come from sinful hopes. For instance, he examines utopian hopes that result in overly zealous practices of world-transformation or world-denying practices arising from otherworldly eschatological hopes. I believe I want to go further than Kelsey in suggesting that even hopes held for genuinely appropriate objects (including the "already and not yet fulfilled eschatological consummation") can still result in sinful activities and emotions in the fall. That said, I believe we share a commitment to identifying the ways in which both Christian and non-Christians can hope sinfully. See Kelsey (2009, 567–589).

73. In many situations, what *should be* appropriate hopes are denied as unrealistic or impossible to attain for individuals; for instance, incarcerated people are often unjustly limited, making their hopes similarly unjustly constrained.

74. In other words, one's hopes set one's life in various ways on particular paths, but one's hopes remain revisable as one and the world around one changes.

75. By climate denier, I do not mean to identify only those who explicitly, theoretically deny the truth of the science of climate change. Rather, as I have argued

elsewhere, there are many forms of 'practical denial' of climate change. See Swenson-Lengyel (2017b).

76. For instance, in a time of few people and abundant resources, a project to build the largest and most beautiful home in the world may be worthy of being desirable and hoped for. However, in a time of many people and scarce resources, such a project, when considered in light of our situation, perhaps should be deemed less or not-desirable. Similarly, a desire for a beachfront property as a second home may both be less desirable and less plausible as climate change alters coastlines and destabilizes housing markets, and yet many hope to attain such a property. Amitav Ghosh describes this unwillingness to confront climate change's impact on possibilities and risk, particularly regarding housing and coast lines. See Ghosh (2016, 44–58).

77. Wendell Berry suggests that mistakenly being optimistic, when one should be hopeful, can lead one to confuse fantasy with reality (in Lamb this volume). I am not sure we should call all individuals who hope wrongly in the ways I am discussing here optimistic, but see in his accounting a resonance with my own on this point regarding the need to reckon with reality and the way in which false hopes encourage fantasy and denial.

78. This need for judgment is emphasized by thinkers giving accounts of hope as a virtue, insofar as they suggest that for hope to properly *be* hope, it must be properly formed, which requires a host of attendant virtues and skills. See, for instance, Lamb (this volume) and Han-Pile and Stern (this volume). I disagree with Han-Pile and Stern that hope askew is no longer hope, but grant that, for hope to be a full good, it depends on the goodness of the moral agent more generally and must be practiced.

79. Here I am emphasizing a Lutheran commitment to *simul justus et peccator*. Even those saved are simultaneously justified and sinner; sanctification is never complete in this life.

80. That this call is also from God may be the case, but one need not recognize that latter to acknowledge the former.

81. Relatedly, David Kelsey suggests that sin distorts our prospective personal identities in hope. Rather than seeing ourselves properly in light of the future of eschatological consummation, we see ourselves variously tied to futures for ourselves that are false and binding (see 2009, 590–602). There is a resonance between Kelsey's account of sinful hope as 'living death' (his term for the way in which hope can support false identities for ourselves) and my own emphasis on the identity-constructing power of hope, both for good and for ill. Vocational hope, one might say, is hope oriented prospectively toward a proper sense of one's personal identity that is life-giving rather than death-dealing.

82. In my emphasis on the importance of this-worldly hope for Christians, I have some overlap with Wendell Berry, as Lamb interprets him in this volume.

According to Lamb, Berry emphasizes the importance of this-worldly hopes in their own right, apart from their 'reference to' eternal life and the eschaton.

83. Of course, there is a way in which one may well argue that all people's vocations have this dual nature, if Jesus was the human as created, the new Adam.

84. See Webb (this volume) for related discussion of senses of the possible and hope. While I am less certain of the typology that Webb provides in the essay and the way in which different 'types' of hope are so closely related to certain activities, I find his account of the way in which one's sense of limitation and possibility can be manipulated or wrong-headed very important to consider when examining hope in a fallen world.

85. I recognize that this will read oddly to some, given that one might see these two petitions in the Lord's Prayer as synonymous. I am emphasizing here, of course, the potential for their divergence *as* petitions.

86. In other words, these investments I make in my own life are responsive to the realities of the world around me. My hopes for social justice in America, once Donald Trump was elected president, changed quite dramatically, insofar as my interpretation of the limitations and hurdles changed with that election.

87. Here Augustine's discussion of defensive virtue in Book 19 of the *City of God* comes to mind. Our virtues in this world are not complete, but instead must be in "unceasing warfare with vices, and those not external vices but internal, not other people's vices but quite clearly our own" (Augustine 1972, 853). So, the virtue of hope in this world must be defensive against the tendencies of fallenness, if it is to be at all virtuous. Yet, that defensive nature showcases its partiality.

88. To recall again note 31, it may be the case that one does also have hope in the eschaton. This hope would be, for instance, for the eschaton to come in one's lifetime or to be made present in some partial way here and now. These, of course, would be compatible with the faith that the eschaton will come and that one will participate in it.

89. I am grateful for the helpful discussion of the ideas found in this essay with my audience at the Society of Christian Ethics (2020), as well as for the engagement from the other contributors to this volume, at our "Is Hope a Virtue?" Colloquium at the Princeton University Center for Human Values (2020). I also thank Alda Balthrop-Lewis, our editor Nancy Snow, and Jacob Swenson-Lengyel for providing incisive feedback on drafts of this paper.

REFERENCES

Augustine. 1972. *Concerning the City of God against the Pagans.* Translated by Henry Bettenson. London: Penguin Books.

Augustine. 1999. *The Augustine Catechism: The Enchiridion on Faith, Hope, and Love*. Translated by Bruce Harbert. Hyde Park, NY: New City Press.

Aquinas, Thomas. 1948. *Summa Theologica*. Translated by the Fathers of the English Dominican Province. New York: Bezinger Brothers.

Aquinas, Thomas. 1960. *The Pocket Aquinas*. Edited by Vernon Bourke. New York: Washington Square Press.

Bovens, Luc. 1999. "The Value of Hope." *Philosophy and Phenomenological Research* 59 (3): 667–681.

Chignell, Andrew. 2023. "Kantian Philosophies of Hope, History, and the Anthropocene." In *The Kantian Mind*, edited by Sorin Bias and Mark Timmons, 529–540. London: Routledge.

Cohen, Stanley. 2001. *States of Denial*. Maldon, MA: Polity Press.

Coleman, Justine. 2020. "Texas Lt. Governor on Reopening State: 'There Are More Important Things Than Living.'" *The Hill*, April 21. https://thehill.com/homenews/state-watch/493879-texas-lt-governor-on-reopening-state-there-are-more-important-things.

Elliot, David. 2017. *Hope and Christian Ethics*. Cambridge: Cambridge University Press.

Ghosh, Amitav. 2016. *The Great Derangement: Climate Change and the Unthinkable*. Chicago: University of Chicago Press.

Griffiths, A. Philip. 1990. "Certain Hope." *Religious Studies* 26 (4): 453–461.

Herdt, Jennifer. 2008. *Putting on Virtue: The Legacy of the Splendid Vices*. Chicago: University of Chicago Press.

Kelsey, David. 2009. *Eccentric Existence*. Vol. 1. Louisville, KY: Westminster John Knox.

Lamb, Michael. 2016a. "Aquinas and the Virtues of Hope: Theological and Democratic." *Journal of Religious Ethics* 44 (2): 300–332.

Lamb, Michael. 2016b. "A Passion and Its Virtue: Aquinas on Hope and Magnanimity." In *Hope*, edited by Ingolf Dalferth and Marlene Block, 67–88. Tubingen: Mohr Siebeck.

Luther, Martin. 1961. *Sermons on Gospel of St. John Chapters 14–16*. Vol. 24 of *Luther's Works*. Edited by Jaroslav Pelikan. Translated by Martin Bertram. St. Louis, MO: Concordia.

Luther, Martin. 1962. *Martin Luther: Selections from His Writings*. Edited by John Dillenberger. New York: Anchor Books.

Luther, Martin. 1963. *Lectures on Galatians, Chs. 1–4*. Vol. 26 of *Luther's Works*. Edited and translated by Jaroslav Pelikan. St. Louis, MO: Concordia.

Luther, Martin. 1967. "Sermons on the Epistle of St. Jude." In *The Catholic Epistles*, vol. 30 of *Luther's Works*, edited by Jaroslav Pelikan, translated by Martin Bertram, 203–218. Saint Louis. MO: Concordia.

Martin, Adrienne. 2014. *How We Hope*. Princeton, NJ: Princeton University Press.

McGeer, Victoria. 2004. "The Art of Good Hope." *Annals of the American Academy of Political and Social Science* 592: 100–127.

Moltmann, Jürgen. 1967. *Theology of Hope*. Translated by James W. Leitch. New York: Harper and Row.

Moltmann, Jürgen. 2004. *In the End, the Beginning*. Translated by Margaret Kohl. Minneapolis, MN: Fortress Press.

Niebuhr, Reinhold. 1996. *The Nature and Destiny of Man*. Vols. 1 and 2. Louisville, KY: Westminster John Knox.

Pieper, Joseph. 1977. *On Hope*. San Francisco: Ignatius Press.

Silcock, Jeffrey. 2017. "Martin Luther on Christian Hope and the Hope for Eternal Life." *Oxford Research Encyclopedia of Religion*. https://oxfordre.com/religion/view/10.1093/acrefore/9780199340378.001.0001/acrefore-9780199340378-e-332.

Swenson-Lengyel, Willa. 2017a. "Beyond Eschatology: Environmental Pessimism and the Future of Human Hoping." *Journal of Religious Ethics* 45 (3): 413–436.

Swenson-Lengyel, Willa. 2017b. "Moral Paralysis and Practical Denial: Environmental Ethics in Light of Human Failure." *Journal of the Society of Christian Ethics* 37 (2): 171–187.

Swenson-Lengyel, Willa. 2021. "The Coming Kingdom: The Future and Human Responsibility." *Journal of Religion* 101 (1): 27–47.

Thomas, Dylan. 1952. *The Poems of Dylan Thomas*. New York: New Directions.

Tillich, Paul. 1959. *Systematic Theology*. Vol. 2. Chicago: University of Chicago Press.

Walker, Margaret Urban. 2006. *Moral Repair*. Cambridge: Cambridge University Press.

Chapter 6

Hope

An Interdisciplinary Examination

LIZ GULLIFORD

6.1 INTRODUCTION

This paper considers hope (and the allied concept of optimism) from multiple perspectives, drawing from literature in philosophy, theology, and psychology. It will compare the nature of the confidence upon which hope and optimism rest, and what is taken to be their ultimate ground within these disciplines. Hope and optimism have risen to prominence as the emerging field of positive psychology has grown, though much can be learned from earlier examinations of hope in psychoanalysis, as will be shown.

Is hopefulness a quality of *individuals*? This paper explores a key distinction between hoping-*that* and hoping-*in*; while the former describes the content of our hopes, the latter, which has its roots in Aquinas, focuses on how hope might be sustained in relation to other agents. Are hope and optimism *virtues*—and if so what kinds of virtue are they understood to be? In our consideration of hope it will also be necessary to consider the question of how we picture the future in

Liz Gulliford, *Hope* In: *The Virtue of Hope*. Edited by: Nancy E. Snow, Oxford University Press.
© Oxford University Press 2024. DOI: 10.1093/oso/9780190069575.003.0007

which hope is said to operate. Is the future conceived as open, closed, or cyclical—and is it perceived to be continuous or discontinuous with the present? Finally, this paper will also consider the role of the imagination in potentiating and sustaining human hopes.

6.2 DEFINING HOPE AND OPTIMISM

This short paper will not attempt lengthy definitions of hope and optimism but will instead focus on similarities and differences between hope and optimism as they pertain to key themes in this paper. Hope and optimism both concern expectations for the future and can be described as concepts of prospection. An *expectation* is a belief concerning a future event or events. Both optimism and hope combine an expectation for the future with an emotional component of desiring or wishing for that future event to happen. This affective constituent may be weak or all-encompassing. Indeed, affective tone may denote a key difference between hope and optimism, as Averill, Catlin, and Chon (1990) propose. Both optimism and hope can be contrasted with dread or fear, which characterizes a blend of expectation with the wish that the future event should not occur.

That hope involves wanting or desiring may represent one source of ambivalence about it, though hope is a concept that gives rise to contradictory opinions for other reasons, as we shall see. Buddhists take the stance that desire is a source of suffering and should be overcome, while many Christians might construe human desire as antithetical to God's will; "*thy* will not my will be done." The psychoanalyst and Roman Catholic priest William Lynch (1974) understood wishing to be the "momentum" to hope and distinguished between wishing and *willfulness*. While the latter describes a limiting stubbornness that is maladaptive, the former is vital to good mental health and potentiates the ability to hope; "when I cannot wish I am moving toward despair" (Lynch 1974, 24). Thus, there is nothing about wishing *in itself* that is problematic for Christian belief. We may hope for and be optimistic about future events that are explicitly (or implicitly) based on potentially quantifiable likelihoods: reasons for hoping-that some desired event may come about. People also use the language of optimism when speaking about favorable statistical odds. That individuals can be pessimistic about a future event but nonetheless say they are *hopeful* suggests hope can be grounded in other ways, as we will see.

Averill, Catlin, and Chon (1990) highlighted a distinction between hope and optimism in terms of their different connotations with possibility and probability. The concept of probability involves calculable likelihoods which provide grounds (evidence) for reasonably held beliefs about whether a given event might happen. In this connection, they note that when a clinician gives an *optimistic* (as opposed to a "hopeful") prognosis, it is assumed she is using *evidence* to support her opinion. Moreover, whereas hope may be deemed appropriate even when the chances of its fulfillment are extremely *un*likely, "optimism" is ruled out in such cases. That there are differences in the way the concepts of optimism and hope are used signifies that a different "species" of confidence underlies them. Gulliford (2013) suggested that where optimism could be characterized as a concept of the "head" (given its association with rational processes involving the weighing of probabilities), hope might be better construed as a concept of the "heart," representing a more consuming emotional orientation toward desired future events.

Averill, Catlin, and Chon (1990) conducted a series of cross-cultural studies of optimism and hope in the United Kingdom and Korea and identified four prototypical "rules of hope." The "prudential rule" holds that hope should be *realistic*, while the "moralistic rule" deems hope to be circumscribed by what is *morally acceptable*. These two rules can be outranked in exceptional circumstances by the "priority rule"; hope may come into play when the likelihood of the desired event is unfavorable (unrealistic), or when what is hoped for would, under normal circumstances, be considered morally unacceptable. Finally, the "action rule" contends that people should *be willing to act to achieve their hopes*. Hoping requires at least some effort or commitment on our part. It is not enough to hope "emptily" (Gulliford 2019, 67).

While the "rules of hope" identified in this empirical work echo common themes identified by philosophers, they do not address the distinctions between hope and optimism that arise from different understandings of the future in which wishes, wants, and desires are operative. The Christian existentialist philosopher Gabriel Marcel (1962) observed that optimistic predictions rest on an assumption that the future is essentially a continuation of the present. Predictions are possible *only* where the contours of the future are predictable. In contrast, hoping may envision a future that is radically *discontinuous* with the present, such as a new world order brought about by the Kingdom of God, or the proletarian Revolution.

Marcel (1962) highlighted that whereas the probabilities he associated with the concept of optimism are *objectively* calculable, and in that respect "external to the self," hope is existential involving the self in a participatory way. Marcel echoes the distinction between the more engrossing emotional response toward desired future events Averill, Catlin, and Chon (1990) linked to hope and *gidae* (in Korean), and the more rational approach of optimism (*himang*). Insofar as hope is deemed difficult to control, to affect thoughts and actions, and to motivate behavior it falls within the parameters of responses classified as *emotional*. Furthermore, in recognizing the "participatory" quality of hope (but not of optimism) Marcel also opens up a line of thinking stretching back to Thomas Aquinas: the idea of *hoping-in* another agency.

When we hope that some event will come about, we specify the *content* of our hope, whereas *hoping-in* directs us toward the dynamics of how hope is sustained, namely, by *hoping in* agencies alongside our own. Thomas Aquinas noted that the temptation to abandon hope may not be as overwhelming when we are able to hope in another's assistance. Naturally, he considered God the final ground of this assistance, but he recognized that we hope in fellow human beings too: "It is unlawful to hope in any man, or any creature, as though it were the first cause of movement towards happiness. It is, however lawful to hope in a man or a creature as being the secondary or instrumental agent through whom one is helped to obtain any goods that are ordained to happiness. It is in this way that we turn to the saints, and that we ask men also for certain things" (*Summa Theologica* II-II, question 17, article 1).

While many would not share Aquinas' belief in God as the ultimate agent in whom humans hope, they might nonetheless agree that we often *hope in* others. For instance, we *hoped in* scientists working around the clock to create a vaccine for the novel coronavirus, though we could not obtain this good through our own efforts. The philosopher Joseph Godfrey (1987) called attention to two models of hope which accord a different role to the agency of self and other in hoping—the "will-nature model" and the "intersubjective model." In the will-nature model, confidence is grounded in the belief that other agencies or instrumentalities are accessible to realize one's own hopes, whereas the intersubjective model conceives of trust as a relationship of union, not of utilizing. This *inter*personal view of hope can be contrasted with a predominantly *intra*personal view of hope in psychology, to which we will now turn.

6.3 OPTIMISM AND HOPE
IN POSITIVE PSYCHOLOGY

Positive psychology has risen to prominence in recent years. Some date its inception to Martin Seligman's inaugural presidential address to the APA in 1998 (see Seligman 1998, 559), when he talked about "launching a science" to correct a psychology that had become almost completely preoccupied with treating pathology. Seligman maintained that a concentration of research efforts on damage repair had neglected what was positive in the individual and how personal strengths could be promoted. Detractors contended that Seligman had overstated the novelty of what he called "positive psychology." Nonetheless, "positive psychology" took hold and has brought about a renewal of research interest in human strengths and virtues, including optimism and hope. The concentration of research in this area has undoubtedly been aided by the creation of an inventory to measure human strengths, the *VIA Classification of Strengths and Virtues* (Peterson and Seligman 2004), which since its beginnings some fifteen years ago has been operationalized in self-report scales, including the original VIA-IS and more recently the VIA-R, VIA-M, and VIA-P (McGrath 2017).

In the 1960s, Seligman studied *learned helplessness* in animals (Overmier and Seligman 1967; Seligman and Meier 1967), a phenomenon that describes what happens when an animal is repeatedly subjected to an inescapable aversive stimulus (usually an electric shock). Eventually, the animal stops trying to avoid the stimulus and behaves as if it is utterly helpless to change the situation, even in subsequent experimental conditions where the aversive stimulus is avoidable. The organism has *learned* that nothing it can do will enable it to escape being shocked. The animal model was extended to examine learned helplessness (depression) in humans but it had to be refined since not *all* people in helpless conditions eventually became helpless. The learned helplessness paradigm was reformulated to include attributional (or explanatory) style, a construct which provided the means of differentiating between those who became helpless and those who persisted in the face of difficulties (Abramson, Seligman, and Teasdale 1978).

Explanatory styles describe characteristic patterns which explain how people attribute the causes of events in their lives, leading to either a positive (optimistic) outlook or a negative (pessimistic) one. Optimistic explanatory style also became known as "Learned Optimism"—the title of Seligman's popular self-help book. The key contention of "Learned Optimism" (Seligman 2006) is that "optimistic explanatory style" can be systematically instilled by examining and changing cognitive attributions.

Pessimistic explanatory style (PES) is maintained by a characteristic pattern wherein individuals attribute the causes of failure *internally* (i.e., to themselves, rather than externally to others or to circumstances) and believe that failure is *permanent* (as opposed to impermanent) and suffuses all domains of their lives (is *global* or *pervasive*, rather than domain-specific). This can be contrasted with optimistic explanatory style (OES), which is characterized by the reverse pattern of *external, impermanent,* and *specific* attributions. By appraising one's thought patterns, explanatory style can be changed and a person can self-consciously take control of how they locate the causes of success and failure in their lives.

Learned Optimism is based on the premise that positive future outcomes are related to a particular profile of dimensions over which an individual can exercise a high degree of control. External attributions protect the self from making internal attributions which locate the cause of negative events within the individual and offer a means of bolstering control and mastery of self-attributions that could be detrimental to future success. Confidence about the future is essentially based on the self's ability to change and manipulate dysfunctional beliefs. Thus, the agency which makes this possible is ultimately *intra*personal.

Alongside Seligman's work on optimistic explanatory style, other allied constructs that have been brought into the fold of positive psychology include "Hope Theory" (Snyder et al. 1991; Snyder 1994, 2002) and the concept of "Dispositional Optimism" (Carver and Scheier 1998, 2003; Scheier, Carver, and Bridges 1994). These psychological theories share the belief that optimism and hope are traits that can be measured and inculcated.

According to the late Charles Snyder, the concept of hope consists of two factors: "agency thinking" and "pathways thinking," and a goal (Snyder, Lopez, and Pedrotti 2011, 185). Agency thinking describes the belief one has in one's ability to reach goals, whereas pathways thinking describes the routes one foresees as necessary to pursue one's objectives—the "will and the ways" of hope, as it has been described (Snyder et al. 1991). Items from the Hope scale (Snyder et al. 1991) which tap agency thinking include the following statements: "My past experiences have prepared me well for my future" and "I've been pretty successful in life." Representative items from pathways thinking include "I can think of many ways to get the things in life that are most important to me" and "Even when others get discouraged, I know I can find a way to solve the problem."

It should be noted that the two items here that concern agency thinking are cast in the past tense and consequently do not actually concern expectations for the future. While one would expect agency thoughts to be influenced by past experiences, the items could be criticized for implying that beliefs about the future are wholly determined by past experiences, an insinuation to which Marcel (1962) and others would object, as we shall see below. Snyder's model is primarily cognitive, according emotion the role of setting the initial tenor of agency and pathways thinking on approaching a goal, and providing feedback (from partial success or failure) that affects ongoing thinking.

This model also conceives of hope as an *intra*personal phenomenon where the individual's will and resourcefulness play key roles in sustaining hope. It could be argued that the model represents a composite of self-efficacy and problem-solving skills, for it surely overlaps significantly with Bandura's definition of perceived self-efficacy, "how well one can execute courses of action required to deal with prospective situations" (Bandura 1982, 122), and an individual's problem-solving abilities.

While neither optimistic explanatory style nor Snyder's Hope Theory are necessarily irreconcilable with a recognition that sources external to the self could provide grounds for optimism or hope, their focus is on how the individual can either interpret the future more positively, Learned Optimism, or activate problem-solving strategies and heightened self-belief to attain desired objectives—Hope Theory (see Gulliford 2013).

"Dispositional optimism" is a further pertinent psychological construct (Carver and Scheier 1998, 2003; Scheier, Carver, and Bridges 1994). Carver and Scheier locate this model within the category of expectancy-value theories of motivation. These theories combine goals, "actions, end states, or values that people see as either desirable or undesirable" with an individual's expectancy, defined as "a sense of confidence or doubt about the attainability of the goal value" (Carver and Scheier 2003, 75). While the importance of a given goal is a major factor in maintaining optimism, so too is an individual's confidence: "When people are confident about an eventual outcome, effort continues even in the face of great adversity" (Carver and Scheier 2003, 76).

Dispositional optimism and dispositional pessimism are two self-regulatory mechanisms through which goals are approached. Optimistic people confidently believe their objectives can be achieved and maintain persistence in pursuing desired outcomes, whereas pessimistic individuals are doubtful about attaining their aims, inhibiting the actions they take toward reaching their goals. Carver and Scheier (2003) draw attention to the fact that the confidence upon which dispositional optimism is founded need not be located exclusively within our own personal agency (as both Learned Optimism and Hope Theory presuppose): "People who are optimistic can be optimistic because they are hard-working, because they are blessed, because they are lucky, because they have friends in the right places, or any combination of these or other factors that produce good outcomes" (Carver and Scheier 2003, 77).

Thus, the concepts of Dispositional Optimism/Pessimism expand the species of confidence upon which their understanding of optimism is grounded, explicitly distancing dispositional optimism from constructs that cast prospection *solely* in terms of personal agency or self-efficacy. While they accord a role to an individual's own "hard work," they contend that optimism can also be based in luck, divine blessing, and other people. Indeed, whether the imprecise "expectation through confidence" which they define as characteristic of optimists could better be construed as hope is perhaps debatable. When confidence inheres in trust rather than being based on external probabilities or self-agency it may arguably come closer to hope than to optimism.

In his presidential address, Martin Seligman highlighted well-being as one of the main goals of positive psychology: "We can show the world what actions lead to well-being, to positive individuals, to flourishing communities" (1998, 560). It is perhaps hardly surprising, then, that within positive psychology, hope and optimism are largely cast as "hedonic resources" which have instrumental benefits in enabling an individual's pursuit of desired goals, happiness, and well-being. As we have seen, both Learned Optimism and Hope Theory construe the concepts of prospection with which they are concerned as largely cognitive, modifiable personal traits that are undergirded and sustained by beliefs about personal agency and—in the case of Hope Theory—aspects of an individual's problem-solving abilities (pathways thinking). On this understanding, if hope and optimism are to be construed as character strengths, they may be best identified as virtues of self-regulation or self-management.

6.4 HOPE, TIME, AND THE FUTURE

In envisioning the future one inevitably engages the imagination. What will the future be like? While we might imagine the future as being a continuation of the present, in certain situations and perhaps especially in times of hardship, we might envisage a future that is radically different from our current circumstances and experience. As we speculate on the nature of the future, we implicitly take into our frame of reference metaphysical questions about the nature and purpose of time. Do we see the future as essentially unwritten, an open book, or do we see it as pre-determined? Does time follow a cyclical course, such that the future is a place of inevitable repetition, or is time going somewhere? Is there a telos to which the future is headed?

The world's great religions and philosophies take different perspectives on this issue. For instance, the ancient Greeks believed their destiny lay in the gods, who controlled the cosmos from above, predetermining the fates of mortals. Within this belief system, the concepts of hope and optimism would seem to be somewhat irrational, though the myth of Pandora's Box shows that whatever the "bigger metaphysical picture" may have been, the concept and experience of hope (and its counterpart, hopelessness) prevailed. The idea of the "wheel of time" is a concept found in Buddhism, Hinduism, and Sikhism wherein time is perceived as cyclical. From this perspective, hopes may be possible, but the idea of a telos, an end-point to which time runs, is incompatible within this frame of reference.

A linear view of time, such as that espoused by Judaism and by extension by Christianity, sees the end-point of time as the coming of the Kingdom of God, however that may be conceived. The future new order inaugurated by the Kingdom is radically different from the present order and stands in sharp contrast to it. The Jewish Marxist philosopher Ernst Bloch ([1959] 1986) conceived the future in similar radical terms, contrasting the merely "New" with "Novum." The former is the new that comes "naturally" through changing seasons, or the growth of acorn into oak. In contrast, the "Novum" describes the radically new that comes about through human will and revolutionary action. Though the Marxist Utopia is realized exclusively by human activity in the historical process, there are elements of Bloch's description of hope that are shared by most Christian theologies insofar as hope is "explosive, total and incognito." Hope stands in discontinuity with the present, involves the whole world in complete fulfillment, and is veiled or hidden in the present.

Kaplan and Schwartz (2008) contrast what they call the "suicidogenic" and tragic Greek perception of time with the suicide-preventing, covenantal, Hebraic vision characterized by freedom, not fatalism. They suggest that the foundation stories of psychoanalysis (such as Oedipus, Elektra, and Narcissus) that derive from the Greco-Roman world are infused with a fatalism that ultimately undermines hope and promotes suicide. The tragic mythic heroes find themselves trapped, the fates having decreed their ends, and a heroic rush to self-destruction is perceived as the sole means of escape. Kaplan and Schwartz (2008) advocate a "biblical psychotherapy" to prevent this tragic end. Essentially, this is a therapy of living in hope, freedom, and possibility (compatible with a linear view of time) rather than submitting to the predetermined inevitability of catastrophic fate. The Hebraic worldview offers possibilities for healing insofar as it conceives the future as open and genuinely new. Understanding the future as closed induces a sense of entrapment and hopelessness. In contrast, the way of hope enlarges the perspective of the hopeless person away from what seems to be inevitable capitulation to despair.

Psychology, whether psychodynamic, behaviorist, or cognitive, tends to concentrate on time insofar as it is implicated in learned patterns of behavior. The empirical method itself requires that data be verified *on the basis of* repeated experimentation. This is the foundation of scientific epistemology. Seligman asserts that an individual's future can be completely different from their past because optimistic explanatory style can be *learned*, but conceives the *future itself* as following an essentially foreseeable and unchanging course. People can control their *attitude toward* the future, but the future itself is not conceived in novel or radical terms. This stands in contrast to philosophies of hope that stress a disjunction between the present and the hoped-for future, exemplified in these quotations from Marcel (1962):

> Hope challenges the 'evidence' against it and is "engaged in the weaving of experience now in process. . . . This does not run counter to an authentic empiricism but to a certain dogmatism which, while claiming to be experience, fundamentally misunderstands its nature." (Marcel 1962, 52)

> Hope throws open the future to be a *real* future, not merely the playing out of pre-determined certainties that "encloses me within time, as though the future, drained of its substance and its mystery, were no longer to be anything but a place of pure repetition." (Marcel 1962, 60)

6.5 HOPE AND WAITING

Waiting is an inevitable precondition of concepts of prospection like optimism and hope. This waiting could be welcomed or endured, and can be construed as an active attitude of vigilance or watchfulness or a passive mindset of resignation. Waiting can be largely individual and private, or communal and shared. Waiting with and imagining with others may transform the hopes we cherish as individuals. In the waiting of hope it is acknowledged that assistance can come from outside our own resources; in other words, that other agencies may cooperate with our own in the realization of our hopes.

In his sermon "Waiting," the theologian Paul Tillich proposes that the condition of waiting *anticipates* what is to come and, in a sense, inaugurates the new hoped-for reality: "Waiting anticipates that which is not yet real. If we wait in hope and patience, the power of that for which we wait is already effective within us" (Tillich 1962, 152–153). While we often experience a period of waiting as intrinsically unsatisfying, Tillich calls attention to how, from a Christian perspective, this time may be uniquely blessed. For example, in his sermon on the blessings and woes of Luke 6 (the Lucan version of Matthew's beatitudes), a distinction is drawn between people who live with their hearts turned toward the world to come and those whose hearts are in the present order. It is those who are dispossessed in the present order who are empowered to turn their hearts toward the coming eon. The waiting of the beatitudes is therefore an expectation of the subversive and radically new future that awaits those whose hearts are turned in anticipation to the age to come.

Hope and optimism imply both waiting and wishing for some end, whether this is a clearly articulated and specific goal or an inchoately perceived future event. It is difficult to give substance to some goals, perhaps because the imagined futures in which they are to be realized stand in such opposition to the present reality, for instance the Marxist Utopia or indeed the Kingdom of God. Other goals may be clear and unambiguous, though the means to their realization may be uncertain—a rescue operation from a collapsed mine, for instance.

Where goals are specific and where it is possible to exercise a high degree of agency over events it is possible *to translate the wanting of hope into action* through plans and strategies, which could be either individual or collective. In contexts where our agency is limited, hope may be characterized by waiting in anticipation of help from without and by putting our hope *in* other agencies.

6.6 COLLECTIVE ASPECTS OF HOPE AND THE ROLE OF THE IMAGINATION

While there can be no doubt that the concepts of hope and optimism (and a whole host of other human strengths) received fresh research interest with the arrival of positive psychology, there were studies of hope in psychoanalytic and clinical contexts before that time. As we have seen, most currently popular psychological theories of prospection envisage hope or optimism as modifiable properties of individuals consequent on changing or enhancing their beliefs about personal agency and enhancing problem-solving capacities. It seems likely that the influence of cognitive psychology and its applied manifestation in cognitive therapies and cognitive behavioral therapies lies at the root of this construal (see Gulliford 2020).

However, though there may be much to be gained from evaluating one's beliefs and identifying ways one can help oneself to envision the future in more favorable terms and with more clearly articulated pathways one might take to realize one's goals, hope is not simply an "internal resource" or individual trait. Hope is sustained *in participation with* others—an insight to which Aquinas perhaps first drew attention. While there are undoubtedly what one might call "autonomous" aspects of hope and optimism, at the same time, when we hope we to some extent "depend" on our environment or on other people to provide the things we desire; we cannot achieve all that we hope for within our own limited powers no matter how much effort we put into the enterprise.

The psychoanalyst and priest William Lynch (1974) wrote a powerful monograph about hope in which he underscored the "interdependence" of hope between agents and the role of the imagination in kindling it. In his work as a therapist, Lynch recognized that a species of confidence is at work in stimulating hope in the therapeutic encounter which can be identified as "confidence as trust." Clients "hope-in" their therapist, seeking help beyond their own resources. This kind of inter-personally grounded confidence can be distinguished from the intra-personally grounded confidence founded in the self's ability to change and manipulate maladaptive beliefs, which has tended to characterize positive psychological understandings of hope.

Lynch observed that a helpless person may indeed be beyond the point of self-help (Lynch 1974, 76). However, they are not beyond receiving help from another, which enlarges the possibilities they perceive in their despair. As a Jesuit, it seems likely that what Lynch observed of hope in his clinical practice may have been influenced by Aquinas' position that the temptation to abandon hope may be assuaged when we are able to hope in another person's assistance. The therapist serves, at least for Lynch, as the proximal ground of hope that is ultimately founded in God.

Lynch (1974) underscores the importance of the imagination in kindling and sustaining hope. In despair, the ability to wish and desire breaks down and constricts the vision of the future a sick person is capable of imagining. Lynch observed from his practice that patients' imaginations can become "fantastical" (characterized by fantasy) and narrowed by rigidly stereotypical fantasies of disaster and inevitable catastrophe, echoing the work of Kaplan and Schwartz (2008) in relation to classical tragedy. This contrasts with a normal healthy and creatively flexible imagination when a person is well.

To recover, the sick person must, in effect, "put on the imagination" of a trusted other person—someone who is able to entertain (through imagination) a different and more hopeful future than that which the client is able to envision on their own. This other agency could be a therapist, a doctor, a sponsor, or a friend. In participating in that vision of a future the client is unable to conceive themselves, the friend becomes a source of hope for the patient and someone in whom they can place their confidence for recovery. Hope therefore exists *between* people and is fundamentally misconstrued when it is understood solely in terms of a capacity or internal resource. In Lynch's own words (Lynch 1974, 23–24):

> Hope not only imagines; it imagines with. We are so habituated to conceiving of the imagination as a private act of the human spirit that we now find it impossible to conceive of a common act of imagining with. But what happens in despair is that the private imagination, of which we are so enamoured, reaches the point of the end of inward resource and must put on the imagination of another if it is to find a way out. Whereas, a more public act of the imagination comes far closer, I think, to describing the saving process that goes on in the modern psychotherapies; two imaginations, that of the patient and the doctor, work together to discover and enlarge the possibilities of a situation.

The tendency to perceive hope as a purely intrapersonal phenomenon (a capacity or individual trait) is also called into question in the work of Arthur Kobler and Ezra Stotland (1964), who undertook a study of an epidemic of suicides in a U.S. psychiatric hospital in the 1960s. They adopted a psychoanalytic, "field theoretical" approach (a psychological theory which examines patterns of interaction between the individual and their environment) and observed that hope for the future was greatly affected by significant others in the troubled person's environment. Whether key people in the psychiatric patient's world *imagined* the worst—if they themselves had lost hope in recovery—was (quite literally) *vital* in determining whether suicide occurred. In interviewing patients in the hospital, the researchers became aware that staff were unwittingly leading patients to engage in entertaining their imaginations in the worst possible ways, as the quote below demonstrates:

> I said what in hell can I possibly do with shoelaces; and then I start thinking—and I never did come up with anything you could do with shoelaces, but I guess there is something you can do with shoelaces. *She got me to thinking about it.* (Kobler and Stotland 1964, 83, my italics)

This patient had apparently not thought about using shoelaces as a ligature. It was only when the laces were removed that they began to share the worst-case imaginings of the orderly who took them away. This is not to say that staff were wrong to do so. However, it does show that the way in which health professionals behave with and respond to patients is critical in sustaining and maintaining hope— or in extinguishing it. People around the troubled person shape the capacities they possess to envision the future. John Donne's meditation that "No man is an island entire of itself" encapsulates the human inter-dependence Kobler and Stotland (1964) found to be so central in kindling hope and preventing suicide in the hospital they studied:

> Too often, in responding to the cry of another human being on the brink of suicide, a person—friend or physician, therapist or patient—acts as if his answer will not influence the other. Too often, the consequences are proof that his conduct is the key to the other's future. After hearing the cry for help, one cannot avoid being fundamentally involved. We are none of us alone, neither clients nor therapists. If we live and act with this

awareness, then none of us will reach the end of hope. (Kobler and Stotland 1964, 265–266)

The current climate of "*self*-help" does little to cultivate this more collective and interpersonal understanding of hope foregrounded in the clinical work of Kobler and Stotland (1964) and Lynch (1974). This perception of hope as existing *between* people, rather than being construed as a purely individual capacity, has a long history and currently popular positive psychological approaches would do well to take this on board.

While it is certainly beneficial to take control of one's own thinking, mindful that our habitual ways of thinking can unseat us, there is more to hope than an individual exercise in cognitive reappraisal (Gulliford 2020). While examining our patterns of thought can be very fruitful, people in the grips of despair would likely be unable to take this dispassionate step back. Alongside the autonomous aspects of hope and optimism exemplified by the positive psychological approaches of Learned Optimism and Hope Theory in particular,[1] it is necessary to highlight the more "dependent" elements of prospection in an uncertain future that is not under our control: "hope is a relative idea. It is always relative to the idea of help. It seeks help. It depends. It looks to the outside world" (Lynch 1974, 31).

6.7 DEPENDENT AND AUTONOMOUS ASPECTS OF HOPE

Hope construed as "hope-in" would seem to be the most fundamental kind of hope. In the symbiosis of mother and baby, the infant depends on the mother to meet their every need, and while of course this expectation is not cognized in infancy, it sets the stage for an emerging sense of what we can expect from our environment—whether we *expect* our needs to be met or not. This lies at the heart of Erik Erikson's psychosocial understanding of hope. According to Erikson (1959) the first stage of psychosocial development in infancy is to negotiate the conflict between basic trust and basic mistrust. Hope stems from trust that the infant can depend on their caregiver to meet basic needs. Thus, hope can only be sustained where a person has learned that they can *depend* upon others.

It seems likely that hope grounded in confidence or trust in other people is therefore the most elemental kind of hope, augmented through the course of development by the more autonomous and agentic aspects of hope and optimism associated with acting on and transforming one's environment by planning, projecting, and buoying up self-beliefs. Learned Optimism and Hope Theory epitomize these self-directed aspects of hope, where we act on the world (and on ourselves) to bring about what we hope for—Averill, Catlin, and Chon's (1990) "action rule."

6.8 IS HOPE A VIRTUE?

There is a long-standing ambivalence toward hope manifest in aphorisms and folk-tales which tell against any unambiguous understanding of hope as a virtue. Hope can "be good sauce but poor food" and the "houses which hope builds are castles in the air."[2] These proverbs point up the insubstantial nature of hope; to hope may be to hope in vain, as Nietzsche pronounced: "Hope: it is in truth the worst of all evils, for it protracts the torment of men" (Nietzsche 1996, 45, §71).

Within the VIA classification of strengths and virtues (Peterson and Seligman 2004), the character strength of hope is defined thus: "I am realistic and also optimistic about the future, believing in my actions and feeling confident things will turn out well" (https://www.viacharacter.org/character-strengths/hope). It is categorized as a virtue of transcendence, alongside appreciation of beauty and excellence, gratitude, humor, and spirituality. However, the way hope is construed in positive psychology would perhaps seem to fit rather better within a category of virtues of self-management or self-regulation.

6.9 CONCLUSION

In this chapter it has been shown that positive psychology has tended to conceive of the allied concepts of hope and optimism *intra*personally, grounding these constructs of prospection in terms of individual agency, volition, goal-setting, and problem-solving (see also Gulliford 2013, 2020). This is extremely useful where personal aims are specific, explicit, and unambiguous, and where it is possible to exercise a high degree of control over events. Snyder's Hope Theory supports individuals in the task of translating desired goals into action by making plans and strategies, while buoying up beliefs about one's capabilities in reaching these goals. The concept of Learned Optimism, while not addressing future goals *explicitly*, enables people to take a step back from the characteristic ways they have attributed causes to events in their lives in their past (reasons for successes and failures), with a view to changing their expectations for events in the future. In this sense Optimistic Explanatory Style also grounds optimism *intra*personally; the resources that sustain optimism ultimately derive from the individual's volitional control of their thinking. Psychological models promote salutary or "positive" styles of thinking that prioritize the self-determined aspects of hope/ optimism over relational aspects.

However, there is more to hope and optimism than these purely intrapersonal factors. That is not to say that this is not important. It is clearly valuable and constructive to reappraise one's thinking as we may not be helping ourselves if we fail to see how these characteristic patterns of thought constrain us. We can take control of the autonomous aspects of hope. That said, we may not be able to bring about all that we hope for through our own efforts. This truth is perhaps recognized in Carver and Scheier's model of Dispositional Optimism (Carver and Scheier 2003), wherein reasons for maintaining optimism can be grounded in sources external to the self, such as luck, God, and other people. These sources are especially critical where we have little—or possibly even no—control over future events, emphasizing the dependent nature of hope and optimism.

Alongside the individual and autonomous aspects of prospection, crucially hope exists *between* agents and can be kindled by significant others around us. This notion of "hoping-in" others was acknowledged by Aquinas. His insight resonates strongly with human experience and does not *require* a religious frame of reference. Especially when human agents have little control over the future, they find themselves hoping-in science, medicine, and other people.

The clinical work of both Lynch (1974) and Kobler and Stotland (1964) underscored the importance of hoping-in others and the role key people around us play in kindling and nourishing hope, or in smothering it. Recent positive psychological models would do well to engage with this earlier psychological literature to expand their concepts and acknowledge those elements of prospection which fall outside the realm of our control. All these positive psychological models of hope and optimism could of course be put into practice collectively in the context of group therapy. The key insight to be gained from the earlier psychoanalytic work is that hope is not limited to our own capacities and we are co-creators in our hoping with others.

One of the reasons our hope and optimism for the future fail is that they require a degree of imagination to be nurtured that may be stifled, narrowed, or damaged by distress. In sickness, the private imagination may become rigid, entertaining only the most limited thoughts about the future. In this very worst-case scenario, the vision of the future becomes so constricted that a person may see only one final way out of their predicament. In this situation, and in the company of another person, the individual is enabled to participate in a different vision of the future by sharing in the imagined future of the trusted other in whom they come to hope. Imagination enlivens our individual and collective hopes. In the words of Emily Dickinson:

> The gleam of an heroic Act
> Such strange illumination
> The Possible's slow fuse is lit
> By the Imagination. (Dickinson 1955, "Number 1687,"
>   688–689)

NOTES

1. It will be recalled that Carver and Scheier's concept of "Dispositional optimism" allows that the confidence which grounds optimism need not be situated wholly within individual agency but may also be grounded in divine blessing or other people.
2. See Averill, Catlin, and Chon (1990), Study III, *Metaphors and Maxims*.

REFERENCES

Abramson, Lyn Y., Martin E. P. Seligman, and John D. Teasdale. 1978. "Learned Helplessness in Humans: Critique and Reformulation." *Journal of Abnormal Psychology* 87 (1): 49–74.

Aquinas, Thomas. 2018. *Summa Theologica: Second Part of the Second Part*. Edited by Anthony Uyl. Woodstock: Devoted Publishing.

Averill, James R., George Catlin, and Kyum Koo Chon. 1990. *Rules of Hope*. New York: Springer Verlag.

Bandura, Albert. 1982. "Self-Efficacy Mechanism in Human Agency." *American Psychologist* 37 (2): 122–147.

Bloch, Ernst. (1959) 1986. *The Principle of Hope*. Vol. 1. Translated by Neville Plaice, Stephen Plaice, and Paul Knight. Cambridge, MA: MIT Press.

Carver, Charles S., and Michael F. Scheier. 1998. *On the Self-Regulation of Behavior*. New York: Cambridge University Press.

Carver, Charles C., and Michael Scheier. 2003. "Optimism." In *Positive Psychological Assessment: A Handbook of Models and Measures*, edited by Shane J. Lopez and Charles R. Snyder, 75–89. Washington, DC: American Psychological Association.

Dickinson, Emily. 1955. *The Poems of Emily Dickinson*. Edited by Thomas H. Johnson. 3 vols. Cambridge, MA: Belknap Press of Harvard University Press. Johnson Poems 1955 edition .https://www.edickinson.org/editions/2/image_sets/12173121.

Erikson, Erik H. 1959. *Identity and the Life Cycle: Selected Papers by Erik H. Erikson*. Madison, WI: International Universities Press.

Godfrey, Joseph J. 1987. *A Philosophy of Human Hope*. Dordrecht: Martinus Nijhoff.

Gulliford, Liz. 2013. "The Head and the Heart of the Matter in Hope and Forgiveness." In *Head and Heart: Perspectives from Religion and Psychology*, edited by Fraser Watts and Geoff Dumbreck, 273–312. West Conshohocken, PA: Templeton Press.

Gulliford, Liz. 2019. *Can I Tell You about Hope?* London: Jessica Kingsley.

Gulliford, Liz. 2020. "Virtue in Positive Psychology." *Acta Philosophica* 29 (1): 91–112.

Kaplan, Kalman J., and Matthew B. Schwartz. 2008. *A Psychology of Hope: A Biblical Response to Tragedy and Suicide*. Grand Rapids, MI: Wm. B. Eerdmans.

Kobler, Arthur L., and Ezra Stotland. 1964. *The End of Hope: A Social-Clinical Study of Suicide*. New York: Free Press of Glencoe.

Lynch, William F. 1974. *Images of Hope: Imagination as Healer of the Hopeless*. Notre Dame, IN: University of Notre Dame Press.

Marcel, Gabriel. 1962. *Homo Viator: Introduction to a Metaphysics of Hope*. Translated by Emma Crauford. New York: Harper and Row.

McGrath, Robert E. 2017. *Technical Report: The VIA Assessment Suite for Adults. Development and Evaluation*. Cincinnati, OH: VIA Institute on Character.

Nietzsche, Friedrich. 1996. "On the History of the Moral Sensations." In *Nietzsche: Human, All Too Human: A Book for Free Spirits*, edited by Reginald J. Hollingdale, 31–59. Cambridge: Cambridge University Press.

Overmier, James B., and Martin E. P. Seligman. 1967. "Effects of Inescapable Shock upon Subsequent Escape and Avoidance Learning." *Journal of Comparative and Physiological Psychology* 63 (1): 23–33.

Peterson, Christopher, and Martin E. P. Seligman. 2004. *Character Strengths and Virtues: A Handbook and Classification.* Washington, DC: American Psychological Association.

Scheier, M. F., C. S. Carver, and M. W. Bridges. 1994. "Distinguishing Optimism from Neuroticism (and Trait Anxiety, Self-Mastery, and Self-Esteem): A Reevaluation of the Life Orientation Test." *Journal of Personality and Social Psychology* 67 (6): 1063–1078.

Seligman, Martin E. P. 1998. "The President's Address: APA." *American Psychologist* 54: 559–562.

Seligman, Martin E. P. 2006. *Learned Optimism: How to Change Your Mind and Your Life.* New York: Vintage Books.

Seligman, Martin E. P., and Steven F. Maier. 1967. "Failure to Escape Traumatic Shock." *Journal of Experimental Psychology* 74 (1): 1–9.

Snyder, C. R. 1994. *The Psychology of Hope: You Can Get There from Here.* New York: Free Press.

Snyder, C. R. 2002. "Hope Theory: Rainbows in the Mind." *Psychological Inquiry* 13 (4): 249–275.

Snyder, C. R., Cheri Harris, John R. Anderson, Sharon A. Holleran, Lori M. Irving, Sandra T. Sigmon, Lauren Yoshinobu, June Gibb, Charyle Langelle, and Pat Harney. 1991. "The Will and the Ways: Development and Validation of an Individual-Differences Measure of Hope." *Journal of Personality and Social Psychology* 60 (4): 570–585.

Snyder, C. R., Shane J. Lopez, and Jennifer T. Pedrotti. 2011. *Positive Psychology: The Scientific and Practical Explanations of Human Strengths.* London: Sage.

Tillich, Paul. 1962. *The Shaking of the Foundations.* Harmondsworth: Penguin.

VIA Institute on Character. n.d. "Hope." Accessed August 22, 2020. https://www.viacharacter.org/character-strengths/hope.

Chapter 7

The Influence of Culture
on Psychological Hope

LISA M. EDWARDS AND KAT R. MCCONNELL

Hope is a concept that has fascinated and compelled humans for thousands of years. Philosophers, spiritual leaders, and scholars have mused upon and debated what hope is and is not. As society moved into the age of scientific inquiry, it was unavoidable that hope would become a topic of scientific curiosity as well. As the science of human behavior and cognition, it also only made sense that the field of psychology would take an interest in exploring hope as a psychological construct. Although many psychologists have discussed and attempted to measure hope in recent decades, C. R. Snyder's (1995) conceptualization of hope rose to prominence within the field. Snyder posited that hope was a cognitive construct comprised of pathways and agency, both of which worked to help individuals move toward their goals. While Snyder believed hope was a universal psychological construct that all could access and develop, it is clear that hope is conceptualized and used in different ways across individuals and groups (Lopez, Snyder, and Pedrotti 2003). In this chapter, we review Snyder's psychological conceptualization of hope and

Lisa M. Edwards and Kat R. McConnell, *The Influence of Culture on Psychological Hope* In: *The Virtue of Hope*. Edited by: Nancy E. Snow, Oxford University Press. © Oxford University Press 2024.
DOI: 10.1093/oso/9780190069575.003.0008

describe how it operates within various cultural contexts. Specifically, we focused on prominent aspects of identity, e.g., race and ethnicity, nationality, religion and spirituality, and disability status, that have been explored in relation to hope within psychological literature (Hays 2016). We discuss how hope might vary across groups from theoretical and measurement perspectives and provide examples of research that explores hope in different populations. Finally, we provide suggestions for how the field can continue to understand the cultural context of hope.

7.1 THE ORIGINS OF SNYDER'S HOPE

C. R. Snyder, a clinical psychologist, began his research on the psychological construct of hope in the 1990s, asserting that hope was not as vague and unmeasurable as earlier psychologists had suggested; rather, it could be effectively studied and measured if it was only broken down into psychological terms. Snyder defined hope as "the cognitive energy and pathways for goals" (Snyder 1995, 355). In other words, he conceptualized hope as a cognitive means of motivation toward and achievement of goals, with feelings playing an important role but not being the main driving force (Snyder 2002; Snyder et al. 2006). This cognitive process of hoping consisted of two elements: agency and pathways.

According to Snyder (2002), goals are the mental targets that help guide human behaviors. They can be large or small, short or long term, and they can vary in importance to a person. Agency comprises the motivational aspect of hope theory, and is referred to as "goal-directed energy" (250). Agency thoughts can propel an individual to initiate and sustain goal-directed activity. "Pathways" refers to an individual's ability to set a plan to reach their goals, including finding ways to overcome obstacles on their way to the goal. Pathways are the routes that people produce to get to their desired outcomes. Taken together, a person with high hope would have both high motivation to pursue a goal (agency) and a decisive plan about how to achieve that goal (pathways), including the ability to create alternate paths to the goal should challenges arise (Snyder 1995, 2002). By measuring these two elements, Snyder posited, one could measure an individual's capacity for hope.

Rather than being an intangible human experience, Snyder's definition of hope represents a behavior that can be learned and taught, and which is influenced by environmental factors such as culture and upbringing (Ritschel 2005). Just as hope can be gained and acquired, hope can also be lost through traumatic events and personal loss (Snyder 2002). The hope process can be affected in positive or negative ways by various factors, including emotion, perception of progress, unexpected events, and stressors (Snyder et al. 2006). For these reasons, psychologists have found hope a worthwhile topic to be measured and studied.

Research over the past thirty years has provided support for Snyder's hope and its relation to numerous positive outcomes in adults and children (Rand and Touza 2018). Utilizing measures of hope developed by Snyder and colleagues (e.g., Adult Hope Scale; Snyder et al. 1991), research has shown that hope is associated with increased academic and athletic performance and various indicators of well-being. Hope is related to but distinct from life satisfaction and optimism, and it has been shown to be useful in coping with numerous health and mental health stressors and illnesses (Rand and Touza 2018). Additionally, hope is associated with positive work performance and social support and connection with others. Importantly, recent research about Snyder's hope has utilized more advanced longitudinal methods to show that hope actually promotes resilience in adults over time (Goodman et al. 2017).

7.2 PSYCHOLOGICAL HOPE IN COMPARISON TO VIRTUE HOPE

In many ways, Snyder's psychological conceptualization of hope may appear different from what many philosophers and spiritual leaders believe of hope. Rather than viewing hope as a virtue or positive trait, Snyder viewed hope as a value-neutral pattern of thinking and behavior that relates to the pursuit of goals. Nor do goals have to be virtuous or moralistic in nature in order to initiate hope; one can be as hopeful for achieving an antisocial goal as another is hopeful for achieving a prosocial goal. Hope is not an innate human virtue so much as it is a mindset and behavior that is taught, learned, and practiced (Shorey et al. 2002). Shorey et al. (2002, 322) argue that while hope is a virtue in the sense that it can be passed down and taught to future generations in order to achieve societal goals, defining hope itself as a virtue "would greatly limit hope's utility in explaining how people pursue goals in their daily lives." To assume that hope necessitates morality would be to project one's own limited scope of values on all persons, neglecting the impact of different cultures and life experience on the creation and pursuit of goals (Shorey et al. 2002).

Authors have compared Snyder's hope to philosophical and religious perspectives, noting areas of similarity and divergence. For example, Martin (2011) discusses two philosophical definitions of hope: epistemic and desiderative. Epistemic hope, a belief in the face of doubt, "declare[s] hope when we are trying to persuade ourselves or others that a desirable outcome is possible. Such declarations occur in response to expressions of doubt or against a backdrop of cynicism" (Martin 2011, 150). Desiderative hope, which is more in line with Snyder's hope, has been described as a hope related to "desire, value, or agency" (150). This type of hope is expressed as something that a person is striving toward. This type of hope serves the purpose of conveying our plans and goals, and how much we value those goals. McGeer (2004) expresses a similar view of hope, referring to it as both an art and a gift and as a skill that can be developed over time.

Religion is another area in which hope has historically been widely discussed and integrated. Hoover-Kinsinger (2018, 316) defines hope from a Christian perspective as "focused on a future goal, but rooted in present acts of faithfulness scattered throughout all of creation, and directed toward both the oppressed and the oppressor." Hope is viewed as a universal experience in which individuals look forward with faith and shape their behavior toward what they are hoping for. It is an endowment from God which offers faith in an intangible salvation to believers (Titone, Stefanik, and McNamara 2013). In discussing this theological view of hope in comparison to Snyder's hope, Hoover-Kinsinger (2018) asserts the belief that hope comes from God rather than from personal drive/goals, but believes that overall, Snyder's model of hope reflects the Christian's call to use hope as a blueprint for agency and action to complete the incomplete. In discussion of Snyder's hope compared to a more broad "religious hope," Watts, Dutton, and Gulliford (2006) agree that the two models of hope are comparable, as religious hope calls the individual to action in response to their hope of things to come. The main distinguishing factor between the two, they assert, is that religious hope comes with the additional psychological tool of *faith*, the "precondition for hope" (287).

Despite the overlap between the virtue of hope and psychological hope, this chapter will address cultural influences on psychological hope specifically. The benefits of psychological hope in a psychological research context is that hope is a quantifiable measure with measurable variables, such as agency and goals. However, the authors are aware that the view of hope as a virtue can be considered a cultural influence itself, such as in certain religions and faith communities wherein hope is taught from a faith-based perspective, and this consideration is kept in mind as the authors explore cultural influences on hope in the following sections.

7.3 CULTURAL INFLUENCES ON HOPE

Snyder's conceptualization of hope describes constructs that all exist within a cultural context: from people's unique goals to the obstacles they face, as well as the ways in which they maintain motivation toward achieving their goals (Edwards and McClintock 2017). Many have argued, therefore, that in order to best understand human strengths and virtues, including hope, it is imperative to consider cultural context (Sandage, Hill, and Vang 2003; Sue and Constantine 2003). In order to do this, one must consider the definition and meaning of hope, how this might apply to other groups, and how research can provide support for these concepts of equivalence. In the following sections, we discuss these issues as they relate to Snyder's popular Adult Disposition Hope Scale (Snyder et al. 1991). First, we describe the development of the Hope Scale, and then we discuss the research that illustrates how hope operates in diverse cultural groups.

7.4 HOPE MEASUREMENT

The Adult Dispositional Hope scale (also known as the Goals Scale or Hope Scale) is a twelve-item self-report measure of hope developed for use with ages fifteen and older (Snyder et al. 1991). Four items on the scale measure agency ("I've been pretty successful in life"), four measure pathways ("I think of many ways to get out of a jam"), and four items are used solely as distractors ("I feel tired most of the time") (Snyder et al. 1991). High scores on the pathways and agency subscales, as well as the total hope score, indicate higher levels of trait hope.

The Hope Scale was developed and normed on six separate samples of undergraduate psychology students and two samples of community individuals receiving psychological treatment. It is assumed the samples were primarily White since no information about race/ethnicity was provided. The average hope score for college students was 24 (4-point Likert scale) and 48 (8-point scale), while the community samples had lower scores but were still relatively hopeful (i.e., approximately a 3 on the 4-point response scale for each hope item). Internal and test-retest reliability for these samples was considered strong, and hope scores were correlated with measures of optimism and other positive constructs as expected (Snyder et al. 1991).

7.5 HOW HOPE OPERATES IN DIVERSE CULTURAL GROUPS

One way to provide support for the utility of psychological constructs across groups is to evaluate equivalence. Several types of equivalence have been described, including functional, conceptual, metric, and linguistic (Ægisdóttir, Gerstein, and Çinarbaş 2008; Lonner 1985). Linguistic equivalence, for example, has to do with how items from an instrument are phrased, as well as reading difficulty, in different language versions (Lonner 1985; Ægisdóttir, Gerstein, and Çinarbaş 2008). Providing support for the linguistic equivalence of the Adult Hope Scale, translations now exist in several languages, including Arabic (Abdel-Khalek and Snyder 2007), Chinese (Sun, Ng, and Wang 2012), Dutch (Brouwer et al. 2008), French (Gana, Daigre, and Ledrich 2013), Japanese (Kato and Snyder 2005), Portuguese (Marques et al. 2014; Pacico et al. 2013), Slovak (Halama 1999, 2001), and Spanish (Galiana et al. 2015).

Other forms of equivalence have to do with the meaning that a behavior or construct has in different cultures (e.g., functional equivalence), the connection in meaning ascribed to behaviors and the construct (e.g., conceptual equivalence), and the psychometric properties of scales of that construct across different groups (e.g., metric equivalence). Providing support for equivalence of a measure is an ongoing process, with each study building upon the body of knowledge about the measure.

In recent years a great deal of research has emerged about Snyder's Hope Scale (Snyder et al. 1991), with many studies exploring questions about equivalence among diverse populations and groups (Edwards and McClintock 2017). In the sections below, we discuss how hope operates in diverse cultural groups by reviewing research from a number of countries and groups. We focus on emerging data which incorporates various aspects of identity as defined by Pamela Hays' (2016) ADDRESSING model. In Hays' model, the primary facets of identity are considered: Age/Generation, Disability (development), Disability (acquired), Religion and Spiritual Orientation, Ethnicity, Socioeconomic Status, Sexual Orientation, Indigenous Heritage, National Origin, and Gender. While research about hope has not been conducted to explore the construct among each of these aspects of identity, the sections below review the work that has been done to date to address many of them.

7.5.1 Nationality

Each country's history, political structure, languages, infrastructure, and wealth influences how its citizens view, set, and pursue goals. Much of the initial research on psychological hope looked at primarily wealthy Western countries, such as the United States, but researchers soon noted that such findings may not be applicable to the culture of other countries and needed to be expanded upon or modified. This section will explore studies which looked specifically at hope within a variety of countries and nationalities.

In research across several countries, support for the construct equivalence (e.g., the two factors of agency and pathways) has been found, as well as evidence for notable differences in structure. Studies in China (Sun, Ng, and Wang 2012), France (Gana, Daigre, and Ledrich 2013), Japan (Kato and Snyder 2005), and Portugal (Marques et al. 2014) provided evidence of the two-factor structure, while research in Brazil (Pacico et al. 2013), Spain (Galiana et al. 2015), and the Netherlands (Brouwer et al. 2008) found that hope was better conceptualized as one factor, or total hope (Rand and Touza 2018). Other research has expanded hope theory by incorporating culture-specific elements from the country of origin. For example, Kato (2006) expanded hope theory in samples of Japanese adults by adjusting items on the Hope Scale to reflect hopeful thinking in relation to others. He found empirical support for this new measure of *interpersonal hope*. Luo et al. (2010) also expanded the model of hope among Taiwanese adults to include transcendental adaptation and persisting effort, two additional subscales that formed the construct of *peaceful hope* and reflected Chinese values of flexibility and calmness. As predicted, these subscales also contributed to lower levels of hopelessness, even above the contributions from agency and pathways (Rand and Touza 2018).

Moving beyond evaluating the construct equivalence of hope in various countries, some researchers have looked specifically at how culture can contribute to the ways hope takes shape in diverse communities. The Kashmir region of India has been plagued in recent decades by political unrest, military conflict, and civilian rebellion, the latter of which was met with human rights violations such as the "enforced disappearances" of rebelling civilians. By one count, up to 81% of Kashmir's citizens had witnessed traumatic events, such as explosions, firing, and combat, firsthand. To cope with a history and culture of trauma, the people of Kashmir seek solace in community, and citizens depend heavily on family and close social connections for support. It is perhaps this social culture, in part, that contributes to hope in the people of this region. For parents of disappeared persons in Kashmir, post-traumatic growth was positively correlated both with close social connections and with psychological hope (Anjum 2017).

Another country through which psychological hope has been explored is South Africa. Between a history of harsh racial division, poor quality of life for many citizens, and a high rate of HIV/AIDS, South African people experience a unique combination of socio-cultural factors and stressors. Despite these adverse factors, the concept of hope has become a theme in South African culture and politics, with President Thabo Mbeki even declaring South Africa to be entering an "Age of Hope" in 2006 (Boyce and Harris 2013). A qualitative study of South African adolescents who grew up exposed to community violence showed that the adolescents closely associated hope with religion and spirituality, and associated a lack of hope with perpetuation of violence and/or suicide (Isaacs and Savahl 2014). In a study of psychological hope in South Africa (Boyce and Harris 2013), it was found that those with the lowest hope were individuals from groups that have been historically oppressed and marginalized in South Africa, such as rural-dwelling people, women, and those who considered themselves to be on a lower social level. For a country in which racial divides have played a vital role, the difference in hope across South African racial groups was very small; this could be due, in part, to recent efforts to rectify the effects of apartheid, resulting in higher hope for Black South Africans and lower hope for the formerly dominant White South Africans (Boyce and Harris 2013).

Africa's smallest country, Swaziland, was the subject of another hope study. The culture of Swaziland is defined by abject poverty, traditional healing practices, low education rates, and extreme limits on women's rights to own property, engage in business, and find employment. Additionally, Swaziland has the highest rate of HIV/AIDS in the world, creating a high number of orphans. The case study in question looked at hope in children in a Swazi orphanage and compared them to Snyder et al.'s (1997) study of children in the United States. Findings showed that the Swazi children showed lower overall hope than children in North America, and that Swazi girls' hope fell below that of their male peers, likely due to the lower status of women in Swazi culture (Titone, Stefanik, and McNamara 2013).

7.5.2 Collectivism and Individualism

Nations are often further divided into two categories in social science research: individualist and collectivistic. This level of difference has been explored in studies about individualist and collectivist values and goals, as well as hope. Bernardo (2010) noted that hope theory was built around research from an individualistic society and suggested that there may be notable differences when investigating hope in collectivistic cultures, such as an extension of agency outside of the individual. Snyder's model, Bernardo et al. (2018, 909) posited, "presumes that positive actions are defined independently of others and are expressions of an individual's intents and preferences." He specifically proposed that the theory of psychological hope be extended to include the dimensions of internal locus-of-hope and external locus-of-hope. According to Bernardo (2010, 945), "the internal locus-of-hope refers to the individual as the agent of goal-attainment cognitions, whereas the external locus-of-hope refers to significant others and external forces as agents of goal-attainment cognitions."

Studies on Bernardo and colleagues' extended theory found that individualistic persons were more likely to have an internal locus-of-hope, and collectivistic persons were more likely to have an external locus-of-hope (Bernardo 2010; Bernardo et al. 2018). Those with external loci-of-hope relied not only on themselves in seeking pathways to their goals, but also utilized the resources and support of their family, peers, and/or a spiritual higher power in order to attain goals (Bernardo 2010).

In a study of loci-of-hope in Eastern Asian students from four different cities (Hong Kong, Macau, Manila, and Johor Bahru), it was found that each locus-of-hope was correlated with different aspects of well-being and coping. For those with internal locus-of-control, students were more likely to possess individualized aspects of well-being, such as self-esteem and self-mastery. Those with an external locus-of-control did not often score well on these aspects of well-being, but they were shown to rely more heavily on external-based aspects of well-being, such as relational self-esteem and communal mastery (Bernardo et al. 2018).

Other researchers have framed generational differences as intersecting with individualist and collectivist orientations and hope. For example, Buyukgoze-Kavas (2016) suggested that Turkey is a unique example of a country containing both collectivistic and individualistic cultures; while historically collectivist, the young Turkish people are striving toward a more individualist mindset. Due to this shift in cultural values, combined with a competitive educational system and low employment rates for young people, Turkish college students' hope was found to be positively correlated with their career adaptability, an arguably individualistic trait (Buyukgoze-Kavas 2016).

Chaudhary, Chadha, and Seth (2017) found that among older adults in India, hope was positively correlated with living with a spouse or other family members and negatively correlated with loneliness and isolation. For these older adults presumably raised in a more collectivistic period in India, the family group was found to be paramount to hope, as the authors expected. This recent data suggests that the nature of psychological hope is dependent upon cultural values. For cultures which value family and group participation, hope comes from these social circles; for cultures which value self-sufficiency, hope comes from one's belief in one's own abilities to achieve goals.

7.5.3 Race and Ethnicity

While Snyder et al. (1991) originally theorized that members of non-White ethnic groups in the United States would have lower hope than their privileged, White counterparts, this theory has not always held true. Importantly, emerging research has explored questions about levels and correlates of hope among various ethnic groups. Here we describe some of these findings that help to illustrate hope within racial and ethnic contexts.

Early research about hope has found there are not strong differences in levels of hope among ethnically diverse college students (Chang and Banks 2007; Visser et al. 2013). In fact, participants from historically marginalized ethnic groups often have as much hope, or even more hope, than White Americans (Adams et al. 2003; Davidson and Wingate 2011). Chang and Banks (2007) posited the idea that rather than systemic oppression and racism hindering hope, early exposure to social barriers may teach people of color at an early age to develop adaptive pathways to goals. In short, being of a racial/ ethnic minority may teach children of color to implement hope as a protective measure (Chang and Banks 2007).

Studies of hope in African Americans as it relates to suicidality have begun to shed light on the complexity of these variables. Although African Americans face numerous life stressors as compared to their Caucasian counterparts, they also have much lower levels of suicidality (Davidson 2011). Researchers have attempted to understand this paradox by exploring protective factors such as hope, among others. In an African American sample of college students, Davidson et al. (2010) found that hope predicted overall lower levels of suicidal ideation, as well as thwarted belongingness and perceived burdensomeness, both components of Joiner's (2005) theory of suicidal behavior. Hope also predicted higher levels of the acquired capability to enact suicide, which is described as the degree to which a person has become habituated to the pain that is present in suicidal behavior. Though these findings may seem counterintuitive, even in his early writings Snyder (1994) noted that suicide could be considered a final act of hope and reflective of goal accomplishment, and studies with primarily Caucasian samples have found similar results (Davidson 2009).

In an analysis of the possible protective role of hope, Hirsch et al. (2012) sought to test whether hope and hopelessness buffered the negative effects of depressive symptoms on suicidality. Their sample was ethnically diverse college students, including a subsample of African American students. Findings revealed that feelings of hopelessness significantly moderated the relationship between depressive symptoms and suicidality, but that trait hope did not. The authors suggested that perhaps hope alone was not enough to overcome the negative effects of depressive symptoms on suicidality. Another moderation study by Hollingsworth et al. (2016) provided support for the fact that hope was protective against the negative effects of perceived burdensomeness and thwarted belonging on suicidal ideation among African Americans. Taken together, these studies suggest that the role of hope is complex with respect to suicidality, and that hope may confer resilience in the context of some variables (e.g., feelings of perceived burdensomeness and thwarted belongingness) but may not in others (e.g., depressive symptoms). Clearly more research is needed in this area.

In a study of hope and suicidality among American Indian and Alaskan Native college students, O'Keefe and Wingate (2013) found that students' hope and optimism were negatively correlated with suicidality and suicide risk factors, as expected. Similar to studies with Caucasian (Davidson et al. 2009) and African American (Davidson et al. 2010) college student samples, hope was also positively correlated with the ability to enact suicide, as measured by questions related to fearlessness in the face of death and tolerance of pain. In other words, although high levels of hope in American Indian/Alaskan Native participants are connected with lower overall feelings of suicidality, the pathways component of hope made it more likely that the participants could carry out a suicide attempt if they decided to do so, by finding ways to achieve a difficult goal despite roadblocks such as pain and fear (O'Keefe and Wingate 2013). These findings illustrate another aspect of the complexity of hope, the fact that pathways and agency are not necessarily always associated with what society would deem to be *positive* outcomes. Just as psychological hope can be utilized to pursue socially acceptable goals, individuals can call upon elements of pathways and agency to pursue more socially taboo goals, such as suicide (Snyder 1994).

Some researchers have probed hope and stress more specifically to identify the role of hope in discrimination. In one study, Danoff-Burg, Prelow, and Swenson (2004) found that African American college students with high hope used more problem-focused coping with racial stressors than those with low hope. In another study, Banks, Singleton, and Kohn-Wood (2008) found that African American college students with high hope experienced more depressive symptoms when reporting discrimination compared to those with low hope. These findings suggest that hope might not always be a buffer to discrimination, particularly when discrimination is too high. Clearly hope is a useful construct for African American college students because of its relation to many positive variables, yet in certain circumstances it might not be able to alleviate high levels of stress (Banks, Singleton, and Kohn-Wood 2008).

7.5.4 Religion and Spirituality

As referenced in the introduction to this chapter, hope has long been associated with religion and spirituality. However, even within the construct of psychological hope, faith can play a role. For example, the Indian people of Kashmir and adolescents of South Africa attributed spirituality and faith as keys to upholding their senses of hope in violent communities (Anjum 2017; Isaacs and Savahl 2014). Some researchers have chosen to measure spirituality and religiosity specifically in relation to hope, as will be explored next.

In a study of hope, spirituality/religious practice, and life satisfaction in adolescents from Portugal, a largely Roman Catholic country, it was found that hope and spirituality were positively correlated with life satisfaction, with religious practice not emerging as a strong predictive factor for hope or life satisfaction. The authors define spirituality as an "inner belief system that a person relies on for strength and comfort" and religiosity as "institutional religious rituals, practices, and beliefs" such as attending church services and participating in traditional religious rites (Marques, Lopez, and Mitchell 2013, 252). While spiritual searching and self-reflection may give adolescents a sense of meaning and purpose with which to set and strive for goals, the simple act of attending church services does not have quite the same effect on hope and life satisfaction without the presence of spirituality (Marques et al. 2013).

In a study comparing hope in relation to disability status in both American Christians and Thai Buddhists (Chen, Brown, and Kotbungkair 2015), Snyder's psychological hope was found to be an important mechanism of coping for both groups, with hope being especially important in self-acceptance of disability for American Christians, but not as much for Thai Buddhists. The authors posit that hope is such an important factor for individuals of both religions due to the emphasis on God and Buddha as merciful beings who provide comfort to their followers, thus allowing followers hope for their futures. As for the disparity in self-acceptance of disability, the authors of the study point out that while Christians are given hope for healing in the afterlife, Buddhists may believe that their current disability is the result of bad karma from a previous life, thus placing the responsibility of their disability on themselves (Chen, Brown, and Kotbungkair 2015). **Disability status.** In addition to dealing with health complications, pain, and life adjustments, individuals with disabilities are often stigmatized by larger society. Hope can be an integral part of living with a disability for many individuals, representing the potential to heal, find new purpose, and adapt under difficult and painful circumstances (Chan et al. 2013; Chen, Brown, and Kotbungkair 2015; Tutton et al. 2012). Snyder himself suggested that his hope theory could be used as a framework for the rehabilitation of medical patients facing significant recovery, by increasing agency and teaching pathways thinking (Snyder et al. 2006).

In an ethnographical study of hope in stroke survivors, Tutton et al. (2012) interviewed both patients and staff on a stroke recovery unit. Stroke patients described how their hope had become hyperfocused on their bodies and their physical recovery. Both patients and staff spoke to the proclivity on the unit toward bleakness and lack of hope as patients struggled to reconcile past goals with their current reality; hope was especially difficult for patients with poor prognosis who were aware that true recovery was unlikely. Although many patients set their goals at full recovery and a "return to normal," nursing staff spoke of helping patients modify their goals to the immediate and short term, such as walking down the hall unassisted, in order to keep morale up without giving patients unrealistic expectations (Tutton et al. 2012).

Just as in stroke survivors, individuals with spinal cord injuries often face lifelong adjustments with little chance of full recovery. Chan et al. (2013) utilized a psychological hope model to examine the causal effects of hope on this population. It was discovered that hope had an indirect causal relationship with life satisfaction for spinal cord injury patients. As hope increased, participants were more likely to engage in community participation, and as participation

increased, life satisfaction increased along with it. Pathways thinking was an especially important element for spinal cord patients, as
they had to come up with alternate ways to exist in the world with
their injuries. The authors encouraged rehabilitation psychologists
to use Snyder's hope construct as a framework for engaging spinal
cord patients in their community and increasing well-being (Chan
et al. 2013).

In the previously discussed study of hope in Thai Buddhists and
American Christians, Chen, Brown, and Kotbungkair (2015) also
measured hope against experiences of neuromuscular disorders.
Findings showed that hope was an important coping mechanism
for participants with disability, with higher hope being correlated
with higher acceptance of disability status. Hope was also found to
be negatively correlated with future time orientation for this population, indicating that hope for individuals with disabilities is more
often focused on the here-and-now and immediate goals, rather than
on the long term (Chen, Brown, and Kotbungkair 2015).

Refugee status. Refugees represent a distinct and unique cultural group. Often caught between their culture of origin and the
culture of the country to which they have been displaced, refugees
additionally deal with trauma from the circumstances which forced
them to flee their home countries, language difficulties, financial
instability, and stigma from citizens of the country to which they
find themselves resettled (Anjum, Nordqvist, and Timpka 2012).
Due to this inherent trauma involved in refugee status, researchers
such as Larson et al. (2007, S383) have proposed that psychological hope may be "antidotes for maladaptation and dysfunction" and
have demonstrated that for Iraqi immigrants resettled in the United
States, psychological hope is inversely related to depression and
anxiety (S383).

Mass violence and terror in the West African countries of Liberia and Sierra Leone produced many such refugees. Researchers Anjum, Nordqvist, and Timpka (2012) strove to understand the effect of resettlement on refugee hope by following West African refugees in the first six years of their resettlement in Sweden. Although the study was qualitative in nature, Snyder's definition of hope was used to inform data analysis of refugees' hopes. It was found that immediately after resettlement, refugees' hopes and goals were focused on factors related to adjustment in their new home, such as educational and professional attainment. However, after six years, refugees' hopes focused more on family reunification. The authors theorize that even after refugees have acclimated to the culture of the place in which they have resettled, the trauma of family separation and continued social isolation still impact refugees' emotional well-being (Anjum, Nordqvist, and Timpka 2012).

Unaccompanied youth refugees also face much potential trauma and psychological distress, both from the circumstances they escaped in their home countries and from being separated from family and guardians. Jani, Underwood, and Ranweiler (2016) investigated psychological hope in refugee minors who had traveled unaccompanied to the United States (largely from Central America) and had been placed in family reunification programs. Using the child version of Snyder's hope scale, it was determined that while 75% of the participants scored high on hope, children who had not experienced abuse either in their home country or since their arrival in the United States were most likely to be hopeful. The authors noted that it is likely the youth in this study experienced relatively high hope and resilience as a result of being placed in a family reunification program. Though this was a pilot study of a new population, further research could begin to better understand hope within the unique context of being a refugee (Jani, Underwood, and Ranweiler 2016).

7.6 CONCLUSION

Over forty years of research about Snyder's concept of psychological hope have provided the field with a greater understanding of this construct. Snyder's hope can be measured in various populations, and studies have found it is associated with numerous positive outcomes in the areas of physical and emotional well-being. In recent years, researchers have also attempted to better understand hope outside of the White, middle-class college student population upon which it was primarily measured and described. Questions about the equivalence of the construct and its measurement across identity groups have begun to illustrate the complexity of hope (Edwards and McClintock 2017).

The field has learned that hope is associated with many positive correlates among individuals from diverse backgrounds and identities, and in many cases it can moderate the negative effects of life stressors. While in many groups the two-factor structure of pathways and agency is the same as how it was originally conceptualized by Snyder, in some populations (e.g., Japanese [Kato 2006] or Taiwanese [Luo et al. 2010]) the definition of hope may need to be expanded or refined. Occasionally, it appears that hope alone may not be able to buffer stress if the effects are too negative. Additionally, hope may be a liability in cases where goals (e.g., suicidality) are not considered functional or healthy. That being said, the very assertion that suicidal behavior is not healthy exists within a cultural context and as such must be seen through that lens.

Hope can look different in various populations, both in how it relates to other behaviors and how it is experienced by people in their lives. Much research still needs to be conducted to understand these nuances between and among cultural groups, and to ensure that hope is considered within its own unique context.

REFERENCES

Abdel-Khalek, Ahmed, and C. R. Snyder. 2007. "Correlates and Predictors of an Arabic Translation of the Snyder Hope Scale." *Journal of Positive Psychology* 2 (4, October): 228–235. doi:10.1080/17439760701552337

Adams, V. H. III, K. L. Rand, K. Kahle, C. R. Snyder, C. Berg, E. A. King, and A. Rodriguez-Hanley. 2003. "African Americans' Hope and Coping with Racism Stressors." In *Between Stress and Hope: From A Disease-centered to A Health-centered Perspective*, edited by R. Jacoby and G. Keinan, 235–249. Praeger Publishers/Greenwood Publishing Group.

Ægisdóttir, Stefanía, Lawrence H. Gerstein, and Deniz Canel Çinarbaş. 2008. "Methodological Issues in Cross-Cultural Counseling Research: Equivalence, Bias, and Translations." *Counseling Psychologist* 36 (2): 188–219. doi:10.1177/0011000007305384

Anjum, Sadaf. 2017. "Role of Hope and Perceived Social Support in Predicting Posttraumatic Growth among Parents of Disappeared Persons in Kashmir." *Indian Journal of Health & Wellbeing* 8 (12): 1463–1467.

Anjum, Tanvir M., Cecilia Nordqvist, and Toomas Timpka. 2012. "The Hopes of West African Refugees during Resettlement in Northern Sweden: A 6-Year Prospective Qualitative Study of Pathways and Agency Thoughts." *Conflict & Health* 6 (1): 1–8. doi:10.1186/1752-1505-6-1

Banks, Kira Hudson, Jennifer L. Singleton, and Laura P. Kohn-Wood. 2008. "The Influence of Hope on the Relationship between Racial Discrimination and Depressive Symptoms." *Journal of Multicultural Counseling & Development* 36 (4): 231–244. doi:10.1002/j.2161-1912.2008.tb00085.x

Bernardo, Allan B. I. 2010. "Extending Hope Theory: Internal and External Locus of Trait Hope." *Personality & Individual Differences* 49 (8): 944–949. doi:10.1016/j.paid.2010.07.036

Bernardo, Allan B. I., Susanna S. Yeung, Katrina Fernando Resurreccion, Ron R. Resurreccion, and Aqeel Khan. 2018. "External Locus-of-Hope, Well-being, and Coping of Students: A Cross-cultural Examination within Asia." *Psychology in the Schools* 55 (8): 908–923. doi:10.1002/pits.22155

Brouwer, Danny, Rob R. Meijer, Anke M. Weekers, and Joost J. Baneke. 2008. "On the Dimensionality of the Dispositional Hope Scale." *Psychological Assessment* 20 (3): 310–315. doi:10.1037/1040-3590.20.3.310

Buyukgoze Kavas, Aysenur. 2016. "Predicting Career Adaptability from Positive Psychological Traits." *Career Development Quarterly* 64 (2): 114–125. https://doi.org/10.1002/cdq.12045.

Chan, Jacob Y. C., Fong Chan, Nicole Ditchman, Brian Phillips, and Chih-Chin Chou. 2013. "Evaluating Snyder's Hope Theory as a Motivational Model of Participation and Life Satisfaction for Individuals with Spinal Cord Injury: A

Path Analysis." *Rehabilitation Research, Policy, and Education* 27 (3): 171–185. doi:10.1891/2168-6653.27.3.171

Chang, Edward C., and Kira Hudson Banks. 2007. "The Color and Texture of Hope: Some Preliminary Findings and Implications for Hope Theory and Counseling among Diverse Racial/Ethnic Groups." *Cultural Diversity & Ethnic Minority Psychology* 13 (2): 94–103. doi:10.1037/1099-9809.13.2.94

Chaudhary, Nisha, N. K. Chadha, and Salma Seth. 2017. "Hope: Faith in What Will Be." *Indian Journal of Positive Psychology* 8 (2): 203–207.

Chen, Roy K., Alicia D. Brown, and Wilaiporn Kotbungkair. 2015. "A Comparison of Self-Acceptance of Disability between Thai Buddhists and American Christians." *Journal of Rehabilitation* 81 (1): 52–62.

Danoff-Burg, S., H. Prelow, and R. Swenson. 2004. "Hope and Life Satisfaction in Black College Students Coping with Race-related Stress." *Journal of Black Psychology* 30: 208–228. https://doi.org/10.1177/0095798403260725.

Davidson, Collin L., and LaRicka R. Wingate. 2011. "Racial Disparities in Risk and Protective Factors for Suicide." *Journal of Black Psychology* 37 (4): 499–516. doi:10.1177/0095798410397543

Davidson, Collin L., Laricka R. Wingate, Kathy A. Rasmussen, and Meredith L. Slish. 2009. "Hope as a Predictor of Interpersonal Suicide Risk." *Suicide & Life-Threatening Behavior* 39 (5): 499–507. doi:10.1521/suli.2009.39.5.499

Davidson, Collin L., LaRicka R. Wingate, Meredith L. Slish, and Kathy A. Rasmussen. 2010. "The Great Black Hope: Hope and Its Relation to Suicide Risk among African Americans." *Suicide & Life-Threatening Behavior* 40 (2): 170–180. doi:10.1521/suli.2010.40.2.170

Edwards, Lisa M., and Jessica McClintock. 2017. "A Cultural Context Lens of Hope." In *Handbook of Hope,* edited by Matthew W. Gallagher and Shane J. Lopez, 95–104. New York: Oxford University Press.

Galiana, Laura, Amparo Oliver, Patricia Sancho, and José Tomás. 2015. "Dimensionality and Validation of the Dispositional Hope Scale in a Spanish Sample." *Social Indicators Research* 120 (1): 297–308. doi:10.1007/s11205-014-0582-1

Gana, Kamel, Stéphanie Daigre, and Julie Ledrich. 2013. "Psychometric Properties of the French Version of the Adult Dispositional Hope Scale." *Assessment* 20 (1): 114–118. doi:10.1177/1073191112468315

Goodman, Fallon R., David J. Disabato, Todd B. Kashdan, and Kyla A. Machell. 2017. "Personality Strengths as Resilience: A One-Year Multiwave Study." *Journal of Personality* 85 (3): 423–434. doi:10.1111/jopy.12250

Halama, Peter. 1999. "Snyder's Hope Scale." *Studia Psychologica* 41 (4): 329–332.

Halama, Peter. 2001. "Slovenská verzia Snyderovej Škály Nádeje: Preklad a adaptácia. = The Slovak version of Snyder's Hope Scale: Translation and adaptation." *Československá Psychologie* 45 (2): 135–142.

Hays, Pamela A. 2016. *Addressing Cultural Complexities in Practice: Assessment,* *Diagnosis, and Therapy.* 3rd edition. Washington, DC: American Psychological Association.

Hirsch, Jameson K., Preston L. Visser, Edward C. Chang, and Elizabeth L. Jeglic. 2012. "Race and Ethnic Differences in Hope and Hopelessness as Moderators of the Association between Depressive Symptoms and Suicidal Behavior." *Journal of American College Health* 60 (2): 115–125. doi:10.1080/07448481.2011.567402

Hollingsworth, David W., LaRicka R. Wingate, Raymond P. Tucker, Victoria. M. O'Keefe, and Ashley B. Cole. 2016. "Hope as a Moderator of the Relationship between Interpersonal Predictors of Suicide and Suicidal Thinking in African Americans." *Journal of Black Psychology* 42 (2): 175–190. doi:10.1177/0095798414563748

Hoover-Kinsinger, Sandra E. 2018. "Hoping against Hope: An Integration of the Hope Theology of Jürgen Moltmann and C. R. Snyder's Psychology of Hope." *Journal of Psychology & Christianity* 37 (4): 313–322.

Isaacs, Serena Ann, and Shazly Savahl. 2014. "A Qualitative Inquiry Investigating Adolescents' Sense of Hope within a Context of Violence in a Disadvantaged Community in Cape Town." *Journal of Youth Studies* 17 (2): 269–278. doi:10.1080/13676261.2013.815703

Jani, Jayshree, Dawnya Underwood, and Jessica Ranweiler. 2016. "Hope as a Crucial Factor in Integration among Unaccompanied Immigrant Youth in the USA: A Pilot Project." *Journal of International Migration & Integration* 17 (4): 1195–1209. doi:10.1007/s12134-015-0457-6

Joiner, Thomas E. 2005. *Why People Die by Suicide.* Cambridge, MA: Harvard University Press.

Kato, Tsuskasa. 2006. "Role of Hope and Coping Behavior in Interpersonal Stress." *Japanese Journal of Health Psychology* 19 (1): 25–36. https://doi.org/10.11560/jahp.19.1_25.

Kato, Tsukasa, and C. R. Snyder. 2005. "The Relationship between Hope and Subjective Well-being: Reliability and Validity of the Dispositional Hope Scale, Japanese Version." *Japanese Journal of Psychology* 76 (3): 227–234. https://doi.org/10.4992/jjpsy.76.227

Larson, Julie H., Mohamed Farrag, Hikmet Jamil, Talib Kafaji, Husam Abdulkhaleq, and Adnan Hammad. 2007. "E. Hope and Fostering the Well-being of Refugees from Iraq." *Ethnicity & Disease* 17: S383–S384.

Lonner, Walter J. 1985. "Issues in Testing and Assessment in Cross-cultural Counseling." *Counseling Psychologist* 13 (4): 599–614. doi.org/10.1177/0011000085134004

Lopez, Shane J., C. R. Snyder, and J. T. Pedrotti. 2003. "Hope: Many Definitions, Many Measures." In *A Handbook of Models and Measures,* edited by Shane J.

Lopez and C. R. Snyder, 91–106. Washington, DC: American Psychological Association.

Luo, Yueh-Chuan, LiLi Huang, Yi-Cheng Lin, and Kwang-Kuo Hwang. 2010. "The Duality of Hope: The Development and Validation of a New Scale." *Chinese Journal of Psychology* 52 (3): 265–285.

Marques, Susana. C., Shane. J. Lopez, Anne. M. Fontaine, Susana Coimbra, and Joanna Mitchell. 2014. "Validation of a Portuguese Version of the Snyder Hope Scale in a Sample of High School Students." *Journal of Psychoeducational Assessment* 32 (8): 781–786. doi.org/10.1177/0734282914540865

Marques, Susana, Shane J. Lopez, and Joanna Mitchell. 2013. "The Role of Hope, Spirituality and Religious Practice in Adolescents' Life Satisfaction: Longitudinal Findings." *Journal of Happiness Studies* 14 (1): 251–261. doi:10.1007/s10902-012-9329-3

Martin, Adrienne M. 2011. "Hopes and Dreams." *Philosophy and Phemenological Research* 83 (1): 148–173. doi.org/10.1111/j.1933-1592.2010.00422.x

McGeer, Victoria. 2004. "The Art of Good Hope." *Annals of the American Academy of Political and Social Science* 592 (1): 100–127.

O'Keefe, Victoria M., and LaRicka R. Wingate. 2013. "The Role of Hope and Optimism in Suicide Risk for American Indians/Alaska Natives." *Suicide & Life-Threatening Behavior* 43 (6): 621–633. doi:10.1111/sltb.12044

Pacico, Juliana Cerentini, Micheline Roat Bastianello, Cristian Zanon, and Claudio Simon Hutz. 2013. "Adaptation and Validation of the Dispositional Hope Scale for Adolescents." *Psicologia: Reflexão e Crítica* 26 (3): 488–492. doi:10.1590/S0102-79722013000300008

Rand, Kevin L., and Kaitlin K. Touza. 2018. "Hope Theory." In *The Oxford Handbook of Positive Psychology*, edited by C. R. Snyder, S. J. Lopez, L. M. Edwards, and S. C. Marques, 425–442. Oxford: Oxford University Press.

Ritschel, Lorie. 2005. "Lessons in Teaching Hope: An Interview with C. R. Snyder." *Teaching of Psychology* 32 (1): 74–78. doi:10.1207/s15328023top3201_15

Sandage, Steven J., Peter C. Hill, and Henry C. Vang. 2003. "Toward a Multicultural Positive Psychology: Indigenous Forgiveness and Hmong Culture." *Counseling Psychologist* 31 (5): 564–591. doi:10.1177/0011000003256550

Shorey, Hal S., C. R. Snyder, Kevin L. Rand, Jill R. Hockemeyer, and David B. Feldman. 2002. "Authors' Response: Somewhere over the Rainbow: Hope Theory Weathers Its First Decade." *Psychological Inquiry* 13 (4): 322. doi:10.1207/S15327965PLI1304_03

Snyder, C. R. 1994. *The Psychology of Hope: You Can Get There from Here.* New York: Free Press.

Snyder, C. R. 1995. "Conceptualizing, Measuring, and Nurturing Hope." *Journal of Counseling & Development* 73 (3): 355–360. doi:10.1002/j.1556-6676.1995.tb01764.x

Snyder, C. R. 2002. "Target Article: Hope Theory: Rainbows in the Mind." *Psychological Inquiry* 13 (4): 249. doi:10.1207/S15327965PLI1304_01

Snyder, C. R., Betsy Hoza, William E. Pelham, Michael Rapoff, Leanne Ware, Michael Danovsky, Lori Highberger, Howard Ribinstein, and Kandy J. Stahl. 1997. "The Development and Validation of the Children's Hope Scale." *Journal of Pediatric Psychology* 22 (3): 399–421. doi:10.1093/jpepsy/22.3.399

Snyder, C. R., C. Harris, J. R. Anderson, S. A. Holleran, L. M. Irving, S. T. Sigmon, L. Yoshinobu, J. Gibb, C. Langelle, and P. Harney. 1991. "The Will and the Ways: Development and Validation of an Individual-differences Measure of Hope." *Journal of Personality and Social Psychology* 60 (4): 570–585. https://doi.org/10.1037/0022-3514. 60.4.570

Snyder, C. R., Kenneth A. Lehman, Ben Kluck, and Yngve Monsson. 2006. "Hope for Rehabilitation and Vice Versa." *Rehabilitation Psychology* 51 (2): 89–112. doi:10.1037/0090-5550.51.2.89

Sue, Derald W., and Madonna G. Constantine. 2003. "Optimal Human Functioning in People of Color in the United States." In *Counseling Psychology and Optimal Human Functioning*, edited by W. B. Walsh, 151–169. Lawrence Erlbaum Associates Publishers.

Sun, Qiwu, Kok-Mun Ng, and Chuang Wang. 2012. "A Validation Study on a New Chinese Version of the Dispositional Hope Scale." *Measurement & Evaluation in Counseling & Development* 45 (2): 133–148. doi:10.1177/0748175611429011

Titone, Connie, Laura Stefanik, and Robert McNamara. 2013. "Assessing and Improving Hopefulness: A Case Study of Swazi Youth." *International Education* 43 (1): 65–84.

Tutton, Elizabeth, Kate Seers, Deborah Langstaff, and Martin Westwood. 2012. "Staff and Patient Views of the Concept of Hope on a Stroke Unit: A Qualitative Study." *Journal of Advanced Nursing* 68 (9): 2061–2069. doi:10.1111/j.1365-2648.2011.05899.x

Visser, Preston L., Priya Loess, Elizabeth L. Jeglic, and Jameson K. Hirsch. 2013. "Hope as a Moderator of Negative Life Events and Depressive Symptoms in a Diverse Sample." *Stress & Health: Journal of the International Society for the Investigation of Stress* 29 (1): 82–88. doi:10.1002/smi.2433

Watts, Fraser, Kevin Dutton, and Liz Gulliford. 2006. "Human Spiritual Qualities: Integrating Psychology and Religion." *Mental Health, Religion & Culture* 9 (3): 277–289. doi:10.1080/13694670600615524

Positive Fantasies about the Future Breed Hope

GABRIELE OETTINGEN

What we do not see, we hope for.—The Crossroads Initiative (2016)

8.1 INTRODUCTION

This sentence from the Parallel Verses of the Romans indicates that hope can be a guide in times *when we do not see* what the future might hold. For example, hope is ascribed to be an important part of the teaching of St. Cyprian, bishop of Carthage under conditions of great uncertainty around the year of AD 248. He led Christians of North Africa through a period of persecution from Rome and a severe pandemic that afflicted the Roman Empire from about AD 249 to 262. It was a time when people had to face a future with potentially deadly outcomes for individuals and the society. In his treatise on mortality, St. Cyprian writes that in death the individual will be rewarded for the earthly sacrifice. By instilling positive thoughts and images about the far future despite present times of severe hardships and bleak

Gabriele Oettingen, *Positive Fantasies about the Future Breed Hope* In: *The Virtue of Hope*. Edited by: Nancy E. Snow, Oxford University Press. © Oxford University Press 2024. DOI: 10.1093/oso/9780190069575.003.0009 prospects, St. Cyprian wanted to motivate his fellow Christians to endure and he wanted to reassure them of their worth in the eyes of God (Cyprian 2013). Many Christians under St. Cyprian's guidance, despite facing the uncertainty of their times, remained hopeful, clinging to their thoughts and images, that is, to their fantasies of a better future after death.

To this date, the theme of hope granted by God did not lose its relevance. Pope Francis preached in his 2020 Easter Vigil during the coronavirus pandemic: "Tonight we acquire a fundamental right that can never be taken away from us: *the right to hope*. It is a new and living hope that comes from God. It is not mere optimism; it is not a pat on the back or an empty word of encouragement with a passing smile. No. It is a gift from heaven, which we could not have earned on our own" (Francis 2020).

Beyond the religious context, the term "hope" has been used for utopian thinking (e.g., Bloch 1996) but also for more trivial secular themes (Marcel 1978; for a summary, see Eliott 2005). For example, hope is a frequent term in everyday language meaning exactly what Pope Francis did not mean, "pats on the shoulder," expressing our wishful thinking whereby the wishful thinking can be directed to ourselves (e.g., I hope I will get a good grade) or to others (e.g., I hope you will get the job). In everyday language, we are using the term hope for future outcomes that we have control over (e.g., I hope I will exercise) or no control over (e.g., I hope the weather will be nice). Still, even when we talk about hope in everyday life, it is linked to something unseen that expresses our desire to experience a possible positive future or to not experience a possible negative future.

Whether referring to divine or secular hope in this chapter, I define hope as positive thoughts and images (fantasies) about the future that can even occur when a person's subjective probabilities (expectations) of reaching the desired future are low (Oettingen 1997a, b). These positive thoughts and fantasies emerge irrespective of the perceived likelihood of the hoped-for event occurring (Klinger 1990; Oettingen and Mayer 2002; Singer 1966). However, I will argue that the behavioral consequences of hope differ depending on how a person mentally approaches their positive fantasies and whether a person expects a bright or a bleak future.

The present chapter has three parts. First, I will introduce the definition of hope as positive thoughts and images about the future (fantasies) and discuss the mechanisms and origins of hope understood that way. The analysis of hope would be incomplete without considering its behavioral functions. Thus, in second, I will discuss Fantasy Realization Theory (FRT) that specifies the various behavioral functions of hope. I will show that positive future fantasies contrasted with the obstacles standing in the way of realizing these fantasies lead people to exert energy and action, while only indulging in positive future fantasies keeps them passively waiting. Third, I will speculate about hope as a virtue arguing that hope can be regulated and cultivated and thereby adjusted to the context that people find themselves in.

8.2 HOPE AS POSITIVE FUTURE FANTASIES

Before beginning, a caveat is in order. Definitions of hope in psychology are rooted in cognitive learning theories and thus typically rely on expectancies (see also Gulliford, and Edwards and McConnell, both in this volume). Expectancies are referred to as beliefs or judgments that the probability of attaining a desired future is high (e.g., Atkinson 1957; Bandura 1977; for a summary, see Oettingen, Sevincer, and Gollwitzer 2018). Grounded in learning from experiences of the past, these expectations are a solid basis for action as they signal that it is reasonable to invest in those areas of life that have proven successful.

The conceptualization of hope used in this chapter differs from hope as expectancy judgment. The argument is that a person's positive thoughts and images about the future (future fantasies) are underlying hope. And that hope can arise no matter whether the expectations of the desired future are high or low as long as they are in the realm of the possible (i.e., above zero; Stotland 1969). In other words, hope in terms of positive expectations and in terms of positive fantasies both qualify as positive thinking about the future. However, they clearly differ in their definition, assessment, origins, and importantly in their behavioral and affective consequences.

8.2.1 *Definition, Assessment, and Origins*

Definition. More than two decades ago, Oettingen (1999; see also Oettingen and Mayer 2002) differentiated between beliefs about the future (expectations) and unrestricted thoughts and images about the future (fantasies). Beliefs versus images in the stream of thought were distinguished already by William James (1890, 283): "Everyone knows the difference between imagining a thing and believing in its existence, between supposing a proposition and acquiescing in its truth." In line with William James, we conceptualize fantasies as thoughts that appear in a person's mind irrespective of the person's beliefs. William James (1890) focused on beliefs versus the stream of thought regarding the past. On the contrary, Oettingen and her colleagues focused on beliefs about possible future events (expectations) versus the stream of thought containing future events (fantasies).

Specifically, positive fantasies are positively experienced thoughts and images about the future in the stream of thought that emerge irrespective of whether people expect them to occur or not (Klinger 1990; Oettingen and Mayer 2002; Singer 1966). They are unrestricted by experiences of the past and factual knowledge. For example, smokers may happily fantasize how they graciously reject the offer of a cigarette despite expecting—based on their experience of the past—that they will eventually be seduced to say yes.

Assessment. Expectations have been assessed by asking participants to report their judgments of the likelihood that a specified future will happen or not, that is, participants self-report a subjective commitment to the probability of an event occurring in the future or not. On the contrary, fantasies do not imply any relation to reality, nor any probability judgment or commitment regarding reality. Measures of fantasies have to capture the stream of thought. Oettingen and Mayer (2002; see also Oettingen and Wadden 1991) solved this measurement task by prompting participants to produce and write down their stream of thought in response to hypothetical stories that could either end happily or not so happily. This way of measuring spontaneous thoughts and images was modeled in line with classic projective tests (e.g., the Thematic Apperception Test, TAT; Murray 1943; McClelland 1980; Schultheiss et al. 2009). The TAT uses pictorial stimuli to generate people's stream of thought, and then these thoughts and fantasies are content analyzed for underlying motives (e.g., achievement, affiliation, or power motives). Oettingen and Mayer (2002), however, rather than using content analysis by outside raters, asked participants to rate themselves how positive or negative their fantasies were (e.g., student participants who had a crush rated their own thoughts in response to an open-ended hypothetical story where they could either obtain or not obtain the attention of the admired person). This semi-projective assessment tool integrates the benefits of projective tests (or operant measures; McClelland 1980) with the benefits of traditional self-report measures (or respondent measures; Oettingen and Mayer 2002).

Origins. While there is plenty of evidence that hope defined as expectations is based on past experiences and performances (Bandura 1977; Mischel 1973; Oettingen and Mayer 2002; Schunk and DiBenedetto 2018; Snyder 1989, 2002), there is much less empirical work on the origins of hope defined as positive future fantasies. Reasoning that these fantasies about the future should be an indication of a person's need states, Kappes, Schwörer, and Oettingen (2012) observed that arousing people's needs triggered future fantasies of positive valence in which people satisfied these needs. A series of four experiments showed this pattern of results regarding physiological and psychological needs alike. For instance, in one study, participants were asked to refrain from drinking any liquids for four hours before coming to the lab, and then were offered salty pretzels to further increase the need for water. Half of the participants then received a bottle of fresh water while the other half were kept thirsty. When asked to freely associate thoughts and images to a scenario that could potentially relate to drinking water versus an irrelevant topic, participants in need of water generated more water-related positive thoughts than the satisfied group but only with respect to the scenario that was relevant to quenching their thirst. In other studies, participants whose needs for meaning were aroused reported more positive fantasies of switching to a more meaningful job, and participants whose needs for interpersonal relationships were aroused positively fantasized about getting together with their friends and family.

Summary. While hope in terms of expectations includes judgments of a high likelihood of a desired event to occur or an undesired event not to occur, hope in terms of positive future fantasies includes thoughts and images in the stream of thought that people generate independent of their judged likelihood that these will come true. Expectations are assessed by self-report measures on classic Likert scales (e.g., from 1 *not at all* to 7 *very much*), while positive fantasies are best assessed by semi-projective tests that allow people to write down their stream of thought and then evaluate the valence of these free thoughts and images. Hope as positive future fantasies originates from our unfulfilled needs and thus provides a signal to act toward satisfying these needs, whether they are physiological or psychological.

8.2.2 Behavioral and Affective Consequences: Pleasure Now, Pain Later

The differentiation between hope as expectations versus hope as fantasies is only meaningful if the constructs have different consequences for people's thoughts, feelings, or actions (e.g., effort and success in fulfilling the desired future). In a variety of domains, positive expectations are associated with increased information seeking, heightened effort and persistence, and eventually with more success (Bandura 1997; Carver, Blaney, and Scheier 1979). Further, positive expectations have been linked to happiness, productivity, and creativity (Taylor and Brown 1988; Seligman 1991). In line with popular beliefs that positive thinking has pervasive positive effects (e.g., Byrne 2006; Canfield, Hansen, and Newmark 2010), one might surmise that hope in terms of positive future thoughts and fantasies will similarly benefit people's effort, success, and well-being.

Behavior. It may come as a surprise, then, that the *more* people positively fantasized about successfully attaining their desired future, the *less* effort they invested and the *less* successful they were. This pattern of results has been observed in the achievement domain, the health domain, and the interpersonal domain, for people of different backgrounds and cultures, for different measures of future fantasies, and for people's everyday life as well as their long-term development. For example, in the achievement domain, the more university students fantasized about doing well on their final exam (Oettingen and Mayer 2002), the less well they actually did. Positive fantasies predicting lower achievement were also found in a sample of diverse students from a disadvantaged background who had enrolled in a vocational program for business education (Kappes, Oettingen, and

Mayer 2012). And in university graduates, the more they imagined a smooth transition into their professional life, the lower were their wages two years later, and the fewer job offers they had received, which was partly explained by their sending out fewer job applications. In other words, they had put less effort into looking for an adequate job (Oettingen and Mayer 2002).

Similar findings exist in the interpersonal domain: the more positively university students dreamed about starting a romantic relationship with a person they had a crush on, the less likely it was that they started a romantic relationship with this person. In the health domain, the more positively women who had just enrolled in a weight-loss program fantasized about their successes in the program, the fewer pounds they had shed after three months and after one year (Oettingen and Wadden 1991). Finally, the more positively hip-replacement patients fantasized about a smooth recovery from their impending surgery, the less well they could move their new joint, the fewer stairs they could walk, and the less well they recovered as judged by their physical therapists (Oettingen and Mayer 2002).

Other researchers have also found that positive future dreams and images predict low effort and success. For example, Taylor et al. (1998) observed that thoughts and images about a positive future outcome led to comparatively less planning and lower academic achievement than simulations about the cumbersome process of getting to the outcome. Similarly, when coping with stressors, hopeful thoughts and images about an "if-only" scenario were less effective in actively coping with the stressor than facing what had actually happened. Taken together, these findings lead to the question of whether the function of hope in terms of positive fantasies is to soothe people's mood rather than get them to actively pursue the desired future.

Affect. In four studies we observed that hope in terms of positive future fantasies is indeed linked to concurrent positive affect and fewer depressive symptoms (Oettingen, Mayer, and Portnow

2016). Our findings are in line with other research showing that positive thoughts and images measured by self-report questionnaires are associated with alleviated symptoms of depression—at least in the short run (Caprara et al. 2012; Golding and Singer 1983).

Importantly, however, Oettingen, Mayer, and Portnow (2016) found that when affect and depressive symptoms were measured over time (up to seven months), hope in terms of positive fantasies predicted *less* and not more positive affect and *increased* rather than decreased symptoms of depression. In all four studies, they used well-validated Depression Inventories to measure affect and depression (e.g., the Children's Depression Inventory [CDI], the Center for Epidemiologic Studies Depression Scale [CES-D], or the Beck Depression Inventory [BDI]). And in three of the four studies, they assessed hope by semi-projective tools prompting future fantasies as described before. In the fourth study, the positivity of fantasies was measured by daily diaries showing that the results also apply to everyday life. Trying to find mechanisms by which hope might cause depressive symptoms over time, the authors observed that weak effort and little success of the participating students were partly responsible for the positively fantasizing students becoming comparatively more depressed over the next two months.

Findings from different areas of psychology support the notion that positive, idealizing, future fantasies have long-term drawbacks. Looking at clinical psychology, positive thinking about the self, although it goes along with less suicidal ideation after a suicide attempt, predicts a higher likelihood of a follow-up suicide attempt over the period of the following fifteen months (O'Connor, Smyth, and Williams 2015). In the psychology of aging, elderly participants foreseeing future happiness showed lower health and less longevity (Lang et al. 2013). Similarly, Cheng, Fung, and Chan (2009) found that adults age sixty years or older who rated their future self as positive felt better at the moment, but it predicted less well-being a year later. Older adults who indulge in their idealizing thoughts and images of a better future may fail to prepare for the impediments that are unavoidable in later life. They also may feel more disappointed and frustrated when these impediments turn up. On the contrary, older adults who look at the future self by considering inevitable declines and losses are less upset when their living conditions in fact decline. Taken together, hope in terms of positive fantasies about the future may be a double-edged sword: it is soothing for the moment but a risk factor in the long run.

Mechanisms. How can it be that hope is only a pillar for short-term affect rather a valid tool for eventual success and happiness? In response to these questions, Oettingen and Mayer (2002) content analyzed their participants' fantasies about the future. Interestingly, successful participants mentioned obstacles and difficulties in realizing the future more often than the less successful participants. We therefore wondered whether hope in terms of positive future fantasies feign success in the here and now and thus sap the energy and the action that is needed to actively bring about the desired future. In fact, it has long been argued that exerting effort is a prerequisite for realizing one's desired future outcomes (Brehm and Self 1989; Oettingen 2012).

Two experimental studies (Sciarappo et al. 2015) with college students showed that positive fantasies of receiving a monetary reward (vs. fantasies questioning the reward) led to delaying a series of hypothetical other rewards. That is, hopeful fantasies about being rewarded made participants patiently wait longer for potential other rewards. This finding suggests that participants were momentarily satisfied with the sum of money they imagined having received (Green et al. 1996; Green, Myerson, and Vanderveldt 2014). Apparently, the hopeful future fantasies allow for the experience of having already achieved the hoped-for future. In another set of studies, Kappes,

Kappes, and Oettingen (2015) observed that mental attainment does not necessarily need to be conscious but can also occur outside of people's awareness.

Beyond cognitive variables speaking to mental attainment as a result of positive future fantasies, four experimental studies looked at motivational mechanisms showing that positive future fantasies (e.g., about how the next week is going, about high achievement, about one's appearance) sapped participants' energy. These findings apply to low energy measured by systolic blood pressure (SBP; Wright 1996) and self-reported energization. Importantly, the decreased energization predicted lower effort and success in attaining the hoped-for future (e.g., in solving relevant tasks during the upcoming week).

Qualifier: Challenging Obstacles. Physical or mental energy is only essential for reaching a desired future when there are challenges on the way. On the contrary, when tasks are easy and straightforward to solve, positive future fantasies should suffice to reach one's desires. For example, when giving to charities is easy, indulging in positive fantasies about the meaning of one's contribution or the recognition of oneself as donor should be enough for spending on the good cause. However, when giving is challenging and costly, such hopeful fantasies may decrease rather than increase the donors' generosity. In three experiments, Kappes, Sharma, and Oettingen (2013) found that positive, hopeful fantasies (vs. control thoughts such as factual thoughts) led to lower giving in terms of time, effort, and money when high resources were demanded, but positive fantasies did not reduce giving when it was easy. Follow-up analyses showed that students in the positive fantasy conditions (but not in the control conditions) perceived the request for many resources as too demanding, which was not the case when few resources were asked for. These results point to an important qualifying factor: hope leads to passivity and low effort only when it is demanding to realize the hoped-for future. When acting is easy, positive fantasies are enough to seize the desired future.

Summary. Hope as defined by positive future thoughts and images works like a short-term bandage. It goes along with an improved mood as people feign having already attained the longed-for future. However, hope as positive fantasies is a risk factor when reality hits, as people have attained their longed-for future just in their mind. This mental attainment then is linked to low energy, low effort, and eventually also low success, which is partly responsible for people getting more depressed over time. In our analysis of hope we have largely focused on situations where people can bring about the desired future via their own actions. After these empirical analyses put such a sad light on hope, I will now turn to the behavioral functions of hope in terms of positive future fantasies.

8.3 BEHAVIORAL FUNCTIONS OF HOPE

The previously reported findings on the origins of positive future fantasies clarify that positive future fantasies are an expression of our needs and thus give action direction. At the same time, they sap our energy needed to reach the desired future. In this part of the chapter, I will argue that complementing hopeful fantasies with thoughts about the obstacles in their way energizes people to actively pursue their hoped-for futures. This proactive part in hope was postulated by philosopher Ernst Bloch (1954, 1996) in *The Principle of Hope*, where he conceives of hope as future dreams: "How richly people have always dreamed of this, dreamed of the better life that might be possible" (Bloch 1996, 3). Bloch also postulates that it is the proactive part of daydreams that causes successful pursuit of a better future (Schnoor 1988). I will now describe how we can bring out this proactive part in hopeful fantasies.

8.3.1 Fantasy Realization Theory

Mental contrasting. Fantasy Realization Theory (FRT; Oettingen 1999, 2012; Oettingen, Pak, and Schnetter 2001) postulates that positive future fantasies as they signal our unfulfilled needs give action direction. However, because positively fantasizing about the future saps our energy for acting, we need to confront ourselves with the obstacles of reality. In short, the theory holds that by generating positive future dreams and fantasies and then mentally facing the obstacles of reality, people will be energized to implement their fantasies. In addition, confronting the obstacles will unveil whether the obstacles are surmountable and what means can be used to overcome them. If the obstacles are perceived as surmountable (i.e., expectations of success are high), people will fully commit to and pursue fulfilling their wishes; however, when obstacles are perceived as insurmountable (expectations of success are low), people will let go of wish fulfilment. They then can either adjust their hopes and dreams, postpone their realization to a better point in time, or let go of wish fulfillment. In this way, people save their resources as they can turn to a more promising and feasible alternative future. This strategy of mentally juxtaposing one's dreams and future fantasies with the obstacles of reality is called "mental contrasting." Mental contrasting helps to set priorities as people now pursue feasible futures but refrain from wasting their time and efforts on futures that can never be reached.

These ideas have been supported by many experimental studies across a variety of life domains (e.g., achievement, health, interpersonal), age, SES, cultures, in patients with mental and physical vulnerabilities, and across various ways to induce or teach mental contrasting. The findings emerged for cognitive, emotional, motivational, and behavioral measures of fantasy realization, and irrespective of whether these measures were based on observation, physiological indicators, self-reports, or content analyses. Finally, the findings were replicated in the laboratory and in real life (e.g., schools, hospitals, community samples), regarding short-term and long-term outcomes, and for trivial as well as life-changing fantasies (overview by Oettingen 2012, 2014; Oettingen and Sevincer 2018).

Taken together, to proactively pursue a hoped-for future, sheer future dreams are not enough. We need to mentally contrast these dreams with the obstacles that might stand in their way. Only then can we understand that our dreams are not already accomplished. We also will recognize what can be done to overcome our obstacles or whether we better let our dreams and wishes go. Mental contrasting will help us clean up our lives and save time, energy, and other resources (Brehm and Self 1989; Wright 1996).

Indulging. The wise allocation of resources via mental contrasting is helpful when people have a choice, that is, when disengaging is worthwhile because viable alternatives exist. However, what should people do in inescapable contexts in which there are no alternatives, where one can neither attain nor let go of a hoped-for future (Oettingen 1997a, b)? Inescapable contexts may, for example, exist in tight norm-oriented cultures where norms and rituals specify exactly what a person must do, when, where, and in what way, without allowing individuals to choose and act by themselves (Oettingen 1997a; Gelfand et al. 2011; Triandis 2000). Here, indulging in hopeful, positive fantasies will keep people away from giving up as these fantasies promote passivity and waiting for better times. People will neither actively engage nor actively disengage from reaching their hoped-for future. In other words, when prospects are bleak and obstacles are insurmountable and there are *no action alternatives* (e.g., because of terminal disease, severe poverty, cultural constraints), sheer positive fantasies will allow people to endure by passively waiting for better times. Or take as an example the 2020 COVID-19 pandemic. For us who are not experts in the medical or financial fields there were no valid means we could apply to broadly stop the virus and its consequences on a societal level. At the same time, we could not disengage from the idea that the society would return to a better life. How can we keep up our hopes? Indulging in positive fantasies is the answer to this question. Mental contrasting would lead us to recognize the insurmountable obstacle and disengage us from our positive fantasies for a better life. In inescapable situations, then, our findings suggest, just dreaming about a better future will support us in *staying in the field*. In fact, indulging in positive fantasies makes us patiently endure until a better life returns. It will prevent us from showing frustration, aggression, and then sinking into depression, all processes that have been linked to disengagement from a highly valued incentive (Klinger 1975).

Things are different in situations where our action can make a difference. For example, protecting others and ourselves from getting infected is a positive fantasy that can in most cases be achieved. Here, mental contrasting is the strategy of choice. This is because the positive future (e.g., protection), contrasted with the obstacle standing in the way (e.g., mask is uncomfortable), will help us proactively wear our masks upon leaving the house.

Summary. Hope in terms of positive future fantasies facilitates patient waiting for the hoped-for future, but when contrasted with the obstacles of reality, positive future fantasies produce active engagement to attain the hoped-for future when the obstacle is surmountable and active disengagement when the obstacle is insurmountable. Following these different behavioral functions of hope, people can use indulging in hopeful thoughts to ride out inescapable situations, where neither engagement nor disengagement is possible. However, for those futures that allow active engagement or active disengagement (with reengagement for better alternatives), indulging in positive fantasies means wasting one's energy and resources as people do not seize promising projects nor do they disengage from unpromising ones.

In a recent prototype analysis of hope, the variables of belief, positive future, desire, and possibility were identified as core elements of hope in U.S. and Dutch adults, with desire as the central element (Luo et al. 2022). A prototype analysis is a bottom-up analysis of laypeople's interpretations of hope. However, the central question remains: How do these different variables that laypeople associate with hope play together in affecting thought and feeling, and under which circumstances? A similarly important question is how hope as positive future fantasies relates to the idea that hope is a virtue. Fantasy Realization Theory hopefully is a step toward better understanding the answers to both questions.

8.4   HOPE AS A VIRTUE

The *Concise Catholic Dictionary* defines hope as "[t]he theological virtue which is a supernatural gift bestowed by God through which one trusts God will grant eternal life and the means of obtaining it, providing one cooperates. Hope is composed of desire and expectation together with a recognition of the difficulty to be overcome in achieving eternal life" (Broderick 1944, 77). Similar to the core values of hope as named in the prototype analysis reported above, the three variables constituting the definition of the theological virtue of hope, desire (as indicated by positive future fantasies), expectations (indicated by the beliefs of having the possibility or means to achieve the desire), and recognition of the difficulty to be overcome in achieving the desire (indicated by obstacles of reality), are in line with Fantasy Realization Theory.

Cultivating hope. Specifically, FRT and the findings reported above predict that people who integrate these three variables in their mind become active in pursuing their hoped-for future. Thus, cultivating hope as positive future fantasies contrasted with the obstacles, unveiling one's expectations, should qualify as a virtue. Our findings also indicate that hope in terms of sheer fantasies about a desired future, bare of expectations and recognition of difficulty, will lead to passive and patient waiting for the hoped-for future. The challenge then is to flexibly adjust one's positive future fantasies in terms of indulging versus mental contrasting to the respective context: indulging in inescapable situations, and mental contrasting when the obstacles can be overcome or viable alternatives exist.

The virtue of hopefulness. Similarly, Chignell (this volume) defines the virtue of hopefulness: "*Hopefulness*, in turn, is the trait of being hopeful with respect to various desired outcomes across many different contexts. In some but not all traditions, hopefulness regarding permissible outcomes is commended as a virtue." The virtue of hopefulness may then encompass the adjustment of indulging in fantasies about a desired future versus mental contrasting, depending on what the situation demands. If the situation calls for patient waiting (e.g., for the results of an exam), hopefulness would be expressed in indulging; if the situation calls for active preparation (e.g., studying for taking the exam), hopefulness would be expressed in mental contrasting.

Cascades of hopes. Indulging in positive fantasies allows people to patiently wait for the eventual advent of the better future. Even if people do not frequently imagine the hoped-for future, having a mental representation imprinted by these fantasies might already be enough to allow people to endure in their patient waiting. Importantly, they may also recognize and seize unforeseen opportunities while waiting for the hoped-for future. For example, if a person who has long been unemployed indulges in hopeful fantasies that she eventually will find a job despite low chances of getting reemployed, she might readily recognize feasible opportunities toward employment that she would otherwise miss. If she then mentally contrasts successfully seizing the tangible and feasible opportunities, beyond patiently waiting, the likelihood of eventually finding employment should be increased.

Hope across cultures. Hope in terms of indulging versus mental contrasting should differ across cultures. For example, tight cultures that put normative constraints on their people may foster indulging, while cultures enforcing autonomy and choice may enforce mental contrasting (Oettingen 1997a). Indulging will let people in tight cultures endure the situations that lack freedom of action; mental contrasting will guide people in loose cultures to choose among the many options and then find their individual path to implement the chosen options.

Summary. Hope as positive fantasies can be cultivated by indulging in positive fantasies, or by mentally contrasting these fantasies with obstacles of reality. We argue that the flexible adjustment of these two types of hope can be an advantage for fulfilling hopes, and that practicing such flexibility might create the virtue of hopefulness. Hope in the form of indulging about grand futures can nourish more feasible lower-tier hopes that can be fulfilled via mental contrasting. Whether indulging or mental contrasting is the preferred way of hoping might also depend on the cultural context, whether it is tight and norm-oriented or loose and autonomy focused.

8.5 CONCLUSION

The most prevalent approaches on hope in psychology are based on people's expectancies that are rooted in past experiences. However, I conceptualize hope as positive fantasies about a desired future that can appear in the stream of thought even if there is maximal uncertainty that this event will occur. These fantasies acquire different behavioral functions (hope-directed waiting vs. hope-directed acting) depending on how they are treated in the mind and depending on the given situational context they are used in. Hopefulness as a virtue, then, is achieved when people practice how to flexibly adjust their hopeful fantasies to the respective context. Coming back to St. Cyprian: "What we do not see, we hope for." He taught his followers to indulge in positive fantasies about an afterlife they could not see, thereby helping them to patiently endure the unbearable challenges of their times. In St. Cyprian's own words: "[I]f we hope for what we do not see, we wait for it in patience" (The Crossroads Initiative 2016).

REFERENCES

Atkinson, John William. 1957. "Motivational Determinants of Risk-Taking Behavior." *Psychological Review* 64, part 1 (6): 359–372. doi:10.1037/h0043445

Bandura, Albert. 1977. "Self-Efficacy: Toward a Unifying Theory of Behavioral Change." *Psychological Review* 84 (2): 191–215. doi:10.1037//0033-295x.84.2.191

Bandura, Albert. 1997. *Self-Efficacy: The Exercise of Control*. New York: W. H. Freeman/Times Books/ Henry Holt.

Bloch, Ernst. 1954. *Das Prinzip Hoffnung*. Berlin: Aufbau-Verl.

Bloch, Ernst. 1996. *The Principle of Hope*. 3rd edition. Cambridge, MA: MIT Press.

Brehm, Jack W., and Elizabeth A. Self. 1989. "The Intensity of Motivation." *Annual Review of Psychology* 40 (1): 109–131. doi:10.1146/annurev. ps.40.020189.000545

Broderick, Robert C. 1944. *Concise Catholic Dictionary*. Milwaukee, WI: Bruce.

Byrne, Rhonda. 2006. *The Secret*. New York: Atria Books.

Canfield, Jack, Mark Victor Hansen, and Amy Newmark. 2010. *Chicken Soup for the Soul: Think Positive. 101 Inspirational Stories about Counting Your Blessings and Having a Positive Attitude*. Cos Cob, CT: Chicken Soup for the Soul.

Caprara, Gian Vittorio, Guido Alessandri, Nancy Eisenberg, A. Kupfer, Patrizia Steca, Maria Giovanna Caprara, Susumu Yamaguchi, Ai Fukuzawa, and John Abela. 2012. "The Positivity Scale." *Psychological Assessment* 24 (3): 701–712. doi:10.1037/a0026681 22250591

Carver, Charles S., Paul H. Blaney, and Michael F. Scheier. 1979. "Reassertion and Giving Up: The Interactive Role of Self-Directed Attention and Outcome Expectancy." *Journal of Personality and Social Psychology* 37 (10): 1859–1870. doi:10.1037/0022-3514.37.10.1859

Cheng, Sheung-Tak, Helene H. Fung, and Alfred C. M. Chan. 2009. "Self-Perception and Psychological Well-being: The Benefits of Foreseeing a Worse Future." *Psychology and Aging* 24 (3): 623–633. doi:10.1037/a0016410

The Crossroads Initiative. 2016. "What We Do Not See, We Hope For—St. Cyprian." January 31. https://staging.crossroadsinitiative.com/media/articles/not-see-hope-st-cyprian/.

Cyprian. 2013. *The Complete Works of Saint Cyprian of Carthage*. Merchantville, NJ: Evolution.

Eliott, Jaklin. 2005. *Interdisciplinary Perspectives on Hope*. New York: Nova Science.

Francis. 2020. "Pope Francis's Easter Vigil Homily: Full Text." April 11. https://www.vaticannews.va/en/pope/news/2020-04/pope-francis-homily-easter-vigil-full-text.html.

Gelfand, Michele, Jana Raver, Lisa Nishii, Lisa Leslie, Janetta Lun, Beng Lim, Lili Duan, Assaf Almaliach, Soon Ang, Jakobina Arnadottir, Zeynep Aycan, Klaus Boehnke, Pawel Boski, Rosa Cabecinhas, Darius Chan, Jagdeep Chhokar, Alessia D'Amato, Montse Ferrer, Iris Fischlmayr, and Susumu Yamaguchi. 2011. "Differences between Tight and Loose Cultures: A 33-Nation Study." *Science* 332: 1100–1104. doi:10.1126/science.1197754

Golding, Jacqueline M., and Jerome L. Singer. 1983. "Patterns of Inner Experience: Daydreaming Styles, Depressive Moods, and Sex Roles." *Journal of Personality and Social Psychology* 45 (3): 663–675. doi:10.1037/0022-3514.45.3.663

Green, Leonard, Joel Myerson, David Lichtman, Suzanne Rosen, and Astrid Fry. 1996. "Temporal Discounting in Choice between Delayed Rewards: The Role of Age and Income." *Psychology and Aging* 11 (1): 79–84. doi:10.1037/0882-7974.11.1.79 8726373

Green, Leonard, Joel Myerson, and Ariana Vanderveldt. 2014. "Delay and Probability Discounting." In *The Wiley Blackwell Handbook of Operant and Classical Conditioning*, edited by Frances K. McSweeney and Eric S. Murphy, 307–337. John Wiley & Sons.

James, William. 1890. *The Principles of Psychology*. New York, NY: H. Holt.

Kappes, Heather Barry, Andreas Kappes, and Gabriele Oettingen. 2015. "When Attainment Is All in Your Head." Unpublished manuscript.

Kappes, Heather Barry, Gabriele Oettingen, and Doris Mayer. 2012. "Positive Fantasies Predict Low Academic Achievement in Disadvantaged Students." *European Journal of Social Psychology* 42 (1): 53–64. doi:10.1002/ejsp.838

Kappes, Heather Barry, Bettina Schwörer, and Gabriele Oettingen. 2012. "Needs Instigate Positive Fantasies of Idealized Futures." *European Journal of Social Psychology* 42 (3): 299–307. doi:10.1002/ejsp.1854

Kappes, Heather Barry, Eesha Sharma, and Gabriele Oettingen. 2013. "Positive Fantasies Dampen Charitable Giving When Many Resources Are Demanded." *Journal of Consumer Psychology* 23 (1): 128–135. doi:10.1016/j.jcps.2012.02.001

Klinger, Eric. 1975. "Consequences of Commitment to and Disengagement from Incentives." *Psychological Review* 82 (1): 1–25. doi:10.1037/h0076171

Klinger, Eric. 1990. *Daydreaming: Using Waking Fantasy and Imagery for Self-Knowledge and Creativity.* Los Angeles: Jeremy P. Tarcher.

Lang, Frieder R., David Weiss, Denis Gerstorf, and Gert G. Wagner. 2013. "Forecasting Life Satisfaction across Adulthood: Benefits of Seeing a Dark Future?" *Psychology and Aging* 28 (1): 249–261. doi:10.1037/a0030797 23421319

Luo, Siria Xiyueyao, Femke Van Horen, Kobe Millet, and Marcel Zeelenberg. 2022. "What We Talk about When We Talk about Hope: A Prototype Analysis." *Emotion* 22 (4): 751–768.

Marcel, Gabriel. 1978. *Homo Viator: Introduction to a Metaphysic of Hope.* Gloucester, MA: Peter Smith.

McClelland, David C. 1980. "Motive Dispositions: The Merits of Operant and Respondent Measures." In *Review of Personality and Social Psychology*, edited by Ladd Wheeler, 10–41. Beverly Hills, CA: Sage.

Mischel, Walter. 1973. "Toward a Cognitive Social Learning Reconceptualization of Personality." *Psychological Review* 80 (4): 252–283. doi:10.1037/h0035002

Murray, Henry A. 1943. *Thematic Apperception Test Manual.* Cambridge, MA: Harvard University Press.

O'Connor, Rory C., Roger Smyth, and J. Mark G. Williams. 2015. "Intrapersonal Positive Future Thinking Predicts Repeat Suicide Attempts in Hospital-Treated Suicide Attempters." *Journal of Consulting and Clinical Psychology* 83 (1): 169–176. doi:10.1037/a0037846

Oettingen, Gabriele. 1997a. "Culture and Future Thought." *Culture & Psychology* 3 (3): 353–381. doi:10.1177/1354067x9733008

Oettingen, Gabriele. 1997b. *Psychologie des Zukunftsdenkens* (The Psychology of Thinking about the Future). Goettingen: Hogrefe.

Oettingen, Gabriele. 1999. "Free Fantasies about the Future and the Emergence of Developmental Goals." In *Action and Self-Development: Theory and Research through the Life Span*, edited by Jochen Brandtstädter and Richard M. Lerner, 315–342. Thousand Oaks, CA: Sage.

Oettingen, Gabriele. 2012. "Future Thought and Behaviour Change." *European Review of Social Psychology* 23 (1): 1–63. doi:10.1080/10463283.2011.643698

Oettingen, Gabriele. 2014. *Rethinking Positive Thinking: Inside the New Science of Motivation.* New York: Penguin Random House.

Oettingen, Gabriele, and Doris Mayer. 2002. "The Motivating Function of Thinking about the Future: Expectations versus Fantasies." *Journal of Personality and Social Psychology* 83 (5): 1198–1212. doi:10.1037//0022-3514.83.5.1198

Oettingen, Gabriele, Doris Mayer, and Sam Portnow. 2016. "Pleasure Now, Pain Later: Positive Fantasies about the Future Predict Symptoms of Depression."

Psychological Science 27 (3): 345–353. doi:10.1177/0956797615620783 26825106

Oettingen, Gabriele, Hyeon-ju Pak, and Karoline Schnetter. 2001. "Self-Regulation of Goal Setting: Turning Free Fantasies about the Future into Binding Goals." *Journal of Personality and Social Psychology* 80 (5): 736–753. doi:10.1037//0022-3514.80.5.736

Oettingen, Gabriele, and A. Timur Sevincer. 2018. "Fantasy about the Future as Friend and Foe." In *The Psychology of Thinking about the Future*, edited by Gabriele Oettingen, A. Timur Sevincer, and Peter M. Gollwitzer, 127–149. New York: Guilford Press.

Oettingen, Gabriele, A. Timur Sevincer, and Peter M. Gollwitzer, eds. 2018. *The Psychology of Thinking about the Future*. New York: Guilford Press.

Oettingen, Gabriele, and Thomas A. Wadden. 1991. "Expectation, Fantasy, and Weight Loss: Is the Impact of Positive Thinking Always Positive?" *Cognitive Therapy and Research* 15 (2): 167–175. doi:10.1007/bf01173206

Schnoor, Heike. 1988. *Psychoanalyse der Hoffnung: Die psychische und psychosomatische Bedeutung von Hoffnung und Hoffnungslosigkeit*. Heidelberg: Asanger.

Schultheiss, Oliver C., Diana Yankova, Benjamin Dirlikov, and Daniel J. Schad. 2009. "Are Implicit and Explicit Motive Measures Statistically Independent? A Fair and Balanced Test Using the Picture Story Exercise and a Cue- and Response-Matched Questionnaire Measure." *Journal of Personality Assessment* 91 (1): 72–81. doi:10.1080/00223890802484456

Schunk, Dale H., and Maria K. DiBenedetto. 2018. "Expectations in the Academic Domain." In *The Psychology of Thinking about the Future*, edited by G. Oettingen, A. T. Sevincer, and P. M. Gollwitzer, 153–173. New York: Guilford Press.

Sciarappo, John, Elyse Norton, Gabriele Oettingen, and Peter M. Gollwitzer. 2015. "Positive Fantasies of Winning Money Reduce Temporal Discounting." Unpublished manuscript.

Seligman, Martin E. P. 1991. *Learned Optimism*. New York: Knopf.

Singer, Jerome L. 1966. *Daydreaming: An Introduction to the Experimental Study of Inner Experience*. 2nd edition. New York: Crown/Random House.

Snyder, Charles R. 1989. "Reality Negotiation—From Excuses to Hope and Beyond." *Journal of Social and Clinical Psychology* 8 (2): 130–157. doi:10.1521/jscp.1989.8.2.130

Snyder, Charles R. 2002. "Target Article: Hope Theory. Rainbows in the Mind." *Psychological Inquiry* 13 (4): 249–275. doi:10.1207/s15327965pli1304_01

Stotland, Ezra. 1969. *The Psychology of Hope*. San Francisco: Jossey-Bass.

Taylor, Shelley E., and Jonathon D. Brown. 1988. "Illusion and Well-being: A Social Psychological Perspective on Mental Health." *Psychological Bulletin* 103 (2): 193–210. doi:10.1037/0033-2909.103.2.193

Taylor, Shelley E., Lien B. Pham, Inna D. Rivkin, and David A. Armor. 1998. "Harnessing the Imagination: Mental Simulation, Self-Regulation, and Coping." *American Psychologist* 53 (4): 429–439. doi:10.1037/0003-066X.53.4.429

Triandis, Harry. 2000. "Cultural Syndromes and Subjective Well Being." In *Culture and Subjective Well-Being*, edited by Ed Diener and Eunkook M. Suh, 13–36. Cambridge, MA: MIT Press.

Wright, Rex A. 1996. "Brehm's Theory of Motivation as a Model of Effort and Cardiovascular Response." In *The Psychology of Action: Linking Cognition and Motivation to Behavior*, edited by Peter M. Gollwitzer and John A. Bargh, 424–453. New York: Guilford Press.

Chapter 9

Hope and the Utopian Impulse

There is a strong conceptual link between utopianism and hope. . . .
[I]t is clearly impossible to be a committed utopian without some
sense of hope. (Bell 2017, 8)

9.1 INTRODUCTION

It is often taken for granted that an intrinsic, positive relationship
exists between "utopia" and "hope." They nurture and feed off each
other, hope driving the utopian impulse, utopianism inspiring hope.
Utopianism has been described as "a vocabulary of hope" (Halpin
2003, 44) and "a form of hope" (Cates 2015, 25). It is commonplace to refer to utopian texts as "visions" of hope (McKenna 2001,
1). Craig Hammond (2017, 6) argues that hope is always already
imbued with utopian potential, while Henri Desroche (1979, 23)
describes the two as "twin sisters." David Pinder (2005, vii) suggests
that rekindling the utopian imagination is necessary in order "to sustain a sense of hope" amid increasingly hopeless conditions. Indeed,
utopianism has been heralded as a means of recapturing the category

Darren Webb, *Hope and the Utopian Impulse* In: *The Virtue of Hope*. Edited by: Nancy E. Snow,
Oxford University Press. © Oxford University Press 2024. DOI: 10.1093/oso/9780190069575.003.0010

of hope for critical social theory (Anderson 2006; Browne 2005). For Tom Moylan (2000, 157), "radical hope" operates as "the correlate sociopolitical position" of the utopian genre, and utopian ideas are seen as essential for the cultivation of new "movements of hope" (Fournier 2002).

What I want to do here is dig beneath these surface-level associations. The chapter argues that hope is a complex category of human experience that is not an unmitigated good and is not always or necessarily aligned with a utopian sensibility.[1] In its broadest sense—in the sense that we need to distinguish it from belief, desire, expectation, wish, optimism, faith, etc.—hope can be understood as a positive orientation, open to disappointment, toward an uncertain and (ordinarily) future good. However, the objective of hope (that toward which hope is directed) and the characteristics of its positive orientation (its associated emotional, cognitive, and behavioral dimensions) can vary in significant ways. The mode in which hope is experienced at any particular time, in any particular culture, within any particular group, is the result of a complex process of social mediation. What this means is that different individuals and social classes, at different historical junctures, embedded in different social relations, enjoying different opportunities and facing different constraints, will experience hope in different ways. Hope is not a singular undifferentiated experience but a socially mediated human capacity—"an ambivalent capacity" not in and of itself "virtuous" (Swenson-Lengyel, this volume)—experienced with varying affective-cognitive-behavioral dimensions.

The concept of utopia carries with it still some pejorative connotations. Rather than referring to a rigid blueprint that suppresses difference and seeks to impose coercive order on the diversity of human life, utopia here denotes both a mode of immanent praxis and a collectively elaborated guiding vision, each reinforcing the other in an iterative pedagogical process. The term "utopian *impulse*" is neither teleological nor essentialist. I am not implying that a utopian impulse is a "transhistorical anthropological constant" (Papastephanou 2009, 43) or "a defining, constitutive feature of humanity" (Bauman 2003, 11), nor am I presenting this impulse in terms of some inchoate future calling to the present (Bloch 1995). Rather, I suggest that in and through the process of social life (the process of creating and sustaining families, friendships, communities, commitments, and forms of cooperation), imaginary landscapes take shape. These landscapes comprise complex, fluid, and often contradictory patterns of desires, needs, fears, hostilities, dreams, ethical norms, symbolic meanings, etc., and the landscapes emerge through a collective process of engagement, struggle, contestation, and shared learning. The utopian impulse—we might also call it the utopian *moment*, the utopian *shift*, the change in momentum implied by the word "impulse"—arises when utopian desire and a utopian horizon are located and *felt* within these imaginary landscapes. I emphasize the affective dimension because we might describe the utopian impulse as "the discovery of a new structure of feeling" (Williams 1991, 266), a structure of feeling that emerges when the imaginary landscapes born of the processes and struggles of social life point to the reconstitution of the *totality* of material conditions giving rise to experiences of alienation, exploitation, degradation, minoritization, and oppression.

If the utopian impulse is best understood as a social process, then one can talk about the ways in which different modes of hoping help nurture, support, constrain, or negate such a process. Different modes of hoping possess different utopian orientations. Here I part company a little with Ernst Bloch, the German Marxist philosopher whose work underpins much of the field of utopian studies. Although Bloch (1995) recognized hope as a highly differentiated human experience, he also maintained that "every hope implies the highest good" (108) and constitutes a "cipher" or "attempted signature" (1352) of the Absolute All. For Bloch (1995, 112), even the weakest hope outstrips its mundane limited content and "essentially refers" to the Authentic. While arguing that the *content* of hope is historically and ideologically constructed, Bloch never let go of the association between the *experience* of hope and utopia. In what follows, I develop a taxonomy of modes of hoping and offer some thoughts on their utopian orientation. Contra Bloch, I suggest that we can talk quite seriously about *anti-utopian hope*—about modes of hoping that negate "the utopian impulse"—just as much as we can talk about utopia and hope as twin sisters.[2] Arguing that hope in its transformative mode most clearly aligns with the utopian impulse, I conclude with a brief excursus on Occupy Wall Street to illustrate how pedagogical intervention is required in order to mobilize transformative hope.

Before exploring each mode of hoping in its specificity, it is important to differentiate at an overarching level between "open-ended" and "goal-directed" hope, between modes of hoping lacking a determinate objective and modes of hoping directed toward a concrete specific goal (akin to the distinction made by Gulliford, this volume, between *hoping-in* and *hoping-that*). Regarding the latter, the proper objective of hope is commonly taken to be a desire that is both significant to the hoper and future-oriented (Waterworth 2004, 5–6).[3] What, however, does it mean to hope for such? Here I differentiate three modes of goal-directed hope: "sound," "resolute" and "transformative." Regarding the former, the experience of open-ended hope is underpinned by a sense that we as human beings are wayfarers who remain as yet undefined, have within us what we could become, and are traveling the path to ourselves (Dauenhauer 1986; Marcel 1962). Hope is the human attribute which simultaneously reconciles us to our ontological status as a traveler and propels us along the path to ourselves. In broad terms, it is characterized by "an openness of spirit with respect to the future" and offers "an intangible umbrella that protects hoping persons by casting a positive glow on life" (Godfrey 1987, 64; Dufault and Martocchio 1985, 380). There is a profound difference, however—in terms of the way in which this openness of spirit and positive glow are experienced—between what I term "patient" and "critical" hope. While acknowledging from the outset that the taxonomy offered here is an artifice that cannot possibly capture hope in all its complexity, I do regard it as useful as an analytical frame.

9.2 PATIENT HOPE

Patient hope is directed toward an objective which lies "beyond our capacity to grasp" (Boscaljon 2015, xv). It is a hope devoid of images. This hope may be characterized as an openness of spirit with respect to the outcome of the ontological journey (Godfrey 1987, 144; Schumacher 2003, 36), or it may be characterized as an openness of spirit with respect to the journey itself, i.e., the general conviction that being en route makes sense and has meaning (Dauenhauer 1986; Havel 1990; Mittleman 2009). Either way, Gabriel Marcel—the French philosopher and dramatist regarded by some as having offered "possibly the most important exploration of hope" (Grady 1970, 56)—captures one of the defining features of this mode of hoping when he states that the nature of its objective "transcends imagination" and "every kind of representation," so that in hoping "I do not allow myself to imagine what I hope for" (Marcel 1962, 45–46).[4] To imaginatively represent to oneself the objective of one's hope implies an illusion open to disappointment. To refuse this temptation is to embrace, in true openness of spirit, the meaningfulness of one's status as *homo viator*. For Marcel, therefore, hope refuses to lay down any conditions, makes no claims on the future, and insists on nothing.

The positive glow cast by hope has three dimensions: it is underpinned by a basic trust in ourselves, others, life, and the underlying goodness of the world (Mittleman 2009; Sacks 2000; Schumacher

2003); it affords a feeling of safety and security of and in one's being (Kast 1994; Marcel 1962); and it instills a patient calm. Precisely because of the security afforded by its positive glow, hope allows one to relax and to let life take its course, providing the hoping human with the "freedom to let events unfold in their own time" (Kast 1994, 146). For Marcel hope represents a "positive non-acceptance" of life's trials and tragedies, a non-acceptance which is to be distinguished from revolt because its characteristics are silence, modesty, timidity, humility, patience, relaxation, and security (Marcel 1962, 38). It is hope in this patient mode that sustained Plenty Coups amid the collapse of Crow culture, enabling him to stand firm and endure disaster guided by a hope directed toward "a goodness in the world that transcends one's ability to grasp what it is" (Lear 2006, 100).

As one might expect, patience is the key behavioral dimension of this mode of hoping. To hope is to appeal to the existence of a certain creative power in the world, and while it is hope's "mission" to respond to conditions of adversity, the response requires no "sense of effort" on the part of the hoper (Marcel 1962, 31, 36). In seeking delivery from present darkness, "hope is not interested in the how" and is not searching for a concrete solution to life's trials, for the "technical question" of ends and means is alien to the character of hope (Marcel 1962, 51–52). To hope is to be patient, "to take one's time," to trust in the underlying goodness of the world, and to rest assured that a solution to life's trials just will be found (Marcel 1962, 39). In contrast to the impatient desire for gratification, hoping in this mode demands steadfast patience and fortitude (Boscaljon 2015, xiii). For Lear (2006, 92–94, 100–103), Plenty Coups' hope was *radical* by virtue of the sheer commitment needed to survive the destruction of a way of life by holding onto the hope that something good will emerge even if this outstrips our current capacity to understand it.[5]

Bernard Dauenhauer (1986) presents the case for secular patient hope. For Dauenhauer, to be human is to be essentially and radically, always and necessarily, en route. Rejecting the notion of a human telos, he argues that hope is directed primarily toward other human beings and is characterized by an expectation concerning their efficacious agency. What the hoper looks for in the agency of others is not the realization of a determinate goal, for hope transcends all such goals and the outcome of human action is always indeterminate. Rather, the hoper expectantly awaits transformations in her relationships with other humans and the non-human world, these transformations being valued for their own intrinsic worth. To hope is thus to ascribe intrinsic value to one's enroutedness, to place one's trust in the efficacy of human agents while accepting its contingent indeterminacy, and to possess the conviction that whatever journey we are taken on by ourselves, via others, will be of positive worth. Emphasizing the similarities between his own reading of hope and what he regards as the Old Testament understanding, Dauenhauer (1984, 456) argues that hope is associated with quietness, "standing firm," and "waiting for." As such, for Dauenhauer (2005, 87), as for Marcel, "hope demands patience."

Patient hope possesses an anti-utopian functionality. However one conceives it—as system, process, or orientation—utopia is a distinctly imaginative-desiderative phenomenon. Imagination and desire are constitutive of any understanding of utopia. One of the defining features of patient hope, however, is precisely the way in which it "transcends imagination" and "transcends desire." For Marcel (1967, 278), "Hope is of a different order from desire." They are qualitatively different orders of experience. It is instructive here to look at Ruth Levitas' (1990, 8) definition of utopia as "the expression of the desire for a better way of being." This is possibly the most-quoted and most widely adopted definition of utopia there is, and yet Marcel would have dismissed it as an oxymoron. He would have argued that "a better way of being," *qua* the objective of hope, transcends desire and cannot find "expression" in its terms. As the activity of the covetous "I" impatiently seeking satisfaction and fulfillment, desire belongs solely to "the domain of having." Only hope—the hope of the patient "we" who have abandoned ourselves in unconditional confidence to the mystery of Being, thus entering into loving communion with an Other in whom we trust—only absolute hope of this kind is capable of expressing humanity's ontological journey toward a better way of being.

Similarly, when Levitas (1990, 199–200) talks of the need for utopias to carry hope as well as express desire if any change at all is to be effected, Marcel would have argued that this was impossible. As phenomena rooted firmly in the impatient imagination—and precisely because they *are* expressions of desire—utopias at best would have been deemed capable of carrying what he scathingly refers to as a "miserable substitute" or "the toxic succedaneum" of authentic hope (Marcel 1962, 56). Rather than grounding and driving utopianism, hope in its patient mode refuses, resists, and negates the utopian impulse. Utopia in both its prescriptive and heuristic forms liberates the imagination and opens a space in which the existing order of things is criticized and challenged. Patient hope, however, transcends the imagination and opens up a space within which the existing order of things is domesticated. Marcel argues that hope cannot ground a movement for social transformation and that it is an illusion to think that readjusting the material, social, and institutional conditions of life can alleviate human suffering: "There can be no question here of my attempting to define anything resembling a political line of action. What we have to deal with is rather an inner attitude" (Marcel 1978, 244). Individuals are confronted with a choice; one either welcomes or rejects the gift of hope. To welcome and embrace this gift is to orient oneself toward the world in a spirit of humble, courageous, trusting patience. For Marcel, to hope is not to transform the world itself (either imaginatively or materially) but is rather to transform one's "inner attitude" toward it.[6]

9.3 CRITICAL HOPE

Like patient hope, critical hope is characterized by an openness of spirit with respect to the future. For Protestant theologian Jürgen Moltmann (1970), who came to prominence in the 1960s as one of the leading figures in the "political theology" movement (and whose *Theology of Hope* has been read as a theological parallel to Bloch's *Principle of Hope*), the proper objective of hope is a new heaven and new earth, a future which is radically new and unpredictable. For Ernst Bloch (1995, 1375), the objective of hope is the Novum Ultimum, the Absolute and Authentic human All, the nature of which is "still utterly opaque" and "remains still concealed." For each, however, the openness of spirit that characterizes hope does not imply that one can say nothing about its objective. Moltmann argues that in the resurrection of Christ one finds God's promise to humanity that oppression, humiliation, and degradation will be overcome. To hope in Christ is thus to demand this. For his part Bloch argues that hope, the human longing born of the No to deprivation and the experience of unfulfillment, is necessarily directed toward a world without degradation, suffering, and anxiety. For both, humans can grasp the future, not in positive terms but as "the negation of the negative" (Moltmann 1970, 114).

Hope's positive glow offers here no comforting refuge but rather stimulates a restless protest against present suffering. In the cognitive-affective domain, the experience of hope is captured by the phrase "something's missing." For Moltmann (1967, 19), hope as an emotional experience is grounded in "the contradiction between the word of promise and the experiential reality of suffering and death." If the resurrection of Christ promised the negation of suffering, then "[t]hose who hope in Christ can no longer put up with reality as it is, but begin to suffer under it, to contradict it" (Moltmann 1967, 21). As the promise of a future which is not-yet, the objective of hope

285

stimulates in the affective domain a "passionate suffering and passionate longing" which manifests in the behavioral domain as "the criticism of present misery" (Moltmann 1967, 16; 1970, 114–115). For Bloch, hope is experienced as a restless, future-oriented longing for that which is missing. This emotion takes on a cognitive dimension when it is consciously known and recognized as the feeling that draws us on into what is better. In the behavioral domain, conscious-known hope is always critical of that which exists precisely because it comprehends itself as an interior force pushing the hoper toward the not yet discovered and as yet concealed Absolute All. The hoper has no clear idea of what this Absolute All might be, but experiences its lack and its forward pull as the compulsion to critically negate the negative.[7]

Moltmann (1967, 21) tells us that the experience of hope as the protest against lack "stabs inexorably into the flesh of every unfulfilled present." While for Marcel, a restless, critical conflict with the world would be regarded as a sin against hope, these are the defining features of critical hope. To take a literary example, in George Orwell's *Nineteen Eighty-Four* Winston Smith is animated by critical hope. His hope is directed toward "the place where there is no darkness" and Winston is stimulated by the pull of this future promised by O'Brien in his dreams. "The place where there is no darkness was the imagined future, which one could never see, but which, by foreknowledge, one could mystically share in" (Orwell 1949, 107). In the affective domain, what this meant for Winston was that "always in your stomach and in your skin there was a sort of protest, a feeling that you had been cheated of something that you had a right to" (Orwell 1949, 63). This sense that something's missing, felt in the stomach and the skin as the hoper responds to the pull of a mystical future, stimulates critical protest against the way things are.

Lia Haro (2010) offers an excellent case study of the critical hope underpinning the politics of the Zapatistas. Born of the No to subjugation and suffering, and taking shape in and through the darkness of powerlessness, humiliation, and death, the hope of the Zapatistas expresses a restless, stabbing, agitated rejection of the totality of structures of oppression. The objective of hope assumes no specific utopian content but is rather "something not-yet known, not-yet imaginable within the limits and terms of current horizons," but nonetheless already inscribed "ahead, in the next step we are going to take" (Haro 2010, 194, 203). While the patient hoper may take refuge in the mysterious unimaginability of hope's objective, the Zapatistas restlessly throw themselves deeper into the present world and create "alternative horizons of possibility" through living together in a critical, restless spirit of "Basta!" (Haro 2010, 199).

Critical hope possesses a complex utopian functionality. Moltmann makes it clear that while hope demands a passionate critical engagement with the present, it must avoid becoming fixed on a dogmatic prescription of the positive awaiting humanity. Indeed, he discusses utopianism under the rubric of the sin of presumption, both the presumptuous anticipation of the form to be taken by God's promised freedom and the self-willed praxis which attempts to fulfill this promise within history (Moltmann 1967, 1996). One must be careful here, however, to specify the character of the utopianism being rejected by Moltmann. Philip Wegner argues that utopia performs two pedagogical operations—deterritorialization, or the critical dismantling of existent social norms and institutions, and reterritorialization, or the production of new forms and institutions through the education of desire (Wegner 2002, 17–25). For Moltmann, hope possesses a deterritorializing utopian function but resists the urge to reterritorialize.[8] To live in the light of hope is to critically engage with the suffering of the present while remaining "open for the coming kingdom" (Moltmann 1975, 188). It is, in fact, to be doubly critical—critical of the unfulfilled present but critical also of any movements of presumption which strive to anticipate and realize the fulfillment promised by and only realizable through God.

Critical hope thus rejects the present in light of a future *novum* which refuses positive representation. This can be seen clearly in Haro's analysis of the hope of the Zapatistas. And this is precisely what utopian scholars find most attractive about Bloch: his provocative use of the *novum ultimum* as "a trope for that which is never fully attained," his conceptualization of humanity as a process forever open to the future, and his insistence that to settle for any goal along the way is "to pause fatally on the path to a homeland which still lies ahead" (Moylan 1997, 117). Bloch, of course, fell foul of his own proscriptions against foreclosing the future, but Moylan (1997) is right to emphasize the need for will-full utopians with long-range visions to engage in critiques of their own praxis in order to avoid hypostatization. However, the danger here is that utopian projects carried by an open-ended hope might never offer anything *more* than a No! to deprivation and "the criticism of present misery" (Moltmann 1970, 114–115). I have argued this point many times before (Webb 2009, 2013, 2016, 2017) but, as David Harvey rightly emphasizes, utopia shorn of vision and goal—the deterritorializing utopia carried by open-ended critical hope—remains "a pure signifier of hope destined never to acquire a material referent," an infinitely circulating self-referential process that has "the habit of getting lost in the romanticism of endlessly open projects" (Harvey 2000, 189, 174). I develop this point further in the concluding section.

9.4 SOUND HOPE

The analytic philosopher John Patrick Day famously told us that "a hope is identical with a desire plus a probability estimate," where "A desires in some degree that Q, and A believes that the probability of Q is >0<1" (Day 1969, 89; 1991, 37). This root understanding of hope has formed the basis of much discussion within analytical philosophy. An extensive literature highlights the dangers associated with "false hope," an overconfident probability estimate akin to wishful thinking and liable to lead to frustration, disappointment, and despair (Polivy and Herman 2000). In the "hope = desire + probability estimate" model, false hope is likely to develop when the fervor of the desiderative aspect serves to raise the subjective probability estimate beyond that which is warranted by the available evidence (Averill, Catlin, and Chon 1990, 96; Bovens 1999, 678). Macquarrie (1978, 15) refers to this as "the pathology of hope," in which hope runs riot and loses its grip on reality. Sound hope, on the other hand, requires a careful study of the evidence and an accurate calculation of the likelihood of one's hoped-for objective coming to pass (Godfrey 1987, 30). Precisely in order to avoid the dangers associated with false hope, Bovens (1999, 678) argues that the strength of the hoper's beliefs "should be determined by the available evidence." Sound hope can thus be characterized as a hope directed toward a significant future good involving a probability calculation which, in order to prevent the hoper losing their grip on reality, is based on a careful study of the evidence.

In terms of its associated behavioral response, some argue that sound hope helps counteract risk aversion. Bovens (1999, 672) in particular emphasizes that "the value of hope is that it makes us focus on the possible gains in more than fair gambles." He also claims that "fear is an antidote to the risk proneness that makes us all too eager to take up less than fair gambles" (Bovens 1999, 672). Sound hope is thus a highly regulated counter to risk aversion. The careful survey of the evidence characteristic of sound hope leads the hoper to identify which gambles are worth taking and which are not. One may hope for the entire set {significant future good the estimated probability of which is >0<1} but only a particular subset {more than fair gambles} prompts a behavioral response. The relationship between sound hope and action is thus uncertain and contingent. Some hopes would be considered less than fair gambles and not worth actively pursuing, while those considered more than fair gambles may prompt goal pursuit.

This resonates with the notions of "complex" and "robust" hope that are popular within educational discourse (Arthur and Sawyer 2009; Halpin 2003, 2007; Sawyer et al. 2007; Singh 2007). The key characteristics here are that the objective of hope is realistic, is grounded in a sound assessment of the evidence, recognizes the obstacles confronting its realization, and is vulnerable to evidence that counts against it. Objectives that are overly ambitious are dismissed as less than fair gambles. While inspiring hope is presented as the educator's duty, it is also their responsibility to avoid the kind of hope variously derided as fanciful, naive, unrealistic, and "hokey" (Duncan-Andrade 2009). Even when confronting ecological catastrophe, "our hopes related to planetary health must be generated in the context of what is realistically possible" (Kretz 2019, 163–164). The kind of "sound" hope that educators are called on to embrace and nurture is one that offers no illusions and is grounded in a realistic grasp of structural constraints (Carlson 2005). Hope here has a "steadying" role, resisting optimism and presumption while avoiding pessimism and despair (see Michael Lamb's chapter, this volume). As Aronson (1999, 489) describes it, sound hope has "a lofty sense of possibility" tempered by "a gritty sense of limits."

Given that sound hope is grounded in a sense of realistic possibility, on the basis of a careful study of "the way things are," such hopes are unlikely to be transformative. Precisely because such hopes are tapered to reality, subsequent goal pursuit will tend to reproduce this reality rather than transform it (Waterworth 2004, 81). Indeed, Bovens (1999, 674) notes that "it is notoriously difficult to make sense of utopian hopes" because, quite simply, from the perspective of the sound hoper, they make no sense. Having said this, in a recent discussion of the modes of hoping framework Julia Cook (2018, 384) suggests that sound hope may "orient individuals toward utopian forms of thinking by forming the preconditions under which they may occur." In fact, consistent with this, the educationalists who rally round the notions of "complex" and "robust" hope do indeed make utopian claims on behalf of their ideas.

I have argued elsewhere, however, that sound hope tames and tempers the utopian impulse, recuperating its radicality in the name of utopian realism (Webb 2009, 2016). Within both the "complex" and "robust" hope projects, a concerted effort is made to redefine the utopian. Utopia is no longer a vision of an alternative state or society but is rather "a vision of utopia which has the possibility of achievement in present socio-economic conditions" (Sawyer et al. 2007, 228). This ideological recuperation of utopia is troubling because its effect is to delimit the range of the possible—the possibilities offered by hope are limited to what, given a sound assessment of the evidence, can reasonably be achieved within existing parameters—and to suppress the critical and transformative modes of hoping that can genuinely be associated with the utopian. As Levitas (2013, 127) rightly notes: "Some overtly positive discussions of utopia privilege particular models of the real and place severe limits on utopia's alterity that are anti-utopian in effect."[9]

9.5 RESOLUTE HOPE

It is sometimes argued that hope is best understood as hope against the evidence. Presenting the case for such an understanding, Philip Pettit (2004, 159) suggests that "[t]o have hope is to have something we might describe as cognitive resolve." Given that humans are emotional creatures subject to anxiety, grief, and despondency in the face of brute fact, forming strategies on the basis of evidence-based calculations of "how things are" would often lead us to "collapse in a heap of despair and uncertainty, beaten down by cascades of inimical fact" (Pettit 2004, 160). Hope is precisely that quality which enables human beings to galvanize their cognitions in a way that overcomes the burden of evidence. In many substantial cases, to hope for/that p is to desire p and to possess the cognitive resolve that enables one to set aside one's evidence-based belief in the probability of attaining p and to organize one's feelings and actions on the assumption that p is attainable. For Adrienne Martin (2014), hope in its fullest sense (hoping against hope) will see the hoper assign a justificatory rationale for engaging in goal pursuit *however small the outcome's probability* simply because their attachment to the outcome permits it. This mode of hoping is referred to here as "resolute hope."

The most fully developed model of resolute hope is that offered by psychologist Rick Snyder (see Gulliford's chapter in this volume for the wider context of Snyder's hope theory). He defines hope as "goal-directed thinking, in which people appraise their capability to produce workable routes to goals (pathways thinking), along with their potential to initiate and sustain movement via a pathway (agency thinking)" (Snyder 1989, 143). Snyder spends very little time discussing the desiderative-calculative aspects of hope that so occupy analytical philosophers. That the hoper has a desire for some future object that she sees as good but deems difficult is taken for granted as the necessary starting point for hope. It is a given rather than the subject of philosophical inquiry. Snyder's reading of hope also downplays its relation to objective conditions and foregrounds the self-referential belief of the hoper. To hope is to perceive oneself as capable of producing plausible routes to one's desired goals and to perceive oneself as capable of achieving one's goals by moving along the identified pathways (Snyder 2000).

Of particular interest is Snyder's emphasis on the way in which hope manifests as action. If to hope is to perceive oneself as capable of deriving pathways to desired goals, and to motivate oneself via agency thinking to use those pathways, then those who are hopeful will tend to be more energetic, outgoing, and determined and less risk-averse than those who are not (Snyder 2002). *Ceteris paribus*, those who are hopeful will be more likely to attain their desired objectives than those who are not. We are moving far away here from the conception of hope as "a desire plus a probability estimate." The activity of hope moves beyond the affective-cognitive domain and inhabits the domain of behavior. There is no uncertainty or contingency regarding the relationship between resolute hope and human action. To hope resolutely is to be a dogged anti-determinist. To hope in this mode is to assume that one has the freedom to initiate events on the basis of goals that one sets oneself, and to assume that the world is fluid, plastic, and capable of being molded by one's agency as it moves along the pathways one has identified.

Resolute hope is a self-efficacious private hope. When Pettit talks of cognitive resolve, he thinks primarily in terms of the individual hoping resolutely in the face of personal adversity, while Snyder focuses on the kind of hopeful thinking that enables individuals to attain academic, sporting, and occupational goals. The behavioral activities associated with such a mode of hoping can be personally transformative—cognitive resolve may enable the hoper to act in spite of the evidence and overcome adversity, while effective pathways and agency thinking may enable the hoper, against all odds, to achieve excellent academic grades. In broader social terms, however, this mode of hoping helps sustain and nourish the existing order of things. It is well noted that social cohesion requires that individuals within society possess hope. Capitalism requires that individuals study, sell their labor power, consume, save, and invest (Braithwaite 2004; Hage 2002). It therefore requires that individuals possess both future-oriented significant desires and a perception that these can be attained. The sense that one's hopes are being thwarted or are unachievable generates frustration, disillusionment, and despair. Conversely, the perception that one can attain one's objectives, even in spite of the evidence, if one engages in determined goal pursuit premised on effective pathways and agency thinking, is a source of social stability.[10]

It could be argued that the pragmatic account of hope offered by Patrick Shade (2001, 2006) addresses the privatized individualism found within Snyder's hope theory. Shade emphasizes the importance of nurturing "habits of hope" (resourcefulness, courage, and persistence) that he regards as operating in much the same way as Snyder's pathways and agency thinking. Shade's account, however, is framed from the outset by a sensitivity to the wider social issues that impinge on people's life chances.[11] Even here, though, Shade is concerned primarily with nurturing habits of hope within individuals in order that they can overcome obstacles and attain their own private goals within society as presently structured. And while Snyder insists that the field of hope should be leveled and all individuals inculcated with a sense of self-efficacy, this is intended to facilitate psychological adjustment, reduce the incidence of disillusionment and despair among certain segments of society, and thus bolster social stability (Snyder and Feldman 2000). Resolute hope, then, while personally transformative, serves a socially conservative function.

9.6 TRANSFORMATIVE HOPE

Like resolute hope, transformative hope is a mode of hoping against the evidence. Pragmatist philosopher Richard Rorty argues that the activity of striving to ground one's beliefs in the evidence is characteristic of the pursuit of knowledge and understanding and alien to the field of hope. The task of politics, as he sees it, "is a matter of replacing shared knowledge of what is already real with social hope for what might become real" (Rorty 1998, 18–19). For Rorty (1999, 28), "humans have to dream up the point of human life," and our belief in the possibility of attaining the goal we dream up lies not in the evidence but rather in the inspirational qualities of the goal itself, its capacity to "astonish and exhilarate" and thereby expand the horizons of possibility. The proper objective of hope is a "shared utopian dream," and to hope for such is to possess "a sense that the human future can be made different from the human past, unaided by non-human powers" (Rorty 1998, 106; 1999, 208). A hope is not a desire plus a probability estimate grounded in a survey of the evidence, but rather a utopia plus a sense of possibility grounded in a confidence in the powers of human agency. It is "taking the world by the throat and insisting that there is more to this life than we have ever imagined" (Rorty 1998, 138).

For Gustavo Gutiérrez (2001, 217), the Brazilian theologian whose *A Theology of Liberation* is perhaps the defining text of the liberation theology movement, the meaning of human life on earth is to establish justice. This is a utopian project requiring the realization of "a historical plan for a qualitatively different society." Because "[t]he Gospel does not provide a utopia for us," Gutiérrez (2001, 223) insists that "this is a human work." He thus concurs with Rorty that the point of human life is the utopian project of devising a new way of living it. Similarly, for Gutiérrez as for Rorty, hope is the phenomenon that enables human beings to fulfill this project. Hope is characterized as a confident belief in the transformative power of collective praxis and a consciousness that human beings are self-organizing and self-determining historical agents. This profound confidence in the affective-cognitive domain facilitates utopian praxis in the behavioral domain, incorporating both denunciation (the critical repudiation of the present) and annunciation (the positive anticipation of the not-yet).

For Gutiérrez (2001), hope is "the driving force of a future-oriented history" (200) and "fulfils a mobilizing and liberating function" (203). Indeed, hope not only "makes us radically free to commit ourselves to social praxis, motivated by a liberating utopia," but also "simultaneously demands and judges it" (Gutiérrez 2001, 223). To hope is to regard the world as open to human design and history as an "adventure." While the cognitive characteristics of transformative hope are in some ways similar to those of resolute hope (an anti-deterministic perception of the world as malleable), and its behavioral characteristics share something in common with critical hope (the critical repudiation of the present), transformative hope is distinct from each. Whereas the resolute hoper resolves to continue striving for her personal goals within society as presently structured, the transformative hoper critically negates the present and is driven by hope to annunciate a better alternative. This positive annunciation—an act demanded by transformative hope and expressive of the confidence placed in the capacity of human beings to resolve human problems—is an activity alien to the critical hoper, for whom images of the future never move beyond vague assertions of the negation of the negative.

Transformative hope is a mutually efficacious collective hope. A distinctive feature is the nature of its objective and the manner in which this comes to be shared by the members of a group. The first point is important because theories of goal-directed hope tend to ignore the question of how people come to have the goals that they have. It is simply assumed that people have goals, and hope is then presented as a particular way of relating to these emotionally, cognitively, and behaviorally. In most cases the goals are taken to be personal ones pertaining to mental and physical health or to things such as material acquisition and academic and financial success. In the case of transformative hope, however, the objective is a qualitatively different organization of society and a new way of being. With regard to how such objectives might develop within a group, and come to be shared as a goal worth collectively striving for, Karl Mannheim remains instructive. According to Mannheim (1940, 187):

> [I]t is a very essential feature of modern history that in the gradual organization for collective action social classes become effective in transforming historical reality only when their aspirations are embodied in utopias appropriate to the changing situation.

He suggests that utopias which emerge to shatter the status quo first take the form of "the wish-fantasy" of an individual or movement (Mannheim 1940, 185). These wish-fantasies do not appear out of nowhere, however, but seize on currents present in society, give expression to them, flow back into the outlook of a social group, and are translated by this group into action. Rather than corresponding directly to a concrete body of articulated needs, the active utopia "transmits" and "articulates" the amorphous "collective impulse" of a group. Without the appropriate wish-fantasy of an individual or movement seizing on currents present in society, the "collective impulse" of a group remains just an impulse because it lacks the "situationally transcendent ideas" that alone can guide and direct transformative action (Mannheim 1940, 185–187).[12]

In terms of hope theory, the collective impulse for change is likely to be born of a sense that the shared hopes of a group are unattainable—even allowing for a group-level version of cognitive resolve—within society as it stands. The utopian platform presented by an individual or movement becomes an objective of hope if this articulates the amorphous impulse of the group and is perceived by its members as so doing. Born of the frustrated hopes of a social group, the utopian objective—by means of its exhilarating and astonishing qualities—expands the horizons of possibility and gives rise to a sense that the human future can be made different from the human past, unaided by non-human powers. The cognitive-affective dimension of transformative hope, a profound confidence in the power of collective praxis, thus develops as the objective of hope feeds back into the outlook of the group whose thwarted hopes gave rise to its production. The cognitive dimension of hope in turn grounds and inspires concerted goal-directed action, i.e., the behavioral dimension of hope.

9.7 IN LIEU OF A CONCLUSION

In lieu of a conclusion I want to use Occupy Wall Street (OWS) as a brief case study illustration of the sociological application of the modes of hoping framework. Here I will make four claims. The first is that OWS signaled a utopian shift, a utopian moment, the discovery of a new structure of feeling oriented toward the reconstitution of the social totality. In other words, OWS gave clear expression to the utopian impulse. The second claim is that OWS was born of frustrated *patient* hope. One of the things that comes through clearly in the accounts of movement activists is the hope that had been placed in Barack Obama, a patient hope directed not toward some specific concrete objective but directed toward the figure of Obama himself, in whose person so much promise and meaning had been instilled. As Rebecca Solnit (2011, 82) put it, following the financial crisis of 2008 the hopes of so many "focused on a single political candidate to fix it all for us, as he promised he would." Exactly *how* he would fix it all was unclear and indeterminate, but patient hope is not concerned with the technical question of how. Rather one places one's hope in the agency of an Other and awaits patiently in the secure trust that, in ways that outstrip our current capacity to fully grasp, it *will* all get fixed.

If this mode of hoping is characterized by a patience born of trust, then by 2011 its foundations began to crumble. As Todd Gitlin (2012) put it, for Occupy activists, after three years of waiting, Obama "had foregone their trust" (193), "[t]heir patience had finally worn out" (27). The third claim I would make, then, is that the patient hope placed in Obama gave way to a critical hope born of refusal, of a resounding No! What is striking, in fact, about the contemporary accounts is how exactly the experiences of movement actors mapped onto the characteristics of critical hope described in this chapter. Expressing her response to the betrayed hope placed in Obama, one activist said, "I felt like I had been hit in the stomach" (Flank 2011, 216). The critical hope of OWS was a guttural hope of protest felt in the stomach and the skin. Key words used by activists at the time were "restlessness," "agitation," "unsettling unease," "indignation and anger," "discomfort and annoyance" (Mizen 2015). As one put it: "We have no clear idea how life should really feel. . . . We sense something is wrong only through the odd clue. . . . We notice a vague spiritual nausea . . . emptiness . . . darkness" (Anon. 2011). This was a hope underpinned by the sense that something's missing, born in the darkness of the lived moment, experienced as restless, nauseous, passionate indignation and directed toward the negation of the conditions giving rise to profound injustices.[13]

The core activists within OWS famously rejected the need for a utopian vision of an alternative way of being. They directed their hopes instead toward here-and-now immanent praxis in the firm belief that refusal is a generative act, that a Yes is born of enacting the Nos. What this meant, however, is that the critical hope of OWS never became truly transformative. Occupy remained a "vast, inchoate" movement of "global restlessness" (Solnit 2016, 109), "the site of inchoate, undertheorized encounters" (Chrostowska 2016, 285), but never became a force that took the world by the throat and committed itself to the positive annunciation of a liberating utopia. OWS was, in John Holloway's (2010, 35) terms, a crack, a momentary rupture in capitalist space-time. As Holloway says of the cracks, "there is always an insufficiency about [them], an incompleteness, a restlessness." Without guidance and direction, however, the cracks do not open out into anything new. As Holloway (2010, 22) remarks, "it also happens that people get tired and the crack freezes over again." My fourth and final claim, then, is that critical hope requires pedagogical direction if it is to transmute into transformative hope.

Within OWS, the utopian impulse was never fully articulated and mobilized. Instead, it circulated at the level of poetic evocation, as an inchoate amorphous collective desire. As Mannheim notes, however, the inchoate collective impulse of a group needs utopian direction if it is to become a historically transformative force. There is a role for utopian pedagogy here in giving clear utopian form to popular aspirations, of turning critical hope into transformative hope. This role involves "convoking" the radical imagination, animating, enlivening, drawing together, and building on the amorphous utopian imaginings of community or movement members. To "convoke" is "to call something which is not yet fully present into being" (Haiven and Khasnabish 2014, 61). Mavis Biss (2013, 937) refers to this as "the specifically imaginative excellence required to bring inchoate experience to conceptual consciousness." The radical imagination is required to articulate movement actors' strong if inchoate emotions, to crystallize them and present them back in the form of a vision. This should be seen as a collective endeavor and iterative process within which the pedagogue plays a crucial facilitating role. To my mind, indeed, to commit to a transformative utopian pedagogy is the primary responsibility of the activist-scholar.[14]

NOTES

1. While agreeing with Potkay's general argument, expressed masterfully in his sweeping survey (this volume), that hope is not necessarily a virtue or a good, I find something amiss in his suggestion that "the satiric aspect of utopian fiction from More to Huxley" is "underwritten" by a sense that "hope is morally corrosive." The operation of hope within utopian (and dystopian) fiction is complex and fraught and refuses such a simple characterization. For my own reading of how hope plays out in tense and uneasy ways in More's *Utopia*, see Webb (2008).

2. The significance of Bloch's work to the field of utopian studies cannot be overstated. Indeed, his three-volume epic *The Principle of Hope* can be considered constitutive of the field itself. For Terry Eagleton, however, Bloch is treated too uncritically by scholars. Eagleton (2015) is right to point out that "[n]ot all hope is a foretaste of utopia" (103) and that Bloch was "too eager to assume that almost every historical phenomenon . . . can be milked for its emancipatory value" (94). Eagleton's own critique, however, lacks a certain generosity of spirit, both with regard to Bloch himself and to the work of utopian scholars. Jack Zipes (2019, 177) goes as far as to describe Eagleton as a "mudslinger . . . whose shallow mind reflects a good deal of his knowledge about philosophy, politics, and hope," and despairs of "his nasty drivel to discredit Bloch and his philosophy of hope."

3. In everyday usage, it is true, we often use the word "hope" to refer to objectives about which we could scarcely care less (I hope dinner arrives soon). These mundane uses of hope are probably best characterized as want (Quinn 1976, 61–62). Similarly, while "hope" can be used to refer to retrospective objectives (I hope you had a good journey), such cases are better understood as instances of wishing (Gravlee 2000, 469). And while there are cases (in palliative care, for example) in which hope takes the form of "hope for the present" (Callina, Snow, and Murray 2018), hope is ordinarily directed toward an objective that is future-oriented.

4. Adrienne Martin thus terms this mode of hoping "unimaginable hope" (Martin 2014, 100).

5. Nancy Snow (2019, 11) refers to the hope described by Marcel and Lear as receptivity theories in that "hoping involves forms of receptivity, such as patience, waiting, and openness."

6. The conservative anti-utopian thrust of patient hope comes through clearly in Charles Péguy's epic theological poem, *The Portal of the Mystery of Hope*. Péguy (1996) presents hope as the mysterious virtue that enables humanity to endure a life of endless repetition, a seemingly futile procession of trials and disappointments. Its effect is to soothe and console suffering creatures, on whom bad days fall like persistent slanting autumn rain. A key theme of

the poem is that Christian hope *demands* that the trials of life be endured with patient, quiet serenity. To confront life with anxiety, restlessness, disquiet, and protest is to betray hope. Developing this theme, Glenn Tinder (2001) argues that the defining characteristic of hope is "situational obedience." In submitting through hope to the mysterious creativity of God, we submit also to the harsh demands of the situation in which we find ourselves. The behavioral imperative of hope thus becomes: "To attend to the personal and historical circumstances surrounding us, without trying to see where they are ultimately carrying us, and to do whatever these circumstances require and to acquiesce in whatever sufferings they involve" (Tinder 2001, 89).

7. In an interesting move, Rochelle Green (2019, 113) draws on both Marcel *and* Bloch to develop "a hybrid theory of political hope" relevant for contemporary feminist praxis. I am not entirely convinced by the usefulness of Marcel in this regard (Green acknowledges herself that he was no feminist) and rather read Green's notion of hope as an example of the critical hope presented here. For Green, hope is political praxis "geared toward the alleviation of oppression without necessarily knowing what society would look like post-oppression" (Green 2019, 120).

8. Stewart Sutherland suggests that Christian hope stands at odds with "descriptively full" normative systems but shares much in common with "the idea of a changing progressive and processive developing utopia" (Sutherland 1989, 204). In similar fashion I suggest here that critical hope is consistent with an understanding of utopia as an open-ended process of becoming. There is little in, say, Erin McKenna's *The Task of Utopia* (McKenna 2001) that Moltmann would consider alien to the task of political theology. What McKenna understands by utopia—a future-oriented critical thinking which refuses to focus on a static final goal but rather emphasizes the process of seeking meaning—is pretty much what Moltmann has in mind when he talks of the activity of hope. This understanding of utopia as an unsettling process of critical exploration has become the dominant understanding within the field of utopian studies. Moltmann would have little issue with utopian activist-scholars who tell us that "we look to utopia not as a place we might reach but as an ongoing process of becoming" characterized by "a critical attitude towards the present and a political commitment to experiment in transfiguring the coordinates of our historical moment" (Coté, Day, and de Peuter 2008, 13).

9. How one perceives "possibility" is crucial here. When Halpin argues that sound hope deals with "what is possible on the basis of what is perceived to be realizable" (Halpin 2003, 60), the question is: "perceived" by whom? Mannheim long ago made the distinction between "relative" utopias (conceptions unrealizable within the existing order) and "absolute" utopias (conceptions unrealizable within any given order). He also argued that the ruling elites will always strive to designate as "unreal" (and thus absolutely utopian) those ideas that

cannot be realized within existing social and political parameters (Mannheim 1940, 175–177). There is a sense in which the sound hoper dismisses as "unrealizable" and absolutely utopian any conceptions that lie outside the social and political parameters of advanced capitalism. There is thus a whole range of alternative systemic possibilities that are precluded from consideration. As Rousseau once noted, "the bounds of possibility are less narrow than we imagine" (Rousseau 1993, 261). The sound hoper "asks too few questions about the world as it is, as it might or as it should be," such that "anything more demanding than piecemeal engineering belongs automatically to the sphere of obsolete and dangerous revolutionary aspirations" (Papastephanou 2009, xiv, 81).

10. This is an important point. There is a temptation sometimes to see hope as a radical or subversive force when, in fact, "capitalism thrives on hope" (Braithwaite 2004, 84) and "the powerful people in a society have strong interests in fostering hope and its consequent effort" (Nesse 1999, 430). As Ghassan Hage (2002, 152) rightly remarks, "we need to look at what kind of hope society encourages rather than simply whether it gives people hope or not."

11. Han-Pile and Stern rightly note that "hope is not a matter of volitional control: an agent cannot will or instill hope in themselves, any more than an agent can will themselves to love" (this volume). Snyder and his team often come very close to suggesting that becoming a high-hope agent *is* a matter of simple will and volition. Shade, on the other hand, is far more attuned to the difficulties and complexities involved in "cultivating hope" discussed by Han-Pile and Stern in the third section of their chapter.

12. I have elsewhere argued that Paulo Freire offers a pedagogy of transformative hope (Webb 2010, 2012). Although he warned against the arrogance of utopian prophets, Freire also stressed the need for a utopian vision that can illuminate and guide the hoping subject along the path toward a transformed future (Freire 1994, 78; 1996, 187; Freire and Shor 1987, 13–14). In the face of a reality that sickens and offends, it becomes the responsibility of the educator to announce their utopian vision and to mobilize support for it, thereby transforming it into a shared utopia dream (Freire et al. 1994, 37). For Freire, education is a pedagogic practice through which the impossible, by virtue of the strength and conviction with which it is dreamed and announced, becomes possible. He tells us: "What is implied is not the transmission to the people of a knowledge previously elaborated, a process that ignores what they already know, but the act of returning to them, in an organized form, what they themselves offered in a disorganized form" (Freire 1978, 24–25). The project of "teaching better what the people already know" is a political one aimed at exhilarating, motivating, inspiring, and evoking transformative hope (Freire 2007, 273). The cognitive-affective and behavioral dimensions of transformative hope resonate with Freire's notion of conscientization as the critical

insertion into history of real subjects animated by a profound confidence in the transformative capacities of human agency and committed to confronting and overcoming the "limit situations" that face them (Freire 1972, 71–72). The discourse of conscientization is the discourse of transformative hope, a hope against the evidence that recognizes the obstacles before it and yet grows in strength in spite of these, and a hope experienced by the hoper as "the taking of history into their hands" as they strive for the "untested feasibility" that lies beyond the concrete material data of every limit situation (Freire 1972, 81; 1994, 176; 2007, 71–72).

13. OWS activists were animated by a mode of hoping rejected by many contemporary commentators. It is interesting to see calls for a renewed patient hope in the face of the conditions confronting humanity. Alan Mittleman (2009), for example, offers "a philosophical reconstruction of biblical hope" (7) as a bulwark against the dangers of "unrestrained secular hope" (10) and the "fanatical" (260) hopes of utopian transformation. For Mittleman (2009, 265, 262–263), the hope required for our age is a hope underpinned by secure trust in both "the goodness of being" and the underlying justice of our social and political institutions. Arguing explicitly against the temptation to "impatience" in the face of injustices, Mittleman (2009, 260, 14) presents "hope as a conservative force within a liberal society" restraining the over-zealous critical impatience born of modern secular hope. For his part, Daniel Boscaljon (2015) urges us to turn our attention away from the desire to *have* and to *fix* things in the present and to embrace instead our frailty and fragility in a virtuous spirit of hope and "the attendant virtues of patience, fortitude and perseverance" (xiii). Confronting the future as a mystery beyond our grasp, Boscaljon champions hope as "a nonreligious capacity to endure suffering for uncertain ends" (xvi). Terry Eagleton's (2015, 59) "tragic hope" also has affinities with patient hope as outlined in this chapter. He tells us that "hope is the kind of virtue that involves a cluster of equally creditable qualities: patience, trust, courage, tenacity, resilience, forbearance, perseverance, long-sufferance and the like." Tragic hope—the hope of Plenty Coups, but also, significantly, the hope prescribed to the radical Left—is a hope in the face of the prospect of defeat; a hope that perseveres in spite of everything; a hope that rejects the impatient tendency on the Left to see revolutionary opportunity everywhere; a hope that dispenses with self-deceptive notions of utopian transformation and manifests as "an irreducible residue that refuses to give way, plucking its resilience from an openness to the possibility of unmitigated disaster" (Eagleton 2015, 114). For Eagleton, the appropriate hope for the Left right now is a steadfast patient hope purged of all delusions, a hope underpinned by the thinnest trust, "not that all will be well, but that all might be well enough" (Eagleton 2015, 133).

14. The nature, form, and role of utopian pedagogy, both within formal educational institutions and beyond, has animated much of my recent research

(Webb 2017, 2018, 2019). This is an ongoing project focused increasingly on seeking to understand the pedagogical processes involved in moving beyond critical hope to transformative hope.

REFERENCES

Anderson, Ben. 2006. "'Transcending without Transcendence': Utopianism and an Ethos of Hope." *Antipode* 38(4): 691–710.

Anon. 2011. "Communiqué 1." *Tidal*, no. 1. http://www.e-flux.com/wpcontent/uploads/2013/05/TIDAL_occupytheory.pdf?b8c429.

Aronson, Ronald. 1999. "Hope after Hope?" *Social Research* 66 (2): 471–494.

Arthur, Leonie, and Wayne Sawyer. 2009. "Robust Hope, Democracy and Early Childhood Education." *Early Years* 29 (2): 163–175.

Averill, James, George Catlin, and Kyum Chon. 1990. *Rules of Hope.* New York: Springer-Verlag.

Bauman, Zygmunt. 2003. "Utopia with No Topos." *History of the Human Sciences* 16 (1): 11–26.

Bell, David. 2017. *Rethinking Utopia: Place, Power, Affect.* New York: Routledge.

Biss, Mavis. 2013. "Radical Moral Imagination." *Hypatia* 28 (4): 937–954.

Bloch, Ernst. 1995. *The Principle of Hope.* Cambridge, MA: MIT Press.

Boscaljon, Daniel. 2015. "The Value of Cultivating Longing in a Secularized World." In *Hope and the Longing for Utopia*, edited by Daniel Boscaljon, xiii–xx. Cambridge, UK: James Clarke.

Bovens, Luc. 1999. "The Value of Hope." *Philosophy and Phenomenological Research* 59 (3): 667–681.

Braithwaite, John. 2004. "Emancipation and Hope." *Annals of the American Academy of Political and Social Science* 592: 79–98.

Browne, Craig. 2005. "Hope, Critique, and Utopia." *Critical Horizons* 6 (1): 63–86.

Callina, Kristina, Nancy Snow, and Elise Murray. 2018. "The History of Philosophical and Psychological Perspectives on Hope: Toward Defining Hope for the Science of Positive Human Development." In *The Oxford Handbook of Hope*, edited by Matthew Gallagher and Shane Lopez, 9–25. Oxford: Oxford University Press.

Cates, Diana. 2015. "Hope, Hatred and the Ambiguities of Utopic Longing." In *Hope and the Longing for Utopia*, edited by Daniel Boscaljon, 23–40. Cambridge, UK: James Clarke.

Chrostowska, S. D. 2016. "Utopia, Alibi." In *Political Uses of Utopia*, edited by S. D. Chrostowska and James Ingram, 269–310. New York: Columbia University Press.

Coté, Mark, Richard Day, and Greg de Peuter. 2008. "What Is Utopian Pedagogy?" In *Utopian Pedagogy: Radical Experiments against Neoliberal Globalization*, edited by Mark Coté, Richard Day, and Greg de Peuter, 3–19. Toronto: University of Toronto Press.

Carlson, Dennis. 2005. "Hope without Illusion: Telling the Story of Democratic Educational Renewal." *International Journal of Qualitative Studies in Education* 18 (1): 21–45.

Cook, Julia. 2018. "Hope, Utopia, and Everyday Life: Some Recent Developments." *Utopian Studies* 29 (3): 381–397.

Dauenhauer, Bernard. 1984. "Hope and Its Ramifications for Politics." *Man and World* 17: 453–476.

Dauenhauer, Bernard. 1986. *The Politics of Hope*. London: Routledge.

Dauenhauer, Bernard. 2005. "The Place of Hope in Responsible Political Practice." In *Interdisciplinary Perspectives on Hope*, edited by Jaklin Eliot, 81–97. New York: Nova Science.

Day, John Patrick. 1969. "Hope." *American Philosophical Quarterly* 6 (2): 89–102.

Day, John Patrick. 1991. *Hope: A Philosophical Inquiry*. Helsinki: Philosophical Society of Finland.

Desroche, Henri. 1979. *The Sociology of Hope*. London: Routledge and Kegan Paul.

Dufault, K., and B. C. Martocchio. 1985. "Hope: Its Spheres and Dimensions." *Nursing Clinics of North America* 20 (9): 379–391.

Duncan-Andrade, Jeff. 2009. "Note to Educators: Hope Required When Growing Roses in Concrete." *Harvard Educational Review* 79 (2): 181–194.

Eagleton, Terry. 2015. *Hope without Optimism*. New Haven, CT: Yale University Press.

Flank, Lenny. 2011. *Voices from the 99%*. St. Petersburg, FL: Red and Black.

Fournier, Valerie. 2002. "Utopianism and the Cultivation of Possibilities: Grassroots Movements of Hope." In *Utopia and Organization*, edited by Martin Parker, 189–216. Oxford: Blackwell.

Freire, Paulo. 1972. *Pedagogy of the Oppressed*. Harmondsworth: Penguin.

Freire, Paulo. 1978. *Pedagogy in Process*. London: Writers and Readers Publishing Cooperative.

Freire, Paulo. 1994. *Pedagogy of Hope*. London: Continuum.

Freire, Paulo. 1996. *Letters to Cristina*. New York: Routledge.

Freire, Paulo. 2007. *Pedagogy of the Heart*. New York: Continuum.

Freire, Paulo, and Ira Shor. 1987. *A Pedagogy for Liberation*. Basingstoke: Macmillan.

Freire, Paulo, Miguel Escobar, Alfedo Fernández, and Gilberto Guevare-Niebla. 1994. *Paulo Freire on Higher Education*. Albany, NY: SUNY Press.

Gitlin, Todd. 2012. *Occupy Nation*. New York: HarperCollins.

Godfrey, Joseph. 1987. *A Philosophy of Human Hope*. Dortrecht: Martinus Nijhoff.

Grady, J. E. 1970. "Marcel, Hope and Ethics." *Journal of Value Inquiry* 4: 56–64.

Gravlee, G. Scott. 2000. "Aristotle on Hope." *Journal of the History of Philosophy* 38 (4): 461–477.

Green, Rochelle. 2019. "Cultivating Hope in Feminist Praxis." In *Theories of Hope: Exploring Alternative Affective Dimensions of Human Experience*, edited by Rochelle Green, 111–128. Lanham, MD: Lexington Books.

Gutiérrez, Gustavo. 2001. *A Theology of Liberation*. London: SCM Press.

Hage, Ghassan. 2002. "On the Side of Life—Joy and the Capacity of Being." In *Hope: New Philosophies for Change*, edited by Mary Zournazi, 150–171. London: Lawrence and Wishart.

Haiven, Max, and Alex Khasnabish. 2014. *The Radical Imagination*. London: Zed Books.

Halpin, David. 2003. *Hope and Education: The Role of the Utopian Imagination*. London: RoutledgeFalmer.

Halpin, David. 2007. "Utopian Spaces of 'Robust Hope': The Architecture and Nature of Progressive Learning Environments." *Asia-Pacific Journal of Teacher Education* 35 (3): 243–255.

Hammond, Craig. 2017. *Hope, Utopia and Creativity in Higher Education*. London: Bloomsbury.

Haro, Lia. 2010. "The Affective Politics of Insurgent Hope." In *Hope against Hope*, edited by Janet Horrigan and Ed Wiltse, 183–206. Leiden: Brill.

Harvey, David. 2000. *Spaces of Hope*. Edinburgh: Edinburgh University Press.

Havel, Vaclav. 1990. *Disturbing the Peace*. New York: Vintage.

Holloway, John. 2010. *Crack Capitalism*. London: Pluto.

Kast, Vera. 1994. *Joy, Inspiration and Hope*. New York: Fromm International.

Kretz, Lisa. 2019. "Hope, the Environment, and Moral Imagination." In *Theories of Hope: Exploring Alternative Affective Dimensions of Human Experience*, edited by Rochelle Green, 155–176. Lanham, MD: Lexington Books.

Lear, Jonathan. 2006. *Radical Hope*. Cambridge, MA: Harvard University Press.

Levitas, Ruth. 1990. *The Concept of Utopia*. London: Allen Lane.

Levitas, Ruth. 2013. *Utopia as Method*. Basingstoke: Palgrave.

Macquarrie, John. 1978. *Christian Hope*. London: Mowbrays.

Mannheim, Karl. 1940. *Ideology and Utopia*. London: Kegan Paul.

Marcel, Gabriel. 1962. *Homo Viator: Introduction to a Metaphysics of Hope*. New York: Harper and Row.

Marcel, Gabriel. 1967. "Desire and Hope." In *Readings in Existential Phenomenology*, edited by Nathaniel Lawrence and Daniel O'Connor, 277–285. Englewood Cliffs, NJ: Prentice Hall.

Marcel, Gabriel. 1978. *Man against Mass Society*. South Bend, IN: Gateway Press.

Martin, Adrienne. 2014. *How We Hope: A Moral Psychology*. Princeton, NJ: Princeton University Press.

McKenna, Erin. 2001. *The Task of Utopia: A Pragmatist and Feminist Perspective*. Lanham, MD: Rowman and Littlefield.

Mittleman, Alan. 2009. *Hope in a Democratic Age: Philosophy, Religion, and Political Theory*. Oxford: Oxford University Press.

Mizen, Phil. 2015. "The Madness That Is the World: Young Activists' Emotional Reasoning and Their Participation in a Local Occupy Movement." *Sociological Review* 63: 167–182.

Moltmann, Jürgen. 1967. *Theology of Hope*. London: SCM Press.

Moltmann, Jürgen. 1970. "Religion, Revolution, and the Future." In *The Future of Hope*, edited by Walter H. Capps, 102–126. Philadelphia: Fortress Press.

Moltmann, Jürgen. 1975. *The Experiment Hope*. London: SCM Press.

Moltmann, Jürgen. 1996. *The Coming of God: Christian Eschatology*. London: SCM Press.

Moylan, Tom. 1997. "Bloch against Bloch: The Theological Reception of *Das Prinzip Hoffnung* and the Liberation of the Utopian Function." In *Not Yet: Reconsidering Ernst Bloch*, edited by Jamie O. Daniel and Tom Moylan, 96–121. London: Verso.

Moylan, Tom. 2000. *Scraps of the Untainted Sky: Science Fiction, Utopia, Dystopia*. Boulder, CO: Westview Press.

Nesse, Randolph. 1999. "The Evolution of Hope and Despair." *Social Research* 66 (2): 429–469.

Orwell, George. 1949. *Nineteen Eighty-Four*. London: Secker and Warburg.

Papastephanou, Marianna. 2009. *Educated Fear and Educated Hope*. Rotterdam: Sense Publishers.

Péguy, Charles. 1996. *The Portal of the Mystery of Hope*. London: Continuum.

Pettit, Philip. 2004. "Hope and Its Place in Mind." *Annals of the American Academy of Political and Social Science* 592: 152–165.

Pinder, David. 2005. *Visions of the City*. Edinburgh: Edinburgh University Press.

Polivy, Janet, and C. Peter Herman. 2000. "The False-Hope Syndrome." *Current Directions in Psychological Science* 9 (4): 128–131.

Quinn, Michael Sean. 1976. "Hoping." *Southwestern Journal of Philosophy* 7 (1): 53–65.

Rorty, Richard. 1998. *Achieving Our Country*. London: Harvard University Press.

Rorty, Richard. 1999. *Philosophy and Social Hope*. London: Penguin.

Rousseau, Jean-Jacques. 1993. *The Social Contract and Discourses*. London: J. M. Dent.

Sacks, Jonathan. 2000. *The Politics of Hope*. London: Vintage.

Sawyer, Wayne, Michael Singh, Christine Woodrow, Toni Downes, Christine Johnston, and Diana Whitton. 2007. "Robust Hope and Teacher Education Policy." *Asia-Pacific Journal of Teacher Education* 35 (3): 227–242.

Schumacher, Bernard. 2003. *A Philosophy of Hope*. New York: Fordham University Press.

Shade, Patrick. 2001. *Habits of Hope*. Nashville, TN: Vanderbilt University Press.

Shade, Patrick. 2006. "Educating Hopes." *Studies in Philosophy and Education* 25: 191–225.

Singh, Michael. 2007. "A Sound Research Base for Beginning Teacher Education: Robust Hope, Action Policy Analysis and *Top of the Class.*" *Asia-Pacific Journal of Teacher Education* 35 (4): 333–349.

Snow, Nancy. 2019. "Faces of Hope." In *Theories of Hope: Exploring Alternative Affective Dimensions of Human Experience,* edited by Rochelle Green, 5–24. Lanham, MD: Lexington Books.

Snyder, C. R. 1989. "Reality Negotiation: From Excuses to Hope and Beyond." *Journal of Social and Clinical Psychology* 8 (2): 130–157.

Snyder, C. R. 2000. "The Past and Possible Futures of Hope." *Journal of Social and Clinical Psychology* 19 (1): 11–28.

Snyder, C. R. 2002. "Hope Theory: Rainbows in the Mind." *Psychological Inquiry* 13 (4): 249–275.

Snyder, C. R., and David Feldman. 2000. "Hope for the Many: An Empowering Social Agenda." In *Handbook of Hope,* edited by C. R. Snyder, 389–412. San Diego, CA: Academic Press.

Solnit, Rebecca. 2011. "The Occupation of Hope." In *This Changes Everything,* edited by Sarah van Gelder, 77–82. San Francisco: Berrett-Koehler.

Solnit, Rebecca. 2016. *Hope in the Dark.* Edinburgh: Canaongate.

Sutherland, Stewart. 1989. "Hope." In *The Philosophy in Christianity,* edited by Godfrey Vessey, 193–206. Cambridge, UK: Cambridge University Press.

Tinder, Glenn. 2001. *The Fabric of Hope.* Cambridge, UK: William B. Eerdmans.

Waterworth, Jayne. 2004. *A Philosophical Analysis of Hope.* Basingstoke: Palgrave.

Webb Darren. 2008. "Christian Hope and the Politics of Utopia." *Utopian Studies* 19 (1): 113–144.

Webb Darren. 2009. "Where's the Vision? The Concept of Utopia in Contemporary Educational Theory." *Oxford Review of Education* 35 (6): 743–760.

Webb Darren. 2010. "Paulo Freire and 'the Need for a Kind of Education in Hope.'" *Cambridge Journal of Education* 40 (4): 327–339.

Webb Darren. 2012. "Process, Orientation, and System: The Pedagogical Operation of Utopia in the Work of Paulo Freire." *Educational Theory* 62 (5): 593–608.

Webb, Darren. 2013 "Critical Pedagogy, Utopia and the Politics of (Dis)engagement." *Power and Education* 5 (3): 280–290.

Webb, Darren. 2016. "Educational Studies and the Domestication of Utopia." *British Journal of Educational Studies* 64 (4): 431–448.

Webb, Darren. 2017. "Educational Archaeology and the Practice of Utopian Pedagogy." *Pedagogy, Culture and Society* 25 (4): 551–566.

Webb Darren. 2018. "Bolt-holes and Breathing Spaces in the System: On Forms of Academic Resistance (or, Can the University Be a Site of Utopian Possibility?)." *Review of Education, Pedagogy and Cultural Studies* 40 (2): 96–118.

Webb, Darren. 2019. "Prefigurative Politics, Utopian Desire and Social Movement Learning: Reflections on the Pedagogical Lacunae in Occupy Wall Street." *Journal for Critical Education Policy Studies* 17 (2): 204–245.

Wegner, Philip. 2002. *Imaginary Communities: Utopia, the Nation, and the Spatial Histories of Modernity*. Berkeley: University of California Press.

Williams, Raymond. 1991. *Writing in Society*. London: Verso.

Zipes, Jack. 2019. *Ernst Bloch: The Pugnacious Philosopher of Hope*. Basingstoke: Palgrave Macmillan.

Chapter 10

Adapting Environmental Hope

ALLEN THOMPSON

In contrast with all preceding ages, human activities have now overtaken natural geological and biological processes as the primary driver of global change. The pace of change is unprecedented, and the projected impact of interactions among economic growth, human population and other living systems is mind boggling. (Malcom Potts 2009, 3114)

That the situation is hopeless should not prevent us from doing our best. (Aldo Leopold, in Meine 2010, 478)

To hope is to give yourself to the future, and that commitment to the future is what makes the present inhabitable. (Rebecca Solnit 2016, 4)

10.1 INTRODUCTION

This chapter is about how a virtue of hope is possible in the face of unfolding, impending, and irreversible anthropogenic global environmental change. A common approach defends the moral value of hope by appeal to its role motivating action to mitigate anthropogenic

Allen Thompson, *Adapting Environmental Hope* In: *The Virtue of Hope*. Edited by: Nancy E. Snow, Oxford University Press. © Oxford University Press 2024. DOI: 10.1093/oso/9780190069575.003.0011 environmental damage. This makes the moral value of hope largely instrumental and derivative of consequences. I argue that saving historic nature (the ecosystems, biodiversity, and climate conditions characteristic of the Holocene) cannot be the object of the virtuous person's environmental hopes for the Anthropocene because such hopes involve denial. Nonetheless, a disposition to hope well is a virtue, and hopes about life on Earth under new and unstable environmental conditions should not be abandoned. I describe how a virtue of environmental hope for the Anthropocene is possible, but this requires that the objects and even the concept of hope itself be suitably adapted. We should embrace but pass through despair to grieve the loss of significant parts of historic nature, yet we must act as though we can save it. Then we should develop a radical hope akin to courage that human capacities for adaptation and flourishing, along with other systems of life on the planet, are resilient and up to challenges presented by novel and very difficult conditions of an emerging new ecological world order.

10.2   THE AGE OF HUMAN DOMINATION

Planet Earth is 4.5 billion years old and multicellular life began about 600 million years ago. Geologic time is deep time and difficult to imagine. The existence of anatomically modern *Homo sapiens* begins somewhere from 200,000 to 350,000 years ago, which is only 0.05% of the history of life on Earth. Then for 99.9% of human existence, just as with all other forms of life, human populations were held in check by the carrying capacity of their local environment (Rees 2020).

Moving toward the present, some waypoints are significant. About 12,000 years ago, at the end of the last glacial maximum, relative climate stability made possible the Neolithic Revolution, that is, the birth of agriculture and the beginning of civilization. Even so, the global human population and the scale of human impacts on the environment were held in check by basic technologies, food shortages, disease, and inter-group conflict, until about 500 years ago with the Scientific Revolution (sixteenth century) and especially the Industrial Revolution (eighteenth century), characterized by the widespread use of fossil fuels. The exploitation of fossil carbon for *energy* and the production of artificial *fertilizer* unleashed exponential growth of the global human population. "It took 200,000–350,000 years for human numbers to reach one billion early in the 19th Century, but only 200 years (as little as 1/1750th as much time!) to balloon another seven-fold by the early 21st Century" (Rees 2020). Consider the following graph.

Similar plots of phenomenal growth, representing a wide array of socioeconomic and Earth system trends, illustrate the scale of collective human impacts on the natural environment, especially since the close of World War II, and are referred to collectively as the "Great

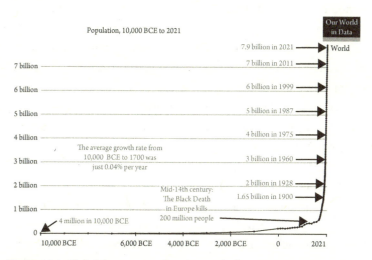

Figure 10.1 Global human population growth from 10,000 BCE to 2019. (Roser 2013)

Acceleration." (Steffen et al. 2015). In sum, the past 75 years—about three human generations—have been utterly outstanding, measured by rates of growth in global human population, economic activity and wealth accumulation, consumer and material consumption, pollution and other waste production that, summed, now have a greater effect on planetary systems than all the other forces of nature combined. Current generations are living through the lift-off stage of life on Earth into the deeply uncertain environmental conditions of the Anthropocene. We live in the midst of rapid and dramatic alterations to fundamental Earth systems, which show no significant signs of slowing. If hope is a virtue, what should we hope about such a future?

10.3 ENVIRONMENTALISM AND HOPE

"Environmentalism" refers to a broad set of concerns about conditions of the natural environment, grounded in and expressing a collection of values and attitudes.[1] People concerned about the natural environment are environmentalists, who can be more or less engaged in behaviors that express, promote, or realize their environmental values and have more or less motivation to undertake behaviors consistent with these values.

In this paper, I consider hope as a virtue of the environmentalist by discussing three basic narrative frameworks of environmentalism in North America, characteristic of the European colonial settlers, spanning from the early twentieth into the twenty-first century. Thinking about environmentalism in terms of narrative frameworks no doubt simplifies complicated social movements and diverse ideologies with very broad strokes. But it provides a way to portray how environmentalists, living in different periods, understand their own projects and the meanings they ascribe to the challenges they face. A narrative approach gives sense and significance to the goals, actions, attitudes, emotions, and dreams of environmentalists, in terms of which to consider their hopes.

I will rely on a standard definition of "hope" as an intentional psychological state consisting of (at least) a desire that some particular state of the world obtain and a belief that the desired state is neither guaranteed nor impossible. To hope for an outcome is to "desire in the context of epistemic uncertainty" (Martin 2014, 5, 11). This standard account combines emotional and motivational (conative) content and intellectual (cognitive) content and finds straightforward articulation in propositional form, that is, through varied constructions of "X hopes *that* Y." It captures the basics of what many people believe is going on in common, even mundane, occasions of hoping, such as "She hopes her candidate will win," or "Mary hopes that Jim will water the houseplants." Although often used interchangeably with optimism and wishing, *hope* has an important connection to agency and pathway thinking (Snyder 1994). In propositional form, the right hopes are a part of virtue at least in part because they set goals to guide appropriate action. By comparison, to *wish* is simply to desire, perhaps even for the impossible, while *optimism* involves an expectation that, by hook or by crook, all will be well.

What seems of enduring interest are a set of intuitions people have about qualities that hope provides in situations when the stakes are high and the prognosis bleak, that is, when the desired outcome is very dear but extremely unlikely. The project of many theorists, then, is to construct an account of what hope is that explains how a person is able to sustain themselves in situations that seem beyond hope. Martin calls such cases "hoping against hope" and characterizes the qualities of such hope as a special focus of our "attention and imagination" on overcoming the dire circumstances and a "special kind of sustaining power" that is "uniquely supportive" as we face discouragement and pessimism (Martin 2014, 5).

Hope, in cases of hoping against hope, seems to offer something of distinct value. It seems uniquely laudable in the worst circumstances because of its ability to keep us oriented toward what we desire and motivated to act in support of what we hope for, against even the steepest odds. However, it also seems that one could hope badly, either by forming false hopes (wishing for the impossible) or in some other way failing to hope well. In this paper I will understand "hopefulness" as a disposition to form particular hopes and a disposition to hope well—for the right things, at the right time, in the right way, etc., as the *phronimos* would hope—as a human virtue, consistent with both eudaimonic (Aristotelian) and social utility (Humean) virtue theory.

Let's call hopes that are in some broad way connected with the natural environment "environmental hopes." Environmental hopes can take a wide variety of objects. They could be about conditions of the natural environment *in* which, *from* which, and *with* which present or future human beings live or about *how* human beings are able to live *given* conditions of the natural environment. Environmental hopes could be about various parts of nature and the natural environment, including plants or non-human animals (e.g., that pollution from some local factory can be abated, or that some critical habitat and the wildlife therein can be protected from development), or about the continued existence of some species of plant or animal (e.g., that Atlantic Bluefin Tuna will not be driven extinct by over-fishing), or the conditions of particular ecosystems or types of ecosystems (e.g., that we can eradicate non-native species of plants and animals from the Galápagos Islands), or the sorts of meteorological phenomena and operation of planetary systems that affect broad material conditions of life on Earth (e.g., that trends in the loss of Arctic sea ice can be reversed or that the global mean surface temperature does not rise more than + 1.5°C).[2]

Furthermore, environmental hopes range from the particular and specific ("We hope to raise more than $10,000 for a lawsuit against the Peabody coal-ash storage facility north of Centerville") to the very general ("I hope climate change does not trigger a sixth mass species extinction event"), and includes hopes that are vague ("We advance this policy with the hope of avoiding the worst possible outcomes of a climate catastrophe"). Finally, hopes with more particular and specific objects are often hoped for as either constitutive of or a means to the objects of more general hopes. For example, Mary hopes to raise awareness about destructive forestry practices because she hopes to build support for protective legislation. This is important to her because she hopes to preserve habitat for endangered spotted owls, hoping this will prevent the owl's extinction, because she believes all species have a right to exist. She also hopes that preserving habitat for the spotted owl, as an indicator species, will help preserve ancient ecosystems and slow biodiversity loss. She hopes success with the owl will inspire more people to work for the environment and maybe even achieve ecological sustainability.

If we stick to purely descriptive language, human influence on nature only causes *change*. But, setting aside classic ecological restoration and management interventions for conservation, most environmentalists view anthropogenic change to undisturbed, natural conditions as degrading and harmful. If true, this reveals an important fact about the value commitments of most environmentalists: all else being equal, the less human influence on natural environments, the better. North American, settler colonial environmentalists value the historic conditions of "undisturbed" natural environments, conditions characteristic of the Holocene prior to fossil fuels and industrialization, above environmental conditions that exhibit the effects of contemporary civilization. To generalize, environmentalists view human impacts that alter received or historic conditions as bad, and, so, environmentalists hope that anthropogenic damage to natural conditions can be stopped, suitably reduced, or reversed. Those who hope for these outcomes locally conceive their success as contributing to the same goals at regional, continental, and global scales. But are these the right kind of environmental hopes, the hopes that a virtuous environmentalist would have, as we march relentlessly into the Anthropocene?

10.4 THREE NARRATIVE FRAMEWORKS

There have been at least three basic narrative forms of environmentalism in colonial North America since the late nineteenth century. I will call these the Protection, System Failure, and Post-Apocalyptic narratives. Drawing ethical conclusions about the hopes of an environmentalist needs to be understood in terms of the prevailing background narrative because what it makes sense to hope for, what it is good or virtuous to hope for, in one context may not make sense nor be properly fitting in another. Akin to the subjective probability assessments internal to genuine hoping (a person can genuinely hope only for what *she believes* is possible, not for what she believes is impossible), other normative dimensions of hope are tied to fitting the agent's worldview; this means the judgment that someone is hoping well is made relative to the person's narrative framework. In this chapter I assume the worth of taking a narrative approach and discuss only three basic narratives of environmentalism (Treanor 2014).

Background assumptions in early twentieth-century environmental history give structure to the **Protection narrative**. Colonial expansion across the western United States threatened nature, to significantly alter landscapes that were mistakenly perceived to be unaffected wildlands (Cronon 1996). European settlers trying to protect "nature" against their own encroachment gave rise to the birth of classic American environmentalism, including the preservation movement of John Muir (1836–1914, naturalist and co-founder of the Sierra Club) and the conservation movement associated with Gifford Pinchot (1865–1946, first head of the U.S. Forest Service). The goal was to protect nature, especially wilderness, wildlife, and natural resources, in the American West, against the pressure of rapidly expanding populations of colonial settlers and their haphazard exploitation of nature for economic gain. Preservation and conservation ideologies are both concerned with growing human impacts on the natural environment, sharing a perception that nature is at risk from too much human activity. Within the Protectionist narrative environmentalists aimed to protect nature against excessive human encroachment or malappropriation; *saving nature* was simply setting it aside.

North American environmentalism has long been informed by science and ecological theory. The Protectionist narrative involves ecological assumptions drawn from Clements' "organismal" theory of plant succession. Frederik Clements (1874–1945) thought that ecosystems—a very new idea at the time—were like individual organisms: a collection of parts functionally organized into a teleological whole. Ecological communities developed progressively according to their type and would reach a mature, or 'climax,' condition representing the *balance of nature*. Disturbance, including anthropogenic, may upset the balance and thus harm a natural ecosystem. When the disturbance ceased, i.e., when human development pulled back, however, the system would reorganize and eventually progress again toward their mature, balanced, and proper condition.

In the Protection narrative, problems of human encroachment or misuse that threaten the value of natural environments were understood to be managerial problems. Given the "forward march of civilization," the ethical question was about how we could conduct ourselves in a way that could also sustain the values of nature. According to conservationist and U.S. President Theodore Roosevelt, the inevitable "human conquest of nature carries with it a moral responsibility to ensure survival of threatened life forms" and wonderous natural landscapes (Jepson 2019, 124). Protecting natural environments requires good management (which, for some, includes leaving large tracts alone), but *protecting nature* was ethically significant because it represented a realization of humane capacities akin to those for empathy, compassion, and self-control. From this perspective, destruction of natural value, an unfortunate side-effect of human progress, was morally problematic. The goodness of humanity must rise to manage the inevitable progress of civilization without a wanton destruction of nature.

Well into the twentieth century, Protection environmentalists hoped to protect important parts of the natural world in its proper, undisturbed condition (at least until we really needed the natural resources). In more concrete terms, Protectionists hope that human civilization will properly self-regulate to maintain the value of nature. The history of legislation establishing protected areas (including U.S. National Parks and, later, Wilderness Areas) and other policy accomplishments (e.g., the Endangered Species Act, the Clean Air Act, etc.), imperfectly delivered what many environmentalists hoped for. Given the Protection narrative, these were reasonable hopes that good environmentalists would entertain. Indeed, many of their hopes were realized, at least for a while.

By the late twentieth century the prevailing narrative shifted to one of **System Failure**. Ecological systems are self-organized but have limits that disturbance events can exceed; complex systems have disturbance thresholds beyond which change will be non-linear, abrupt, and unexpected.[3] Environmentalism became aware of the threat that human activity could push ecological and Earth systems over thresholds, beyond their capacity for self-organization, and cause them to collapse. Natural environments were not just undeveloped landscapes but were now recognized as complex functional systems that could be utterly destroyed.

The change in narrative framework coincided roughly with a shift in ecological theory. Clements' *organismic* theory had given way to Henry Gleason's (1882–1975) *individualistic* theory of ecological change. On this view, individual species migrated geographically according to their own internal evolutionary responses to conditions and the carrying capacity of local environments. Thus, ecosystems are collections of functionally integrated species in particular places and across particular times; ecosystems do not exist as instantiations of natural kinds and, in the long run, there is no balance of nature. Gleasonian ecology gives prominence to the central and persistent role of disturbance; disturbance is the norm, not merely an aberration along the teleological march toward some mature system state. Thus, there is no compositional or functional profile of an ecosystem that scientific ecology could teach us is the proper one.

The System Failure narrative came into the popular imagination through Carson's *Silent Spring*, Ehrlich's *The Population Bomb*, the Club of Rome's *Limits to Growth*, and is illustrated today in the model of Planetary Boundaries (Rockström et al. 2009). With the baby boomers, the environmental movement became populated by broader segments of the population, including college-educated young professionals in urban and suburban areas. In the wake of World War II, awareness of environmental problems grew well beyond concern for the loss of undeveloped land out west. Growing evidence of harmful human effects closer to home fueled dire concerns which increasingly gave rise to narratives of an impending environmental catastrophe (Buell 2003). This marks a central narrative shift, from worry about a *progressive loss of undeveloped landscapes* to existential threats about systemic and cascading environmental collapse framed in apocalyptic terms, the very *abolishment of nature as we know it*.

A prognosis of impending catastrophe gave new urgency to calls for action and frames many environmental problems as binary: we can solve or fail to solve environmental problems before collapse. Recognizing the great inertia of social systems and scientific uncertainty about the exact location of "tipping points," the System Failure narrative encourages two distinct interpretations. Either there is still time to avoid catastrophe, and so the urgent need for significant action now, or it is already too late. Of course, the former solicits the hopeful, and environmentalists will encourage each other to be hopeful that we can change in time. Fatalism, on the other hand, is seen as pessimistic and generally condemned as no help at all. Saving nature, in this narrative, is to avoid system failure and thus preserve natural environments and systems in more or less their historic state. Good environmentalists, then, hope that we can still save nature, which means not pushing environmental systems to failure and collapse. Environmentalists need to hope the fatalists are mistaken; indeed, they are *committed* to the idea that fatalists must be wrong. Otherwise, in a System Failure narrative, there is simply no room for environmental hope.

The hopes typical of System Failure environmentalism will be familiar. Folks hoped we could lower pollution and waste, hoped we could slow deforestation and depletion of the seas, and hoped we could stop the extinction, especially of charismatic species, mostly by protecting habitat, and so on. Hoping, in all cases, was to avoid collapse and the loss of valued natural systems and so, with them, conditions that support human flourishing. More ambitiously, many environmentalists hoped there would be a "green awakening," hoping not only that activism would raise political will but that social consciousness could be enlightened, that more and more people would recognize, for example, the intrinsic value of nature and the right of non-human species to exist, or their responsibility to be active citizens in a just and green society. The fact that more and more people expressed environmental concerns is itself grounds for environmental hope: hopes that the movement could succeed.

Environmentalists hoped that humanity writ large could somehow learn to live "in harmony" with nature or, as Aldo Leopold famously aspired in the Land Ethic, that we could live as "plain and ordinary citizens" in the community of life on Earth. The ready-at-hand hopes of good environmentalists were about solving particular and placed environmental problems (bringing remedy to specific affronts to nature), enacting protective legislation (to prevent future harms), and that everyone would *learn* how, and even *love*, to live more lightly on the planet, that is, inside planetary boundaries. They hoped, and still hope today, for ecological sustainability.

System Failure, arguably, is still the most prominent narrative in contemporary environmentalism but a **Post-Apocalyptic** narrative is emerging (Cassegård and Thörn 2018). In terms of the System Failure framework, pessimists now come into the spotlight with greater confidence. Articulating what its adherents see as a version of ecological and political realism, the new narrative framework acknowledges what seems written on the wall: perhaps there is no longer any chance of avoiding significant environmental catastrophe. So, our puzzle: what happens to environmental hopes when a prominent cultural narrative gives up saving nature?

News about the environment is a regular part of reporting from all major news organizations and appears in two basic tracks: good news and bad news. The bad news is characterized by relatively frequent, high-level reports from collections of scientists or hybrid political and scientific bodies, such as the United Nations Intergovernmental Panel on Climate Change (Steffen et al. 2018; IPCC 2018). These reports unfailingly offer updates that things are worse than we expected, support grievous predictions about future conditions, given our current trajectories, and are very bleak. Couched in a careful language of scientific uncertainty, the window of opportunity to prevent a "cascade of feedbacks" which would accelerate runaway climate change is closing fast or is already closed. The regular appearance of bad news feeds a narrative reflected in popular titles such as *The Uninhabitable Earth* (Wallace-Wells 2019), "What If We Stopped Pretending" (Franzen 2019), and *Learning to Die in the Anthropocene* (Scranton 2015). Against this background, the idea that crises can no longer be prevented begins to take center stage (de Moor 2020). It may not be obvious to everybody, the story goes, but for some the environmental apocalypse is already here and worse conditions are inevitable for everyone.[4]

The string of political failures, chronic social inertia, and more environmental science, all provide compelling evidence to the specter that we cannot avoid ubiquitous human effects and crossing significant system tipping points. With a narrative committed to crossing thresholds of irreversible change, it would seem impossible to be genuinely hopeful about the environmental future. Nonetheless, environmentalists encourage each other of the desperate need, even now more than ever, to be hopeful. Recognizing the severity of the situation, environmentalists admonish each other to develop *hope against hope* that environmental catastrophes can be avoided. Importantly, this call to be hopeful has a strong moral salience: expectation that the good environmentalist will be, or struggle to be, hopeful about the environment. But how can one be hopeful if they are swayed by the growing influence of a Post-Apocalyptic narrative?

10.5 TRYING TO SAVE TRADITIONAL HOPE

The second basic track of environmental news is optimistic, offered as reasons to be hopeful. Some good news is about remarkable technologies, e.g., materials that create surprisingly efficient photovoltaic cells, development of wind turbines that also pull pollutants from the air, or progress toward an electric, zero-emissions airplane, etc. Other reports about social or political developments give a feeling of hope, such as climate activist Greta Thunberg named *Time*'s "Person of the Year," or U.S. President Biden's ambitious climate agenda, or surveys noting an uptick in public concern about climate change. Others still, but very few, concern revised scientific assessments, e.g., "Many Scientists Now Say Global Warming Could Stop Relatively Quickly after Emissions Go to Zero" (Berwyn 2021). Round-up reports are explicitly packaged as providing reason for environmental hope, or at least to feel optimistic, against an acknowledged background of growing desperation (*New Scientist* 2019).

Good news about the environment can, of course, buoy feelings of optimism. There is a lot of positive psychology associated with hopefulness, playing an important role in the normative appeal of efforts to sustain hope. Positive psychology feels good and can help to keep one motivated in action toward desired outcomes. The hopes thus buoyed are that we will prevent pushing systems over thresholds into irreversible change, thus saving more of historic nature. This makes sense within the System Failure framework: hope for sustaining the conditions of a nature we know and love. It is also a familiar form of hoping: that threatening but undesirable futures—involving radical change and loss—can be avoided. Let's call System Failure hopes "traditional environmental hopes": to avoid triggering system failures and hold on to environmental conditions characteristic of the Holocene.

Grave environmental despair, however, especially about climate change, is widespread and on the rise (USGCRP 2016). For the difficulty of sustaining traditional environmental hopes in light of all the bad news, exposure to some spattering of good news now seems inadequate. It's understandable how feelings of anxiety, depression, and fear arise for the environmentalist who then might turn toward and woefully embrace a Post-Apocalyptic narrative frame. To many, it seems reasonable. Consider, for example, Figure 10.2 which represents how sixty years of relevant politics has had no significant consequence on the growth trajectory of accumulated atmospheric carbon dioxide.

In response to Post-Apocalyptic thinking, authors who advocate for traditional environmental hope become strategic. "The message our society [of American culture] is spreading is this: no matter how dreary a situation appears, the *wrong* thing to do is despair. Instead, think positively, envision success and be hopeful" (Brei 2016, 15). I distinguish four tactics by which advocates of traditional environmental hope advance their cause and I respond to each. In the process, I unpack potential misunderstandings about a Post-Apocalyptic narrative.

The first is straightforward and pragmatic. It begins with recognition that it is psychologically difficult to sustain environmental hopes

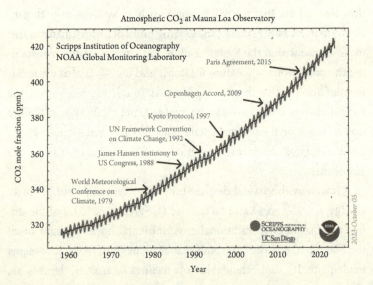

Figure 10.2 NOAA measurements of accumulated global atmospheric carbon dioxide (Adapted from PeterKalmus@ClimateHuman, Nov. 24, 2020)

when they are frequently dashed. Additionally, when one takes in the big picture, it is difficult to recognize or believe there is some course of action, a causal pathway, by which one could make any real difference. To sustain traditional environmental hope, then, advocates advise us to dial back ambition, to focus on local and relatively unentangled problems; activists will be able to clearly see how their actions can be effective and will more frequently have experience of success. To sustain hope, environmentalists are advised to set goals that are more easily achievable.

In light of very grim global assessments, this first tactic downscales hope. The goal is to enable environmentalists to enjoy the psychological benefits of being hopeful, including some counterbalance to dread, anxiety, and depression. However, the idea that hopes for more modest victories could also sustain motivation required to fight global-scale environmental problems is problematic since, by analogy, the tactic advises us to focus on winning battles just because we recognize that we are losing the war. The global forces driving climate and other environmental catastrophe won't be stopped by regional victories (or your change in individual lifestyle consumer choices). This is not a tactic to save long-term, big-picture environmental hope. Here, so far, we might well remain hopeless.

On this point, we can see a duality endemic to System Failure environmentalism: hope to win, to find "climate solutions," or otherwise all is lost. By contrast, Post-Apocalyptic environmentalists are meliorists; the environmental future is not *literally* fated. Those skeptical we can avoid catastrophe typically believe "there is a meaningful difference to be made between more or less catastrophic scenarios" (de Moor 2020, 4). So, the relatively vague hope that we can avoid the worst possible outcomes of climate change is befitting Post-Apocalyptic environmentalism and can support prescriptions identical to those fueled by traditional hopes of avoiding climate catastrophe. Every degree matters. Post-Apocalyptic environmentalism asserts that we need to do what we can to protect nature from excessive and rather reckless anthropogenic drivers, but we don't need to hope historic nature can be miraculously saved, that we are somehow not entering the Anthropocene.

A related second tactic exploits an internal relation between hope and appropriate action: simply engage in behaviors designed to contribute to desired outcomes, or to directly address one's despair, and the ability to sustain hope becomes significantly enlivened. Hope must be cultivated; in a sense, it must be earned. "Hope comes from action, not just words," said the incomparable Greta Thunberg.[5] Straightforwardly, if you are feeling hopeless about climate change, get involved with people who are actively involved in doing things. The prescription is captured by a colloquial principle: *motion makes emotion*—to become hopeful, act like the hopeful. The approach is therapeutic, aiming to deliver hope through a set of practices and exercises, some to honor our emotional pain, as part of building a positive and hopeful psychology (Macy and Johnstone 2012).

The second tactic, like the first, offers practical advice for those looking to feel hopeful and both offer psychologically plausible prescriptions. But even when such a program of earning or cultivating a psychology of greater hopefulness is successful, the hopes made possible are not thereby shown to be an expression of environmental virtue, even though they feel good and help to motivate environmental action. Understanding hope as a virtue, of course, requires a normative account and so methods aimed at simply producing the psychological state fail to distinguish a disposition for hoping well from simply having a psychology of hopefulness (cf. McGeer 2004).

A third tactic attacks the Post-Apocalyptic narrative on epistemological grounds. A narrative that *assumes* environmental catastrophe simply isn't justified by the relevant science. Take climate change, for example: our best atmospheric science says it's technically still possible to reduce global greenhouse gas emissions enough to stay below

+ 2°C. Those who peddle the Post-Apocalyptic narrative that it's too late (or, so-called doomers) move beyond pessimism to adopt an unwarranted *fatalism*. It is a vice to presume catastrophe. Until the science tells us it's impossible to avoid climate catastrophe, there are grounds for hope, and those who traffic in a narrative of doom should stop (Mann and Hassol 2017).

In response to epistemological critics, first we set aside any idea that a broad cultural framework narrative is true or false. It's a social construct that provides context for meaning, significance, and value orientation; it's not entirely subject to empirical disconfirmation because the perspective it provides is not one assembled by an application of empirical methods alone. It's a framework to try to understand what facts natural and social science are helping us to see, as an expression of humanistic and philosophic grappling with our overall situation. Specifically, Post-Apocalyptic environmentalism does not have to deny science that tells us it is still technically possible to cut greenhouse gas emissions consistent with staying below + 2°C because other evidence, about social inertia and political trends, is just as relevant. Those who believe we won't avoid some degree of climate disaster are making a broader, all-things-considered assessment about the future.[6] Post-Apocalyptic environmentalists maintain there are pretty good reasons to believe, for example, we just won't hit the crucial emission targets. Some System Failure catastrophes are to be expected, so we better prepare for terrible outcomes.

Second, we have good evidence that a person's worldview and values are largely immune to alteration by exposure to conflicting empirical facts. It tends to run the other way: the significance of facts and evidence is tempered to conform with one's pre-existing worldview (Bardon 2020). From a perspective of cognitive psychology, then, we have reason for doubt when defenders of traditional hope reject Post-Apocalypse environmentalism as factually mistaken. Why believe an appeal to bare empirical facts would influence the perceived legitimacy of a narrative for those who find it a compelling framework for understanding their world? If Mann and others are really concerned to advance climate action, they should realize that telling people technical facts about reduction curves and carbon budgets does not effectively change attitudes and behavior. What does motivate people, according to the *Environmentalist Platitude* (discussed below), is what they hope for. So, it looks as though the epistemic attack on a Post-Apocalyptic viewpoint is simply a case of one-upping those pessimists as technically mistaken, a critique from which we shouldn't expect much of the desired effect.

Third, while it is not technically impossible for us to radically alter the global economy fast enough to keep greenhouse gas emissions within a + 2°C carbon budget, this is a rather narrow perspective from atmospheric science, failing to acknowledge the many interconnected anthropogenic drivers which pose catastrophic threats to historic Earth and biological systems. I reference two recent examples of a wider perspective. First, over eleven thousand biological and atmospheric scientists signed a report identifying the need for deeply radical social transformation of energy and food production, the economy, and human population growth to avoid profound environmental catastrophe (Ripple et al. 2020). Another interdisciplinary group reviews the strong evidence that "future environmental conditions will be far more dangerous than currently believed. The scale of threats to the biosphere and all its forms of life—including humanity—is in fact so great that it is difficult to grasp for *even well-informed experts*" (Bradshaw et al. 2021, italics added). If reports like these are right, it may not be the Post-Apocalyptic environmentalists who are failing to rightly comprehend the dismal truth about our situation. Post-Apocalyptic environmentalists are not ignorant of the science; they just hold a plausible belief that our civilization will not change course quickly enough to miraculously save nature and itself.[7]

Finally, and leading into the final set of *moral* arguments, it's important to remember that the most prominent Post-Apocalyptic environmentalists are not *proponents* of social and environmental collapse, in any sense that they are rooting for catastrophe. On the whole, such authors only articulate and explore an existing cultural narrative they neither control nor created; rather, they are like bearers of bad news, delivering an unwelcome story that seems to many a plausible and perhaps compelling way to make sense of all the facts as we understand them. A basic Post-Apocalyptic frame is that it is too late to avert natural disasters disrupting society and it makes sense to talk about collapse. Those who anticipate collapse interpret all the relevant facts differently and want to have a conversation about what ecological and social collapse could mean for our ethical and political thinking.[8]

The fourth tactic is to frame traditional environmental hope as a moral imperative. There are two versions, each appealing to bad consequences. The first condemns a Post-Apocalyptic environmentalism for promoting a rhetoric of "climate nihilism" because it contributes to a growing mental health crisis about the environmental future, which is especially harmful to young people. "Promoting doom and despair, and the notion that it's too late to do anything, is literally stealing their future away from them," says atmospheric scientist Michael Mann. "It is taking away agency on their part" (Villarreal 2020). Thus, Post-Apocalyptic narratives are doing wrongful harm (see also Mann and Hassol 2017).

A second moral argument rests on the *Environmentalist's Platitude*; put bluntly: "action is impossible without hope" (Solnit 2016, 4). Let's consider a weaker version of this argument. The first part is psychological: it's difficult enough to sustain motivation for environmental action and despair undercuts motivation, thus diminishing action. Despair is the absence of hope, so hope is necessary to motivate more climate action. The second part is moral: the environmentalist rightly views actions that mitigate climate change as morally good, if not obligatory; hopelessness is morally bad because it defeats some such actions. In this way, despair about a wrecked environment itself contributes to the realization of that horrible future. It is a vice to despair, and so the good environmentalist will not abandon hope.

At root, the Post-Apocalyptic narrative is a set of hypotheses that we are not going to avoid irreversible ecological change (loss of global biodiversity and historic systems) and consequently will suffer a variety of human catastrophes, including episodes of social collapse. Are people who hold such a view, those who anticipate collapse, *thereby* causing harm to others, or are they *acting* in ways that wrongly harm individuals or society, by discussing our environmental nightmare in Post-Apocalyptic terms? The moral complaint against a Post-Apocalyptic narrative assumes (a) the view is incompatible with the kinds of hopes that good environmentalists ought to have, and (b) advocating the narrative is a *cause* of hopelessness, and thereby is (i) wrongfully harming the mental health of individuals, by "robbing them of agency," and (ii) wrongfully harms society, especially future generations, by undercutting people's motivation to fight climate change.

Of course, extreme climate despair, anxiety, and depression can be harmful to mental health. But it looks unlikely that an emerging cultural narrative is the best explanation of climate anxiety and subsequent harms to mental health. The cause is far more plausibly thought to be an honest appraisal of all the evidence we have about widespread and relentless human effects on the environment, including scientific facts about atmospheric physics and historical facts about weak social response and the string of political failures to stop living unsustainably. These facts are not exclusive to the Post-Apocalyptic narrative, but populate Protectionist and System Failure narratives equally. The descriptions of where we are, how we got here, and the prospects we now face are terrifying from any ethically acceptable environmentalism that is consistent with natural and social sciences. Those who lack hope that we can save historic nature, those who anticipate collapse, are not the biggest thing for us to worry about as we face the climate emergency. Our denial and political failures are much worse.

Mental anguish is an appropriate response to the vast environmental destruction our contemporary form of life is enacting on the Earth. A narrative framework that makes sense and affirms those fears is not to *blame* for those fears; it is a framework for making sense of those fears and, then, what it makes sense to hope for going forward. From a Post-Apocalyptic perspective, anxiety and fear about the environmental future is an appropriate, even excellent, human response and it takes courage to be pessimistic, to anticipate collapse. In this sense, environmental pessimism can be understood as a virtue.[9] On the other hand, hope that we can avoid catastrophe, which then insists that we continue so hoping—no matter how bad the news gets—looks more like a willed optimism, rather than a morally excellent response of genuine hopefulness, to our dire predicament (Foster 2015, 29).

Now let's consider the *Environmentalist Platitude* directly: hope is necessary for action, because hopelessness (despair) undercuts motivation. The claim can be understood in at least two ways. As an empirical claim about human psychology, it may be true: loss of hope may defeat, or significantly reduce the motivation needed to support important actions. Even so, this can't show that *traditional environmental hopes* are required. Hopes consistent with a Post-Apocalyptic narrative could motivate appropriate action. Indeed, I argued above, Post-Apocalyptic hopes to minimize forthcoming catastrophes underwrite identical prescriptions to reduce anthropogenic drivers of environmental change. Alternatively, as a conceptual claim, if hope is necessary for action, then wherever there is good environmental action, there is hope. I don't think anyone can doubt that at least some of those who operate with a Post-Apocalyptic narrative are just as motivated and engaged actively in struggles against environmental degradation and the climate emergency. If so, the *Environmentalist's Platitude* implies that there is a way for Post-Apocalyptic environmentalists to have hope.

10.6 ADAPTING HOPE FOR A POST-APOCALYPTIC NARRATIVE

A disposition to be hopeful can be virtuous, but only if one hopes as the virtuous person does. So, I won't argue that we abandon hope about environmental conditions, even if it's only understood as a psychological source of motivation (Nelson and Vucetich 2009). But those who advocate strongly for traditional environmental hopes against the Post-Apocalyptic narrative present a false dichotomy. Nothing about the Post-Apocalyptic narrative excludes having hope, simpliciter. Instead, we need to adjust our ideas about what a good environmentalist should hope for, given a Post-Apocalyptic environmental narrative. In this context, I argue that some environmental despair should be embraced and, furthermore, *some* traditional environmental hopes should be abandoned. In the end, I mention a couple of possible examples of hope that seem befitting a Post-Apocalyptic environmentalism.

A Post-Apocalyptic narrative is scary, especially to those who believe there may be technological solutions to climate change or who are committed to preserving the current social order at all costs.[10] But rejecting a Post-Apocalyptic narrative doesn't change the realities of ever-*growing* global emissions, etc. No longer a question of *if* things are going to get bad, Post-Apocalyptic environmentalism wonders about *how bad* things are going to get, with a steady refrain that the future will certainly be much worse, and for many more, than most people imagine. A Post-Apocalyptic framework asks us to consider what we should do on the plausible assumption that we fail to prevent cataclysmic environmental damage, including exceedingly dangerous anthropogenic climate change. Echoing Aldo Leopold, the trick is to acknowledge what's beyond hope yet still act just as those lost hopes would otherwise inspire (Meine 2010, 478).

Recent literature at the intersection of climate ethics and environmental virtue theory has taken Lear's account of Plenty Coups' *radical hope* as a motivating example of virtue in the face of unavoidable catastrophe (Lear 2006). The Crow form of life, and so their mode of flourishing, was being destroyed by advancing settler colonialists. Plenty Coups correctly saw that the Crow were facing the end of conditions under which they had resources to conceive of what it meant to live well and flourish. His radical hope was a hybrid and new form of courage, leading action under special circumstances of deep uncertainty and the acceptance of devastating loss. Importantly, it is *not* hope that through a dogged determination catastrophe could be miraculously avoided. Instead radical hope involves commitment to the emergence of a new but presently unknowable form of flourishing.

Taking this cue, elsewhere I argue that appropriate adaptation to conditions of the Anthropocene will involve adjusting our ideas about environmental virtues concerning moral responsibility, future generations, and how we value nature (Thompson 2010, 2012, 2021). Adapting environmental virtues implies adapting ideas about the environmental dimensions of human flourishing (Thompson and Bendik-Keymer 2012). Here I am arguing that a virtuous disposition of hopefulness regarding the natural environment must be adapted to the growing implausibility of widespread success in saving historic nature. Such hopes fail to take seriously facts about the wide array of pervasive background anthropogenic drivers of environmental change, including but not limited to climate change. We need new hopes consistent with a narrative accepting that some significant environmental and social systems will collapse, that we are not going to "solve" climate change and need to prepare for an inevitably undesirable environmental future.

Against the broader Western cultural narrative that enshrines "progress, limitless growth, and material betterment for humans as the only rational, enlightened, and politically acceptable goals while making death and limits a cultural taboo," we now confront limits and ends. Instead of rejecting a Post-Apocalyptic framing, Moser asks "that we witness and engage with . . . a serious psychological and cultural struggle within ourselves over what and how to confront endings, what kind of hope to sustain, and how to be and act in the face of . . . accumulating apocalyptic (i.e., revelatory) facts" (Moser 2019, 2).

As we enter an ugly and uncertain future, new environmental hopes are nascent. But we can distinguish traditional environmental hopes, i.e., that bad outcomes can be avoided, from courageous hope that we will act well when they aren't. A Post-Apocalyptic narrative willingly confronts this despair, acknowledging we face almost unimaginable loss, and so welcomes feelings of guilt, shame, and grief, and permits social practices of mourning (Jensen 2019). We can hope to grieve and mourn well, through appropriate human emotions and collective practices which enable people to come to terms with unwelcome change, then face the future and move forward. Furthermore, a Post-Apocalyptic narrative may have strategic value for activists promoting a bold agenda of *transformative* adaptation, focusing on radical social alterations directly addressing root structural inequalities, vulnerabilities, and elusive climate justice (de Moor 2020). We can hope, like Plenty Coups, committing ourselves to the idea that future generations will have the opportunity to lead flourishing lives in ways we are not accustomed to, or can't quite even imagine as possible, for example, without trappings of materialism and capitalist consumer economies. We can hope that a Stoic philosophy, which holds internal goods of rational self-control sufficient for virtue and flourishing, will help people face their hardships. We can hope that other innate human capacities for flourishing are resilient and that ideals of justice, equality, and human rights are not left behind in the wreckage but instead serve to form the basis of new societies that promote the development of core human capabilities.

Nor do natural systems need to be left out. Recent developments in restorative ecology increasingly recognize that non-historic, or "novel," ecosystems are globally widespread and promise ubiquity (Hobbs, Higgs, and Hall 2013). Paul Ehrlich's metaphor of removing successive rivets from an airplane notwithstanding, ecosystems do not have some singular function and do not inevitably crash when one too many species is removed (by extinction) or replaced (by non-natives). Even after disturbance that exceeds systemic thresholds, natural systems can reassemble themselves to exhibit new structural, compositional, and functional profiles. We see that nature can change dramatically and, in the long run, we can hope that nature is resilient in ways we have failed to previously imagine.

It seems obviously too optimistic to imagine a "good" Anthropocene (Hamilton 2016). Still, the natural world is not literally ending; we are pushing it through radical transformations, much of which will be very bad. But for those who will be born well into the future, all the endings that a Post-Apocalyptic view entertains today—the end of valued and historic natural systems and cherished cultural forms of life—will be long gone. For them, as for all children, the future should be full of new beginnings. For their sake, then, we can commit to imagining new environmental hopes for humanity and the natural world we are inextricably a part of.

10.7 CONCLUSION

On my view, traditional environmental hopes amount to hopes for a miracle. In this paper, I have responded to the accusation that the narrative of those who anticipate collapse is dashing people's hopes and thereby driving a wedge in progressive climate movements. It has not been shown we must believe that we can save historic systems in order to undertake appropriate behaviors. In response, I say by definition that the virtuous *do act* as they should and I have assumed that hope is a virtue, as long as one hopes rightly. Further, I have argued that hope is not antithetical to a Post-Apocalyptic perspective, but that environmental hopes have to be adapted accordingly. To those who would believe that a Post-Apocalyptic narrative must undercut action, I say: passivity is only the response of those who are passive. Those who are virtuously hopeful will find something good to hope for.

NOTES

1. There is, of course, no such thing as *the* environment. It is better to think about one's surroundings, the complex of conditions in which one is embedded. Also, there are different senses of *nature* and *natural*. Here I will follow the convention of distinguishing nature from the products of human design and intention, ignoring problematic cases. So, *the natural environment* is shorthand for non-human conditions of life on Earth, including all non-human forms and systems of life, that are not the intentional product of human design.
2. For my discussion there is no need to arbitrate between anthropocentric and non-anthropocentric environmentalists about what grounds relevant values or the best reasons for action. All kinds of environmentalists have all kinds of environmental hopes. In my argument about adapting environmental hope for the Anthropocene, we're not interested in *why* people are brought to the hopes they have, but *how* they hope and *what* they hope for.

3. Linear change is characterized by a direct relationship between an independent and dependent variable. In a nonlinear relationship, changes in the output are not directly proportional to changes of any of the inputs. Once an ecosystem has undergone non-linear change restoration or recovery of the original state is often impossible.

4. Projecting environmental catastrophe *still in the near future* reveals, again, how the main Post-Apocalyptic narrative is colonial. Indigenous Americans "already inhabit what their ancestors would have understood as a dystopian future" (Whyte 2017, 206).

5. https://www.youtube.com/watch?v=KjRDUlkEbu4.

6. Against accusations that he can't scientifically *prove* we are facing collapse, Jem Bendel responds, "All I'm saying is: if we keep going where we are headed, we're gonna get there." Post Carbon Interview, at 19 min/28 sec: https://www.youtube.com/watch?v=dZKYJjDxeos.

7. Kyle Whyte remarks, "[F]or a privileged person to hope for a miracle is disingenuous insofar as they have no way of knowing whether the very maintenance of their privilege renders the miracle even less likely to happen." https://gendread.substack.com/p/how-can-you-hope-when-youre-coming.

8. Consider how Jem Bendell understands his work and a Post-Apocalyptic perspective, for example, in The Post Carbon Institute's "What Could Possibly Go Right?" interview: https://www.youtube.com/watch?v=dZKYJjDxeos.

9. Mara van der Lugt locates the origin of "optimism" and "pessimism" in long-standing philosophical debates about theodicy and the problem of evil, which she traces through thinkers of the seventeenth and eighteenth century and beyond. In her fascinating book *Dark Matters*, she follows these debates to consider how we can approach suffering in a way to offer both hope and consolation and which reveals "a deep sense of the fragility of life" (Lugt 2021, 23). In "Look on the Dark Side" van der Lugt discusses how a *virtue of hopeful pessimism* is befitting our time of ecological devastation: "hopeful pessimism many not be a contradiction," she writes, "but a manifestation of the wild power that is harnessed only when life's darkest forces are gathered into the strange alchemy of hope." It is a virtue from which we may expect nothing "other than the knowledge that we have done what we are called upon to do as moral agents in a time of change. This may just be the thinnest hope, the bleakest consolation—but it may also be the very thing that will serve us best in times to come" (Lugt 2022).

10. Dale Jamieson discusses the "misunderstood" (i.e., under-appreciated) existential and political risks of climate change, i.e., worries about the loss of cultural patterns through which people find meaning and worries that familiar socio-political institutions, such as democracy and capitalism, won't survive. https://www.youtube.com/watch?v=SBfYRtcXL_g.

REFERENCES

Bardon, Adrian. 2020. "Humans Are Hardwired to Dismiss Facts That Don't Fit Their Worldview." *The Conversation*, January 31. https://theconversation.com/humans-are-hardwired-to-dismiss-facts-that-dont-fit-their-worldview-127168.

Berwyn, Bob. 2021. "Many Scientists Now Say Global Warming Could Stop Relatively Quickly after Emissions Go to Zero." *Inside Climate News*. https://insideclimatenews.org/news/03012021/five-aspects-climate-change-2020/

Brei, Andrew T. 2016. "Hope and Pressure." In *Ecology, Ethics, and Hope*, edited by A. Brei, 13–25. New York: Rowman & Littlefield.

Bradshaw, Corey J. A., Paul R. Ehrlich, Andrew Beattie, Gerardo Ceballos, Elieen Crist, Joan Diamond, Rodolfo Dirzo, Anne H. Ehrlich, John Harte, Mary Ellen Harte, Graham Pyke, Peter H. Raven, William J. Ripple, Frédérik Saltré, Christine Turnbull, Mathis Wackernagel, and Daniel T. Blumstein. 2021. "Underestimating the Chance of Avoiding a Ghastly Future." *Frontiers in Conservation Science*, January 13, 1: 615419. doi: 10.3389/fcosc.2020.615419

Buell, Frederick. 2003. *From Apocalypse to Way of Life: Environmental Crises in the American Century*. New York: Routledge.

Cassegård, C., and H. Thörn. 2018. "Toward a Postapocalyptic Environmentalism? Responses to Loss and Visions of the Future of Climate Activism." *Environment and Planning E: Nature and Space* 1 (4): 561–578.

Cronon, William. 1996. "The Trouble with Wilderness: Or, Getting Back to the Wrong Nature." *Environmental History* 1 (1): 7–28.

de Moor, Joost. 2020. "Postapocalyptic Environmentalism: A Movement for Transformational Climate Adaptation." Earth System Governance Working Paper No. 40. Utrecht: Earth Systems Governance Project.

Foster, John. 2015. *After Sustainability: Denial, Hope, Revival*. New York: Earthscan/Routledge.

Franzen, Jonathan. 2019. "What If We Stopped Pretending? The Climate Apocalypse Is Coming. To Prepare for It, We Need to Admit That We Can't Prevent It." *The New Yorker*, September 8.

Hamilton, Clive. 2016. "The Theodicy of the 'Good Anthropocene.'" *Environmental Humanities* 7 (1): 233–238.

Hobbs, Richard, Eric Higgs, and Carol Hall. 2013. *Novel Ecosystems: Intervening in the New Ecological World Order*. Hoboken, NJ; Wiley-Blackwell.

Jensen, Tim. 2019. *Ecologies of Guilt in Environmental Rhetorics*. New York, NY: Palgrave Macmillan.

Jepson, Paul. 2019. "Recoverable Earth: A Twenty-first Century Environmental Narrative." *Ambio* 48: 123–130.

IPCC. 2018. Special Report on Global Warming of +1.5C. https://www.ipcc.ch/sr15/

Lear, Jonathan. 2006. *Radical Hope: Ethics in the Face of Cultural Devastation.* Cambridge, MA: Harvard University Press.

Lugt, Mara van der. 2021. *Dark Matters: Pessimism and the Problem of Suffering.* Princeton, NJ: Princeton University Press.

Lugt, Mara van der. 2022. "Look on the Dark Side." *Aeon*, April 22. https://aeon. co/essays/in-these-dark-times-the-virtue-we-need-is-hopeful-pessimism?fbc lid=IwAR0WnrMaeJEuVkuoGnmIMjz4D_eM6hf3gedLJXeFpqh_iN4P6tbi kAxT8mU.

Macy, Joanna, and Chris Johnstone. 2012. *Active Hope: How to Face the Mess We're in without Going Crazy.* Novato, CA; New World Library.

Mann, Michael, and Susan Joy Hassol. 2017. "Doomsday Scenarios Are as Harmful as Climate Change Denial." *Washington Post*, July 12.

Martin, Adrienne M. 2014. *How We Hope: A Moral Psychology.* Princeton, NJ: Princeton University Press.

McGeer, Victoria. 2004. "The Art of Good Hope." *Annals of the American Academy of Political and Social Science* 592 (1): 100–127.

Meine, Curt. 2010. *Aldo Leopold: His Life and Work.* Madison: University of Wisconsin Press.

Moser, Susanne C. 2019. "The Work after 'It's Too Late' (to Prevent Dangerous Climate Change)." *WIREs-Climate Change* 11 (1): e606.

Nelson, Michael, and John Vucetich. 2009. "Abandon Hope." *Ecologist*, March, 32–35.

New Scientist. 2019. "We Live in Testing Times, but There Are Many Reasons to Be Optimistic." December 18. https://www.newscientist.com/article/mg24432 615-000-we-live-in-testing-times-but-there-are-many-reasons-to-be-optimis tic/#:~:text=One%20thing%20we%20can%20all,will%20continue%20to%20 do%20so.

Potts, Malcom. 2009. "Where Next?" *Philosophical Transactions of The Royal Society* (1532): 3115–3226.

Rees, William E. 2020. "The Fractal Biology of Plague and the Future of Civilization." *Journal of Population and Sustainability* 5 (1): 15–30.

Ripple, William J., Christopher Wolf, Thomas M. Newsome, Phoebe Barnard, and William R. Moonmaw. 2020. "World Scientists' Warning of a Climate Emergency." *BioScience* 70 (1, January): 8–12.

Rockström, J., W. Steffen, K. Noone, Å. Persson, F. S. Chapin III, E. Lambin, T. M. Lenton, M. Scheffer, C. Folke, H. Schellnhuber, B. Nykvist, C. A. De Wit, T. Hughes, S. van der Leeuw, H. Rodhe, S. Sörlin, P. K. Snyder, R. Costanza, U. Svedin, M. Falkenmark, L. Karlberg, R. W. Corell, V. J. Fabry, J. Hansen, B. Walker, D. Liverman, K. Richardson, P. Crutzen, and J. Foley. 2009. "Planetary Boundaries: Exploring the Safe Operating Space for Humanity." *Ecology and Society* 14 (2): 32.

Roser, Max, Hannah Ritchie, and Esteban Ortiz-Ospina 2013. "World Population Growth." Our World in Data.https://ourworldindata.org/world-population-growth.

Scranton, Roy. 2015. *Learning to Die in the Anthropocene: Reflections on the End of Civilization*. San Francisco: City Lights Books.

Snyder, C. 1994. *The Psychology of Hope: You Can Get There from Here*. New York: Free Press.

Solnit, Rebecca. 2016. *Hope in the Dark: Untold Histories, Wild Possibilities*. 3rd edition. Chicago: Haymarket Books.

Steffen, William, Wendy Broadgate, Lisa Deutsch, Owen Gaffney, and Cornelia Ludwig. 2015. "The Trajectory of the Anthropocene: The Great Acceleration." *Anthropocene Review* 2 (1): 81–98.

Steffen W., J. Rockström, K. Richardson, T. M. Lenton, C. Folke, D. Liverman, C. P. Summerhayes, A. D. Barnosky, S. E. Cornell, M. Crucifix, J. F. Donges, I. Fetzer, S. J. Lade, M. Scheffer, R. Winkelmann, and H. J. Schellenhuber. 2018. "Trajectories of the Earth System in the Anthropocene." *Proceedings of the National Academy of Sciences of the United States of America* 1115 (33): 8252-8259. https://doi.org/10.1073/pnas.1810141115.

Thompson, Allen. 2010. "Radical Hope for Living Well in a Warmer World." *Journal of Agricultural & Environmental Ethics* 23 (1): 43–59.

Thompson, Allen. 2012. "The Virtue of Responsibility for the Global Climate." In *Ethical Adaptation to Climate Change: Human Virtues of the Future*, edited by Allen Thompson and Jeremy Bendik-Keymer, 203–222. Cambridge, MA: MIT Press.

Thompson, Allen. 2021. "A World They Don't Deserve: Moral Failure and Deep Adaptation." In *Oxford Handbook of Intergenerational Ethics*, edited by Stephen M. Gardiner. New York; Oxford University Press. https://doi.org/10.1093/oxfordhb/9780190881931.013.28

Thomson, Allen, and J. Bendik-Keymer. 2012. "Adapting Humanity." In *Ethical Adaptation to Climate Change: Human Virtues of the Future*, edited by Allen Thompson and J. Bendik-Keymer, 1–24. Cambridge, MA: MIT Press.

Treanor, Brian. 2014. *Emplotting Virtue: A Narrative Approach to Environmental Virtue Ethics*. Albany, NY: SUNY Press.

USGCRP. 2016. *The Impacts of Climate Change on Human Health in the United States: A Scientific Assessment*. Edited by A. Crimmins, J. Balbus, J. L. Gamble, C. B. Beard, J. E. Bell, D. Dodgen, R. J. Eisen, N. Fann, M. D. Hawkins, S. C. Herring, L. Jantarasami, D. M. Mills, S. Saha, M. C. Sarofim, J. Trtanj, and L. Ziska. Washington, DC: U.S. Global Change Research Program. http://dx.doi.org/10.7930/J0R49NQX

Villarreal, Alexandra. 2020. "Meet the Doomers: Why Some Young US Voters Have Given Up Hope on Climate Change." *The Guardian*, September 21.

Wallace-Wells, David. 2019. *The Uninhabitable Earth: Life after Warming.* New York: Penguin Random House.

Whyte, Kyle Powys. 2017. "Our Ancestors' Dystopia Now: Indigenous Conservation and the Anthropocene." In *The Routledge Companion to the Environmental Humanities*, edited by U. Heise, J. Christensen, M. Niemann, 206–215. New York: Routledge.

Chapter 11

Difficult Hope

Wendell Berry and Climate Change

MICHAEL LAMB

[I]f you can find one good example, then you've got the grounds for hope. (Wendell Berry 2013)

11.1 INTRODUCTION: HOPE AND CLIMATE CHANGE

The news about our changing climate is not encouraging. Reports highlight the alarming impact of human-induced climate change, from warming temperatures, melting glaciers, and rising sea levels to increasingly extreme weather events and the extinction of diverse species.[1] The effects on human life are potentially dire, threatening increased migration and displacement, poverty and starvation, death and disease. Many of these effects have accelerated faster than predicted and are already endangering many of our most vulnerable communities.[2]

Michael Lamb, *Difficult Hope* In: *The Virtue of Hope*. Edited by: Nancy E. Snow, Oxford University Press.
© Oxford University Press 2024. DOI: 10.1093/oso/9780190069575.003.0012

These ecological effects are compounded by social and political realities. Many citizens still lack the political will to address climate change. While the scientific consensus on human-induced climate change is widely accepted, it nonetheless remains a fraught political issue in an increasingly polarized public.[3] Like cracks in the Arctic ice shelves, the divide threatens disaster.

While there are many reasons for inaction,[4] this paper focuses on two of the most persistent: presumption and despair. Many citizens presume that the news about climate change is overblown or politically motivated and thus deny that climate change is happening or discount the risk it poses to our planet. Others presume that human beings will invent some technological or scientific solution that will avert the crisis without requiring any further action in the present.[5] Often veiled as "optimism," such presumption diminishes the motivation to act.

By contrast, many climate scientists and environmentalists are tempted to despair, worrying, perhaps rightly, that we have done too little too late to stave off ecological catastrophe.[6] In the face of apocalyptic predictions, some environmentalists have given up on activism altogether, advising us simply to "enjoy life while you can."[7] Others believe that optimism has fueled complacency and therefore reject hope as the proper posture toward the looming threat. One climate scientist has suggested that "we need courage, not hope, to face climate change" (Marvel 2018). Another scholar has said that "climate change calls for science, not hope" (Porter 2015). A third has described hope as "dangerous and counterproductive," calling for "a revolution that includes abandoning hope" (Nelson 2016, 129, 132).[8] Most pointedly, environmental activist Derrick Jensen has indicted hope on multiple counts, arguing that hope "is what keeps us chained to the system, the conglomerate of people and ideas and ideals that is causing the destruction of the Earth" (Jensen 2006). Equating hope with belief in Santa Claus, he suggests that false hopes not only "bind us to unlivable situations, and blind us to real possibilities," but also "lead to inaction, or at least ineffectiveness." Lest we think it is "only false hopes that keep those who go along enchained," Jensen insists it is *hope itself.*" Hope, he argues, necessarily involves a denial of agency.[9] "[W]hen hope dies," he concludes, "action begins" (Jensen 2006).

These critics rightly target the presumption that passes for hope in much contemporary discourse, highlighting the dangers of naive optimism and false hope.[10] Yet in implicitly equating *all* hope with optimism or wishful thinking, they fail to distinguish the virtue of hope from its semblances, offering no way, for example, to differentiate legitimate hope from false hope or the virtue of hope from the vice of presumption.[11] These conceptual confusions have potentially dangerous consequences. If we assume that hope is necessarily irrational, passive, or pacifying, we risk having no conceptual framework that recognizes the reality of the ecological crisis while acknowledging possibilities to avert or mitigate it. This conceptual deficit can tempt despair, encouraging citizens to give up rather than work to avoid disaster. Without a robust and realistic account of hope and examples of people who embody it, we risk depriving citizens of the conceptual and motivational resources needed to resist environmental presumption and despair.[12]

This chapter seeks to provide an antidote to presumption and despair by drawing on the ideas and example of Wendell Berry, one of America's most influential environmentalists. For the past fifty years, Berry has provided incisive analyses of ongoing ecological devastation and the forms of culture, agriculture, and economy that support it. In his poetry and prose, he has also enacted a particularly artful example of how to sustain hope against the temptations that threaten it. Given how he frequently deflates environmental presumption, no one can accuse Berry of being a naive optimist, but neither does he abandon hope. Instead, he elevates and enacts a conceptually sophisticated yet democratically accessible virtue of hope that enables citizens to acknowledge difficult realities while resisting despair.

This chapter reconstructs Berry's account of hope by synthesizing insights from numerous books, essays, and a rare personal interview at his farm in Kentucky (Berry 2012b).[13] The chapter first identifies health as the standard of virtue and the aim toward which good hope should be directed. The next section recovers Berry's understanding of hope as a practical virtue that resists the vices of presumption and despair. Then the chapter explores hope's relation to action and identifies ways in which hope may be inferred from actions that might, at first glance, seem despairing. After considering how exemplars enact the virtue and provide both grounds for hope and models for emulation, the chapter elevates Berry as one such exemplar, showing how his "structure of encouragement" functions to cultivate the virtue of hope and chasten opposing vices. The chapter concludes by analyzing how Berry's insight and example can help contemporary citizens sustain hope in the face of ecological risks and realities.

11.2 HEALTH AS THE AIM OF HOPE

Like ancient virtue thinkers, Berry assumes that virtues must be directed toward an ultimate aim or end, a telos that provides content and direction to the virtues. Berry identifies this ultimate aim as flourishing or "health."[14] Against modern assumptions that health is merely the absence of bodily disease or that the body's health is separate from the soul's, Berry defends a "positive and far more elaborate" conception that places special emphasis on health's part-whole structure.[15] "To be healthy," he writes, "is to be whole" (Berry 1977, 103). Health obtains when "each part is connected to every other part," unified in "a network of mutual dependence and influence" (Berry 1977, 110). Health thus involves the integration of all parts: "When all the parts of the body are working together, are under each other's influence, we say that it is whole; it is healthy. The same is true of the world, of which our bodies are parts. The parts are healthy insofar as they are joined harmoniously to the whole" (Berry 1977, 110).

Health provides the aspirational ideal and critical standard for individuals and communities (Berry 2007a, 41).[16] Berry frequently describes health as a form of "membership," where people are not isolated individuals but "fellow citizens, sharers in a common wealth, members of one another" (Berry 2002c, 152).[17] He likes to quote the definition he puts into the mouth of one of his most colorful fictional characters, Burley Coulter: "[W]e are members of each other. All of us. Everything. The difference ain't in who is a member and who is not, but in who knows and who don't" (Berry 2004, 356; Berry 2012b).

For Berry, the standard of health and membership provides the ultimate aim of hope: "If you are going to have hope and you're going to make things better, you've got to get the standards right. . . . And the standard's going to be *health*" (Berry 2012b, emphasis original). Berry emphasizes that "the idea of health doesn't mean being cured of sickness; it means bringing things together into coherence" (Berry 2012b). Such coherence serves as virtue's regulative ideal, directing us toward what is good and enabling us to discern what is bad or harmful to health. Importantly, this regulative ideal supplies constraints on the means we might use to realize health. If an action or aim is not conducive to, or compatible with, the health of an individual and their community, it is not virtuous or responsible. Means and ends are interdependent: "Corrupt or false means must inevitably corrupt or falsify the end" (Berry 2012a, 88). This interdependence of means and ends thus places constraints on our actions: "you cannot damage what you are dependent upon without damaging yourself" (Berry 1977, 116). The same constraint applies to social and political communities as well. "Violence against one is ultimately violence against all" (Berry 1977, 106).[18] This relationship between means and ends is crucial for Berry's understanding of ecological hope. Against strictly utilitarian calculations that allow any means to promote a good end, Berry's approach entails that we must not seek objects of hope that undermine the health of the whole or its individual parts.[19]

11.3 HOPE AS A PRACTICAL VIRTUE

With this ecological ideal in view, Berry identifies virtues as dispositions of character that enable us to flourish and enjoy the ultimate good of health. In particular, virtues are capacities that help us overcome difficulties that inhibit wholeness and dispose us toward the kind of attitudes, actions, and relationships that sustain the health of individuals and communities (Berry 1977, 121). For Berry, virtues are partly constitutive of health: they "lead to harmony between one creature and another" and enable us to act in ways that preserve wholeness (Berry 1977, 121).[20] They also serve practical purposes: "A purposeless virtue is a contradiction in terms. . . . If a virtue has been thought a virtue long enough, it must be assumed to have a practical justification—though the very longevity that proves its practicality may obscure it" (Berry 1977, 121).[21]

Perhaps because of such longevity, many people fail to recognize any practical justification for hope, often conceiving it as a fleeting attitude or emotion detached from practical realities. Popular rhetoric reinforces this view, leaving citizens without a sense of how the attitude or rhetoric differs from the virtue. This neglect of hope as a virtue with practical purposes exacerbates criticisms that hope is irrational, feckless, or futile.[22]

Others assume the virtue of hope has a purpose but identify it as solely theological. They assume that the only legitimate hope is for heaven, which implies that we should turn our attention away from this world toward the next, dispensing with any hope not directed toward the transcendent (Berry 2012b).[23] Because some forms of heavenly hope can license a withdrawal from the world, critics worry that otherworldly longing denies the value of earthly goods and the need to combat earthly evils here and now.[24] Berry is one such critic. While he recognizes that hope is a "theological virtue," he denies that it must always have an explicitly or exclusively theological aim: "People who think hope can *only* be theological are like pessimists: they're leading a very restful life. They've given up. That's like putting faith absolutely over work—that's a way of giving up" (Berry 2012b, emphasis added). Against those who focus their hopes exclusively on the next world and fail to preserve this one,[25] Berry attempts to "make hope a much more practical issue" (Berry 2012b).[26]

For Berry, the virtue of hope is "practical" in four senses. First, it has a "practical basis": it is oriented toward practical goods and focused on tangible issues in the world (Berry 2012b). It does not defer its realization solely to heaven but involves social, political, and ecological aims that require immediate attention and action. While Berry's hope is compatible with a theological vision of virtue, its aims are, as Philip Muntzel suggests, "embedded" within the here and now.[27]

Second, the virtue of hope has a practical function: it supplies the motivation and resolve needed to do good work and achieve difficult goods over the long haul. Hope is the virtue that disposes us to pursue goods that are uncertain but possible to attain.[28] For this reason, Berry rejects the idea that hope is "passive": "that's just not the way I've experienced it, and I don't think anybody else has *experienced* it that way" (Berry 2012b, emphasis original). While Berry recognizes the possibility of "false hope" and "passive hope," he denies that these forms constitute the virtue. We cannot just sit and wait for others to act:

You've got to live, and if you attach yourself to people in this world—you marry, you have children, you have neighbors— if you are not careful, you'll get so that you *love* these people. I mean, *really love them*, to the extent that you'll work for them, that you'll exert yourself, that you'll be ashamed of yourself if you don't do justice to them. That's hard. It's a predicament, and it's a practical predicament. And if you're in a predicament, if there's anything to do at all, you *stir*. You get up and go about your work. (Berry 2012b, emphasis original)[29]

For Berry, good work, rooted in love, is motivated by hope.[30] Without hope, we would have no motivation to work since we would believe our efforts to be futile: "People who work have hope. . . . People don't do that if they don't have any hope" (Berry 2012b).

Berry's connection between hope and work highlights a third aspect of the virtue's practical purpose: in order to motivate *good* work, the virtue must also help us avoid doing *bad* work or no work at all.[31] Thus, the virtue of hope functions to chasten temptations toward vices that might produce bad work. Like pre-modern thinkers, Berry emphasizes the vices of "presumption" and "despair."[32]

Throughout his writings, Berry constantly highlights the dangers of "pride" or "presumption," which is often identified with "hubris," the "great ecological sin" and the "great sin of politics."[33] For Berry, much ecological damage and destruction reflects the prideful presumption that we are self-sufficient beings without limits, and that we can use natural resources without consequence to impose our will on the world.[34] Without limits or restraints, we presume the future is ours to conquer through any technological means at our disposal. Whether agricultural, cultural, or political, such "optimism" reflects an oversimplification that confuses "fantasy" with "reality."[35] This distorted vision in turn authorizes a premature rest or refusal to work: optimism assumes "everything is going to turn out fine, so you don't need to worry."[36]

In rejecting optimism, however, Berry does not thereby commend pessimism. Pessimism also involves a premature rest and refusal to work: it says "you might as well give up because it's inevitable."[37] And when we identify a problem with "that weighty adjective *inevitable*," we no longer have any motivation to work to prevent or alleviate it (Berry 1977, 232).[38] The fatalistic acceptance of "inevitability" can authorize "despair" (Berry 2005b, 74).[39]

Berry's diagnosis of presumption and despair is evident in his essay "Healing," where he condemns both the "bad work of pride" and the "bad work of despair—done poorly out of the failure of hope or vision" (Berry 2010a, 10). "Despair," Berry writes, "is the too-little of responsibility, as pride is the too-much" (2010a, 10). Those who despair refuse responsibility and therefore fail to work to achieve goods that are actually possible, while those who are prideful assume too much responsibility and fail to recognize their limits. As a result, Berry writes, "The shoddy work of despair, the pointless work of pride, equally betray Creation" (2010a, 10). "Good work," he concludes, "finds the way between pride and despair" (Berry 2010a, 10).

If hope is to motivate good work and help us resist "violent swings between pride and despair" (Berry 1977, 106),[40] then hope must steady our resolve when we are faced with the vicissitudes of life. As a habit of character, hope provides a stabilizing force that helps us resist fleeting emotions and fluctuating fortunes. "[I]t's a bad move to get into a contest between optimism and pessimism," Berry argues. "The steadying requirement is for hope."[41]

That Berry emphasizes the "steadying" effect of hope points to a fourth reason why the virtue is practical: it must be *practiced*.[42] If hope is to be a virtue—a stable and enduring disposition of character that enables us to hope for the right objects in the right ways in the right places at the right times—then cultivating and sustaining the virtue will require significant practice, disciplined by intelligence and skill, "accurate perception," and the "slow, expensive, uneasy tutelage" of "experience," a process of "education" he describes in an early essay called "Discipline and Hope" (Berry 2012a, 84, 94–99, 158).[43] Here and elsewhere, Berry implies that virtues such as hope must be informed by practical intelligence, the virtue that draws on experience to recognize the morally salient features of a situation and discern how best to respond according to the right standard.[44] In this way, the virtue of hope must be cultivated like the practical arts of farming, which are "learned not only by precept but by example . . . and [require] not merely a competent knowledge of . . . facts and processes, but also a complex set of attitudes, a certain culturally evolved stance, in the face of the unexpected and the unknown" (Berry 2012a, 94).[45] This complex set of attitudes and dispositions is cultivated through disciplined practice, the emulation of exemplars, and reflection on experience.

Berry emphasized this practice of hope in our interview. Hope is "not a feeling," he suggested, but a "virtue." "It's something that happens because you've worked for it" (Berry 2012b). Like other arts and skills, it must be intentionally cultivated, even when we do not feel very hopeful. We must practice hope without feeling hope, he insisted, even if this entails possessing "a certain amount of hypocrisy." Just as we are required to love our neighbors even when we do not feel like it, we must enact good hope when we do not feel very hopeful. "So if you can act like it, maybe you can feel like it sooner or later" (Berry 2012b). Here, Berry echoes a long tradition of virtue thinkers, from Aristotle onward, who argue that playing the part of a virtuous person—"putting on virtue"—is one way to become virtuous.[46]

11.4 THE ENACTMENT OF HOPE

Berry's emphasis on the practice of hope points to another distinctive feature of his account: if hope is not just a feeling but a practical virtue that can dispose us to act, then we can often infer the presence of the virtue from our actions, even when we do not a have conscious awareness or feeling of hope.[47] We can look to our actions—and others' actions—as evidence of hope when we do not consciously experience that attitude or emotion ourselves.[48] Berry believes the enactment of hope is one of the virtue's most important expressions: "When a person learns to *act* on his best hopes he enfranchises and validates them as no government or public policy ever will. And by his action the possibility that other people will do the same is made a likelihood" (Berry 2012a, 118, emphasis original).

The enactment of hope animates "A Poem of Difficult Hope," an essay in which Berry analyzes Hayden Carruth's "On Being Asked to Write a Poem Against the Vietnam War" (Berry 2010c, 58–63). At first glance, Carruth's protest poem appears to refuse the invitation. Writing another poem, like his previous poems against the war, will likely do little good. Yet lest we interpret Carruth's poem simply as an expression of despair, Berry observes a more subtle possibility by inferring what is enacted in it. Noting that "the distinguishing characteristic of absolute despair is silence," Berry recognizes "a world of difference between the person who, believing that there is no use, says so to himself or to no one, and the person who says it aloud to someone else. A person who marks his trail into despair remembers hope—and thus has hope, even if only a little" (Berry 2010c, 59).

In attributing such hope to Carruth, Berry does not deny legitimate reasons for despair. To ignore temptations toward despair would reflect the vice of presumption more than the virtue of hope.[49] Indeed, to refuse the possibility of despair is to refuse authentic hope: "[T]he voice of our despair defines our hope exactly; it seems, indeed, that we cannot know of hope without knowing of despair, just as we know joy precisely to the extent that we know sorrow" (Berry 2010c, 62). Yet, while the *feeling* of despair may sometimes be an appropriate response to a situation when what we hope for is not possible, when such despair becomes a *vice*—a *habit* that informs how we perceive all difficult goods and causes us to treat them as impossible—it threatens to undermine our capacity for both hope and action, filtering out possibility through its thoroughgoing pessimism.[50] According to Berry, Carruth avoids presumption without falling into "the silence of perfect despair, for he is speaking; and he is not talking only to himself, for he has published his poem" (Berry 2010c, 61). Despite its despairing rhetoric, Carruth's poem is an enactment of "difficult hope" (Berry 2010c, 58).

But hope for what? As Berry recognizes, Carruth harbors no hope that his poem will have any success in ending the Vietnam War. That is what makes his hope "unusually complex" (Berry 2010c, 61). "Much protest is naïve; it expects quick, visible improvement and despairs and gives up when such improvement does not come" (Berry 2010c, 62). Carruth's protest resists such despair because he does not hope for immediate success. "History simply affords too little evidence that anyone's individual protest is of any use. Protest that endures, I think, is moved by a hope far more modest than that of public success: namely, the hope of preserving qualities in one's heart and spirit that would be destroyed by acquiescence" (Berry 2010c, 62). Ultimately, Carruth's poem is a protest "against reduction," against the "possibility that we will be reduced, in the face of the enormities of our time, to silence or to mere protest" (Berry 2010c, 63). Carruth's poem, in other words, exemplifies the preservation of character and conscience as an act of hopeful resistance: "By its wonderfully sufficient artistry, the poem preserves the poet's wholeness of heart in the face of his despair. And it shows us how to do so as well" (Berry 2010c, 63).

Berry's analysis of this "poem of difficult hope" has important implications for environmentalism. First, it resists the common assumption that hope is saccharine and sentimental. Carruth's hope is not the cheerful optimism or positive thinking that often passes for hope in contemporary discourse. Hope is "difficult," in part, because it takes hard work to specify its proper objects and to cultivate and sustain the virtue in the face of persistent temptations toward presumption and despair.[51] Difficult hope requires recognizing and resisting temptations on both sides.

Second, Carruth's difficult hope highlights why the virtue is not necessarily tied to immediate success. A virtue is an intrinsically appropriate stance toward our ultimate ends in light of potential obstacles and cannot be reduced simply to an instrumental stance toward more proximate aims. It is *constitutive* of health, not merely *instrumental* to it. Thus, while practical intelligence may sometimes require that we abandon hope for particular proximate goods, it can also encourage us to specify how proximate objects fit with ultimate ends. In Carruth's case, one object of hope is preserving his own "wholeness of heart in the face of his despair" (Berry 2010c, 63). If the virtue of hope is constitutive of "wholeness of heart," then embodying the virtue can be appropriate even when some instrumental aims are less likely to be realized, an insight that is especially important for environmentalism.[52] Critics such as Michael P. Nelson, for example, reject hope because it reflects a dangerous "fixation on consequences" and argue instead that we should focus "on virtue rather than on consequence," acting "rightly and virtuously" without being "hostage" to the "fickle and fragile focus on the results" (Nelson 2016, 130–131). Nelson, however, does not consider that hope might be such a virtue, a way of enacting a right relation to reality that is constitutive of wholeness, not simply a means to proximate results.[53] Carruth's difficult hope enacts such virtue.

Third, if we can infer hope from actions, not just from conscious feelings, thoughts, or expressions, we can discover grounds of hope– –in ourselves and others––that can enable us to resist despair when we may be otherwise inclined to give up.[54] We can ask ourselves and others *why* we are acting in particular ways, and through the process of reflection, conversation, and inference, we can discover additional grounds of hope when possibilities seem dim. Looking to action can even enable us to find common objects of hope when our professed hopes appear divergent—an insight that is especially important for environmentalism. If we can look to our actions and see that we are actually working together toward similar hopes and objectives, then that recognition can encourage us to join together to achieve a difficult good that would be impossible to realize on our own. If, in an organizational context, "[a] large number of people can act together only by defining the point or the line on which their various interests converge" (Berry 1977, 31), then the ability to infer hope from action can help us identify common hopes as points of convergence and thereby expand the possibilities for individual and collective action.

Fourth, the difficult hope expressed in Carruth's poem is relational. Carruth chose not simply to write his poem but to *publish* it, to connect with an audience of readers (Berry 2010c, 61). To facilitate that connection, Carruth writes in a direct and plain-spoken style that produces an accessibility and immediacy of feeling that widens his community of readers, providing opportunities for communal hope in the face of despair.[55] By presenting himself as an example of difficult hope to interrogate and potentially emulate, Carruth gives his community grounds to continue their hopeful resistance when it might otherwise seem futile. In this sense, Carruth's example highlights an important aspect of Berry's difficult hope: it involves hoping not only *for* particular difficult goods, but *in* fellow citizens, relying on their assistance to realize potentially difficult goals that might not be possible alone.[56] Berry's vision of hope is fundamentally relational.[57]

The need to hope in others is perhaps one reason why Berry emphasizes the limits of "individual protest" aimed solely at success (Berry 2010c, 62). The most enduring and successful protest, he suggests elsewhere, is social and political; it involves hoping not only in ourselves or in singular leaders, but in fellow citizens and citizens' organizations devoted to conservation and stewardship (Berry 2012d, 87–88). Yet Berry emphasizes that "public" movements also require "private" movements in the lives of their members.[58] Social hope entails individual responsibility: "[T]he things you hope for in other people, you've got to try to find in yourself" (Berry 2012b). Hoping rightly thus requires enacting hope in one's own life and cultivating the character to sustain it over the long haul.[59] As Berry writes in "A Statement against the War in Vietnam," "In seeking to change the world, we must see that we also change our lives. . . . We have no right to hope for a better world unless we make ourselves better" (Berry 2012e, 86).[60]

11.5 EXEMPLARS OF HOPE

Berry takes the enactment of hope seriously. Across his writings, he intentionally supplies examples that can empower readers to cultivate and sustain the virtue of hope in the face of despair.

For Berry, examples are important for at least two reasons. First, examples supply important grounds of hope, providing rational evidence that a specific aim or way of life is actually possible to attain. If someone has already actualized a particular aim or way of life in the world, then seeing their example can supply reasons to believe that such an object may also be possible for us.[61] Berry emphasizes this function of examples in an interview with Bill Moyers. When asked what he has witnessed over his life that has prevented him from "being fatally pessimistic," Berry replied, "Well, hope. . . . [I]n my work . . . I've always been trying to construct or lay out, map out the grounds of a legitimate, authentic hope. And if you can find one good example, then you've got the grounds for hope. If you can change yourself, if you can make certain requirements of yourself that you are then able to fulfill, you have a reason for hope" (Berry 2013).[62]

Second, examples offer models for emulation. If an exemplar has already enacted the virtue of hope and resisted presumption and despair, her example can not only supply grounds for believing that certain objects are possible, but also provide a pattern for how to cultivate that virtue ourselves. Berry belongs to the long tradition of thinkers who argue that emulating virtuous exemplars is one of the most effective ways to cultivate virtue.[63]

Berry places special emphasis on "living examples" who reveal that certain objects of hope are not only historical or imagined possibilities but actualized possibilities (Berry 1977, 206).[64] In *The Unsettling of America*, he elevates the examples of rural farmers and urban homesteaders who are enacting a more complex and caring relation to their place (Berry 1977, 210–223).[65] Elsewhere, he highlights a "greater number and diversity of exemplary practices," identifying farmers, conservationists, and citizens who tend their land and communities with affection, attention, and skill (Berry 1981, ix). These living examples show that particular ways of life are possibilities that also "exist in proof" (Berry 1977, 180).

For Berry, choosing which exemplars and qualities to emulate requires the use of critical reflection and practical intelligence. Examples are not exemplars without qualification; what they are particular examples *of* and *for* matters.[66] In one interview, Berry affirms Wes Jackson's suggestion that examples from the "margin" are a "source of hope," a reason to believe that alternative ways of life are possible because they have been actualized by others (Berry and Jackson 2012). But he insists that practical intelligence is required to distinguish good examples from the bad. While exemplars can provide a reason to believe that some objects of hope are possible, "you're not under any obligation to be an optimist. And you're not under any obligation to construct a hope for the whole human race. What you are required to do is to be intelligent. And that means you've got to have an array of examples you want more or less to understand. Some are not perfect, and others are awful, and to be intelligent you've got to know why some are better than the others. . . . [T]hat means you've got to think in particular about particular examples" (Berry and Jackson 2012). To recognize particular exemplars as grounds and patterns of hope, in other words, we must consider the particular objects of hope they prove to be possible in particular contexts for particular people. Exemplars cannot be understood in abstraction from their concrete particularities.

In our interview, Berry shared more about his own exemplars of hope. Unsurprisingly, he did not list extraordinary leaders but ordinary citizens—writers, farmers, and friends on the margins of mainstream culture: Wallace Stegner, Wes Jackson, Harry Caudill.[67] Berry focused in particular on exemplars close to his home, "people in Eastern Kentucky . . . who have suffered the destruction of their land, their home country, and have opposed its destruction, and have continued to oppose it after it has been destroyed." Those people, he said, are the real "exemplars" (Berry 2012b).[68]

In this way, Berry practices what Alda Balthrop-Lewis has described as "exemplarist environmental ethics," an approach to ethics that involves narrating "what we admire in those we have long admired in order to make them resonate with contemporary ethical needs" (Balthrop-Lewis 2019, 525–526). Resisting the reduction of environmental ethics to "solution thinking" focused only on solving environmental problems, Balthrop-Lewis elevates another strand of environmental ethics that highlights the importance of virtuous exemplars who show us how to live "in right relation to one another and the world we inhabit," even when we are not able to solve the overwhelming problems before us (Balthrop-Lewis 2019, 531–532, 546). Balthrop-Lewis highlights Francis of Assisi and Henry David Thoreau as two such exemplars. Berry and the living exemplars he elevates are others.[69]

11.6 HELL, BUT NOT HELL ALONE

As a writer aware of how texts shape readers, Berry takes seriously his own responsibility to exemplify hope for his readers: "[M]y essay writing has been very largely trying to discover what the legitimate ground of hope *is* and trying to keep it, somehow, securely underfoot" (Berry 2012b, emphasis original).[70] Berry intentionally structures his essays to cultivate hope and help readers resist temptations toward presumption and despair. He frequently begins with a trenchant critique that exposes the pride and presumption that fuel political, economic, and ecological domination. His incisive analysis of ecological and political evils is meant to change how we see our situation and thereby chasten the presumption that often characterizes those with power or privilege. Yet he recognizes that such vivid descriptions of our ecological, economic, and political challenges can also tempt despair. The sheer scope of present problems can make the status quo seem inevitable, causing readers to abandon hope and thereby compounding the problems that originally prompted despair. Berry thus seeks to dispel despair by identifying latent grounds for hope and concluding with concrete reasons for citizens to act. Rhetorically, he leads his readers through presumption and despair to cultivate a virtue of hope that can register and resist temptations on both sides.[71]

Berry repeats this pattern in several essays. For example, in "Starting from Loss," a foreword to *Kentucky's National Heritage*, he begins with a lengthy survey of "all that we have lost, ruined, or squandered since our European forebears came to live in this place only 235 years ago"

(Berry 2012d, 67). Recognizing that this loss may tempt despair, he suggests that "[t]he publication of this book . . . comes at a time when the need for hope has become urgent. The news from the land under our feet is not good, but the most hopeless thing we can do is ignore this news or pretend it is not so bad" (Berry 2012d, 86). He then concludes by listing ten "authentic reasons . . . for hope," beginning with the importance of proper perception: "We can look around us and see. If we see, by many observable signs, that during our history here we have lost much that we once had, we will see also that much remains" (Berry 2012d, 86). We can also see "that we are not help-less," and "[t]here is hope in seeing what we need to do, and in doing it" (Berry 2012d, 86–87). In particular, Berry encourages us to see what ordinary citizens are doing to support conservation and local economy. Noting the lack of "effective public leadership" in govern-ment and education, he highlights the hope-giving work of conser-vation groups and "formal citizens' organizations," as well as more informal "leadership from the bottom": "individuals and local groups who, without official permission or support or knowledge, are see-ing what needs to be done and are doing it" (Berry 2012d, 87). He concludes by suggesting that perhaps "the finest sources of hope are the people for whom the effort of conservation has ceased to be a separate activity and has come to be at one with their ways of making their living," "foresters, farmers, and ranchers" who "have achieved a kind of unity of vision and work." Berry finds evidence of hope in their enactment of it (Berry 2012d, 88).[72]

Here and elsewhere, Berry starts with loss and concludes with hope, applying what the famous scholar of rhetoric Kenneth Burke describes in another context as a "structure of encouragement" (Burke 1973, 160).[73] Criticizing those who diagnose the harsh reali-ties of life but offer no hints of a cure, Burke urges writers to recog-nize how their images and words affect readers:

Suppose, that, gnarled as I am, I did not consider it enough sim- ply to seek payment for my gnarledness, the establishment of communion through evils held in common? Suppose I would also erect a structure of encouragement, for all of us? How should I go about it, in the sequence of imagery, not merely to bring us most poignantly *into* hell, but also *out* again? (Burke 1973, 160)

Berry repeatedly practices a similar structure of encouragement in his essays, crafting a sequence of arguments and images that leads readers into hell and out again.[74]

Berry finds a similar rhetorical structure in the work of William Carlos Williams. Bemoaning trends among contemporary "realists" who perpetuate a "literature of unrelieved pain and horror" that "dwells upon whatever is worst," Berry argues that Williams nei- ther denies harsh realities nor dwells excessively upon them (Berry 2011, 120). Williams's poetry leads readers through the "defeat and despair" that accompany the "descent" of age, for example, while also revealing new possibilities that "waken as night advances."[75] For Williams, Berry concludes, "[t]he imagination may show us Hell, but not Hell alone. It shows us, beyond Hell, the beckoning light, to be reached even by descent" (Berry 2011, 120).

Like Williams, Berry offers a critical assessment of contempo- rary ecological and political realities, but he does not dwell on defeat and despair. He also supplies legitimate grounds for hope, deliber- ately structuring his essays to give readers the experience needed to cultivate the virtue.[76] By leading readers through presumption and despair and showing them how to identify and avoid both tempta- tions, he provides an example to emulate and an exercise of hope to practice.

In our interview, Berry indicated that his structure of encourage- ment is intentional: "I feel like a jazz musician sometimes. How am I going to get [to hope]? Here I am lost. Here I am in the dark wood of error—how am I going to keep myself from being stopped there? You've got to keep going till you get back to where you can line up with the great ones who have really upheld our dignity and worth as human beings" (Berry 2012b). It is no accident that Berry's mention of a "dark wood of error" alludes to Dante, who makes his readers go through hell and purgatory in order to reach paradise. Berry follows Dante's example, showing his readers hell but not hell alone.[77]

11.7 CONCLUSION

Against the simplifications of optimism and pessimism and the fatalism of presumption and despair, Wendell Berry commends a virtue of hope that motivates good work and supplies the examples necessary to cultivate and sustain it. With this vision in view, I want to conclude, as Berry often does, by identifying concrete ways that his ideas and example might inspire virtuous hope in our time.

First, Berry's emphasis on health as the aim of hope provides a valuable standard by which to evaluate and direct our hopes. The constraints implied by the part-whole structure of his regulative ideal are especially important when specific ecological solutions or technologies might advance the health of some people or places but disproportionately harm the health of others, especially in more vulnerable communities. If the health of particular people and places cannot be understood apart from the health of the whole, then we cannot sacrifice or diminish the health of many to advance the health of some. Understanding health as wholeness provides important ethical and ecological constraints on what we may hope for.

Second, conceptualizing hope as a practical virtue helps to rescue hope from critics who dismiss it as irrational or imprudent. By showing that hope need not be exclusively theological or otherworldly, Berry chastens those who set their hopes solely on a transcendent heaven or transhuman future. Instead, his virtue functions to motivate good work and resist vices of presumption and despair, both of which generate a fatalism that encourages premature rest rather than good work. His distinctions provide a more capacious conceptual vocabulary that enables citizens to distinguish the virtue of hope from "optimism" and "presumption" without thereby licensing "pessimism" or "despair." This expansive conception provides a nuanced way to evaluate hope's objects and cultivate the appropriate stances toward them.[78] Moreover, understanding hope as a "steadying" virtue informed by practical intelligence and cultivated through disciplined practice highlights the kind of work required to sustain hope amid persistent temptations that threaten it. If resisting these temptations requires hard work, it puts more responsibility on us, as both individuals and communities, to do that work in ourselves and with others. Berry's relational conception of hope highlights the importance of hoping in others to achieve difficult goods that cannot be achieved on our own.

Third, Berry points to concrete ways that we can cultivate and sustain the virtue of hope. In particular, he highlights the importance of proper perception, of seeing not only the damage and devastation around us but also the examples of those already enacting a different way of life. Berry's emphasis on hope's enactment elevates these ordinary examples, including those, such as Hayden Carruth, who might not seem very hopeful. By encouraging us to see how hope can be connected to action, Berry challenges the assumption that hope inhibits action while highlighting a subtler way of recognizing hope in others. If we can infer hope from actions to conserve land or preserve the local ecosystem, even among citizens who do not profess an explicit commitment to "environmentalism," then we can find additional points of convergence that can facilitate larger and more powerful coalitions. The ability to infer common hopes may be especially useful when partisan divisions threaten to forestall urgent action on climate change. Looking to hopeful actions rather than partisan professions may provide a constructive way forward.

Fourth, Berry highlights the importance of exemplars in providing both relevant models to emulate and proof that particular objects of hope can be actualized. His emphasis on living exemplars is especially important in the context of environmental communication when many advocates are inclined to offer detailed scientific information about the damaging effects of climate change without offering examples of ordinary citizens whose lives are challenging the status quo. That actual examples are available provides evidence that such ways of life are possible and thus legitimate objects of hope.

Fifth, Berry's "structure of encouragement" alerts us to how rhetoric might encourage or inhibit such hope. Berry is especially concerned about the cynicism that dwells only upon what is bad and thereby portrays ecological and political problems as inescapable. "The logical end of the ain't-it-awful conversation . . . is despair": "People . . . begin to talk about the 'inevitability' of what they are against, and they give up" (Berry 2005b, 74). By resisting inevitability, Berry models the way to highlight political, social, and ecological wrongs while simultaneously supplying concrete reasons to hope. His rhetoric may be especially useful for environmental activists and communicators who are tempted either to abandon their efforts or double-down on fear, emphasizing a looming climate catastrophe to jolt audiences into action. As recent research shows, although "fear appeals" can increase awareness of climate change, they do not always increase audiences' motivation to act; they can even be counter-productive if they are not paired with more positive guidance on how citizens can respond.[79] In this context, Berry's structure of encouragement can provide a useful model for climate communicators who want to diagnose environmental threats without producing a debilitating despair.

Finally, Berry himself offers a living example that proves the possibility of authentic hope and supplies a model that ordinary citizens can emulate. And as he acknowledges, "if you can find one good example, then you've got the grounds for hope" (Berry 2013).[80] As a farmer, writer, and activist who deliberately makes his ideas accessible to democratic citizens, Berry provides one good example of an environmentalist who resists the despair of our current moment and embodies alternative ways of living, using the full suite of his intellectual and persuasive powers to defend the people and places he holds dear. For this reason, we can apply what Berry says of Hayden Carruth's "poem of difficult hope" to his own work: "By its wonderfully sufficient artistry, [it] preserves the poet's wholeness of heart in the face of his despair. And it shows us how to do so as well" (Berry 2010c, 63). If Berry can enact such difficult hope, perhaps we can, too.[81]

NOTES

1. See, e.g., Reidmiller et al. (2018); Masson-Delmotte et al. (2018); Jarvis (2018).
2. Masson-Delmotte et al. (2018); Jamail (2019).
3. In the United States, 71% believe climate change is happening, while 56% acknowledge it is caused by human beings (Ballew et al. 2019). On partisan polarization, see Dunlap, McCright, and Yarosh (2016).
4. For one summary, see Ballew et al. (2019).
5. On the "false hope" that "technology will solve the problem," see Derber (2015, 22).
6. For analyses of "environmental pessimism" and "hopelessness," see Swenson-Lengyel (2017) and Kretz (2013). On potential sources of "environmental despair," see Andre (2016) and Treanor (2016).
7. James Lovelock quoted in Aitkenhead (2008). Cf. Smith (2014).
8. For our purposes, it is significant that Nelson cites both Derrick Jensen and Wendell Berry in defense of his position. By contrast, I draw on Berry to challenge Jensen's critique of hope.
9. According to Jensen, "hope is a longing for a future condition over which you have no agency; it means you are essentially powerless" (2006). While

some objects of hope may be beyond our capacity for agency, not all are. See Swenson-Lengyel (2017, 420–421, 427–428).

10. On various dangers of hope, see Potkay (this volume).

11. On how the virtue of hope generally differs from corresponding vices and semblances, see Lamb (2016b). On conceptual differences between hope and its semblances in relation to climate change, see Orr (2007); Derber (2015); Andre (2016, 4–6); Brei (2016b); Fiala (2016); Nolt (2016); Treanor (2016); Beever (2016); Kretz (2016); Swenson-Lengyel (2017). These accounts acknowledge the dangers of false hope or optimism but explicitly focus on despair as the primary vice that opposes hope. My account identifies "presumption" as another opposing vice and suggests that hope finds a way between both. This account aligns with Brei's attempt to find "a 'sweet spot' between paralyzing despair on one hand and pacifying fantasy on the other" (2016b, 16).

12. For an insightful overview of the psychological relationships of both hope and despair to environmental action and inaction, see especially Kretz (2013, 2016). For a short but powerful popular article, see Solnit (2018).

13. For an insightful analysis of Berry's account of hope, see Muntzel (2009). I developed my analysis before encountering Muntzel's, but the two accounts are complementary, though distinctive, with different evidence and emphases.

14. See, e.g., Berry (2012a, 157). Kimberly Smith (2003, 155–165) also describes Berry as a virtue thinker, though she emphasizes "grace" as his ultimate telos.

15. See, e.g., Berry (1977, 103; 2005b, 77–78). Cf. Berry (2002c) and Muntzel (2009, 193–194).

16. As Berry writes elsewhere, "[O]ur sense of wholeness is not just the sense of completeness in ourselves but also is the sense of belonging to others and our place; it is an unconscious awareness of community, of having in common." Berry suggests this "double sense of singular integrity and of communal belonging is our perfect standard of health for as long as we live" (2002c, 144–145).

17. Cf. Berry (1977, 105–106; 2004, 348, 356, 362; 2010b, 135).

18. Berry also emphasizes this point when condemning racism in *The Hidden Wound*: "[A] community, properly speaking, cannot exclude or mistreat any of its members. This is what we forgot during slavery and the industrialization that followed, and have never remembered" (2010b, 135).

19. "Hopeful people," Berry suggests, "have some kind of vision of wholeness and health and goodness and beauty, at least the incentive to pursue truth—not know it but at least pursue it" (2012b).

20. That virtue is *constitutive* of wholeness, not simply *instrumental* to it, distinguishes Berry's account of virtue from more consequentialist or utilitarian conceptions. For a helpful discussion of Berry's work in light of contemporary moral philosophy, see Smith (2003, 115–128). On making excellence rather

than utility and profitability the proper standard of education and virtue, see Berry (1977, 142–169).

21. "Morality," he writes elsewhere, "is long-term practicality" (Berry 2012a, 157).

22. For accounts of hope as a relevant virtue for contemporary citizens, see, e.g., Mittleman (2009); Stout (2010, xv–xix, 254–259, 278–286); Kadlac (2015, 337–354); Snow (2018, 407–427); and Han-Pile and Stern (this volume). My account of Berry is informed by my analysis of the virtue of hope in the work of Augustine and Aquinas. See Lamb (2016a; 2016b, 2018a, 2018b, 2022).

23. Cf. Muntzel (2009, 191).

24. For a thoughtful analysis of the experience of Christian hope not tied exclusively to eschatology, see Swenson-Lengyel (2017). For an analysis of forms of otherworldly hope in relation to climate change, see Nolt (2016).

25. See, e.g., Berry (1981, 267–281; 2002a). For discussion, see Smith (2003, 171–177).

26. Rather than opposing this view to Christian hope, he suggests that Jesus made hope a "practical issue" as well. Similarly, he recognizes that charity, like hope, is both a "theological virtue" and a "practical virtue" (Berry 1981, 274).

27. See Muntzel (2009, 191, 193–206). For a complementary account of Christian hope, see Swenson-Lengyel (this volume).

28. Berry insists that "you've got to hope for something that's *possible*" and notes that, for hope to be a virtue, it must not be directed toward the "wrong thing" (2012b, emphasis original). Cf. Muntzel (2009, 192).

29. Strikingly, Jensen affirms the importance of love as the motivation for action; he simply disconnects hope from love. Berry, by contrast, roots his conception of hope, like all emotions, in affection and love. Here, Berry's account of hope has deep similarities with that of Augustine and Aquinas. See Lamb (2016a, 2018a, 2022).

30. See also Muntzel (2009, 191).

31. "The ability to do good," Berry writes, "is not the ability to do nothing. It is not negative or passive. It is the ability to do something well—to do good work for good reasons" (1981, 275).

32. See Muntzel (2009, 193–199, 204–206); cf. Lamb (2016a, 2022). While Berry does not present presumption and despair as hope's corresponding vices in a systematic way, in our interview he affirmed they "are temptations rightly enough" (Berry 2012b). On hope as the virtue between vices of "unwarranted optimism" and "despair," see also Han-Pile and Stern (this volume).

33. See, e.g., Berry (1977, 53–59, 97–106, 174; 1981, 270; 2003a, 49; 2003b, 183–184; 2010a, 9–13; 2012c, 53). Elsewhere, he describes "*hubris*" as "the most dangerous moral circumstance" (2012a, 151).

34. See, e.g., Berry (1977, 53–59, 76–79, 94–109); cf. Muntzel (2009, 197–199). On the importance of limits in relation to hope, see Swenson-Lengyel (this volume).

35. See Berry (1977, 3, 13–14, 51–79; 2003c, 79–80; 2005a, 114; 2012a, 94–101; 2012e, 77); Berry and Jackson (2012).
36. See Berry and Jackson (2012).
37. See Berry and Jackson (2012). In the interview, Wes Jackson affirms Berry's distinction between optimism and hope. As Jackson notes, "[O]ptimism and pessimism aren't arguments. They're just two different ways to surrender to simplicity" (Berry and Jackson 2012).
38. See also Bittman (2014).
39. Cf. Berry (2012a, 117–118). Berry suggests that the violence of political rhetoric and division causes a "political and social despair" that "is the greatest peril a country can come to, short of the inevitable results of such despair should it continue very long" (2012a, 88–89).
40. Berry offers an illuminating analysis of Shakespeare's *King Lear*, in which the Earl of Gloucester is an example of someone who swings between "pride" and "despair" (1977, 98–99).
41. Berry, as quoted in Shattuck (2012). For an account of hope as a virtue that helps us avoid "fluctuations" of emotion and understanding, see Han-Pile and Stern (this volume).
42. Berry notes that charity is not only a theological virtue but also "a practical virtue because it must be practiced" (1981, 274).
43. See also Berry (1981, 274–275) on the development of charity, and Muntzel (2009, 194–195).
44. "In order to be good," Berry writes, "you have to know how—and this knowing is vast, complex, humble, and humbling; it is of the mind and the hands, of neither alone" (1981, 275). Berry identifies Wes Jackson as an exemplar "of a thoroughly informed, technically competent, practical intelligence working by the measure of high ecological and cultural standards" (1981, 248).
45. See also Berry (1977, 43–45, 87, 191–193).
46. See Herdt (2008).
47. If hope is "dispositional," as Nolt argues in another context, "one need not be conscious of it at a particular time in order to have it then" (2016, 47). On hope and action, see also Webb (this volume).
48. Hope, however, need not necessarily result in action. See Swenson-Lengyel (2017, 427–428).
49. See also Lamb (2016a, 325; 2016b, 86); and Han-Pile and Stern (this volume), who argue that "knowing when to stop hoping and to adopt another attitude is precisely part of the virtue of hope."
50. Berry believes we should not actively "*cultivate* despair and sorrow in order to know hope and joy . . . for there will always be enough despair and sorrow" (2010c, 62–63). On the difference between despair as a passion and a vice, see Lamb (2016b, 86n118).

51. As Muntzel affirms, "hope is difficult because the temptations to presumption and despair remain" (2009, 195). Han-Pile and Stern (this volume) agree that "exercising hope as a virtue is a difficult thing to do as it requires significant epistemic and ethical skills."

52. This analysis fits with Andrew Fiala's discussion of hope as an environmental virtue: "There is nobility and virtue in struggling and remaining hopeful, even in the face of calamity. Hope is not always efficacious. But hopefulness is a virtue. . . . Hopefulness may have a payoff in terms of good consequences. But hope is also an end in itself. It is useful and good to remain hopeful—even in the face of catastrophe" (2016, 29; cf. 33–36, 42). Such an account also resonates with Nolt's "duty" or "imperative to hope," though his account of "optimizing hope" is more consequentialist than Berry's (Nolt 2016, 48–52).

53. In rejecting hope, Nelson suggests that an ethic of "virtue" is "the only moral anchor imaginable in the sea change rolling our way" (2016, 131). Ironically, he neglects the fact that, from St. Paul and St. Augustine onward, the "anchor" has been an influential metaphor for the virtue of hope, providing a steadying and stabilizing force against the temptations of presumption and despair. See Lamb (2022, 55).

54. In *The Hidden Wound*, for example, Berry acknowledges that we may possess "the unspoken, even the unthought, hope" for forgiveness (2010b, 9), which implies that hope may be enacted even if we do not experience it as a conscious mental state. I make a similar argument about inferring hope from action in Lamb (2022, 198, 244).

55. See Berry (2010c, 59–61).

56. Muntzel (2009, 190–193, 203–204) also emphasizes this relational aspect of Berry's account. On hoping in others more generally, see Lamb (2016a; 2022, 99–113) and Gulliford (this volume).

57. See especially Berry (2010a, 12), where he emphasizes how the prideful and despairing pursue "this work alone" rather than in relation to others and thereby experience the "failure" of "loneliness." In this way, Berry's account aligns with Kretz's "relational" account of hope (see Kretz 2016, 136–137).

58. See Berry (2003a, 49–50).

59. See Berry (2003a; 2012f, 76–77).

60. Cf. Derber (2015, 23).

61. For discussion of examples, see Stout (2010, 142, 283–284). See also Lamb et al. (2022, 124–128).

62. As Berry writes elsewhere, "A man cannot despair if he can imagine a better life, and if he can enact something of its possibility" (2002b, 725).

63. See Zagzebski (2017).

64. Cf. Berry (1977, 180).

65. Cf. Berry (1977, viii, 233), where he lists a set of specific "exemplars."

66. See Stout (2004, 168–173; 2010, 111).

67. Elsewhere, Berry criticizes traditions that are "strongly heroic" and emphasize the "extraordinary actions of 'great men,'" which, while significant, "cannot

very well serve as examples of ordinary behavior. Ordinary behavior belongs to a different dramatic mode, a different understanding of action, even a different understanding of virtue" (1981, 276). Berry's emphasis on ordinary exemplars aligns with research suggesting that "relevant" and "attainable" exemplars are more effective for cultivating virtue than distant heroes or unattainable exemplars. See Han et al. (2017); cf. Stout (2010, 283–284).

68. Berry emphasizes the importance of exemplars in his distinction between optimism and hope in relation to humanity as a whole: "I will not be optimistic, for its history is full of ugliness and cruelty and violence and waste; it has inflicted terrible damage on itself and on the world. But I will be steadfastly hopeful, for as a member of the human race I am also in the company of men, though comparatively few, who through all the sad destructive centuries of our history have kept alive the vision of peace and kindness and generosity and humility and freedom—the sense of how comely and satisfying men's lives would be if they were all free and at peace, and if they cared enough for the world and for each other. It is in behalf of that vision that I wish to speak" (2012e, 77).

69. The success of the modern environmental movement requires a wide variety of exemplars to inform and engage a wide variety of citizens with diverse backgrounds, roles, and commitments. In addition to the rural farmers, citizens, and advocates that Berry elevates, we also need urban and suburban exemplars as well as scientists, entrepreneurs, educators, advocates, politicians, policymakers, non-profit leaders, and others who embody the virtue of hope.

70. Berry expresses a similar sentiment elsewhere: "All my work comes from my loves and hopes. My essays come from a desire to understand what I love and hope for and to defend those things" (Berry 2007d, 120; cf. 2007b, 212).

71. For a parallel analysis in the work of Augustine, see Lamb (2018b, 616–623; 2022, 160–164, 271–273).

72. Berry's assessment aligns with Brei's (2016b, 20) emphasis on having "reasons" for "genuine hope," including accurate and realistic evaluations of "past experiences."

73. For the introduction to Burke, I am indebted to Stout (2004, 55). I develop a similar analysis of Augustine's rhetorical structure in Lamb (2018b; 2022, 160–162).

74. While it is unclear whether Berry has read Burke, he has studied other writers who have employed similar structures of encouragement—Dante, Milton, and Emerson. On Emerson's structure of encouragement, see Stout (2014).

75. The last two quotations in this sentence are from Williams' "Coda" for "Asphodel, that Greeny Flower," cited by Berry (2011, 120).

76. If, as Jeffrey Stout suggests, "[t]he delicate task of the social critic is to adopt a perspective that makes the dangers of our situation visible without simultaneously disabling the hope of reforming it" (2010, 259), then Berry performs this task with aplomb.

77. On Dante's hope, see Potkay (this volume).

78. I make similar arguments in Lamb (2016b; 2022, 266).

79. See, e.g., Moser (2007); O'Neill and Nicholson-Cole (2009); Moser and Dilling (2011, 164–165); and McQueen (2017; 2021). See also Lamb (2022, 272–273).

80. As Stout argues, "When despair is the disease one hopes to remedy, anecdotes can be antidotes" (2010, 283).

81. I am grateful to Wendell Berry for the opportunity to interview him at his home in Kentucky, and for the generosity he displayed during our conversation and subsequent correspondence. A generous grant from Princeton's University Center for Human Values supported the initial research and travel for this interview. I am also grateful to William Morgan for careful research assistance and a number of friends and colleagues for helpful discussion of Berry, virtue, and hope, including Alexis Andres, John Bowlin, Edward Brooks, Michaelle Browers, Bradley Burroughs, Joshua Carpenter, JanaLee Cherneski, Andrew Chignell, Joseph Clair, Kendall Cox, Adam Cureton, Thomas Frank, Andrius Galisanka, Jon Garthoff, Clifton Granby, Eric Gregory, Lynn Casteel Harper, Ryan Harper, Davey Henreckson, Lucas Johnston, John Knox, Hannah Lafferrandre, Brooks Lamb, Melissa Lane, James Linville, Matthew Longo, Philip Lorish, Stephen Macedo, Victoria McGeer, Alison McQueen, Stan Meiburg, Reid Morgan, John Nolt, Melissa Orlie, David Phillips, Adam Potkay, Max Robitzsch, Cameron Silverglate, Frederick Simmons, Kimberly Smith, Nancy Snow, Jeffrey Stout, Willa Swenson-Lengyel, Bob Pepperman Taylor, Kenneth Townsend, Nate Van Yperen, Cornel West, Elizabeth Whiting, Derek Woodard-Lehman, and audiences at Middlebury College (2014), American Political Science Association annual meetings (2016, 2019), Wake Forest University (2019), University of Tennessee (2019), a Hope Colloquium at the Princeton University Center for Human Values (2019), and the colloquium "Is Hope a Virtue?" sponsored by the Princeton Project in Philosophy of Religion (2020). This project was made possible through the support of Wake Forest University and grants from the John Templeton Foundation and Lilly Endowment Inc. The opinions expressed in this publication are those of the author and do not necessarily reflect the views of Wake Forest University, the John Templeton Foundation, or Lilly Endowment Inc.

REFERENCES

Aitkenhead, Decca. 2008. "James Lovelock: 'Enjoy Life While You Can: In 20 Years Global Warming Will Hit the Fan.'" *The Guardian*, March 1. https://www.theguard ian.com/theguardian/2008/mar/01/scienceofclimatechange.climatechange.

Andre, Elizabeth. 2016. "The Need to Talk about Despair." In *Ecology, Ethics, and Hope*, edited by Andrew Brei, 1–11. Lanham, MD: Rowman & Littlefield.

Ballew, Matthew T., Anthony Leiserowitz, Connie Roser-Renouf, Seth A. Rosenthal, John E. Kotcher, Jennifer R. Marlon, Erik Lyon, Matthew H. Goldberg, and Edward W. Maibach. 2019. "Climate Change in the American Mind: Data, Tools, and Trends." *Environment: Science and Policy for Sustainable Development* 61 (3): 4–18.

Balthrop-Lewis, Alda. 2019. "Exemplarist Environmental Ethics: Thoreau's Political Asceticism against Solution Thinking." *Journal of Religious Ethics* 47 (3): 525–550.

Beever, Jonathan. 2016. "Have Hope, Not Too Much, Mostly for Plants." In *Ecology, Ethics, and Hope*, edited by Andrew Brei, 111–125. Lanham, MD: Rowman & Littlefield.

Berry, Wendell. 1977. *The Unsettling of America: Culture and Agriculture*. San Francisco: Sierra Club Books.

Berry, Wendell. 1981. *The Gift of Good Land*. Berkeley, CA: Counterpoint.

Berry, Wendell. 2002a. "Christianity and the Survival of Creation." In *The Art of the Commonplace: The Agrarian Essays of Wendell Berry*, edited by Norman Wirzba, 305–320. Berkeley, CA: Counterpoint.

Berry, Wendell. 2002b. "An Entrance to the Woods." In *The Norton Book of Nature Writing*, edited by Robert Finch and John Elder, 718–728. New York: W. W. Norton.

Berry, Wendell. 2002c. "Health Is Membership." In *The Art of the Commonplace: The Agrarian Essays of Wendell Berry*, edited by Norman Wirzba, 144–158. Berkeley, CA: Counterpoint.

Berry, Wendell. 2003a. "In Distrust of Movements." In *Citizenship Papers*, 43–51. Berkeley, CA: Counterpoint.

Berry, Wendell. 2003b. "Is Life a Miracle?" In *Citizenship Papers*, 181–189. Berkeley, CA: Counterpoint.

Berry, Wendell. 2003c. "A Long Job, Too Late to Quit." In *Citizenship Papers*, 77–84. Berkeley, CA: Counterpoint.

Berry, Wendell. 2004. "The Wild Birds." In *That Distant Land: The Collected Stories*, 337–364. Berkeley, CA: Counterpoint.

Berry, Wendell. 2005a. "Local Knowledge in the Age of Information." In *The Way of Ignorance and Other Essays*, 113–125. Berkeley, CA: Counterpoint.

Berry, Wendell. 2005b. "The Purpose of a Coherent Community." In *The Way of Ignorance and Other Essays*, 69–79. Berkeley, CA: Counterpoint.

Berry, Wendell. 2007a. "Interview with Wendell Berry." Interview by Vince Pennington. In *Conversations with Wendell Berry*, edited by Morris Allen Grubbs, 36–49. Jackson: University of Mississippi Press.

Berry, Wendell. 2007b. "In the Service of Hope—A Conversation with Wendell Berry." Interview by Marlene Muller and Dennis Vogt. In *Conversations with Wendell Berry*, edited by Morris Allen Grubbs, 201–213. Jackson: University of Mississippi Press.

Berry, Wendell. 2007c. "Rendering Us Again in Affection: An Interview with Wendell Berry." Interview by Katherine Dalton. In *Conversations with Wendell Berry*, edited by Morris Allen Grubbs, 187–200. Jackson: University of Mississippi Press.

Berry, Wendell. 2007d. "Toward a Healthy Community: An Interview with Wendell Berry." Interview by *The Christian Century*. In *Conversations with Wendell Berry*, edited by Morris Allen Grubbs, 114–121. Jackson: University of Mississippi Press.

Berry, Wendell. 2010a. "Healing." In *What Are People For?*, 9–13. Berkeley, CA: Counterpoint.

Berry, Wendell. 2010b. *The Hidden Wound*. Berkeley, CA: Counterpoint.

Berry, Wendell. 2010c. "A Poem of Difficult Hope." In *What Are People For?*, 58–63. Berkeley, CA: Counterpoint.

Berry, Wendell. 2011. *The Poetry of William Carlos Williams of Rutherford*. Berkeley, CA: Counterpoint.

Berry, Wendell. 2012a. "Discipline and Hope." In *A Continuous Harmony*, 83–161. Berkeley, CA: Counterpoint.

Berry, Wendell. 2012b. Interview by Michael Lamb. Lanes Landing Farm, Port Royal, KY. October 7.

Berry, Wendell. 2012c. "The Loss of the Future." In *The Long-Legged House*, 53–73. Berkeley, CA: Counterpoint.

Berry, Wendell. 2012d. "Starting from Loss." Reprinted in *It All Turns on Affection: The Jefferson Lecture and Other Essays*, 67–88. Berkeley, CA: Counterpoint.

Berry, Wendell. 2012e. "A Statement against the War in Vietnam." In *The Long-Legged House*, 75–87. Berkeley, CA: Counterpoint.

Berry, Wendell. 2012f. "Think Little." In *A Continuous Harmony*, 69–82. Berkeley, CA: Counterpoint.

Berry, Wendell. 2013. "Wendell Berry, Poet & Prophet." Interview by Bill Moyers. October 3. http://billmoyers.com/episode/wendell-berry-poet-prophet/.

Berry, Wendell, and Wes Jackson. 2012. "A Conversation with Wendell Berry and Wes Jackson." Interview by Joshua Yates. *Hedgehog Review* 14 (2, Summer).

Bittman, Mark. 2014. "Let's Reject the 'Inevitable.'" *New York Times*, September 16. https://www.nytimes.com/2014/09/17/opinion/mark-bittman-lets-reject-the-inevitable.html.

Brei, Andrew, ed. 2016a. *Ecology, Ethics, and Hope*. Lanham, MD: Rowman & Littlefield.

Brei, Andrew. 2016b. "Hope and Pressure." In *Ecology, Ethics, and Hope*, edited by Andrew Brei, 13–25. Lanham, MD: Rowman & Littlefield.

Burke, Kenneth. 1973. "Semantic and Poetic Meaning." In *The Philosophy of Literary Form: Studies in Symbolic Action*, 3rd edition, 138–167. Berkeley: University of California Press.

Derber, Charles. 2015. "Hope Requires Fighting the Hope Industry." *Tikkun* 30 (2, Spring): 22–23.

Dunlap, Riley E., Aaron M. McCright, and Jerrod H. Yarosh. 2016. "The Political Divide on Climate Change: Partisan Polarization Widens in the US." *Environment: Science and Policy for Sustainable Development* 58 (5): 4–23.

Fiala, Andrew. 2016. "Playing a Requiem on the *Titanic*: The Virtue of Hope in the Age of Ecological Calamity." In *Ecology, Ethics, and Hope*, edited by Andrew Brei, 29–42. Lanham, MD: Rowman & Littlefield.

Grubbs, Morris Allen, ed. 2007. *Conversations with Wendell Berry*. Jackson: University of Mississippi Press.

Han, H., J. Kim, C. Jeong, and G. L. Cohen. 2017. "Attainable and Relevant Moral Exemplars Are More Effective Than Extraordinary Exemplars in Promoting Voluntary Service Engagement." *Frontiers in Psychology* 8, article 283 (March): 1–14.

Herdt, Jennifer. 2008. *Putting on Virtue: The Legacy of the Splendid Vices*. Chicago: University of Chicago Press.

Jamail, Dahr. 2019. "Climate Disaster Is Upon Us." *The Nation*, January 15. https:// www.thenation.com/article/climate-disaster-is-upon-us/.

Jarvis, Brooke. 2018. "The Insect Apocalypse Is Here." *New York Times Magazine*, November 27. https://www.nytimes.com/2018/11/27/magazine/insect-apo calypse.html.

Jensen, Derrick. 2006. "Beyond Hope." *Orion Magazine*, May–June. https://orionm agazine.org/article/beyond-hope/.

Kadlac, Adam. 2015. "The Virtue of Hope." *Ethical Theory and Moral Practice* 18 (2): 337–354.

Kretz, Lisa. 2013. "Hope in Environmental Philosophy." *Journal of Agricultural and Environmental Ethics* 26 (5): 925–944.

Kretz, Lisa. 2016. "Singing Hope's Praises: A Defense of the Virtue of Hope for Environmental Action." In *Ecology, Ethics, and Hope*, edited by Andrew Brei, 133–150. Lanham, MD: Rowman & Littlefield.

Lamb, Michael. 2016a. "Aquinas and the Virtues of Hope: Theological and Democratic." *Journal of Religious Ethics* 44 (2): 300–332.

Lamb, Michael. 2016b. "A Passion and Its Virtue: Aquinas on Hope and Magnanimity." In *Hope*, edited by Ingolf U. Dalferth and Marlene A. Block, 67–88. Tübingen: Mohr Siebeck.

Lamb, Michael. 2018a. "Between Presumption and Despair: Augustine's Hope for the Commonwealth." *American Political Science Review* 112 (4): 1036–1049.

Lamb, Michael. 2018b. "Beyond Pessimism: A Structure of Encouragement in Augustine's *City of God*." *Review of Politics* 80 (4): 591–624.

Lamb, Michael. 2022. *A Commonwealth of Hope: Augustine's Political Thought*. Princeton, NJ: Princeton University Press.

Lamb, Michael, Jonathan Brant, and Edward Brooks. 2022. "Seven Strategies for Cultivating Virtue in the University." In *Cultivating Virtue in the University*, edited by Jonathan Brant, Edward Brooks, and Michael Lamb, 115–156. New York: Oxford University Press.

Marvel, Kate. 2018. "We Need Courage, Not Hope, to Face Climate Change." *On Being*, March 1. https://onbeing.org/blog/kate-marvel-we-need-courage-not-hope-to-face-climate-change/.

Masson-Delmotte, V., P. Zhai, H.-O. Pörtner, D. Roberts, J. Skea, P. R. Shukla, A. Pirani, W. Moufouma-Okia, C. Péan, R. Pidcock, S. Connors, J. B. R. Matthews, Y. Chen, X. Zhou, M. I. Gomis, E. Lonnoy, T. Maycock, M. Tignor, and T. Waterfield. 2018. *Global Warming of 1.5°C: An IPCC Special Report on the Impacts of Global Warming of 1.5°C above Pre-Industrial Levels and Related Global Greenhouse Gas Emission Pathways, in the Context of Strengthening the Global Response to the Threat of Climate Change, Sustainable Development, and Efforts to Eradicate Poverty*. Intergovernmental Panel on Climate Change. https://www.ipcc.ch/site/assets/uploads/sites/2/2019/02/SR15_Citation.pdf.

McQueen, Alison. 2017. "Salutary Fear? Hans Morgenthau and the Politics of Existential Crisis." *American Political Thought: A Journal of Ideas, Institutions, and Culture* 6 (Winter): 78–105.

McQueen, Alison. 2021. "The Wages of Fear? Toward Fearing Well about Climate Change." In *Philosophy and Climate Change*, edited by Mark Budolfson, Tristram McPherson, and David Plunkett, 152–177. New York: Oxford University Press.

Mittleman, Alan. 2009. *Hope in a Democratic Age: Philosophy, Religion, and Political Theory*. New York: Oxford University Press.

Moser, Susanne C. 2007. "More Bad News: The Risk of Neglecting Emotional Responses to Climate Change Information." In *Creating a Climate for Change: Communicating Climate Change and Facilitating Social Change*, edited by Susanne C. Moser and Lisa Dilling, 64–80. New York: Cambridge University Press.

Moser, Susanne C., and Lisa Dilling. 2011. "Communicating Climate Change: Closing the Science-Action Gap." In *The Oxford Handbook of Climate Change and Society*, edited by John S. Dryzek, Richard B. Norgaard, and David Schlosberg, 161–174. Oxford: Oxford University Press.

Muntzel, Philip A. 2009. "Embedded Hopefulness: Wendell Berry and Saint Thomas Aquinas on Christian Hope." In *Wendell Berry and Religion: Heaven's Earthly Life*, edited by Joel James Shuman and L. Roger Owens, 190–208. Lexington: University Press of Kentucky.

Nelson, Michael P. 2016. "To a Future without Hope." In *Ecology, Ethics, and Hope*, edited by Andrew Brei, 129–132. Lanham, MD: Rowman & Littlefield.

Nolt, John. 2016. "Hope, Self-Transcendence and Environmental Ethics." In *Ecology, Ethics, and Hope*, edited by Andrew Brei, 43–63. Lanham, MD: Rowman & Littlefield.

O'Neill, Saffron, and Sophie Nicholson-Cole. 2009. "'Fear Won't Do': Promoting Positive Engagement with Climate Change through Visual and Iconic Representations." *Science Communication* 30 (3): 355–379.

Orr, David W. 2007. "Optimism and Hope in a Hotter Time." *Conservation Biology* 21 (6): 1392–1395.

Porter, Eduardo. 2015. "Climate Change Calls for Science, Not Hope." *New York Times*, June 23. https://www.nytimes.com/2015/06/24/business/combating-climate-change-with-science-rather-than-hope.html.

Reidmiller, D. R., C. W. Avery, D. R. Easterling, K. E. Kunkel, K. L. M. Lewis, T. K. Maycock, and B. C. Stewart, eds. 2018. *Impacts, Risks, and Adaptation in the United States: Fourth National Climate Assessment*. Vol. 2. U.S. Global Change Research Program. nca2018.globalchange.gov.

Shattuck, Kathryn. 2012. "Out on the Prairie, Moon, Music, and Lectures, Too." *New York Times*, October 2. http://www.nytimes.com/2012/10/03/us/prairie-festival-draws-crowds-to-land-institute-in-kansas.html.

Smith, Daniel. 2014. "It's the End of the World as We Know It . . . and He Feels Fine." *New York Times*, April 17. https://www.nytimes.com/2014/04/20/magazine/its-the-end-of-the-world-as-we-know-it-and-he-feels-fine.html.

Smith, Kimberly K. 2003. *Wendell Berry and the Agrarian Tradition: A Common Grace*. Lawrence: University Press of Kansas.

Snow, Nancy E. 2018. "Hope as a Democratic Civic Virtue." *Metaphilosophy* 49 (3): 407–427.

Solnit, Rebecca. 2018. "Don't Despair: The Climate Fight Is Only Over If You Think It Is." *The Guardian*, October 14. https://www.theguardian.com/commentisfree/2018/oct/14/climate-change-taking-action-rebecca-solnit.

Stout, Jeffrey. 2004. *Democracy and Tradition*. Princeton, NJ: Princeton University Press.

Stout, Jeffrey. 2010. *Blessed Are the Organized: Grassroots Democracy in America*. Princeton, NJ: Princeton University Press.

Stout, Jeffrey. 2014. "The Transformation of Genius into Practical Power: A Reading of Emerson's 'Experience.'" *American Journal of Theology and Philosophy* 35 (1): 3–24.

Swenson-Lengyel, Willa. 2017. "Beyond Eschatology: Environmental Pessimism and the Future of Human Hoping." *Journal of Religious Ethics* 45 (3): 413–435.

Treanor, Brian. 2016. "Hope in the Age of the Anthropocene." In *Ecology, Ethics, and Hope*, edited by Andrew Brei, 95–110. Lanham, MD: Rowman & Littlefield.

Zagzebski, Linda. 2017. *Exemplarist Moral Theory*. Oxford: Oxford University Press.

INDEX

For the benefit of digital users, indexed terms that span two pages (e.g., 52–53) may, on occasion, appear on only one of those pages.

Figures are indicated by *f* following the page number

INDEX

religion, in cultural influence on hope, 241–45. *See also* Buddhism; Christianity; Islam; Judaism
Religion and Nothingness (Nishitani), 152–53
Religion within the Limits of Reason Alone (Kant), 7
religious hope, 231, 253–54
resignation, despair compared to, 103–4n.33
resilience, hope as secular virtue and, 82
resisting reactive emotions, hope as secular virtue and, 82–83
resolute hope
  action and, 293
  cognitive resolve and, 32–33, 291–92, 293–94
  concept of, 32–33, 291–92
  as private hope, 293–94
  Snyder and, 32–33, 292–94
  social order and, 293–94
  transformative hope compared to, 296
respondent measures, 257
reterritorialization, utopianism and, 287–88
Revised Standard Theory (RST), 15–16, 110, 118–21
Rioux, C., 136n.28
risk
  of hope, 102n.23
  sound hope counteracting aversion to, 289–90
The Road (McCarthy), 77–78, 87–90, 101n.18, 103n.32
robust hope, 290–91
Romantic era, hope as virtue in, 50, 62–63
Roosevelt, Theodore, 33–34, 319–20
Rorty, Richard, 32–33, 294–95
Rousseau, Jean-Jacques, 302–3n.9
RST. *See* Revised Standard Theory

sadness, as passion, 5
Sartre, Jean P., 83, 102n.25
Scheier, Michael F., 29–30, 209–10, 221–22
Schiller, Friedrich, 62–63
Schopenhauer, Arthur, 37n.1
Schwartz, Matthew B., 212, 216
Schwörer, Bettina, 257–58
Scientific Revolution, 312–13
Scranton, Roy, 323–24

secular patient hope, 282–83
secular virtue. *See* hope as secular virtue
Segal, G., 21–22, 39n.17
self
  African exemplars of, 152
  Buddhism and, 152–54
  detachment and, 153–54
  in Islam, 152
self-belief, 209, 220
self-report measures, 257
Seligman, Martin, 206–7, 210–11, 213
Seneca, 52
Seth, Salma, 238–39
Shade, Patrick, 4, 32–33, 294, 303n.11
Shariati, Ali, 150, 152
Sharma, Eesha, 263–64
The Shawshank Redemption, 12, 17, 101n.20, 104–5n.35, *See also* Prisoners example
Shelley, Percy, 50, 62–63
Shorey, Hal S., 230
Sierra Club, 318–19
Sierra Leone, refugees from, 245
significance, of specific episodic hope, 110–12
Silcock, Jeffrey, 187n.18
Silentio, Johannes de. *See* Kierkegaard, Søren
Silent Spring (Carson), 321
Singleton, Jennifer L., 241
situational obedience, hope and, 301–2n.6
skewed desire, 176–77, 194n.62
slavery, hope and, 156–57
Smith, M., 22
Smoker example
  Focus Theory of hope and, 125
  RST and, 120–21
Snyder, Charles R. *See also* Hope Theory
  on agency thinking and pathways thinking, 29–31, 208, 227–29
  on ethnicity, 239
  hope definition of, 228, 229
  hope measures developed by, 229, 232–33, 234
  Hope Theory's origin and, 228–29
  influence of, 246
  psychological hope compared to hope as virtue and, 230–32
  resolute hope and, 32–33, 292–94
  on suicide, 239–40

395